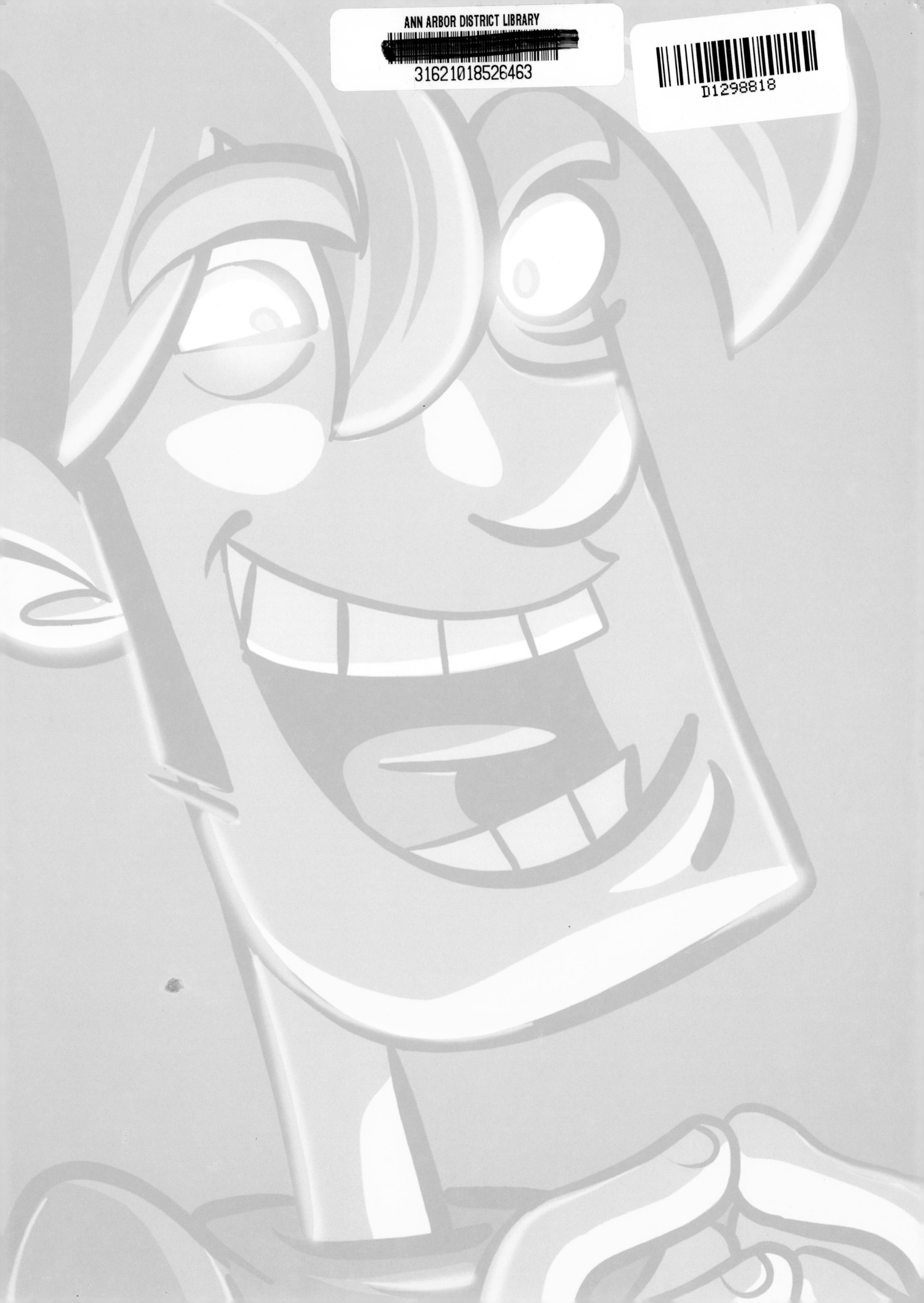

THE SPLENDID MAGIC OF PENNY ARCADE

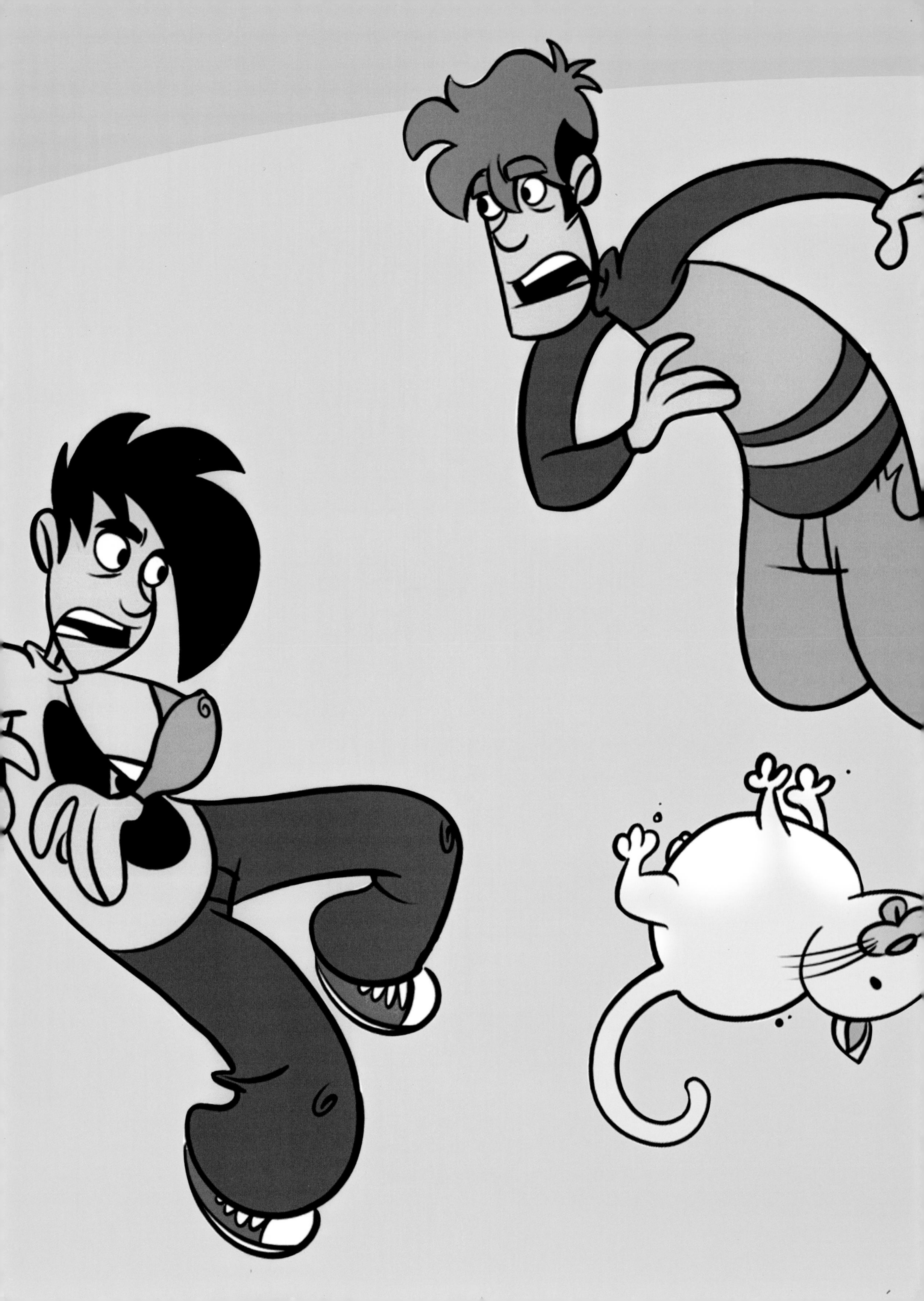

THE SPLENDID MAGIC OF PENNY ARCADE

MIKE KRAHULIK

JERRY HOLKINS

The 11 ½ Anniversary Edition

DEL REY · PENNY ARCADE BOOKS

BALLANTINE BOOKS • NEW YORK

Copyright © 2010 by Penny Arcade, Inc.

Published in the United States by Del Rey, an imprint of The Random House Publishing Group, a division of Random House, Inc., New York.

DEL REY is a registered trademark and the Del Rey colophon is a trademark of Random House, Inc.

Penny Arcade copyright © 1998 Penny Arcade, Inc. PENNY ARCADE, and all related characters and the distinctive likenesses thereof: TM and © 1998 Penny Arcade, Inc. Licensed by Penny Arcade, Inc. All rights reserved.

ISBN 978-0-345-51226-0

Printed in the United States of America on acid-free paper

www.delreybooks.com

1 2 3 4 5 6 7 8 9

First Edition

Book design by Foltz Design

Foreword

It's not news that I'm a huge fan of *Penny Arcade* and its creators, Jerry Holkins and Mike Krahulik: not only does a Krahulik cover grace one of my books (the hardcover edition of *Agent to the Stars*), but I gave both Holkins and Krahulik's *Penny Arcade* alter egos a shout-out in my novel *The Ghost Brigades,* with a character named "Gabriel Brahe."

So yes, I dig these crazy kids. But *why* do I dig them so much? Well:

1. Speaking of them as individuals, I admire their work. Mike's art has evolved into a form that's both distinctive and accessible (think that's easy? Try it), and as for Jerry, there's been more than once when I've looked at a phrase he's penned and said, "Oh, yes, I am so very stealing *that.*"

2. Speaking of them as a team, *Penny Arcade* resides in the personal category I like to call "bladder-threatening humor," a category that includes *The Hitchhiker's Guide to the Galaxy, Eddie Izzard: Dress to Kill,* and *A Fish Called Wanda.*

3. They make a living playing video games and then writing and drawing cartoons about it, and in doing so helped create the webcomic genre. Well done them.

4. More than that, they use that dream gig to *without exception* give the smartest, punchiest, *on-point* criticism of games and the gaming industry out there. They savage the industry as only someone who loves games could. Does it matter? Ask someone on the receiving end.

5. Anyone can say "fuck you" to unfair criticism. Jerry and Mike are some of the *very* few who use that fuck-you attitude for good. See: their Child's Play charity, which has raised millions of dollars for hospitalized children and got its start after the two of them were fed up with gamers being portrayed as shut-in serial killers in training.

6. Which is another thing I like about Mike and Jerry: That whole "we'll show *you*" thing, which (with the critical help of PA business director Robert Khoo, the secret sauce to Mike and Jerry's all-beef patties) has led to Child's Play, PAX, and a whole bunch of other initiatives that take the geek stereotype of a passive, antisocial loser and punt it into the inky darkness. Show of hands: How many non-geeks have pioneered a creative genre, built a successful charity, and created one of the largest conventions on the planet, all in less time than it takes a standard newborn male to reach puberty? Yes, well. That's what I thought.

In short: Jerry and Mike. I admire their talent, I love their work, and I *bow to them* for the good they're doing in the world. I'm a huge fan because they've earned the admiration, period, end of sentence. If you're reading this book, you're probably a fan, too. But if you aren't yet, by the time you're done here, I'm betting you will be, for the same reasons I am.

I say to you: Welcome to the club.

—John Scalzi
November 23, 2009

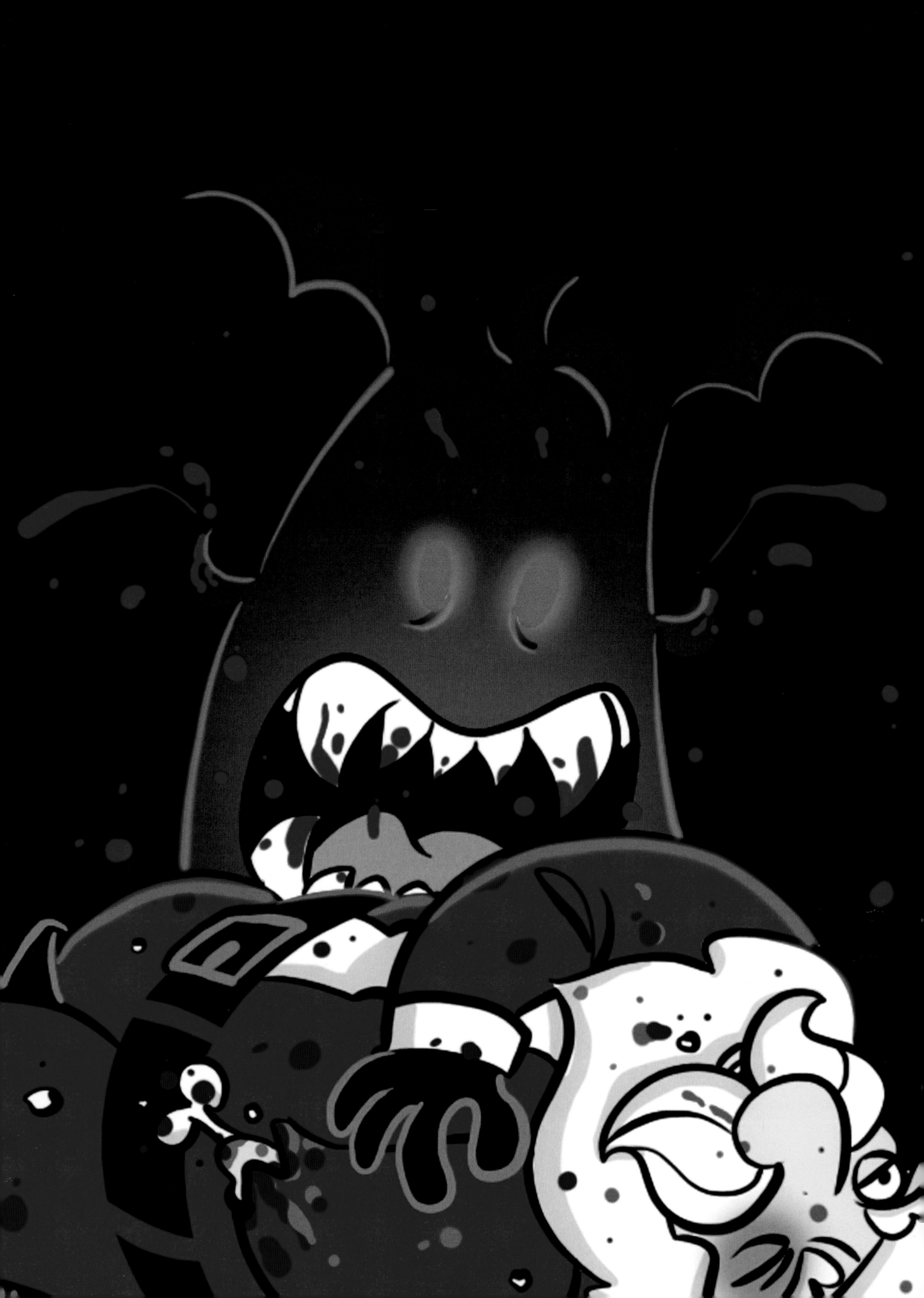

CONTENTS

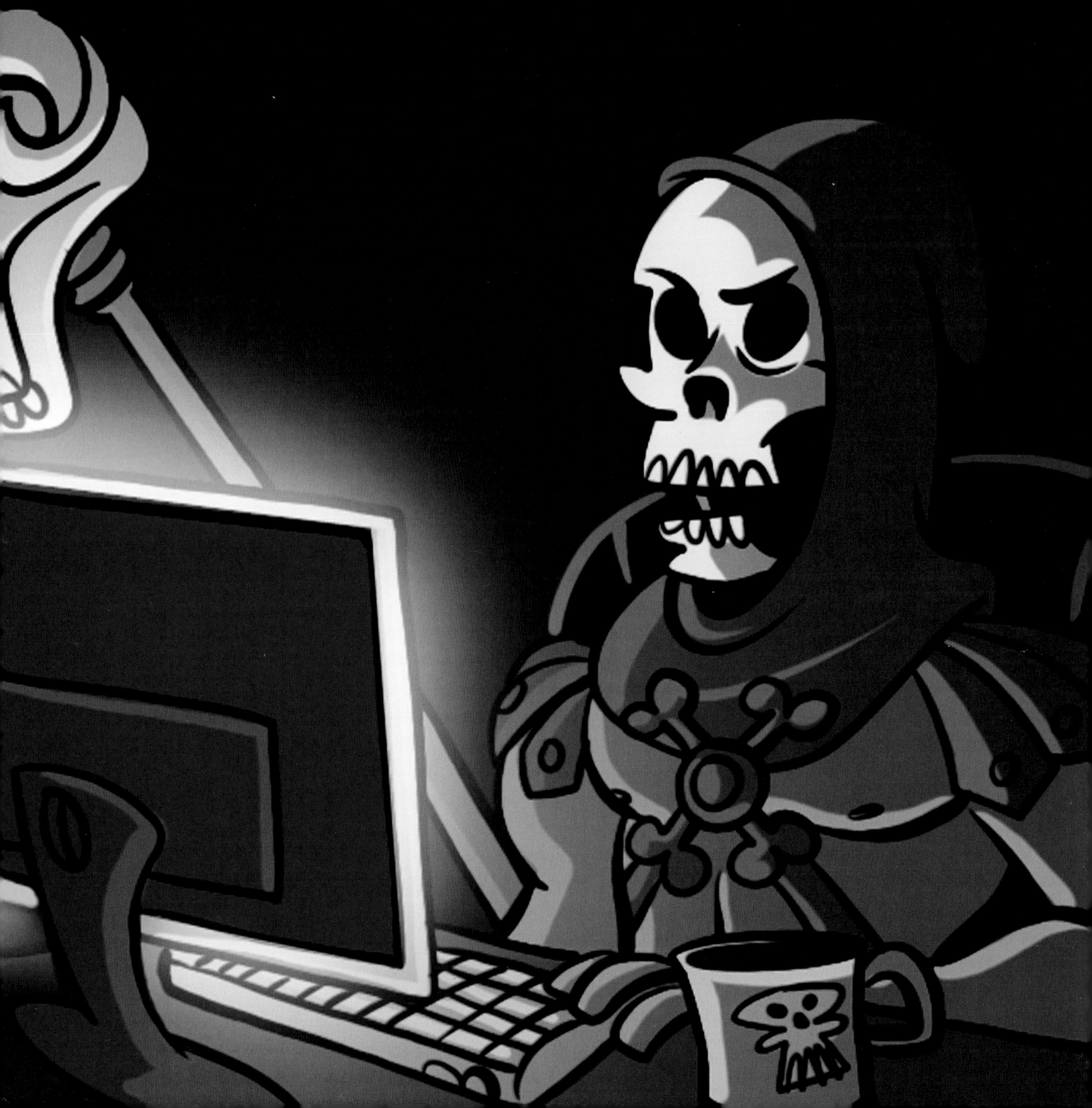

Hello. My name is Jerry Holkins, and I write a comic strip called *Penny Arcade*.

Our comic is *collected* in books—certainly this book contains many such strips—but most people read it on the computer. This was very odd when we started doing it in 1998, much less so now. The term *webcomic* did not yet exist to describe what we had done, inadvertently, by uploading images to the Web where they would be visible to others. In time, this would come to be understood as an incredibly big deal.

We are often asked questions of various kinds about the strange life we lead as online image wranglers. Some questions deal with the remainder of our meals, specifically, are we going to eat them? Others refer to our bizarre, frenzied rituals, or the waxy sheen that gives our flesh the cast of death. Beyond this introduction, burning questions such as these receive a proper airing.

This book is, in some ways, like a common FAQ that has metastasized into some terrible, physical form. Under what circumstances would two misanthropes *ever* create a charity? We touch on this. How did a handful of people who liked playing video games end up starting the premiere public gaming event in the United States? That is a great question, actually, and we will *tell* you how. The questions become more and more granular, up to and including items like "What kinds of things do you have on your shelves?"

In this exhaustive tome, answers to these questions and more await the reader.

We're a little afraid, in general, to think about *Penny Arcade* as a concept. This fear is rooted in the idea that, were we to analyze it for any prolonged length of time, it would somehow evaporate and be gone. We've decided to reverse this position, temporarily, and this is why: We did something strange, something interesting. Sometimes by accident, certainly, but not always. We should take a moment to write it all down before we forget.

You may come along, if you like.

Jerry Holkins
Seattle, WA

That looks fine to me.

Mike Krahulik (via email)
Seattle, WA

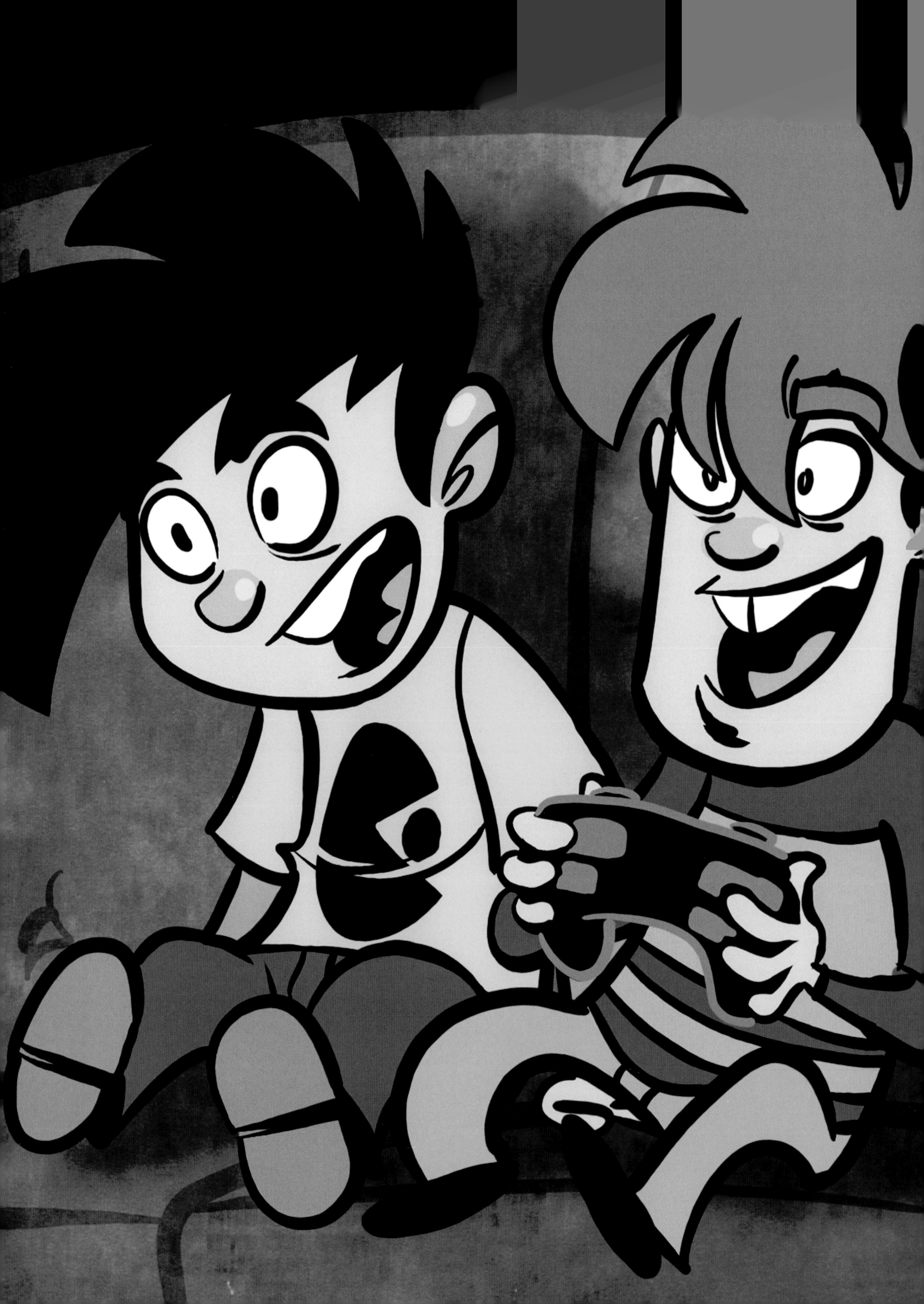

THE
SPLENDID
MAGIC OF
PENNY
ARCADE

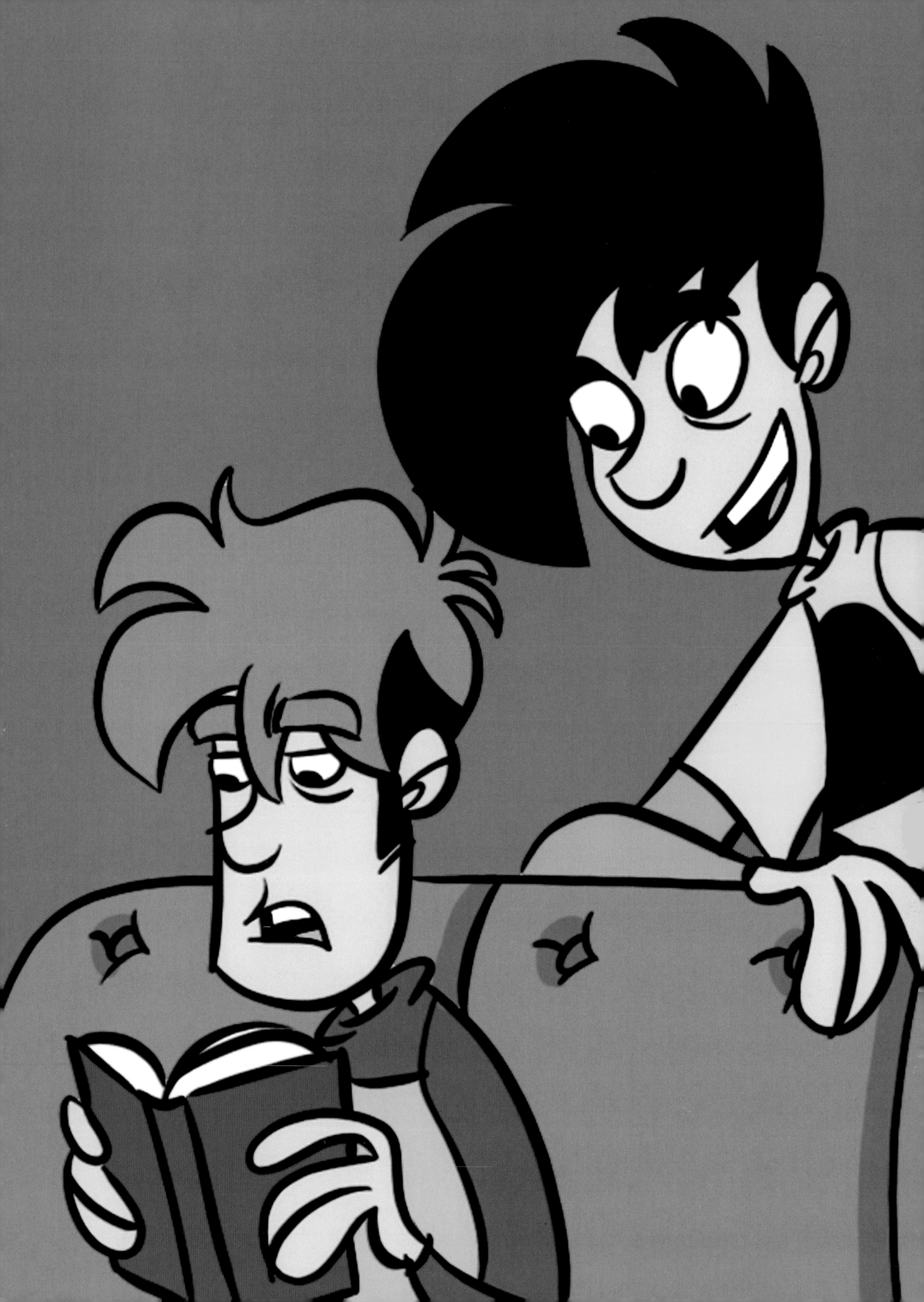

PENNY ARCADE: A HISTORY

by Chris Baker

ORIGIN STORY

The year 1993 was a momentous one for video games. Classics like Star Fox, X-COM: UFO Defense, Shinobi III: Return of the Ninja Master, and Day of the Tentacle were released that year. Doom pioneered networked multiplayer gaming. Early adopters snapped up the consoles that would usher in the next generation: Atari Jaguar and 3DO. And at Mead High School in Spokane, Washington, two dorks named Mike Krahulik and Jerry Holkins met for the first time in a spring semester journalism class.

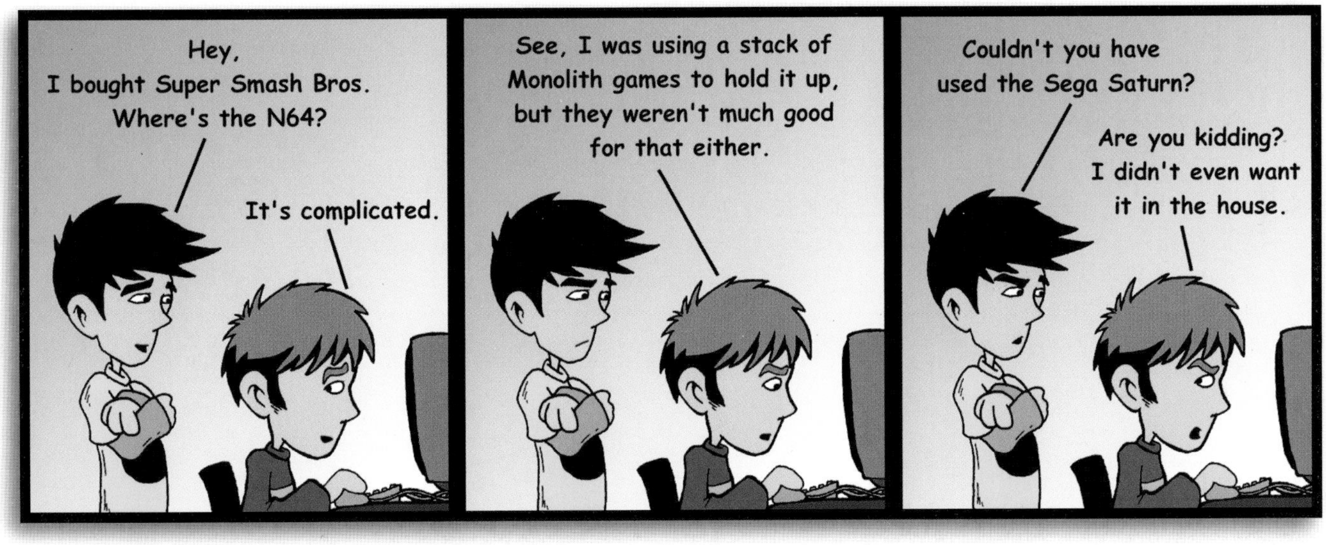
Hey,
I bought Super Smash Bros.
Where's the N64?
It's complicated.
See, I was using a stack of
Monolith games to hold it up,
but they weren't much good
for that either.
Couldn't you have
used the Sega Saturn?
Are you kidding?
I didn't even want
it in the house.

The two would find their calling in that journalism class, but what they discovered wasn't journalism per se. It had more to do with games. The classroom had computers equipped with bleeding-edge 1993 hardware—CD-ROM drives. Their indulgent instructor let the kids spend class time exploring a hot new adventure game, an audiovisual extravaganza called Myst. For a few precious hours, high school wasn't stultifying. It was fun. That was a tiny taste of what the future would hold.

Jerry was a senior and a staff writer on the school's newspaper. He was a hyperarticulate nonconformist, constantly jotting down song lyrics and perfectly happy to make a spectacle of himself. Mike was a sophomore hoping to contribute illustrations to the paper. He was quiet and fastidious, content to withdraw into the solitude of drawing. But the two did have some things in common. They both wore glasses, they were both very low on the social totem pole at their school, and they both loved to play video games. They clicked.

Jerry asked to see Mike's portfolio of drawings. "I didn't really grow up reading comics," Jerry says. "I mean, I was a total dork, don't get me wrong. But I didn't have a tremendous amount of exposure to the comic book medium. Still, I knew that what I was looking at was good."

The two quickly sensed that their skills and their personalities complemented each other, that they could maybe form some kind of team. "I had already decided that I was going to be a comic book artist," says Mike. "I needed someone to write me stories—that was the boring part of the job, as far as I was concerned."

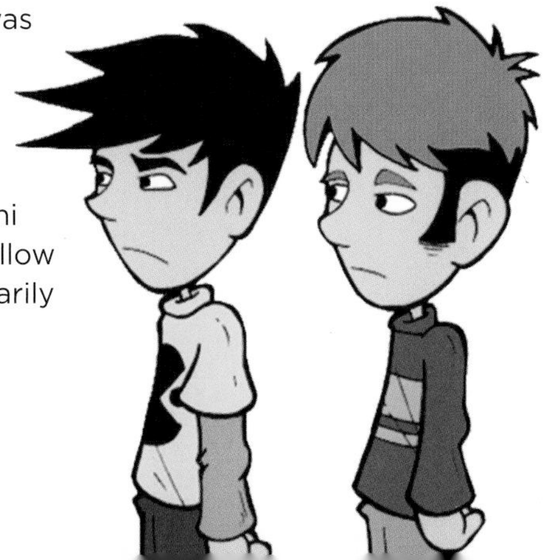

Their first collaboration was an article for the school paper. "It was a newspaper production class, so it was basically a free pass to go wherever you wanted off campus to track down stories," says Jerry. They left school and drove a mile down Route 395 to Wonderland, a family fun center with mini golf, bumper boats, and an arcade. They were going to report back to their fellow students at Mead High about this place, with their journalistic attentions primarily

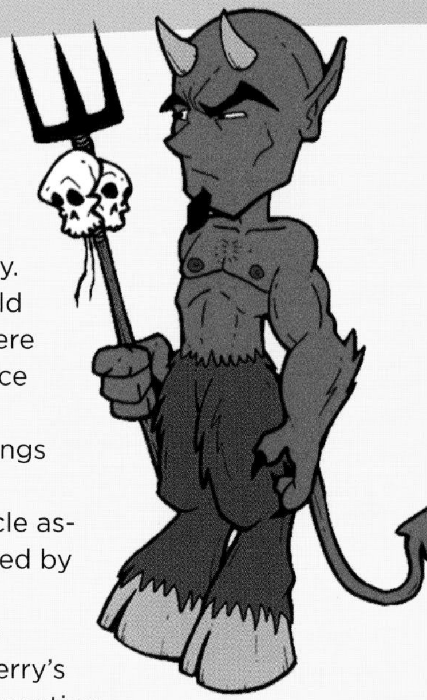

focused on the arcade. "It was a pretty flimsy reason to not be at school," concedes Jerry.

Mike got increasingly nervous as the day went on. He couldn't believe that they would actually get away with this. "I was a good kid, I never broke any rules," he insists. "And here I was playing hooky. I was like, 'They're gonna know where we've been, they'll smell the ice cream on my breath.'"

Jerry had a little more experience with bending the rules. "You're worrying about things before they happen," he told Mike.

Sure enough, there were no repercussions when they returned to campus. Their article assessing the merits of Wonderland ran in the next edition of the school paper, accompanied by Mike's illustrations. They got away with it.

Seventeen years later, they're still getting away with it. It's amazing how many of the elements of their future partnership were captured in that first collaboration. Mike and Jerry's distinctive talents and diametrically opposed personalities meshed well. They were commenting on games, the places that gamers liked to hang out at, and the issues that are vitally important to gamers. The two managed to convince everyone that they were behaving responsibly when they were actually just goofing around and having fun. The first seeds of what would be *Penny Arcade* were planted that day over sessions of Killer Instinct and Virtua Racer.

This is how *Penny Arcade* came to be.

JERRY

"His name means 'oracle' or 'one who writes,' like the prophet," says Jerry's mother, Peta Countryman. Her son was born on February 6, 1976, and she knew right away that he was some kind of prodigy. "He was reading *Time* magazine when he was still practically a toddler. He started school when he was four and a half, and he was in all of the gifted programs."

Jerry wasn't just smart—he was a keen observer of the world around him, alive to absurdities that other people take for granted. "When he was about seven, he was reading a Toys "R" Us insert in the newspaper," says his mother, "and he just burst out laughing at this one ad. I swear, he laughed about it for weeks afterward."

Jerry remembers the ad. It was for a game console, something that couldn't fail to catch his eye. The accompanying photo showed the system hooked up to a television. There was a disclaimer on the ad that read "TV not included." The fact that the retailers had to idiotproof their ad with a warning that spelled out something that was obvious to any second grader with an Odyssey[2] was so ridiculous that it was hilarious.

"Jerry doesn't take things at face value," explains his wife, Brenna. "He asks, 'Is that the way it has to be?'" That off-kilter perspective comes in handy these days—he makes a living by noticing the odd details that other people take for granted. You can almost imagine that stupid Toys "R" Us ad copy becoming fodder for a *Penny Arcade* strip if he'd spotted it twenty years later. But during grade school, being precocious and observant just marked him as an outsider. When his classmates weren't ridiculing him, they were whacking him with their lacrosse sticks. If that bothered him, he didn't let it show.

"He never cried," his mom remembers. "He was always laughing, even when he was being reprimanded. And he was *so* funny! Once I was working late, and I asked if he would draw me a bath for when I got home. He literally drew a bathtub on a piece of paper for me."

When he wasn't joking around, Jerry devoured every book he could get his hands on, from fantasy to history to sci-fi to philosophy. The free-form poetry of e. e. cummings was a particular revelation. "Just the idea that capitalization and paragraphs and even the arrangement of words on a page could be arbitrary—that was huge for me," he says.

Jerry penned some verses himself. "He wrote so beautifully!" says Peta. "For holiday gifts, I'd tell him, 'Jer-Bear, all I want is a poem.' I was a single mom at that point, supporting Jerry and his sister as a florist. One of his poems was about how I could do anything with a glue gun."

Most of the rhyming couplets Jerry wrote were song lyrics. He loved music. He picked out tunes on a hand-me-down guitar and sang in the school choir. "He had a beautiful voice," says his mom. "He had lead roles in these school musicals, and he would never tell us about it beforehand. It would just be, 'Oh by the way, I have to be at school in fifteen minutes for this thing.'"

He wasn't just a right-brained artsy kid. He had a clear aptitude for technology, and his family encouraged it. "My grandma had a matriarchal edict," Jerry recalls. "She declared that every grandchild of hers was to have a computer in the house." They all got Commodore 128s. Jerry used his to write school papers, access a primitive online service

TIME LINE

1993 (March) — Mike Krahulik and Jerry Holkins meet in a high school journalism class in Spokane, Washington. Mike needs a writer and Jerry needs something to write for.

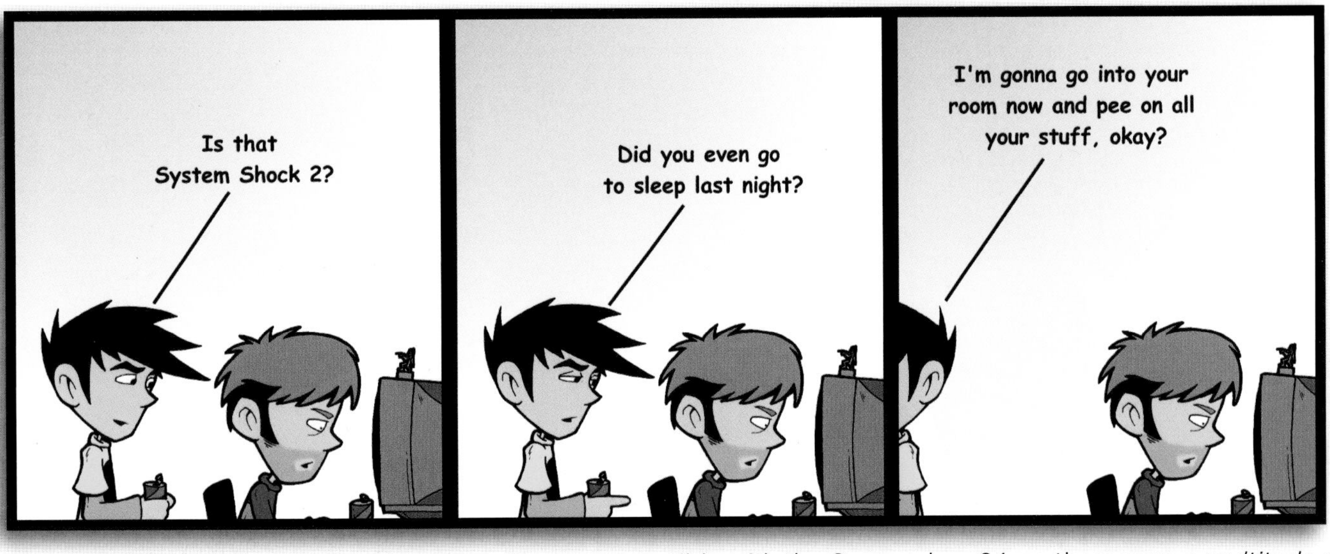
Is that
System Shock 2?
Did you even go
to sleep last night?
I'm gonna go into your
room now and pee on all
your stuff, okay?

called Q-Link, and play games. Ah, games. "It was compatible with the Commodore 64, so there were a *multitude* of games for it."

By the standards of American parents in the 1980s, Jerry's mom was fairly tolerant of games. She bought him some, and if his grades were good—which they always were—she'd let him skip school and play them once in a while. Interactive entertainment was fine, as far as she was concerned. "I could see that the Choose Your Own Adventure books were really fascinating for him," says Peta. But she refused to allow Dungeons and Dragons in her home. "I did raise him in the church, and that was one thing you just couldn't play."

Jerry has a slightly more pungent recollection about that particular restriction. "Like many young men, I found a place inside my bed where I could hide things," he says. "One day, Mom harvested a number of D&D books from that secret realm, ostensibly while she was putting laundry away. She told me that the reason we had all been getting sick lately, and the reason my father had left us, is that I had insisted on bringing these devil books into the house. Like I was some kind of necromancer just because I liked fiction."

But he didn't let that faze him any more than he let all of the bullying and teasing get to him. He became something of an iconoclast at Mead High. "My goal in school was to make people uncomfortable."

"He was not a run-of-the-mill kid. He was a...I want to say beatnik," says Mike's father, Don Krahulik.

"Jerry was sort of like that 'king of the dorks' kid in *Sixteen Candles,*" recalls Brenna. "But just in the sense that he was entirely his own person, and he absolutely didn't care what people thought. Like, he would tie a tea bag to his glasses so that it would hang down over his nose. He did that several times in high school." ("They're very aromatic," he insists.)

Jerry hung out with the handful of bohemian kids in Spokane. "He always had a girlfriend, and lots of friends," says Brenna. "But they were a weird bunch of friends that weren't necessarily into legal activities."

"If he had parties, he would leave no evidence," says Peta. "He was the best son ever. But sometimes when he tells me stuff about what was going on back then, I'm like, 'Stop! You're taking away my perfect image of you!'"

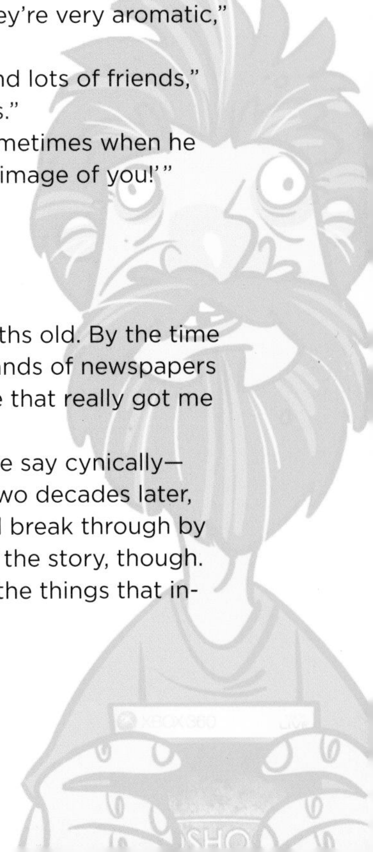

MIKE

The comic strip *Garfield* debuted in newspapers in July 1978, when Mike Krahulik was eight months old. By the time Mike was old enough to read the strip, it had become an enormous success, appearing in thousands of newspapers and spawning a merchandising empire. "*Garfield* was the first comic that I really took to, the one that really got me excited," says Mike. "I bought all the books and posters."

The strip's creator, Jim Davis, consciously set out to create a blockbuster. He shrewdly—some say cynically—conceived of a high concept that would appeal to the widest possible audience. It's ironic that two decades later, Mike would have his own successful comic strip, complete with tie-in merchandise, and that he'd break through by catering not to a mass audience but to a small niche of his fellow geeks. That's getting ahead of the story, though. When Mike was a kid, he was simply enthralled by the images of that fat, lazy cat. It was one of the things that inspired him to start doodling.

"Drawing is his life, always has been," says his mother, Dawn Krahulik. "He was a loner. He did what he had to do in school so he could get by, then just spent hours drawing."

Mike didn't just draw to amuse himself—he approached it like a calling, and he worked hard to hone his skills. In the mid-1980s, he discovered a PBS educational show called *Draw Squad.* The host "Comander Mark" Kistler taught kids illustration techniques like foreshortening, shadowing, and contours. Mike watched it religiously with a pad in hand.

His other fixation was video games. He had a fierce competitive streak, and he brought the same intensity to playing that he brought to drawing.

Mike's father, Don Krahulik, bought him consoles, but he was not without misgivings. "I didn't think highly of the games," remembers Don. "I didn't encourage him to sit there in front of the TV. I was always trying to get him to go outside."

"I tended to be a tad more understanding," says Dawn. "I remember sitting with Mike all afternoon watching reruns of *Saturday Night Live* and *The Kids in the Hall.* We shared a love of dry wit and one-liners."

"Mom introduced me to humor, to a lot of comedians that cussed and swore," recalls Mike. "If my dad ever saw *The Kids in the Hall,* he would have lost his shit. I mean, it's got a bunch of men who dress as women."

This education in TV comedy helped Mike develop a knack for snappy comebacks and withering put-downs. Persecution by his schoolmates also helped him hone that skill. He remembers being held down while someone kicked a soccer ball into his face at close range. And there was the time that someone stole the clothes from his locker during PE, and he was forced to wear his gym outfit for the rest of the day. "I developed humor and bitter sarcasm as a defense mechanism," he says.

"He had it hard in school, and he hid 90 percent of that from us," Dawn puts in. "He pretty much went it on his own."

"My goal in high school was to be unnoticed," says Mike. "I didn't want people to talk to me, but I didn't want them to think ill of me."

He wasn't much of a joiner, but he did get on the golf team and pursued the sport with characteristic fervor. "My parents would drop me off at the golf course at five in the morning," recalls Mike. "I'd play eighteen, maybe twenty-seven holes, then go to school. And then after school, the bus would drop me off at the golf course and I'd play till it got dark. I tend to fixate on things."

"He won some little trophies, and was on his way to being the next Tiger Woods," says Don. "But then it got to the point where he would have to put some *real* work into it to get to the next level."

Mike has no regrets about abandoning the sport. "I realized that golf was not my future, and I started to really focus on art."

"He doesn't believe in getting distracted by trivial things," agrees Dawn. She says he insisted that the reason he didn't date wasn't due to shyness; it was because it didn't seem practical unless he'd found his soul mate. "His attitude was, *Why should I waste some girl's time—and my time—if it's not going to go anywhere?*"

When Mike was in high school, he got a chance to actually meet his childhood idol, "Commander Mark" Kistler, when the drawing instructor was in town to do a presentation at a local elementary school. "He was this eager young cub, charmingly starstruck by me," recalls Kistler. "He reacted to meeting me the way I might've reacted to meeting William Shatner when I was his age."

Mike showed Kistler a stack of his drawings and sketches. "I remember thinking, *Whoa! This fourteen-year-old has college-level skills,*" says Kistler. "I could totally see him going into animation or comics. In fact, when I got behind on a book project, I called his mom up and had him help out."

"For a big chunk of a semester, I was doing drawings for that book in art class, regardless of what the curriculum was," Mike says. "For a while, I even stayed home from school to do the book."

As the project progressed, Mike was given more and more leeway to plot out the images on his own. "He must have done a hundred pen-and-ink illustrations," Kistler recalls. "He was so passionate about drawing. And now he's a world-famous Web cartoonist! Alumni of my classes have gone on to Pixar, Disney, and Marvel Comics. But Mike's definitely my most famous student. Well, him and Miley Cyrus."

TIME LINE

1997 (June) — Mike and Jerry decide to cohabitate in the real Apartment 26 in Spokane.

6

EARLY COLLABORATIONS

Mike and Jerry would go on to create a highly successful webcomic. It's debatable whether they became as famous as Miley Cyrus, but they definitely became authoritative figures in the media that grew up around video games. At the time that they first met, though, both the Internet and gaming were still in their infancy. "Our future had not materialized yet," says Jerry.

They continued to collaborate on the school paper for the rest of the semester. One of their creations was a recurring comic strip called *David and Goliath,* which chronicled the exploits of a cop and a giant robot. It was…coolly received by the rest of the student body. "The final strip was just an insult to those who could not perceive the quality of our work," says Jerry.

After he graduated, Jerry worked as a dishwasher and janitor before finding a better gig with a tech consulting firm. He was delighted to escape the confines of Mead High, but he would often go back to have lunch with Mike. "I felt bad that he still had to go to school," says Jerry. "I would bring him snacks and pizza from the outside world."

Mike continued to do illustrations and editorial cartoons for the school paper. He and Jerry also began dreaming up their own comic books. Jerry didn't have the strong grounding in the form that Mike did, but he gamely pitched ideas. "One of our comics was going to be called *G4,*" says Mike. "It was about kids with special mutant genes that could be activated by the government. I finally had a writer to help me, so I didn't have the heart to tell Jerry that this was the exact same story as the comic *Gen¹³*. He was so proud when he dreamed up this character who had the power of magnetism."

"Yes, I came up with Magneto completely independent of Marvel," says Jerry.

They admit that most of their creations were "overwrought superhero comics" in this vein, conceived in the style of the publisher Image, which was very hot at the time. There was also their hallucinatory character Chickenman, who did battle with monsters that only he could see. "I used to try to get our comics into a local compilation called *Ape-X,*" says Mike. "In my mind, the guys doing this compilation had totally *made it.*"

Meanwhile, Jerry had begun dating his future wife, Brenna. "We were in a high school production of *Guys and Dolls* together," recalls Brenna. "I was a Hot Box dancer, he was a gambler. But I didn't really get to know him until after he graduated and we had a chance to really talk to each other at this coffee shop called Java Junkies."

She was a bit hesitant to get involved with someone who wore sweatpants and Christian heavy metal T-shirts for ironic effect. But his conversational skills overcame his carefully cultivated air of eccentricity. "He was very funny and intelligent," says Brenna. "My favorite thing about him is his voice. Just the sound of it. To this day, he'll be telling me about the plot to some game, and pause to ask if he's boring me. He never is. I just love to listen to him."

Jerry wooed Brenna with all his geeky might. For their first date, he invited her over to play with LEGOs in his basement. "I thought that constituted a romantic afternoon," he says.

"He was definitely trying to impress me with his intellectual prowess," says Brenna. "He would quote Kant, give me books of poetry, write me songs. But he was also constantly buying me little presents. When I was a cashier at Shopko, he had me ring up a teddy bear. Then he turned around and gave it to me at the end of the checkout line."

During this time, Jerry was also playing with his bands, the Righteous Corn Farmers and the Fine Print. "He was the front man, the lead singer," according to Brenna. "It was exciting to see him jumping around and trying to dance. He did this little hop with the microphone that was delightful. But I always felt like the vocals were too low and the background music was too loud. I just wanted to hear him sing. I always thought that if he got famous, it would be for singing."

Jerry's romance with Brenna never interfered with his and Mike's friendship. "He would come over to my house to play games all the time," says Mike. "We also spent a lot of time on the phone. We'd sit through an entire *Twilight Zone* marathon on the Sci Fi Channel, just trading quips over the phone."

Some of Jerry's blasé attitude about what other people thought about him started to rub off on Mike. "My dad thought that Jerry was a bad influence," says Mike. "I stopped caring about dressing nice. I would wear shirts with holes." Don also didn't approve of Mike's all-consuming desire to draw, especially as it became clearer that he was pinning all his hopes of finding a career onto cartoons. "He wanted me to do something reliable, like go work in an office."

"Playing video games and making comics didn't look like raw materials for success," concedes Jerry. "In fact, what we were doing looked very similar to fucking around."

"Yeah, I completely understand where my dad was coming from now," says Mike. "At the time I didn't, because in my mind there was no way I was going to fail."

THE APARTMENT

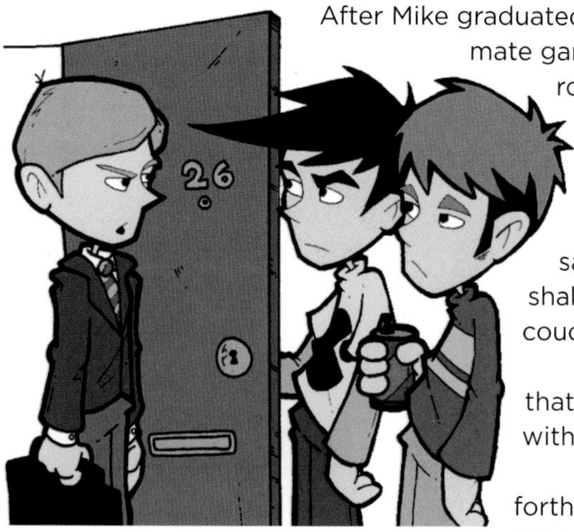
26

After Mike graduated from Mead High in 1995, he and Jerry got a place together. It was the ultimate gamer crash pad. There were two bedrooms, a room for their PCs, and a living room where they hooked up their consoles. The furniture consisted of a few desks, a few mattresses, a ratty couch, and a beanbag chair. The two were not noted for their tidiness. "It was *so* nasty," recalls Brenna. "The bathroom was foul."

"We had a cat that liked to pee everywhere, especially in the beanbag," says Mike. "Then that would congeal into, like, a piss jelly. You would have to shake the pee out of it before you sat down. The cat did the same thing to the couch. We tried to give the couch to Goodwill. It was rejected."

But they were so focused on playing games and cracking each other up that they barely noticed their living conditions. "Mike was having a blast living with Jerry," says Dawn. "The two of them had the best time ever."

"I remember going over there once, and they were just rolling back and forth across the carpet, giggling like maniacs," says Brenna. "And then they saw me and instantly looked all guilty, like they just got caught."

"They didn't have a pot to piss in, but it didn't bother them," says Don. "Money wasn't something they worried about."

Actually, Jerry had a decent job doing IT work for the school district at this point. He paid a greater share of the rent than Mike, partially so that he'd have someone there to game with, but also because he had an unshakable, if amorphous, sense that they were destined to do great things as a creative unit. "I subsidized him," says Jerry. "The return has been profound."

Mike endured some lousy jobs. For a while, he was the guy who picked up golf balls on the driving range. (Which is to say, he was the guy who came home with welts all over his body because golfers used him for target practice.) His parents convinced him to take some art courses at Spokane Falls Community College. It wasn't a good fit—the curriculum there wasn't geared toward comics-style illustrators. "But there was a really awesome arcade on campus," says Mike. "They had Tekken 2."

Brenna went off to college in 1996. Jerry didn't. He simply didn't have the money, and he would've needed to quit his lucrative IT job and become completely destitute to qualify for financial aid. "For a while he was kind of self-conscious about it," says Brenna. "But he would've hated college, all the self-aggrandizing posturing that goes on there." The two dated long-distance the whole time she was away, and saw each other every other weekend. "I met a lot of guys there," she says. "None of them were as good as Jerry."

Mike eventually found a job he really enjoyed at Toys "R" Us. Nintendo's 3-D stereoscopic gaming system was the hotness at the time. "I was a Virtual Boy attendant," he says gleefully. "They hired me as a temp to stand next to the Virtual Boy kiosk with a light-up hat and vest. Some kids would stumble away sick after playing for just a few minutes. Other people would sit at it all day, like they were hypnotized by it."

Mike was in his element. "I knew more about games than anyone else there, and I loved to talk about them, give advice to moms. They hired me on as a regular employee."

He moved up and became a "ticket rider." To prevent theft, all the good toys and games were kept in a booth behind bulletproof glass. Buyers presented tickets for the items they wanted, and Mike retrieved them. His perch in the booth gave him a great vantage point to scope out his future wife, Kara O'Donnal, who worked the checkout line. "Apparently, he'd just sit in there and watch me," says Kara. "That was a little stalkerish."

Mike couldn't work up the courage to talk to her until they met in the ticket line to see the *Star Wars* special edition re-release. "He said he would save me a seat...he was very sweet," says Kara. "On the next Valentine's Day, a mutual friend got us together on a date. He tricked us into it—he told Mike that I tried to call him, and told me that Mike tried to call me."

Mike had finally found a girl who was worth his time. "He hid his art skills at first," says Kara. "He thought people would look at him differently if they knew he could do that. But later that month, he left a drawing on the seat of my car. It had a boy holding a heart, and it said 'I love you.' Mike was just a very considerate, awesome guy."

Kara remembers the first game they played together—Tekken 2. And she remembers having a lot of fun hanging out with Mike and Jerry. "I loved their place," she says. "I mean, it was a hole and I had to clean it every time I went over, but I could just totally be myself there. And they were always cracking each other up. One of them would say

TIME LINE **1998 (November) — The First Strip is created and hosted by LoonyGames.com.**

something, and then the other one would say something that rhymed with the word the first one had just said, and they'd go on like that for hours."

TURNING POINT

Mike and Jerry were both dating girls they really liked, they had plenty of games, and they had jobs that didn't make them want to kill themselves. But their dreams of comic book superstardom were stagnating. "None of the projects we were doing together were ever even halfway completed," says Mike. "They were constantly petering out."

They also weren't really honing and refining their craft. "I don't know that our work together was getting any better," says Jerry. "There was no outside force compelling us to do stuff."

But they were also discovering that comic books might not be their only outlet. There was this thing called the World Wide Web, and it was full of people who were just like them.

Mike and Jerry were early adopters. "I remember having to *buy* a browser," says Jerry. "We both had a pretty good understanding of HTML. This was back when a regular person could still understand HTML."

They discovered sites like Blue's News and Telefragged, which were dedicated to dissecting every last nuance of PC gaming. They also discovered Usenet, where geeks gathered to flame each other. "We definitely tried to make our perspective known there," says Jerry. "We'd weigh in on the merits of Blue's News versus Duke Nukem, the 3-D shift—that was a really big deal for us."

Their earliest experience in building an online community was Clan Walrus. "We were playing Quake over modems," says Jerry, "and in order to start a clan you had to have five user names. We only knew each other, so we put in our names and then just pulled names out of terrible comics: Abaddon the Destroyer, the Anti-Pope, and Desiccator. We started getting messages like, 'What clan are you, can I join?' It actually ended up becoming a real clan." They set up a website for their clan with design by "The Art Angel Gabriel" and commentaries penned by one Tycho Brahe. The noms de plume stuck.

The two increasingly came to realize that there was a large bloc of gamers out there, and while they didn't always agree about everything, they all spoke a common language. "Before that, we didn't have the sense that there was a community of kids who play games. The people in arcades weren't a community—they were your opponents," says Jerry. He gets enraged all over again remembering people who defeated him on arcade fighters and forced him to spend another quarter. "These were people who could literally steal your money. I mean, *actually rob you.*"

When *NextGen* magazine posted a call for funny comic strips, Mike and Jerry had a good sense of what would tickle the collective funny bone of the gamer audience. *NextGen* rejected their offerings, but the two knew they had finally created something that was worth sharing with that audience. They shopped their strips around to some of the gamer websites they'd discovered. Jason "loonyboi" Bergman at Loonygames ran them, and demanded more.

And that was how *Penny Arcade* began. Mike and Jerry weren't being paid for their work, but the exposure and the experience of having regular deadlines would prove to be invaluable. "That was the external structure we needed, something that would force us to create work continually," says Jerry.

WWW.PENNY-ARCADE.COM

After six months, *Penny Arcade* parted ways with Loonygames. (There was a fundamental disagreement about the necessity of profanity in the strip.) They had no idea how popular their creation had become until they moved to their own site in 1999. It turned out they were getting hundreds of thousands of page views a month.

The next couple of years were eventful. Mike and Jerry got married (not to each other), moved to Seattle, and quit their day jobs to work on *Penny Arcade* full-time. Those years were also very stressful. To put it mildly, Mike and Jerry were not good businessmen. They signed away book-publishing rights to a guy who moved to Alaska and refused to pay them. They hooked up with a dubious Net company and nearly lost the rights to their intellectual

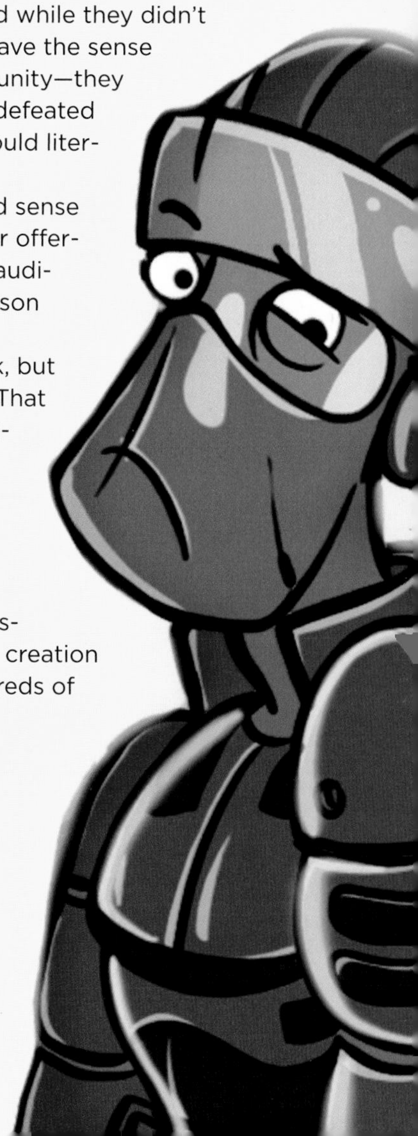

TIME LINE **1999 (February) —** Gabe proposes to Kara on *Penny Arcade*.

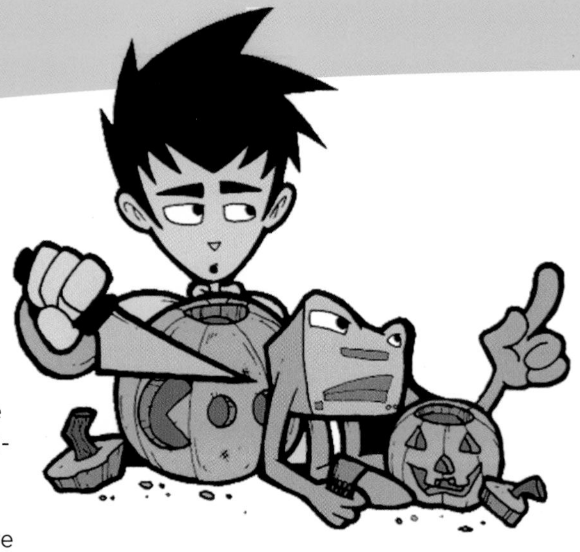

property, including the name *Penny Arcade.* "Jerry and I are good at making comics and being funny...and that's *it,*" Mike concedes. Even worse, the time they spent wrestling with financial issues took away from time that could've been spent making the strip.

They were living off donations from readers and contemplating the prospect of getting day jobs again when they met Robert Khoo. A business analyst at a market strategy firm, he was discussing a deal with the pair over lunch at the Golden Chopsticks restaurant in Redmond, Washington. "I realized right away that they had no idea what they were doing," he says. He was particularly appalled with their sideline in creating and displaying ads for game companies. "They were charging about 98 percent less than they should have been."

Robert coaxed them into a second meeting and presented them with a fifty-page business plan. He offered to quit his analyst job and work for them free for two months. "Looking back, they really shouldn't have trusted me," he says.

They did. Jerry looks back in astonishment at what easy prey they would've been for an unscrupulous person looking to get his hands on the business. "Luckily, Robert perceived greater value in fixing us to the front of his chariot and riding us forever," he says.

Within six months, *Penny Arcade* was a profitable enterprise. Mike's dad, who'd been a frequent and vocal critic of Mike and Jerry's business acumen, may have been more relieved than anyone by this turn of events. "There was finally light at the end of the tunnel," he says. "Robert is a great guy."

The rest of the story is there for everyone to see on Penny-Arcade.com. The guys could now focus more of their energies on the strip itself, and the writing and artwork just got better and better. They were able to get an office, expand it to accommodate a Ping-Pong table, then moved to an even nicer office with *a Ping-Pong stadium.* They were able to hire more people and pursue increasingly ambitious side projects like the Child's Play charity, the PAX conference, and even making their own video game.

In the end, *Penny Arcade* was just a continuation of Mike and Jerry's first collaboration at Mead High. It seemed like a goof, an excuse to lose themselves in the world of games, but it turned out to be much more than that. For one uncomfortable moment, it looked like their project would get them in trouble. But ultimately, there was no need to worry. They are still getting away with it.

Chris Baker's 2007 article on *Penny Arcade* for *Wired* was "the most honest interview...anyone has managed to get out of us," according to Mike. He is currently a senior editor for *Wired* magazine.

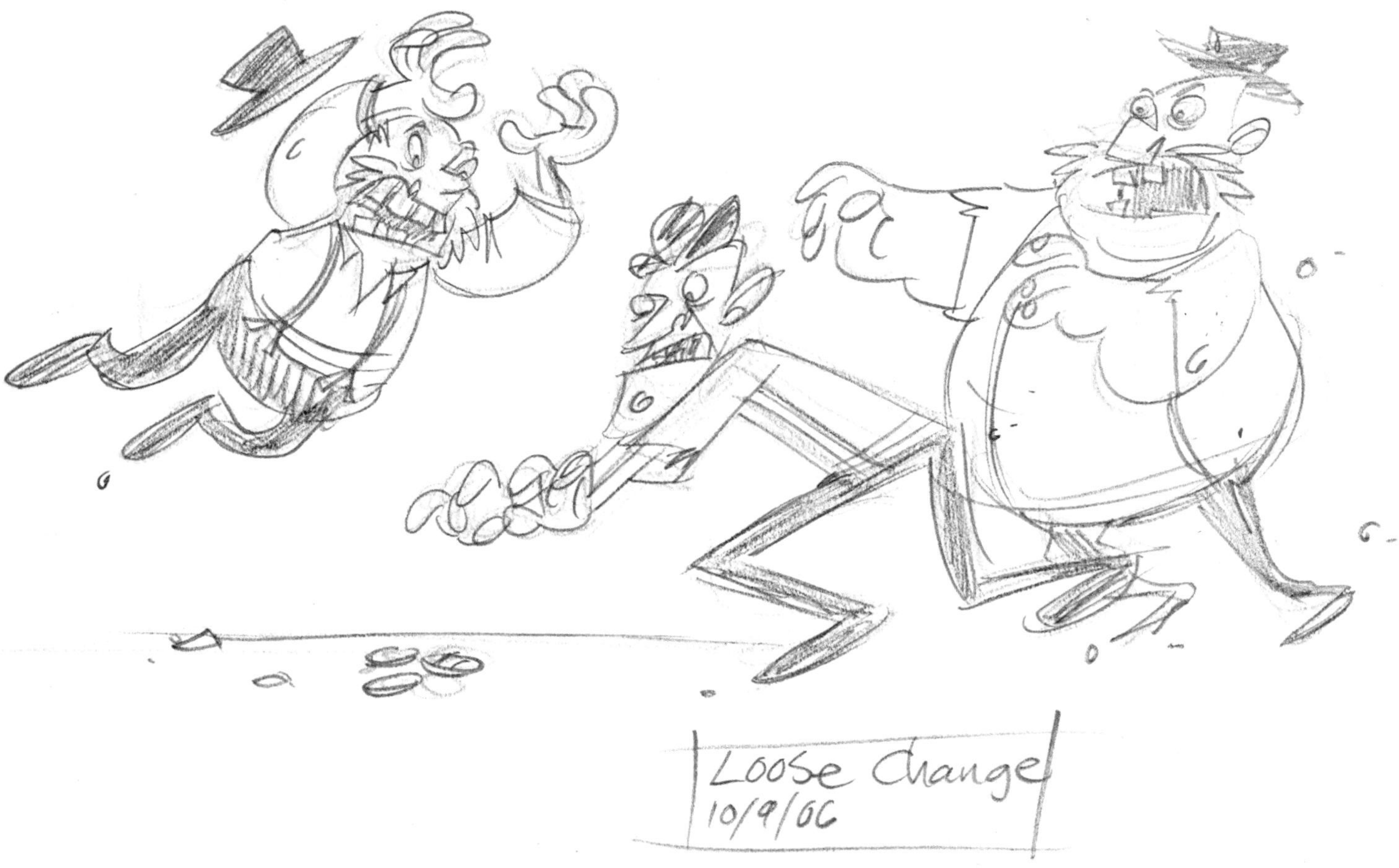
Loose Change
10/9/06

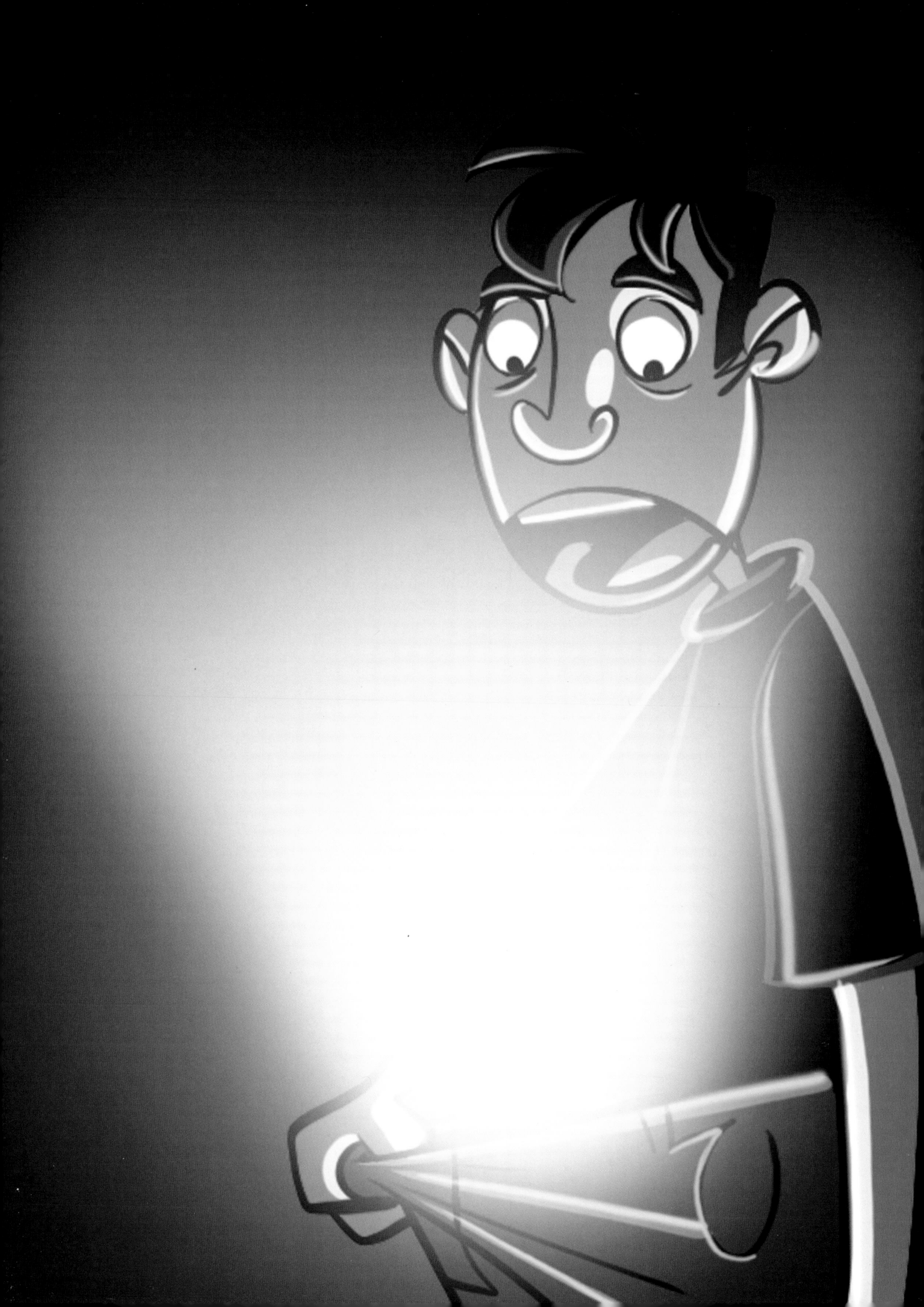

THE (CONTINUING) EVOLUTION OF GABE AND TYCHO

by Mike Krahulik

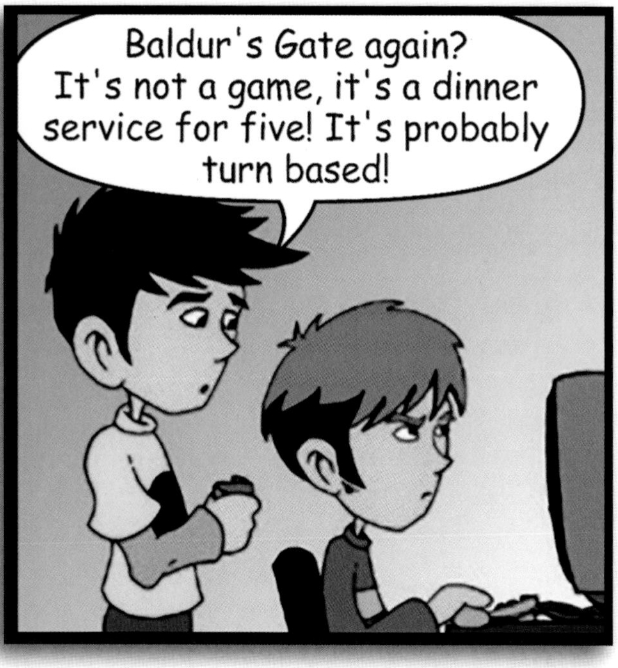
Baldur's Gate again?
It's not a game, it's a dinner service for five! It's probably turn based!

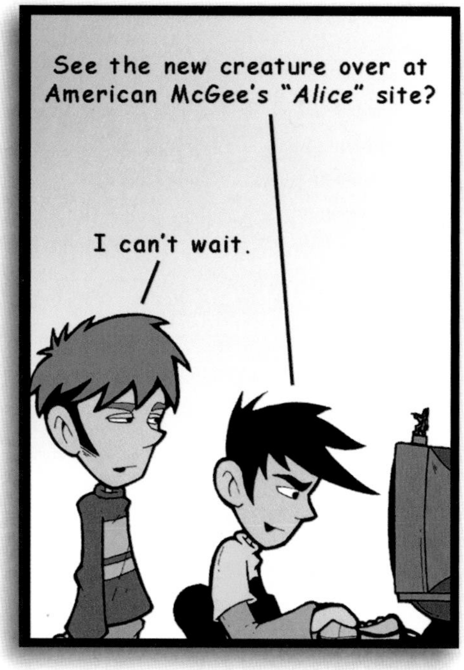
See the new creature over at American McGee's "Alice" site?
I can't wait.

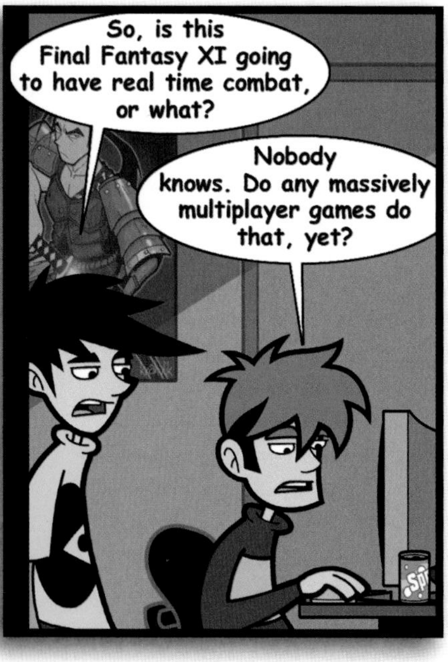
So, is this Final Fantasy XI going to have real time combat, or what?
Nobody knows. Do any massively multiplayer games do that, yet?

I have to be honest and say that when we started the comic strip back in 1998, I didn't know a thing about cartooning. As a young man, I had spent the majority of my time reading and copying the artwork from comic books. Back then I was trying very hard to draw like Jim Lee, Todd McFarlane, and (God help me) Rob Liefeld. When we decided to enter a cartooning contest, I did my best, but it was a real departure for me.

When I look at the characters from back in 1999 and 2000, I just see way too many unimportant lines. Cartooning is about simplification and making a few lines really matter. Every line you draw needs to be important; it needs to matter. Back when PA started, I didn't understand that yet, and so the characters ended up looking lumpy.

In 2001 I discovered an artist named Stephen Silver via the *Clerks* cartoon that had just come out. I was blown away by Stephen's designs, and I spent hours trying to deconstruct them and discover what exactly he was doing that I found so appealing. What I discovered was that each of his characters had a unique silhouette. That was probably the first lesson I tried to incorporate into my work. Until then, Gabe and Tycho essentially had the same head shape. They each had different hair, but that was really it. This is when I redesigned Tycho's face so that it was a straight line with a curved back line. Gabe also got a refresh—his face became more V-shaped.

Studying Stephen's work also taught me the importance of line economy. Their backs and fronts are single sloping lines. I got rid of all the extra little tics and crosshatches that really didn't add anything. I also started using a much bolder line to frame the characters and a thinner line for the interior details.

TIME LINE **1999 (May) — The *Penny Arcade* forums are created. Today it is one of the largest online communities in existence.**

I think that's the guy who played the dragon in Panzer Dragoon Orta. Go ask him!
No! You go ask him.
How do you unsubscribe from Asheron's Call 2?
I don't think you can.
FOR LOST O
MANAGEM

In early 2003 I took a big chance and tried just coloring my pencil sketches. This was a really fun period artistically because I was trying a bunch of new digital coloring tools and techniques. This style proved to be very unpopular with our readers, though, and so I ended up giving up on it after a few comics. By February 2003 I was back to my old style, but I was still trying to push myself. My goal was to try and make the comic look like still frames from an animated show. I really wanted to convey the idea that the characters were moving around and "acting" in the frames you couldn't see.

Have sex, Goddamit!
What's wrong?
I'm playing the Singles, and I can't get these kids to swap tartar sauce.

As you can see, in 2004 I discovered what all those extra buttons in Photoshop were for. At this point I flipped Gabe's hair so that it pointed down and also finalized the number of points it had. I did the same with Tycho, and looking back on it now, I'm surprised it took me that long. Like I said, I was playing around with Photoshop at this point, trying to teach myself different coloring techniques. Rendering shadows and highlights this completely didn't last long, either. It was all good practice, but it just took way too long, and I don't think it really added that much to the comic.

You delivered such a mighty blow, that you caused your opponent to be ejected from the server?
That's right. I hit him so hard he fell off the Internet.
I think he's he's screaming for help.
What, so now you speak Chinese?

By this point I was really becoming fascinated with cartooning and animation. Rather than a thick line for the outside lines and a thinner one on the inside, I tried to focus on varying my line. I finally started to play with the pressure sensitivity on my tablet and made a real effort to teach myself about line weight. It wasn't very obvious in 2005 and 2006, but was there and I was learning. I was also pushing myself during this period to improve my facial expressions.

TIME LINE **1999 (July) —** Penny Arcade launches *The Bench*, an open-source cartoon with Gabe and a squirrel and a variety of props as stock art. More than four thousand strips are created.

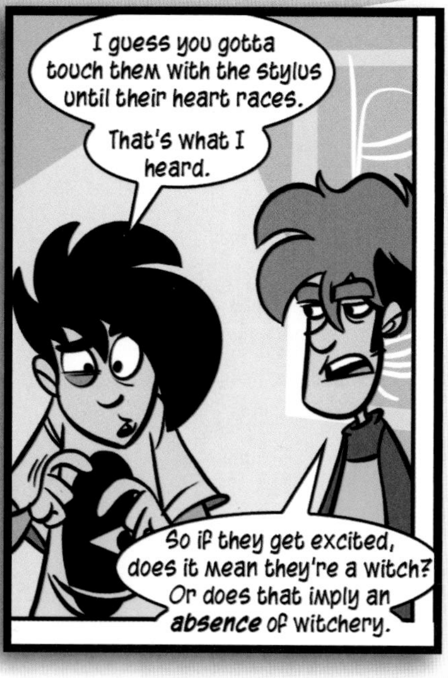
I guess you gotta touch them with the stylus until their heart races.
That's what I heard.
So if they get excited, does it mean they're a witch? Or does that imply an *absence* of witchery.

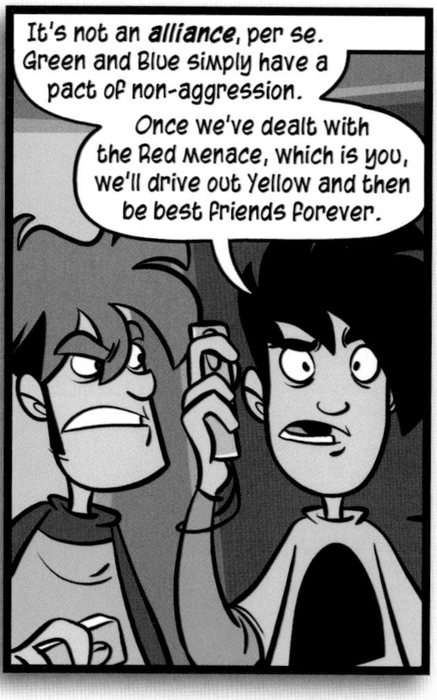
It's not an *alliance*, per se. Green and Blue simply have a pact of non-aggression.
Once we've dealt with the Red menace, which is you, we'll drive out Yellow and then be best friends forever.

Through 2007 and 2008 I was really just refining my line work. I think at this point after years of fiddling, I was finally starting to zero in on the characters as well. Gabe's eyes have gotten bigger to reflect his naïveté and whimsical nature. Tycho's eyes have shrunk, I suppose, to convey the exact opposite. I was still trying to push my expressions as well as the characters' acting. I spent a lot of time thinking about the dialogue and trying to imagine the characters delivering in my head. *What do they do with their hands? What is their body language like?* All that stuff helps to reinforce the joke.

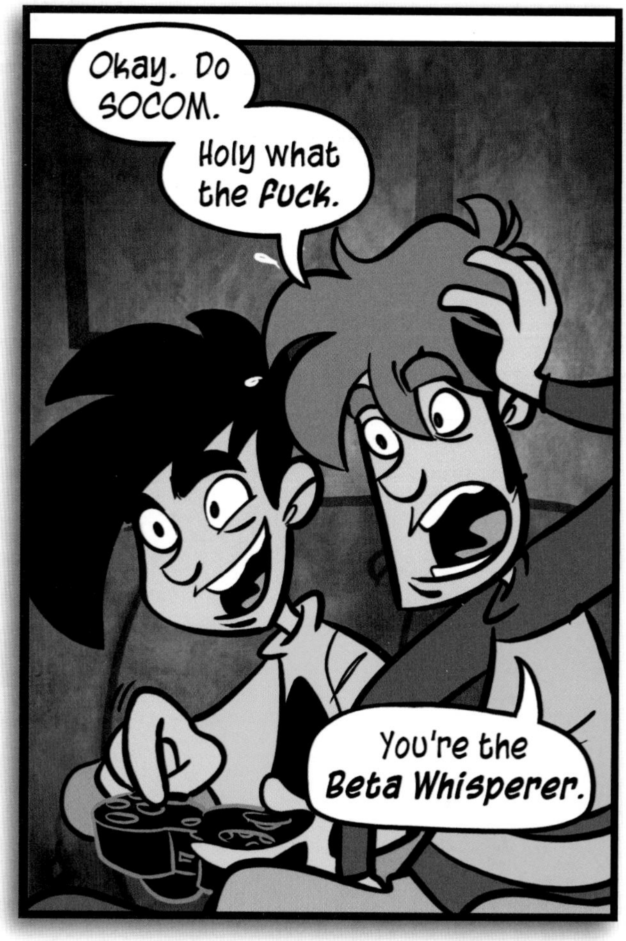
Okay. Do SOCOM.
Holy what the *fuck*.
You're the *Beta Whisperer*.

From the end of 2008 to now, it's just been a matter of trying to refine all this stuff: line weight, character emotion and acting, pushing my expressions. I've also started trying to incorporate texture into the backgrounds. I think this helps make the characters pop out more. It's an old trick but it took me a long time to figure out how to make it work in the context of *Penny Arcade*.

It's really a never-ending journey. I imagine I could do another one of these retrospectives in 2019, and track another ten years of progression. The secret is to hate yourself and the work you produce. If everything you make is trash, then you'll continually push yourself to produce something that won't fill you with shame. If you're lucky, after a lifetime of self-doubt, maybe you'll produce something you can be proud of before you fall over dead.

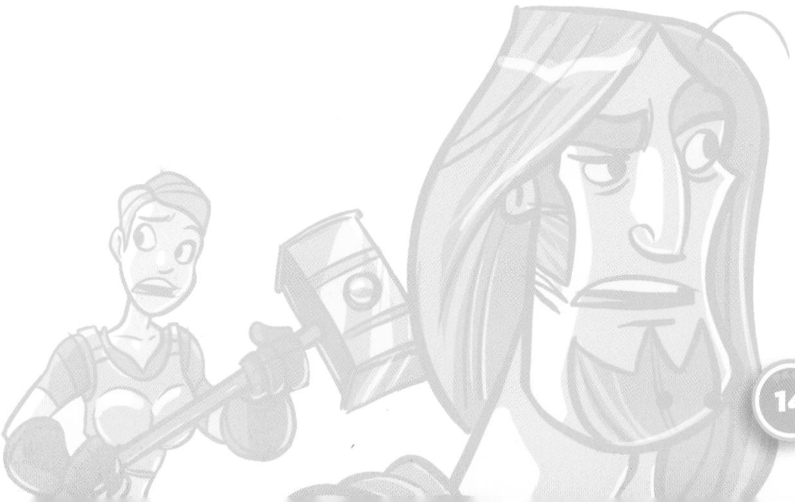

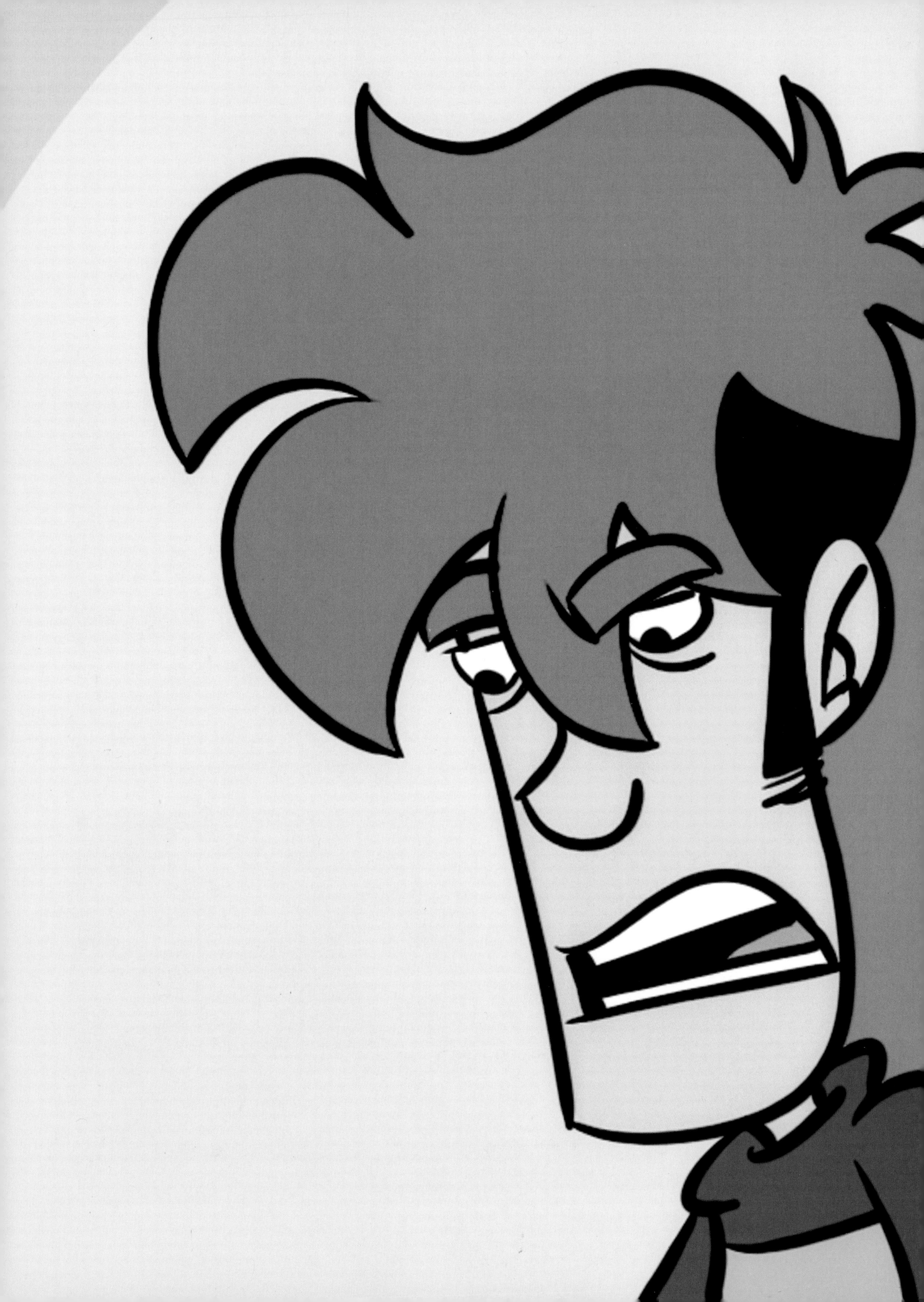

THE CARDBOARD TUBE SAMURAI

by Jerry Holkins

One of our unlikely, runaway accidents, the Cardboard Tube Samurai came to be after Mike found a cardboard tube in a dumpster and began to beat me with it. That's pretty shameful. As an unflinching account of the site's formative years, though, this book must project the *whole truth.*

Cardboard Tube Samurai strips are a chance for us to indulge ourselves a little bit, to experiment with tone and art—to play, essentially. They also teach us to pace full pages, something we don't get an opportunity to do in the normal course of our work. They've taught us a lot, and we are still learning.

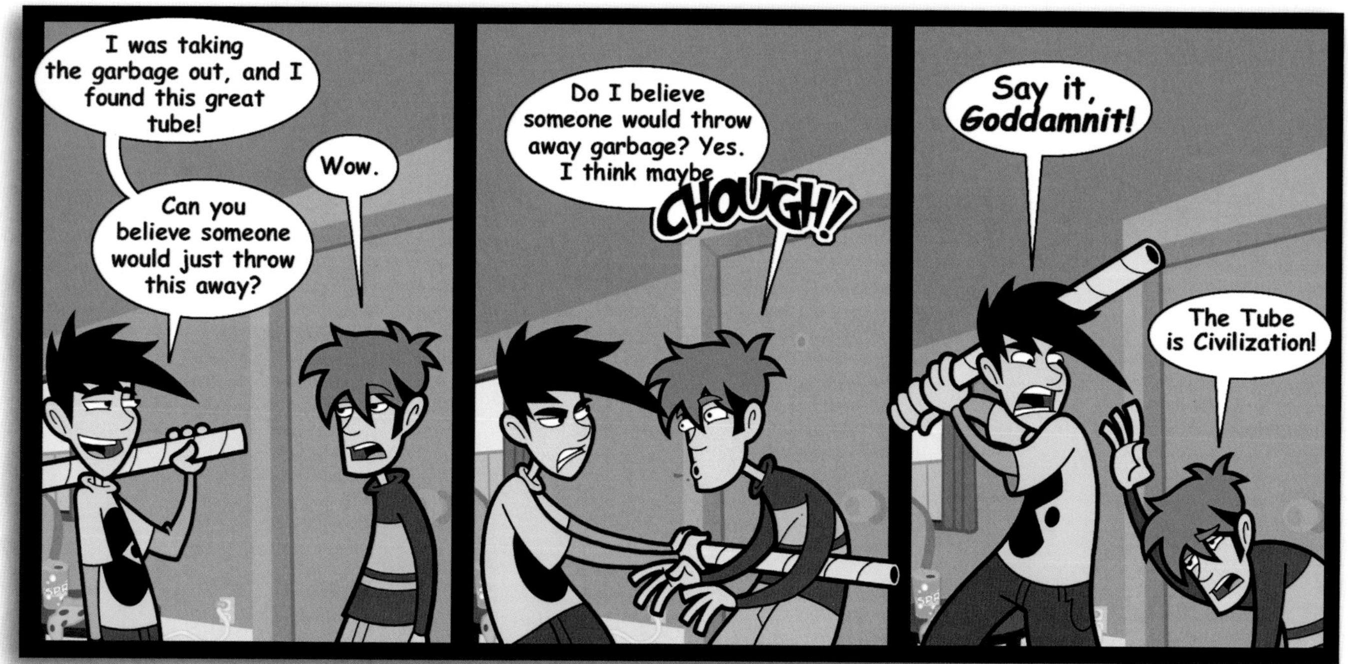
I was taking the garbage out, and I found this great tube!
Wow.
Can you believe someone would just throw this away?
Do I believe someone would throw away garbage? Yes. I think maybe
CHOUGH!
Say it, Goddamnit!
The Tube is Civilization!

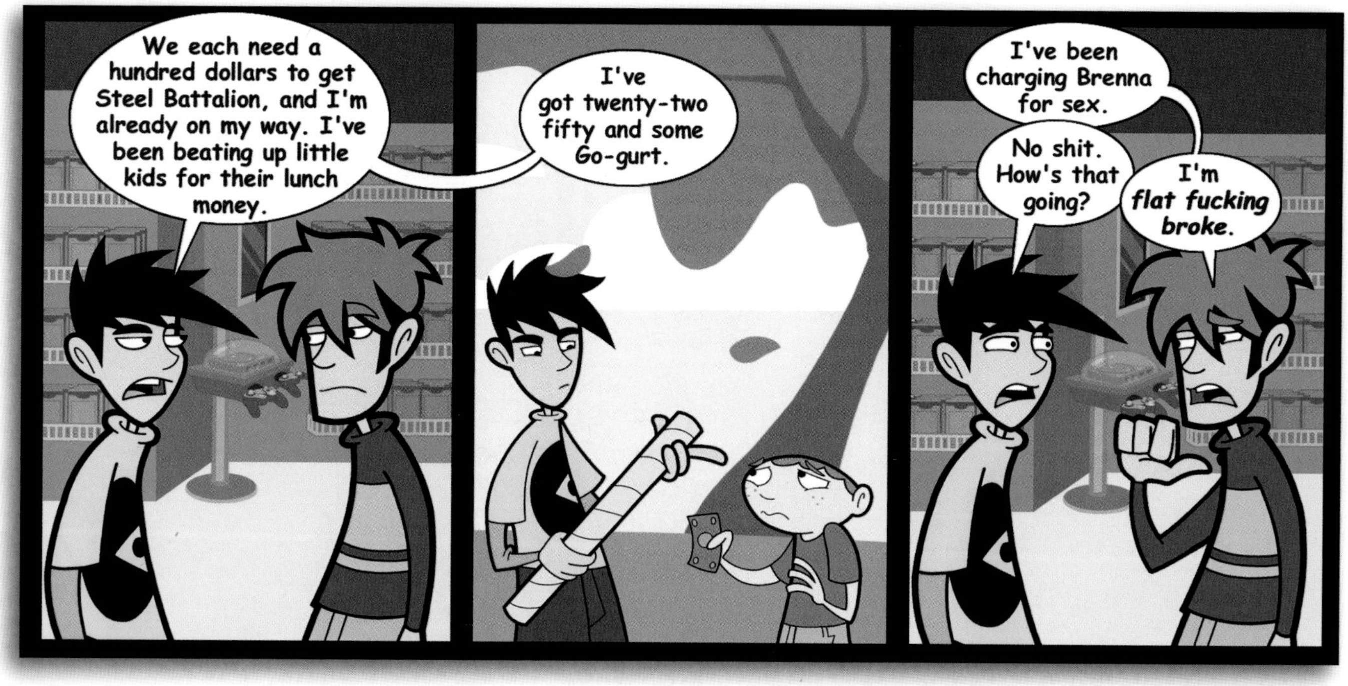
We each need a hundred dollars to get Steel Battalion, and I'm already on my way. I've been beating up little kids for their lunch money.
I've got twenty-two fifty and some Go-gurt.
I've been charging Brenna for sex.
No shit. How's that going?
I'm flat fucking broke.

TIME LINE

1999 (October) — Jerry and Brenna are married, combining their last names, Holcomb and Parkinson, to form Holkins.

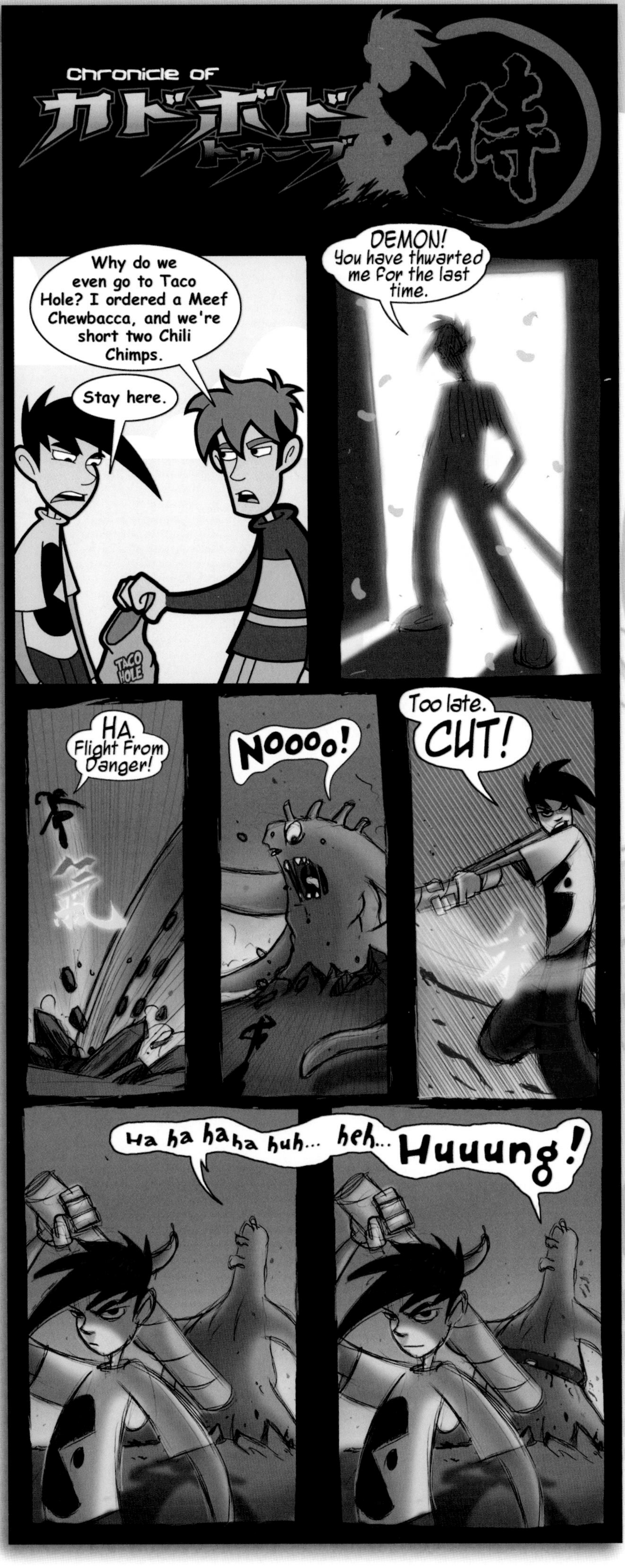
Chronicle of
侍
Why do we even go to Taco Hole? I ordered a Meef Chewbacca, and we're short two Chili Chimps.
Stay here.
TACO HOLE
DEMON! You have thwarted me for the last time.
HA. Flight From Danger!
Noooo!
Too late. CUT!
Ha ha haha huh... heh... Huuung!

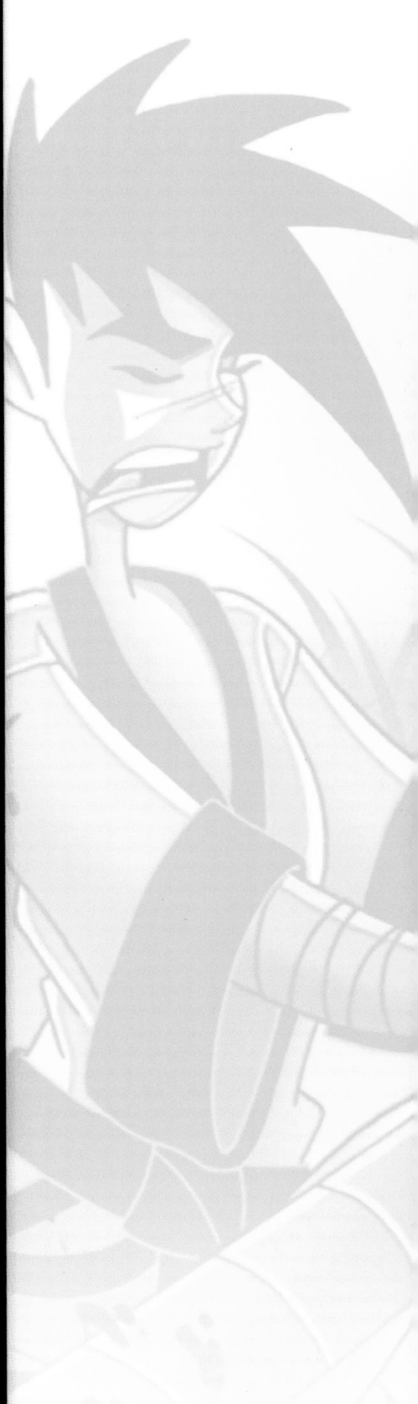

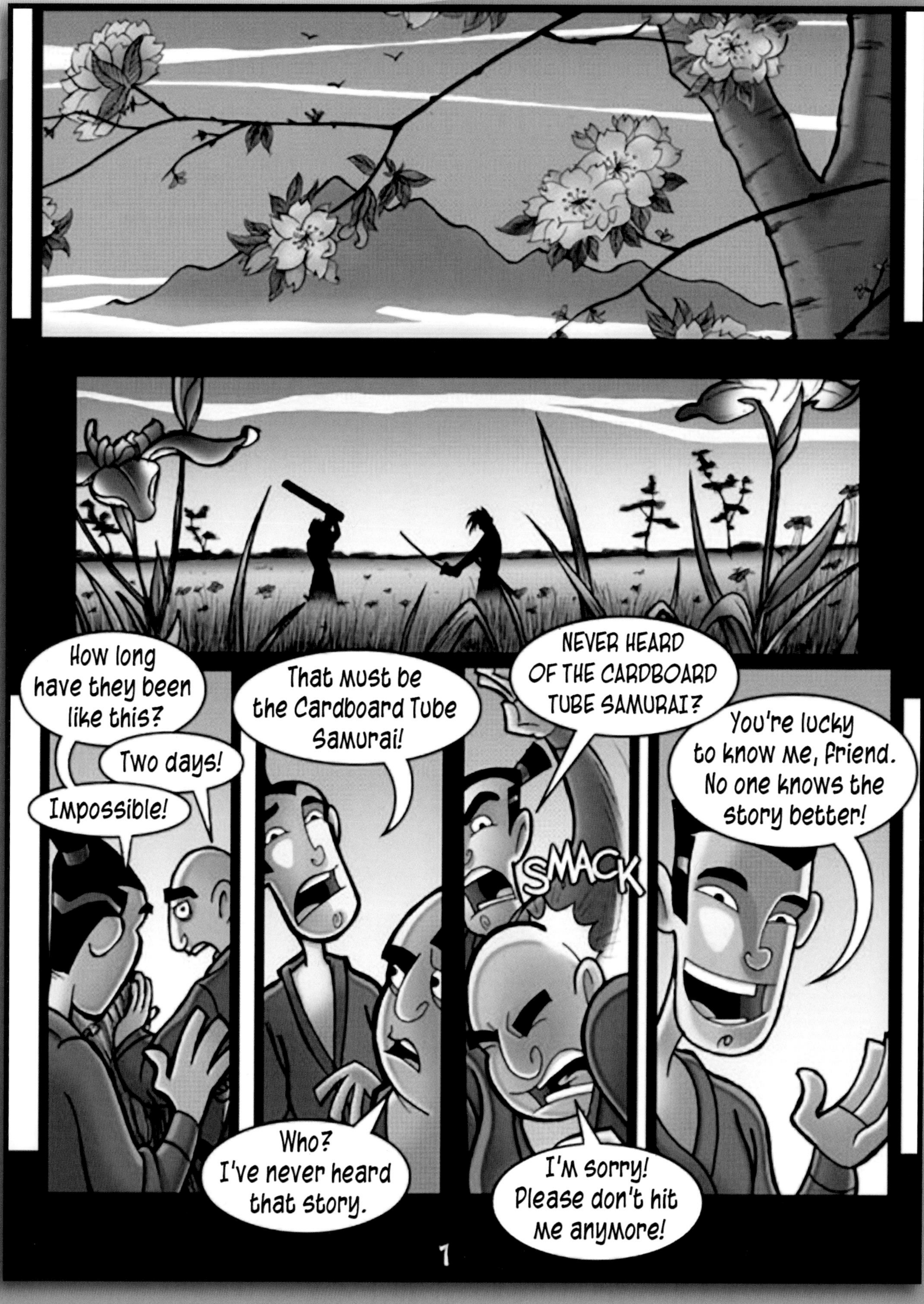
How long have they been like this?
Two days!
Impossible!
That must be the Cardboard Tube Samurai!
Who? I've never heard that story.
NEVER HEARD OF THE CARDBOARD TUBE SAMURAI?
SMACK
I'm sorry! Please don't hit me anymore!
You're lucky to know me, friend. No one knows the story better!
7

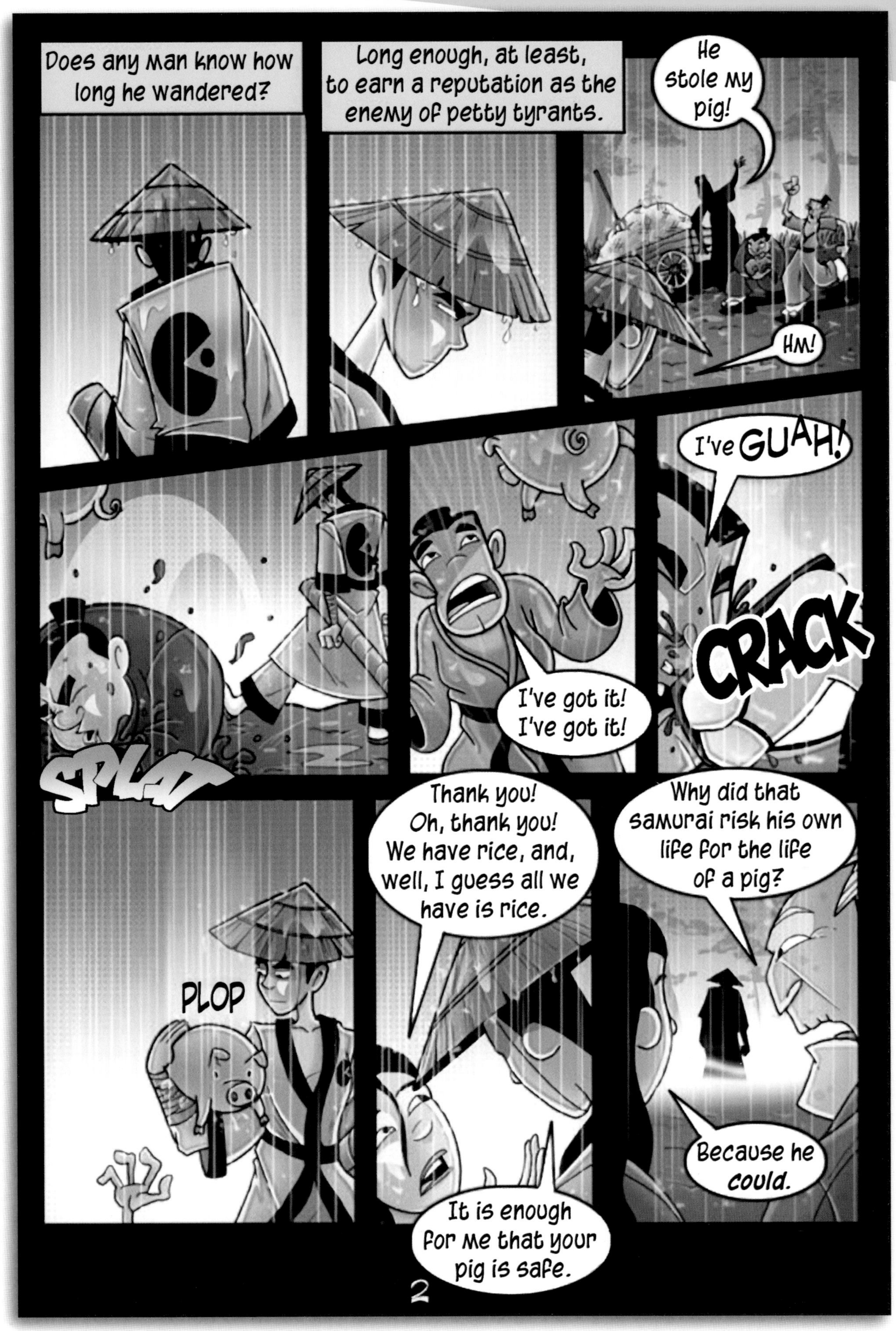
Does any man know how long he wandered?
Long enough, at least, to earn a reputation as the enemy of petty tyrants.
He stole my pig!
HM!
I've got it! I've got it!
I've GUAH!
CRACK
SPLAT
PLOP
Thank you! Oh, thank you! We have rice, and, well, I guess all we have is rice.
It is enough for me that your pig is safe.
Why did that samurai risk his own life for the life of a pig?
Because he could.
2

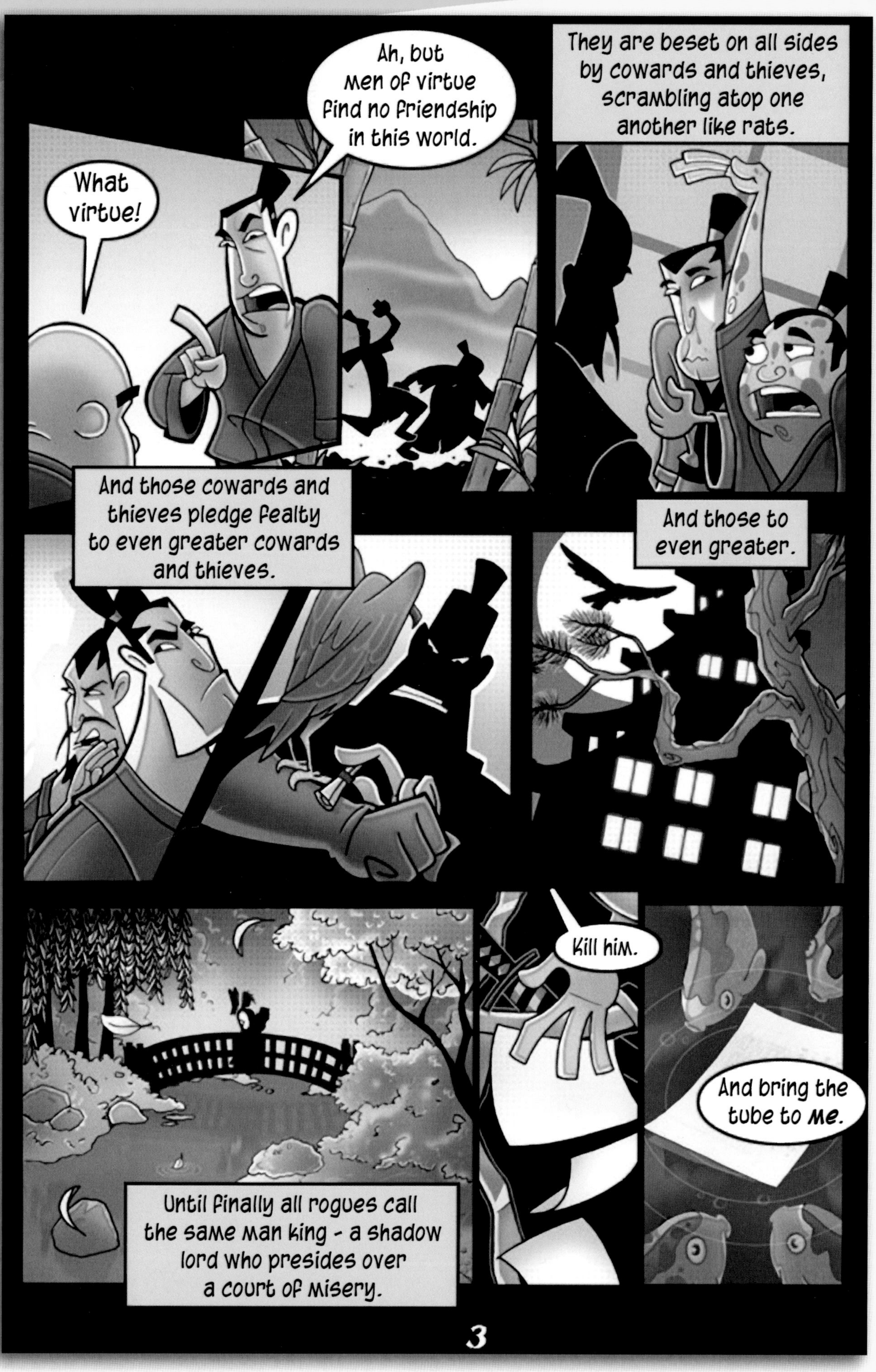
What virtue!
Ah, but men of virtue find no friendship in this world.
They are beset on all sides by cowards and thieves, scrambling atop one another like rats.
And those cowards and thieves pledge fealty to even greater cowards and thieves.
And those to even greater.
Until finally all rogues call the same man king - a shadow lord who presides over a court of misery.
Kill him.
And bring the tube to me.
3

TIME LINE **1999 (November)** — The first piece of Penny Arcade merchandise, the Got Game? T-shirt, is created.

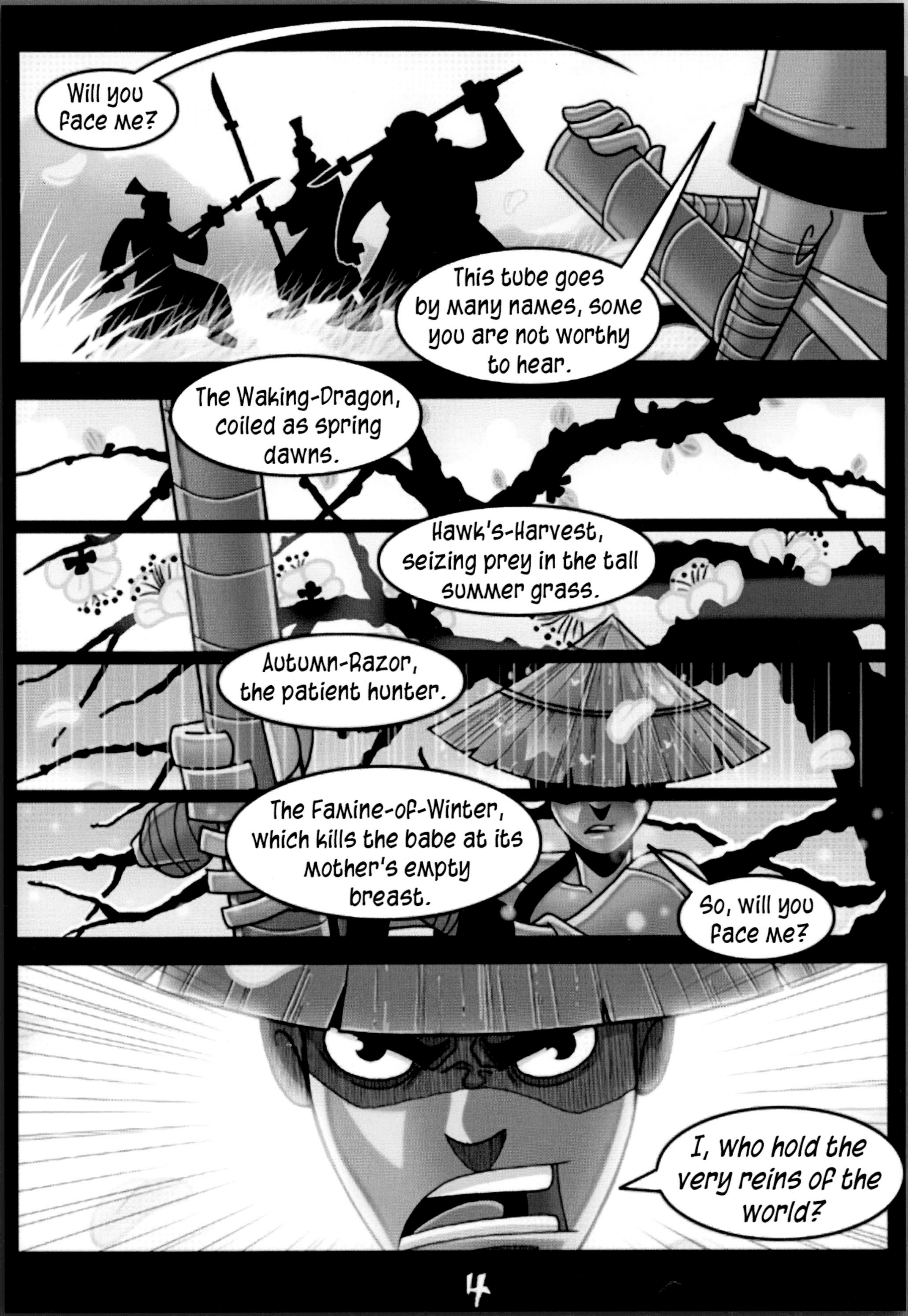
Will you face me?
This tube goes by many names, some you are not worthy to hear.
The Waking-Dragon, coiled as spring dawns.
Hawk's-Harvest, seizing prey in the tall summer grass.
Autumn-Razor, the patient hunter.
The Famine-of-Winter, which kills the babe at its mother's empty breast.
So, will you face me?
I, who hold the very reins of the world?
4

TIME LINE **1999 (November) —** *Penny Arcade* hits one hundred strips.

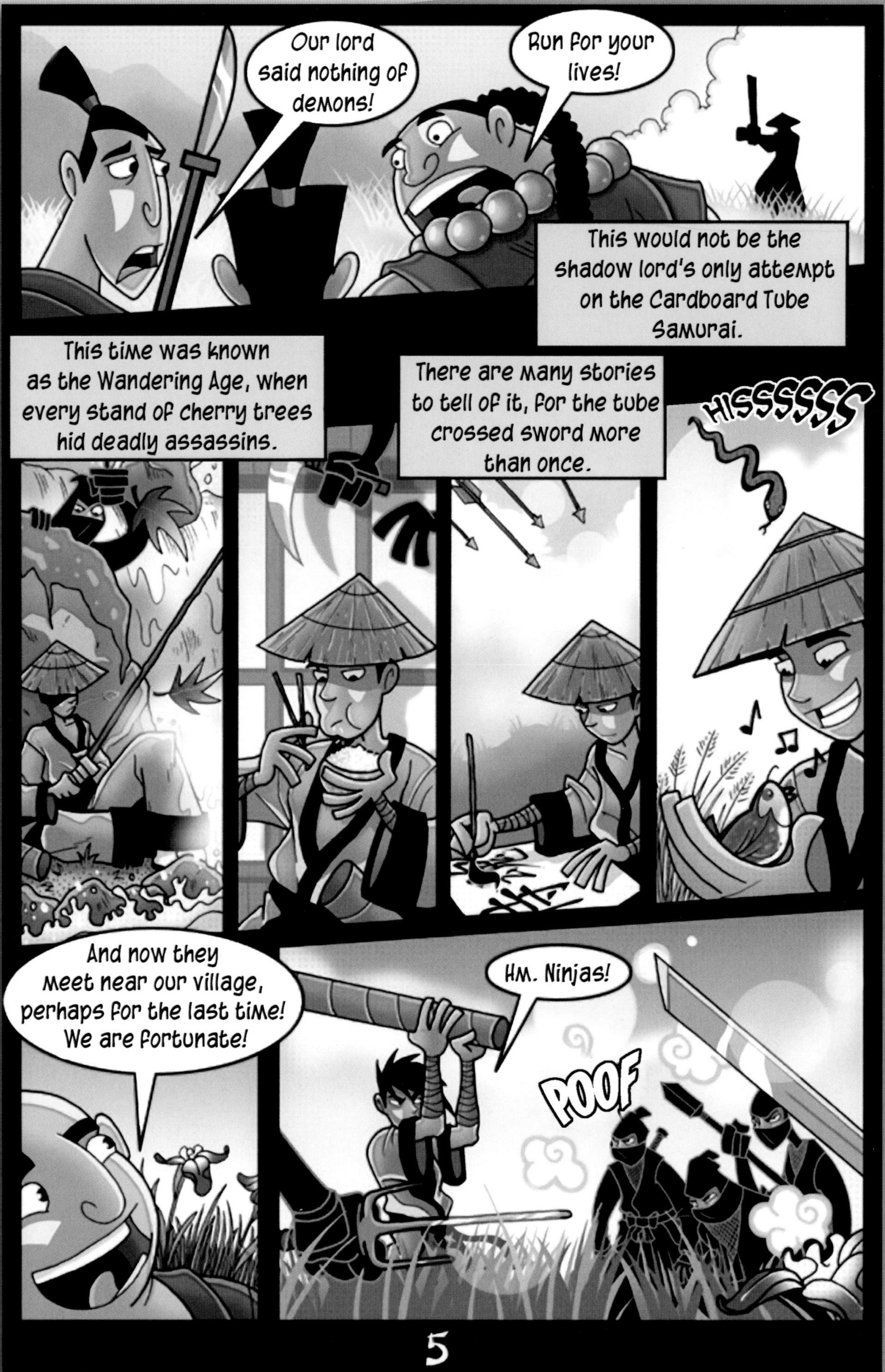
Our lord said nothing of demons!
Run for your lives!
This would not be the shadow lord's only attempt on the Cardboard Tube Samurai.
This time was known as the Wandering Age, when every stand of cherry trees hid deadly assassins.
There are many stories to tell of it, for the tube crossed sword more than once.
HISSSSSS
And now they meet near our village, perhaps for the last time! We are fortunate!
HM. Ninjas!
POOF
5

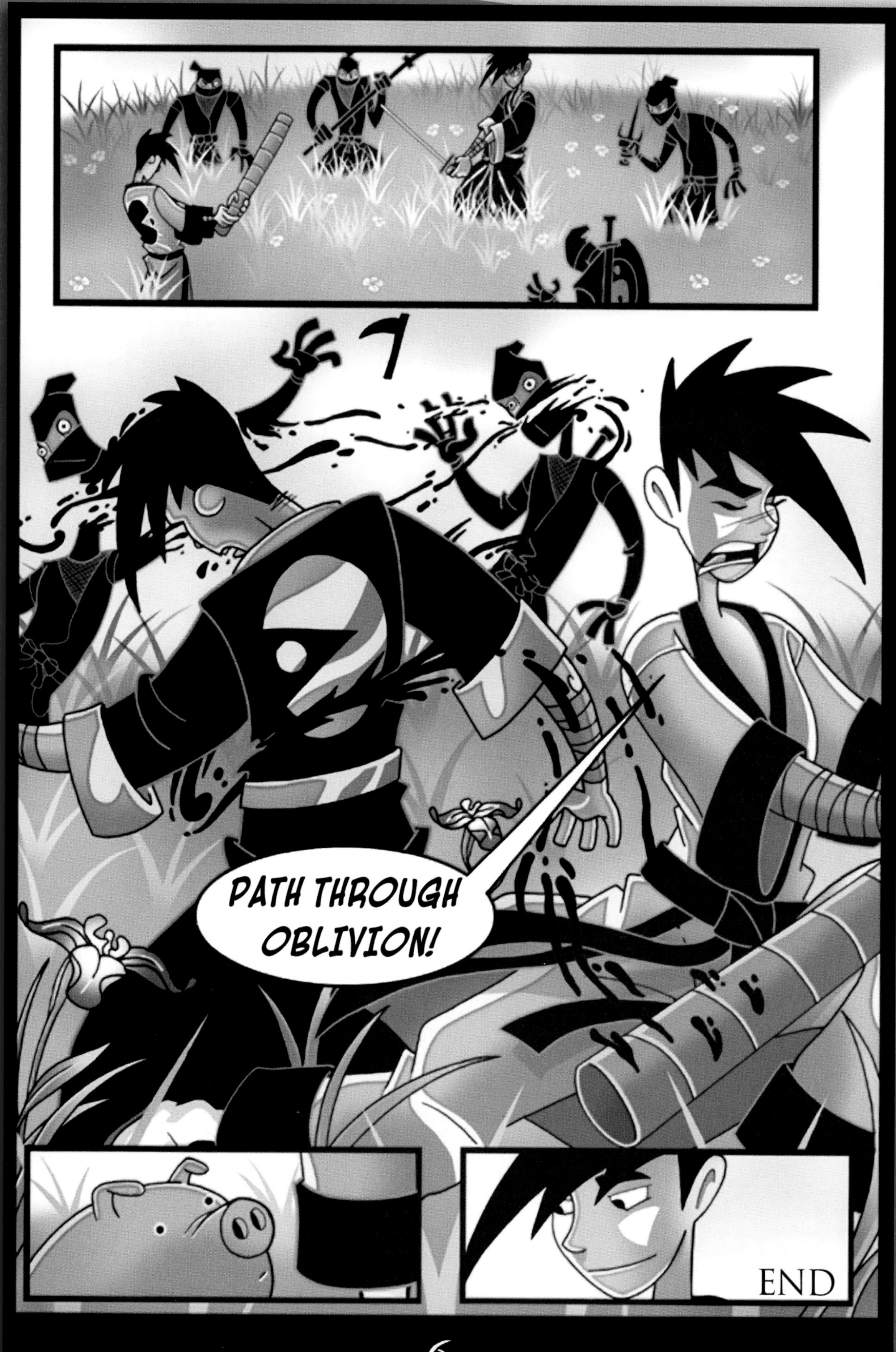
PATH THROUGH OBLIVION!
END
6

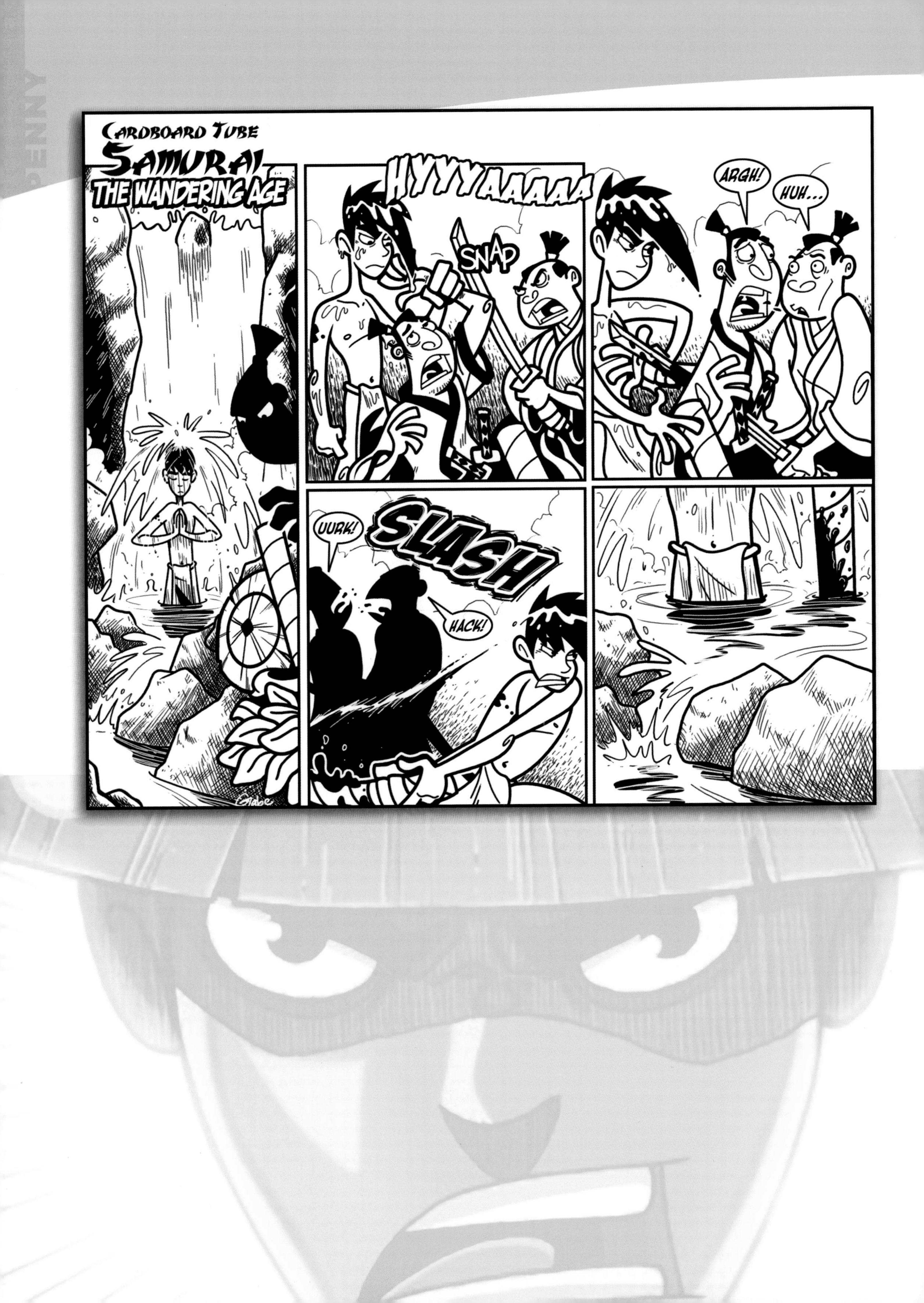
Cardboard Tube
Samurai
The Wandering Age
HYYYAAAAAA
SNAP
ARGH!
HUH...
UURK!
SLASH
HACK!
Gabe

THE WANDERING AGE

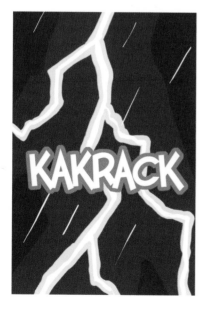

End

TIME LINE **2000 (March)** — Jerry quits his day job as a technician for a school district in Spokane.

25

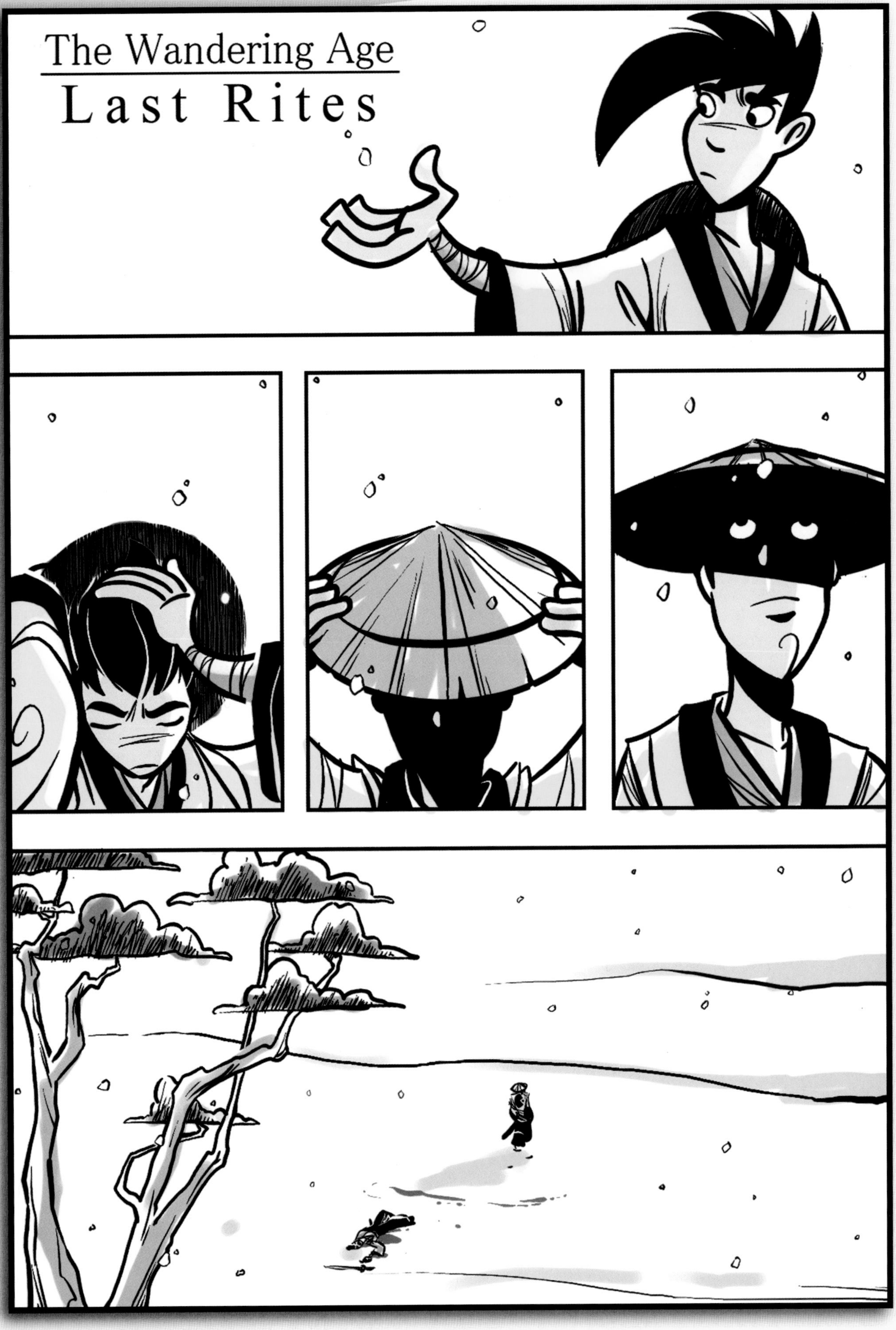
The Wandering Age
Last Rites

TIME LINE **2000 (March)** — Mike and Kara are married. Jerry shaves his head shortly afterward.

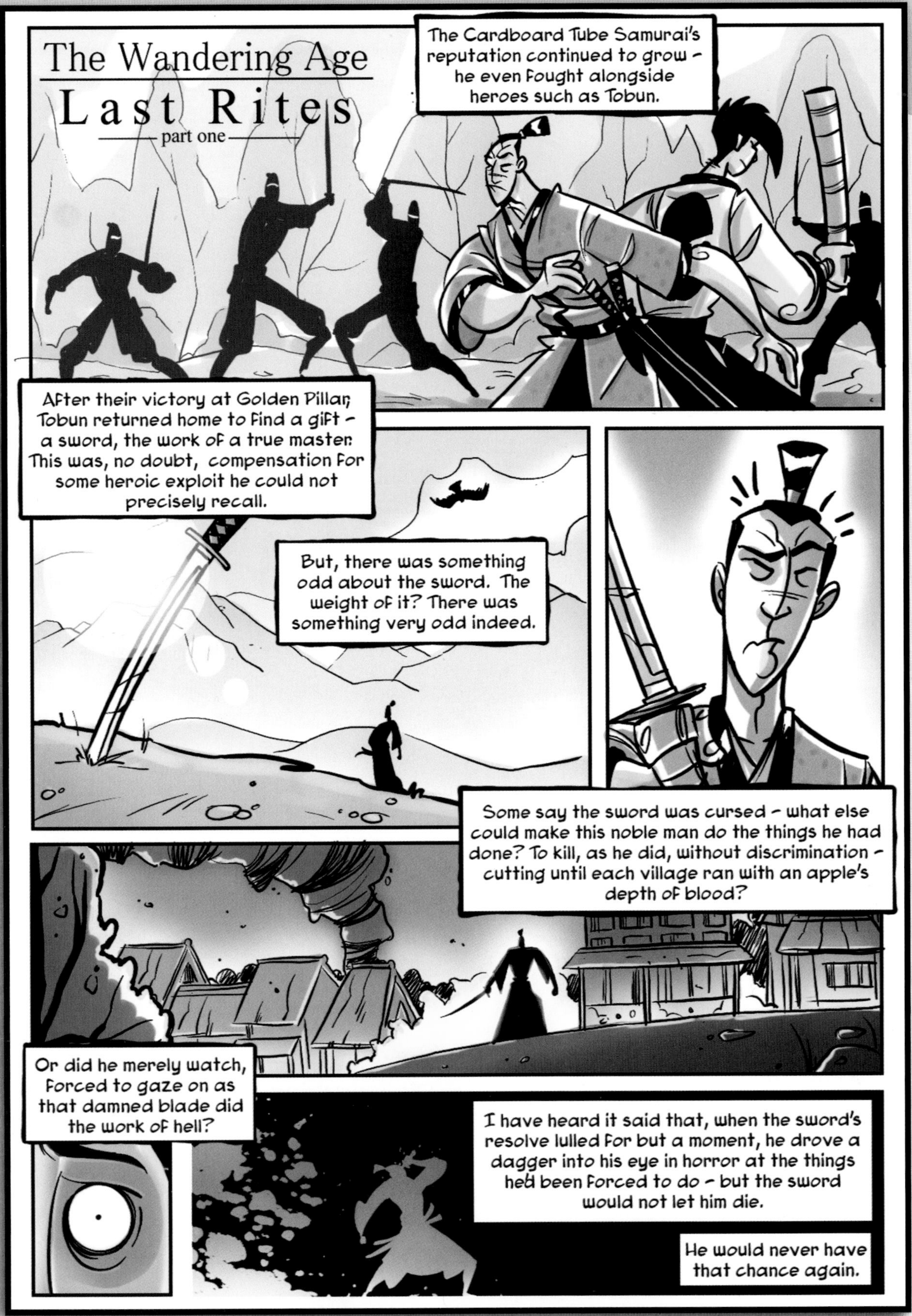
The Wandering Age
Last Rites
part one
The Cardboard Tube Samurai's reputation continued to grow - he even fought alongside heroes such as Tobun.
After their victory at Golden Pillar, Tobun returned home to find a gift - a sword, the work of a true master. This was, no doubt, compensation for some heroic exploit he could not precisely recall.
But, there was something odd about the sword. The weight of it? There was something very odd indeed.
Some say the sword was cursed - what else could make this noble man do the things he had done? To kill, as he did, without discrimination - cutting until each village ran with an apple's depth of blood?
Or did he merely watch, forced to gaze on as that damned blade did the work of hell?
I have heard it said that, when the sword's resolve lulled for but a moment, he drove a dagger into his eye in horror at the things he'd been forced to do - but the sword would not let him die.
He would never have that chance again.

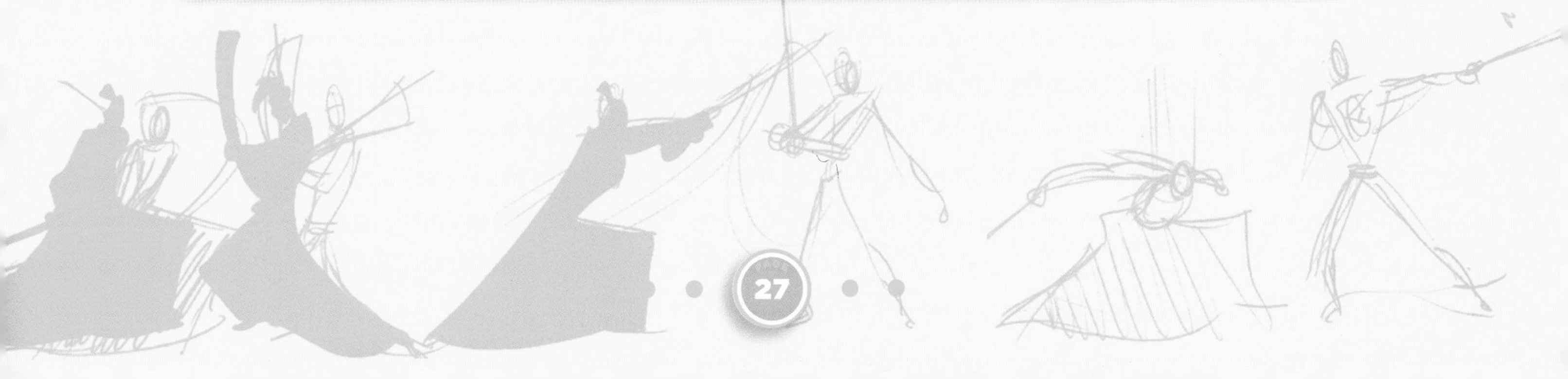

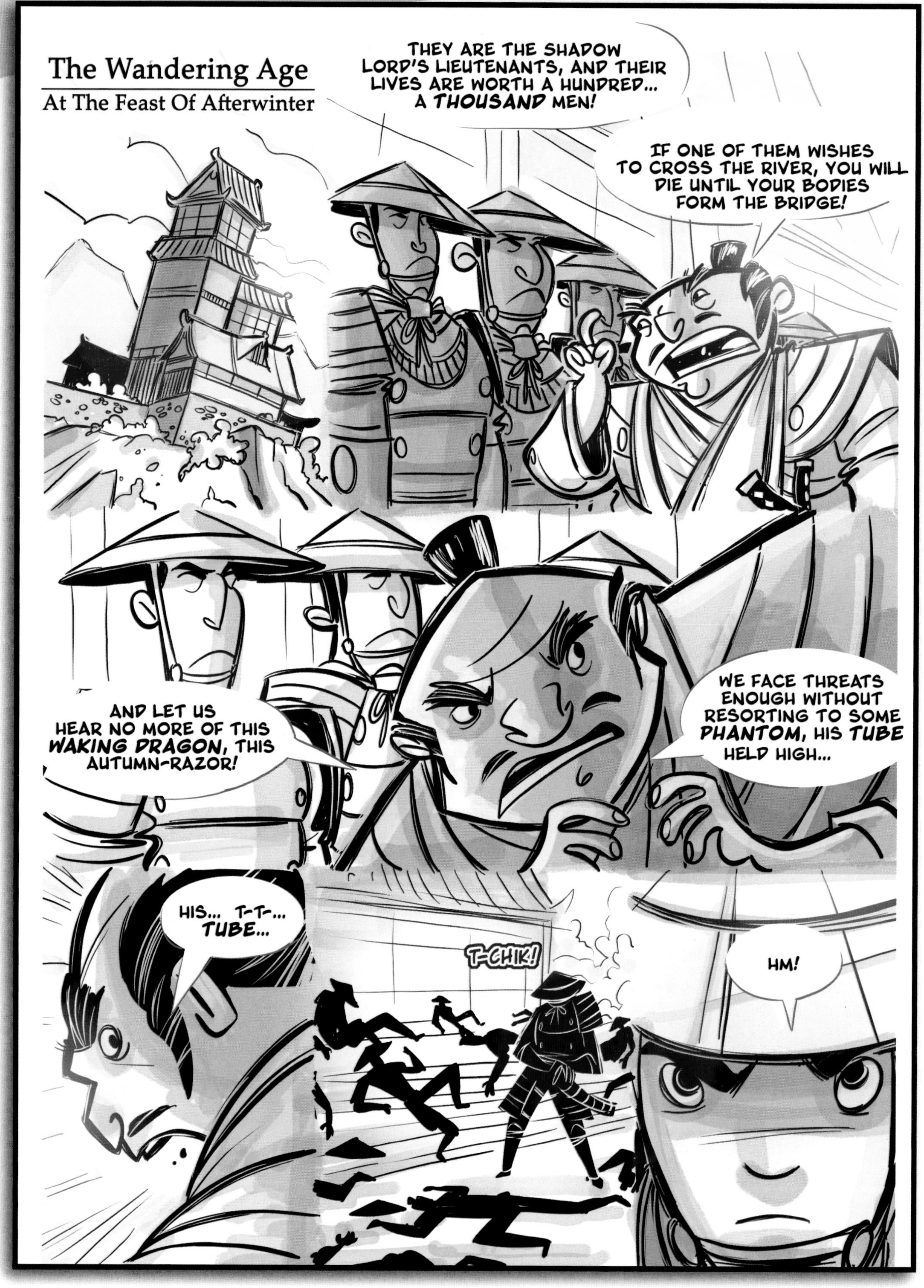
The Wandering Age
At The Feast Of Afterwinter
THEY ARE THE SHADOW LORD'S LIEUTENANTS, AND THEIR LIVES ARE WORTH A HUNDRED... A THOUSAND MEN!
IF ONE OF THEM WISHES TO CROSS THE RIVER, YOU WILL DIE UNTIL YOUR BODIES FORM THE BRIDGE!
AND LET US HEAR NO MORE OF THIS WAKING DRAGON, THIS AUTUMN-RAZOR!
WE FACE THREATS ENOUGH WITHOUT RESORTING TO SOME PHANTOM, HIS TUBE HELD HIGH...
HIS... T-T-... TUBE...
T-CHIK!
HM!

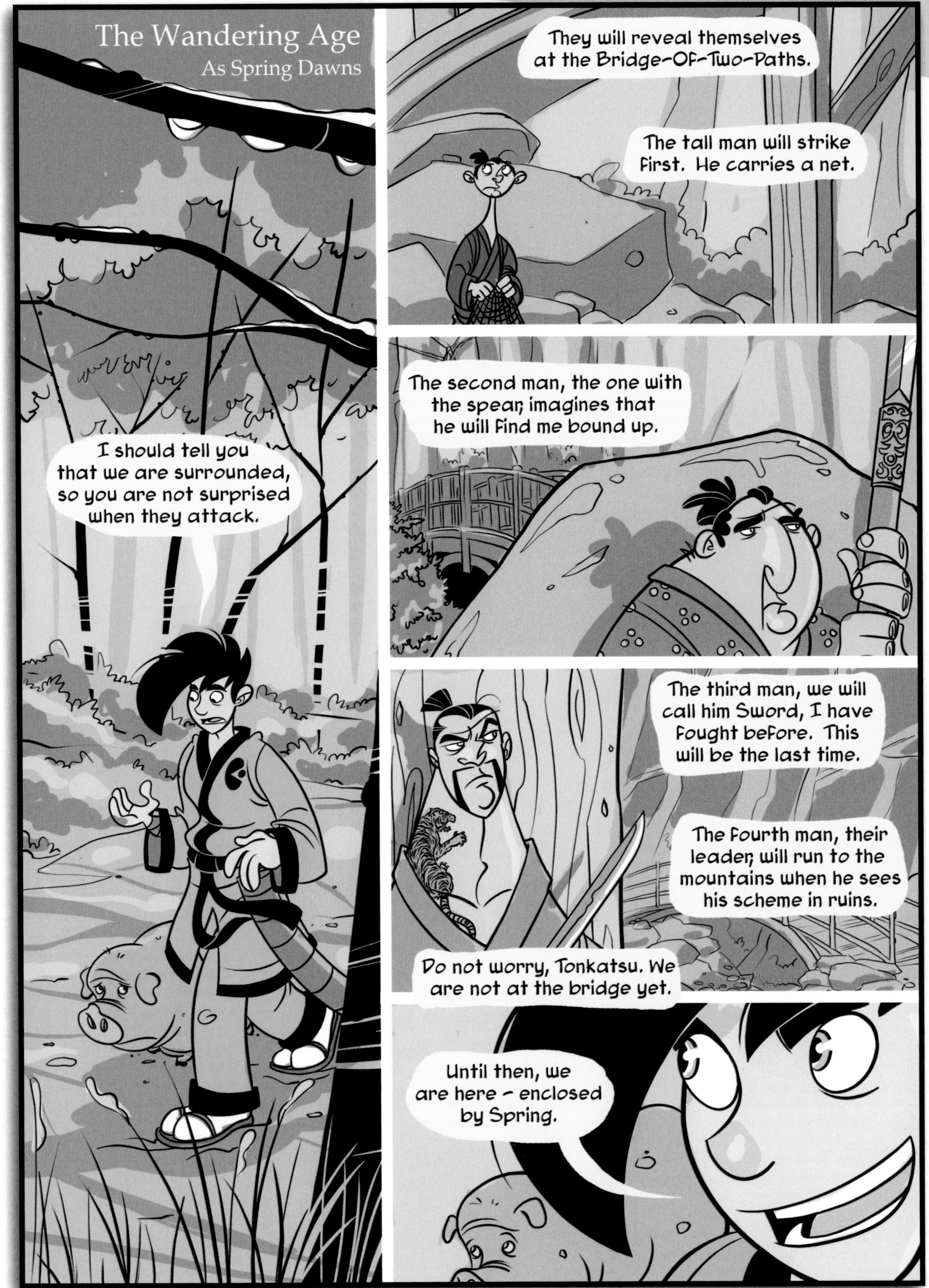

The Wandering Age
As Spring Dawns
I should tell you that we are surrounded, so you are not surprised when they attack.
They will reveal themselves at the Bridge-Of-Two-Paths.
The tall man will strike first. He carries a net.
The second man, the one with the spear, imagines that he will find me bound up.
The third man, we will call him Sword, I have fought before. This will be the last time.
The fourth man, their leader, will run to the mountains when he sees his scheme in ruins.
Do not worry, Tonkatsu. We are not at the bridge yet.
Until then, we are here - enclosed by Spring.

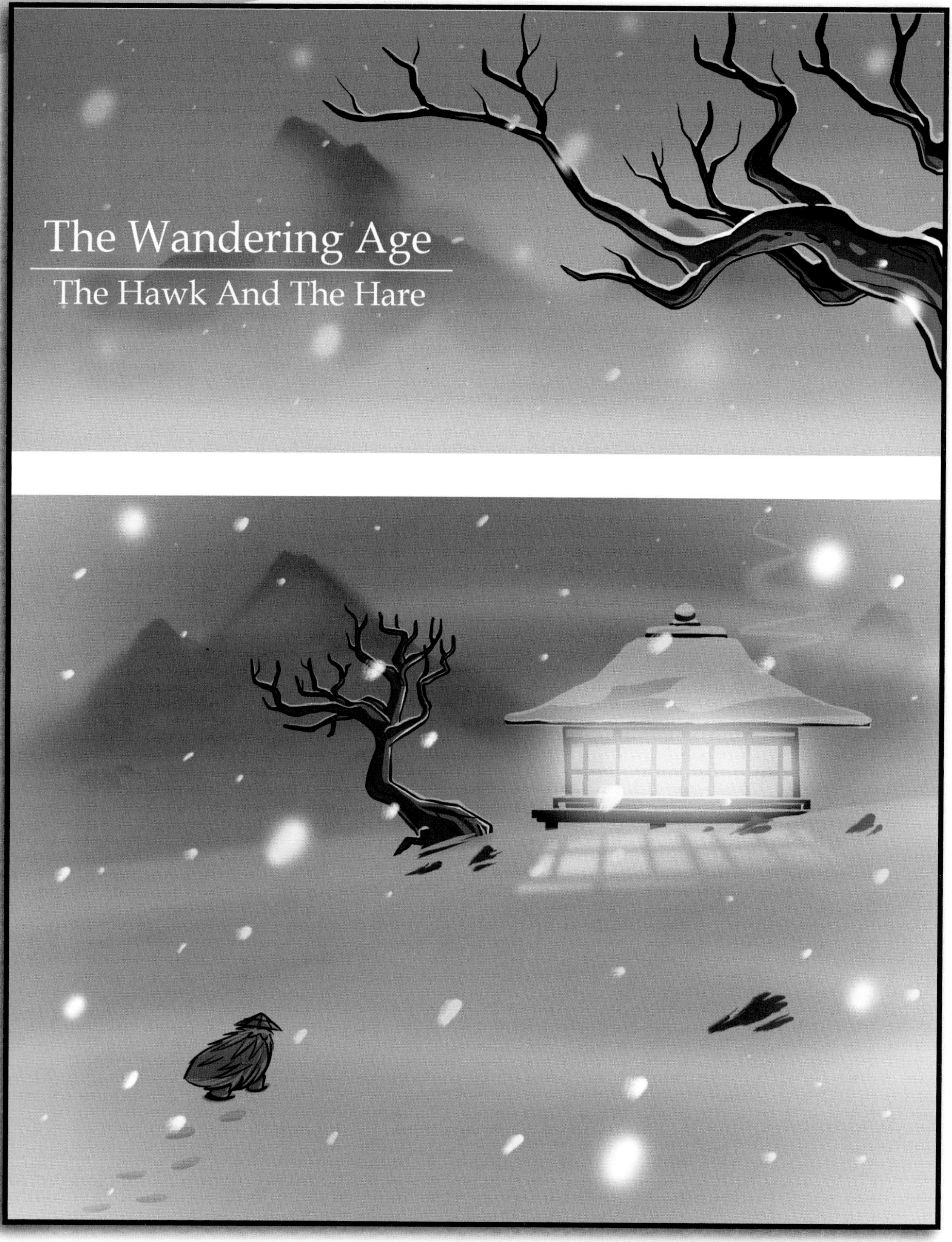
The Wandering Age
The Hawk And The Hare

TIME LINE **2000 (June) —** Mike takes a side job at GameSpy.com as an artist, using most of his income to buy video games.

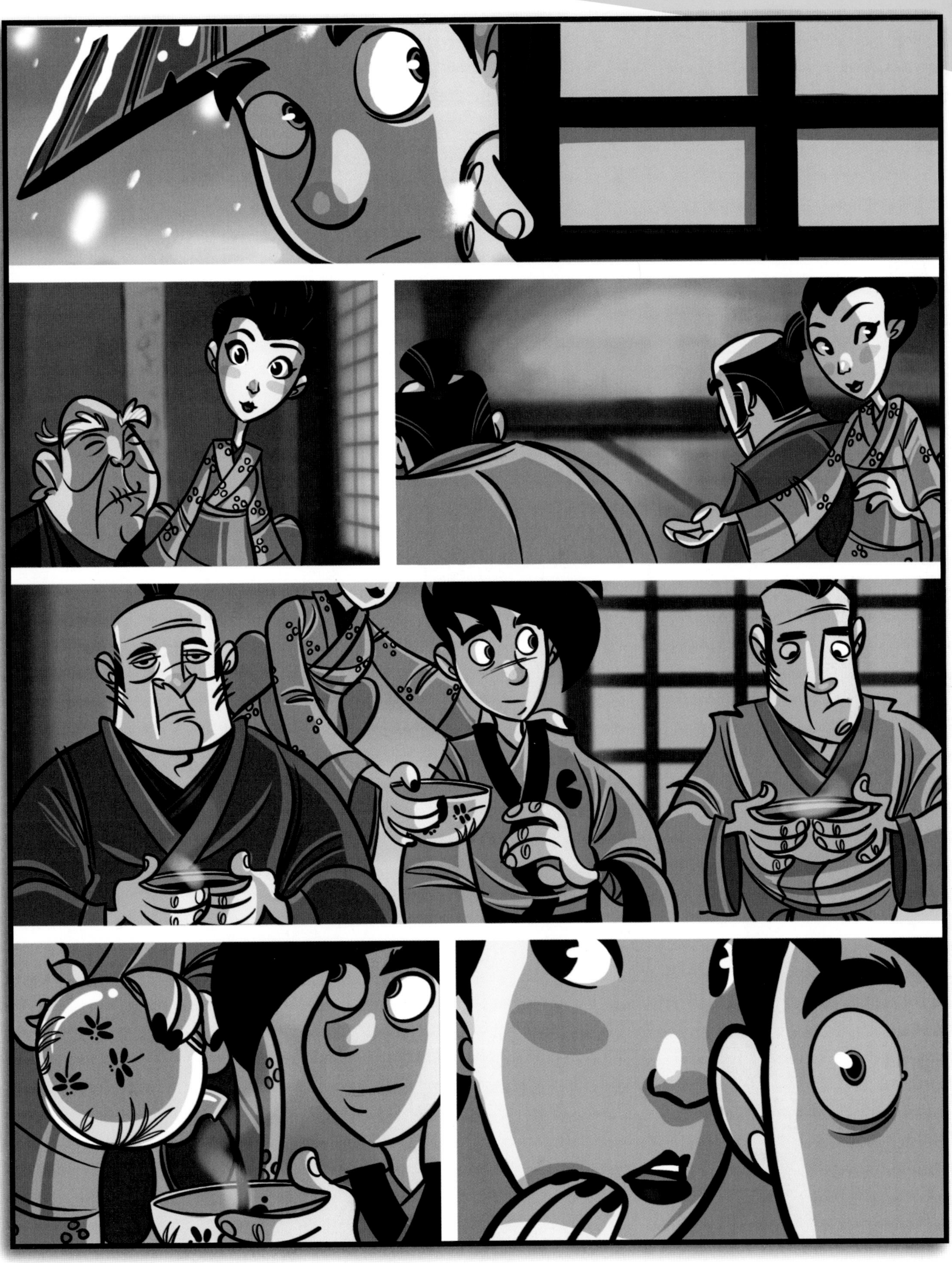

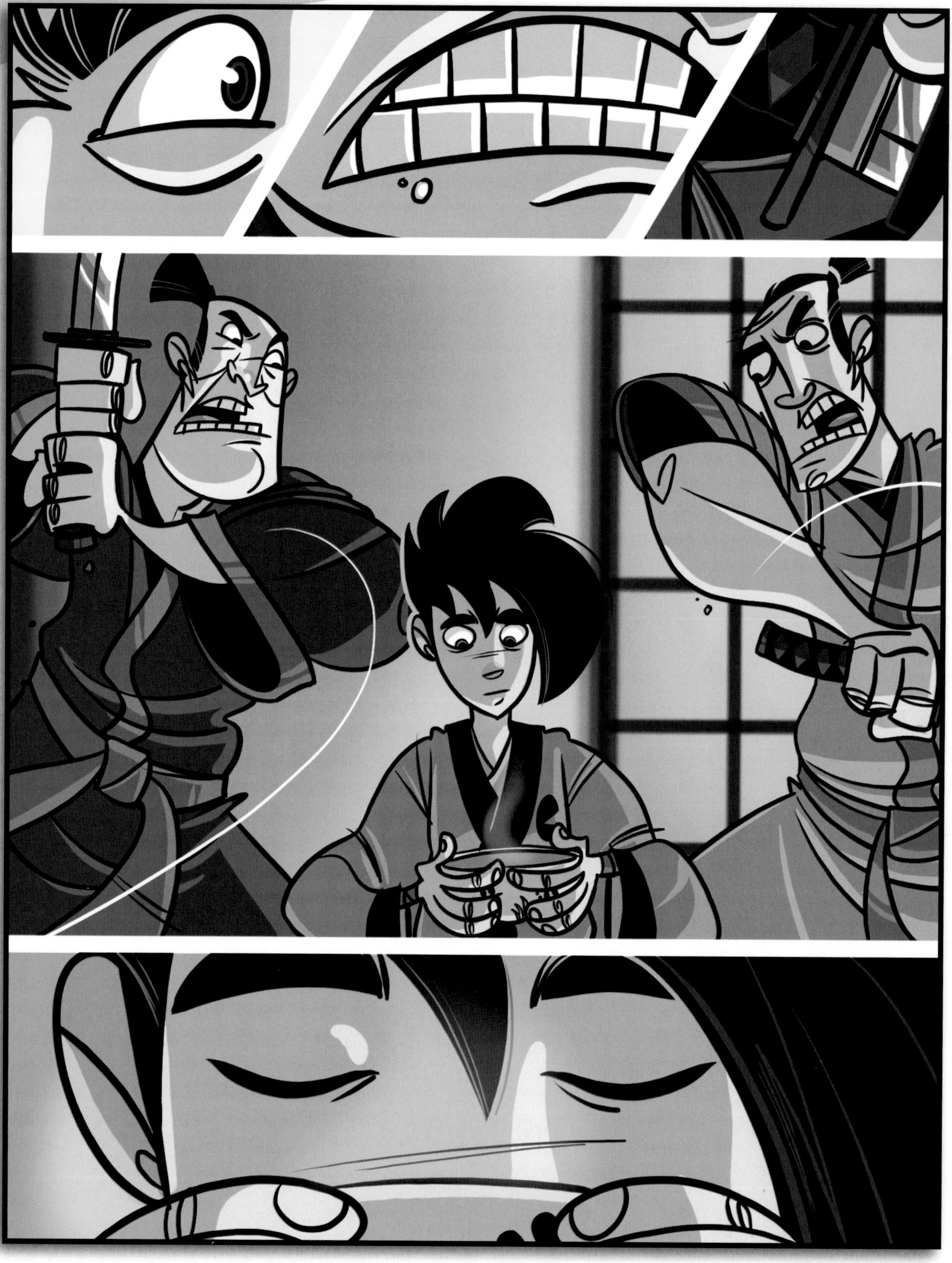

TIME LINE **2000 (July)** — Penny Arcade accidentally sells their company to eFront in what they believed was a hosting deal.

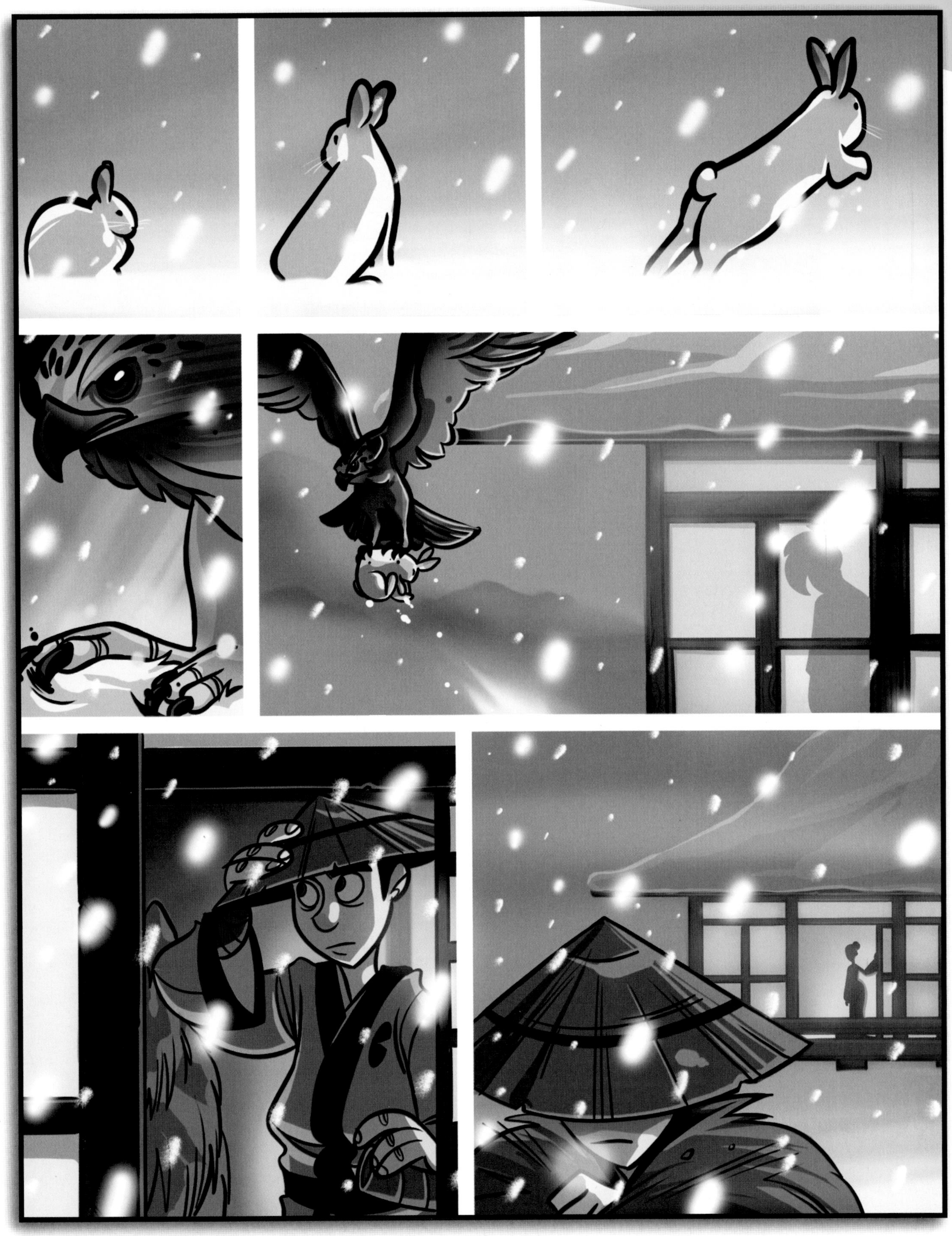

2000 (September) — Jerry moves from Spokane to a rat-infested home in Seattle.

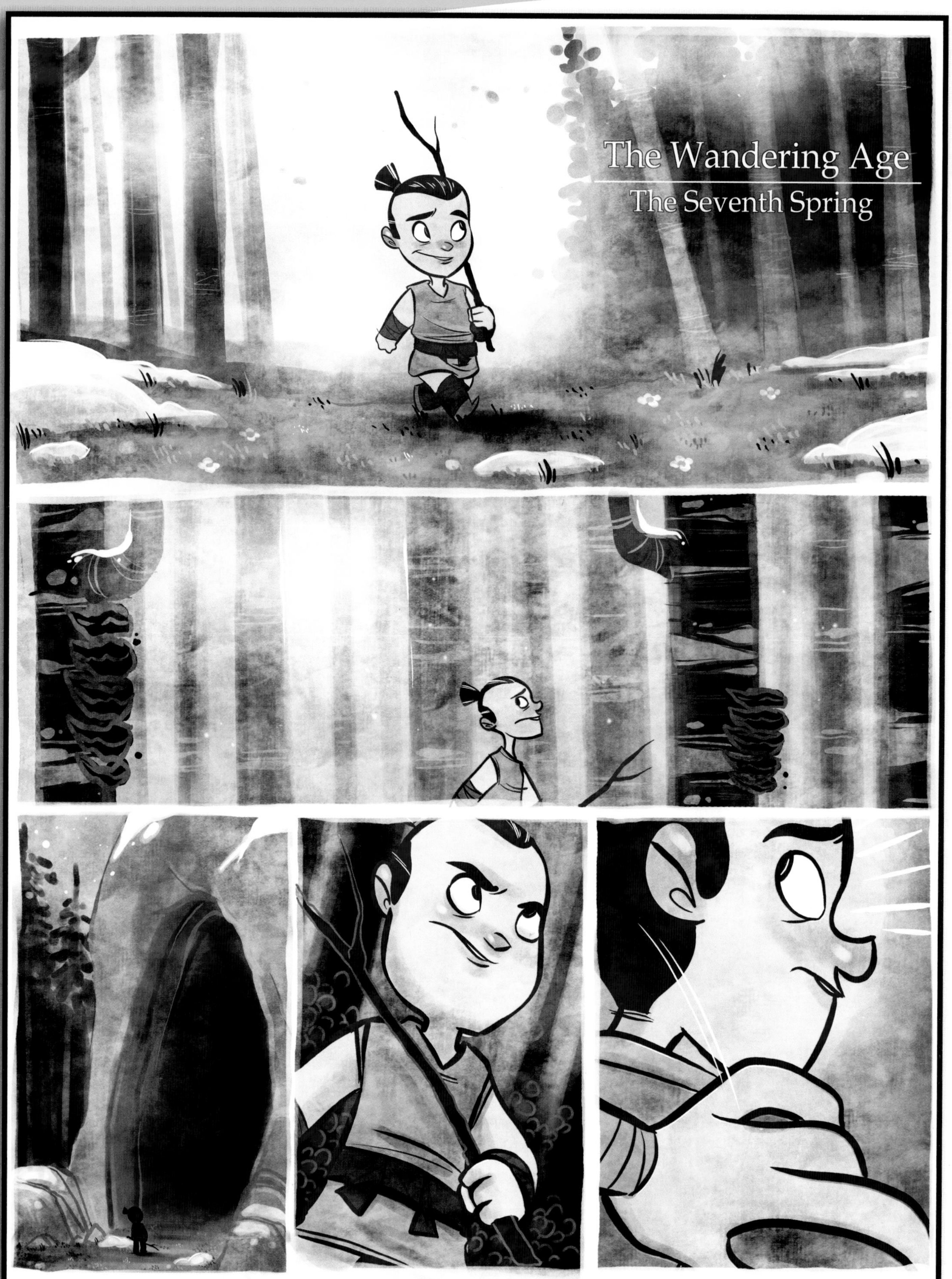
The Wandering Age
The Seventh Spring

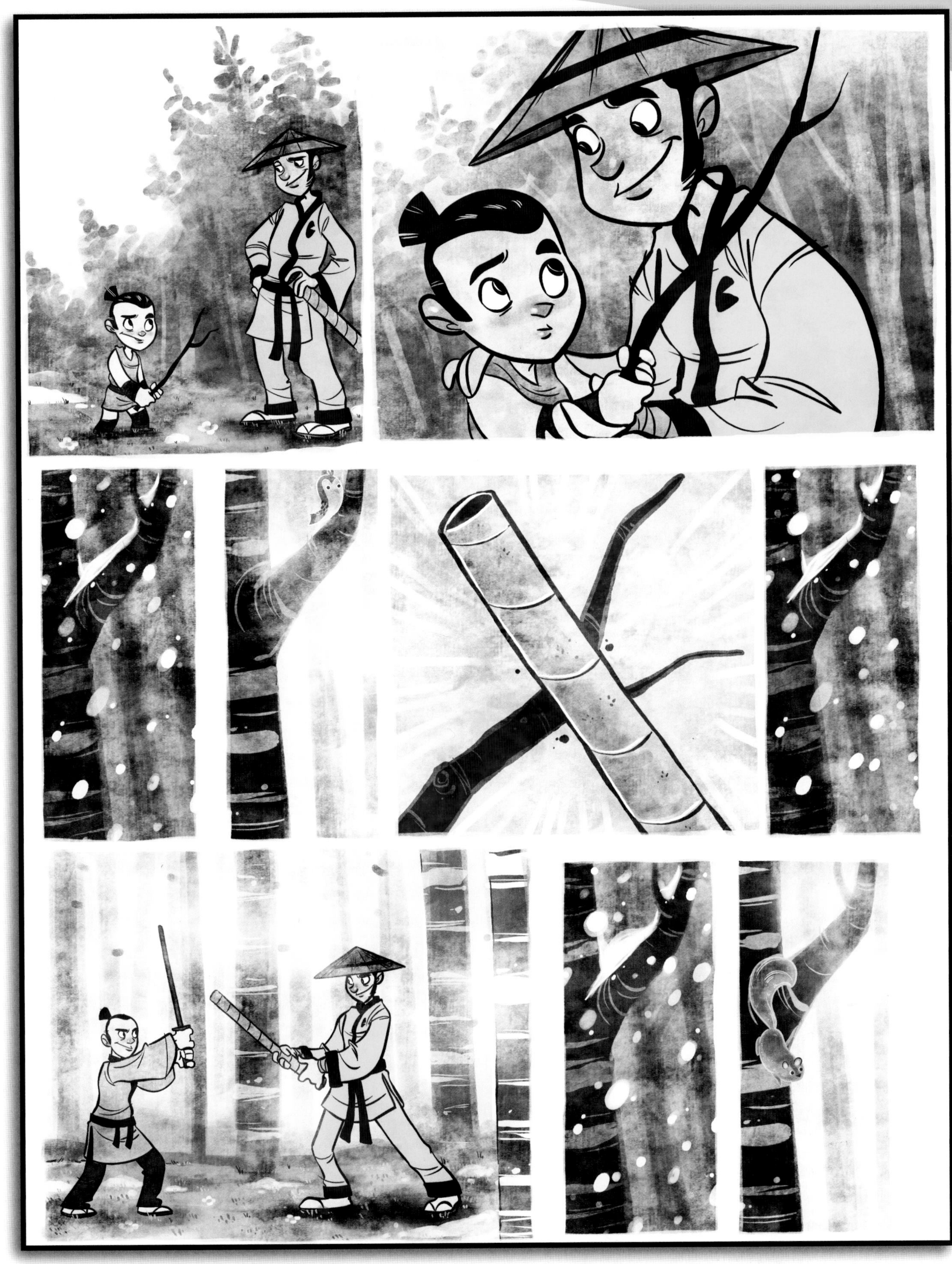

TIME LINE

2000 (December) — Penny Arcade accidentally sells their book publishing rights to a small company in Spokane.

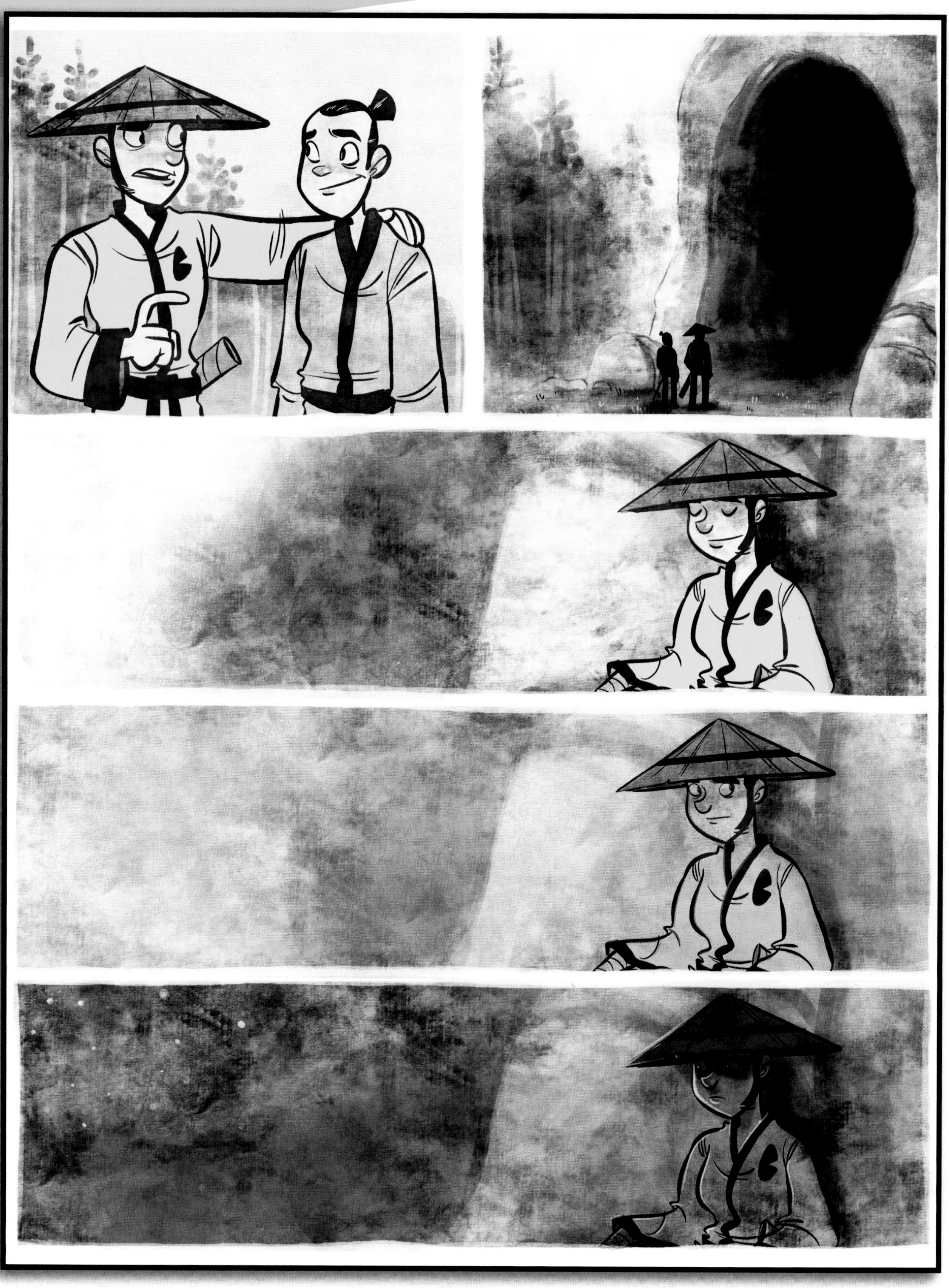

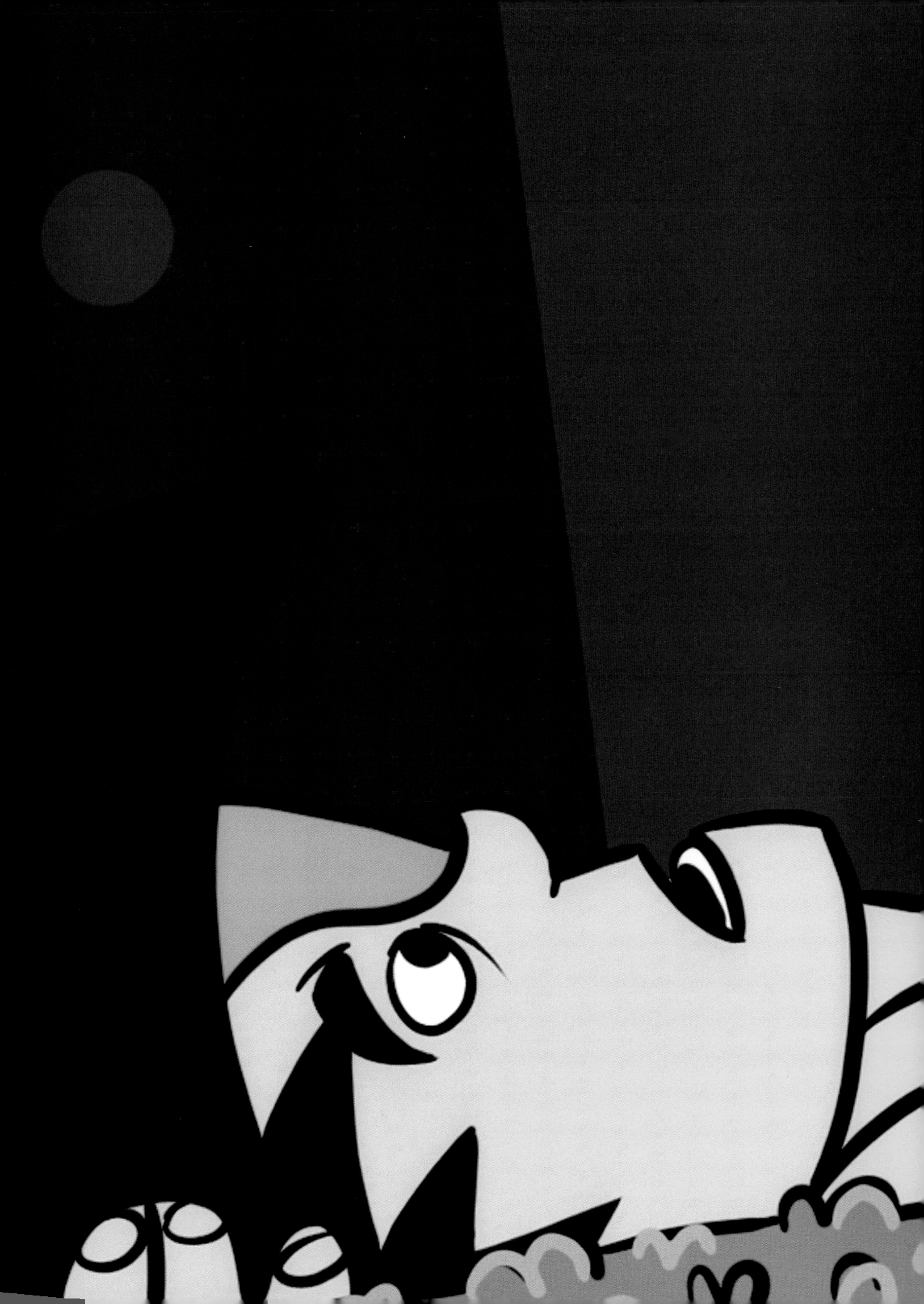

THE CHARACTERS OF *PENNY ARCADE*

by Jerry Holkins

Fruit Fucker

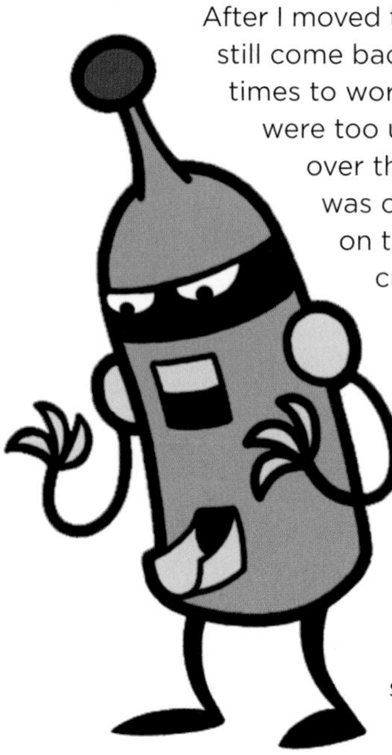

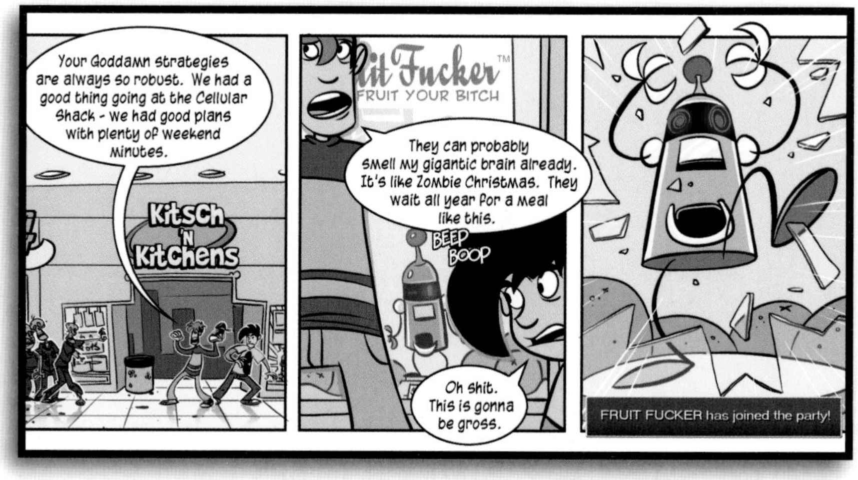
Your Goddamn strategies are always so robust. We had a good thing going at the Cellular Shack - we had good plans with plenty of weekend minutes.
Kitsch 'N Kitchens
...it Fucker™
FRUIT YOUR BITCH
They can probably smell my gigantic brain already. It's like Zombie Christmas. They wait all year for a meal like this.
BEEP BOOP
Oh shit. This is gonna be gross.
FRUIT FUCKER has joined the party!

After I moved to Seattle, I would still come back to Spokane sometimes to work on projects that were too ungainly to be done over the phone. When I was over there to work on the first book, road crews had utterly destroyed the street in front of Gabe's apartment, and they were leaving huge notes in ALL CAPITAL LETTERS in everyone's mailboxes, telling them to keep their goddamned cars off the street, *or else.*

We wondered how they would make good on their implied threat. Did they have some special machine to destroy cars people had left out—a hydraulic monster that would mount cars and puncture them, a kind of *car fucker?* Was there a special company that specialized in devices of this kind? What other shit did they make? Hence, the *Fruit Fucker.*

Div

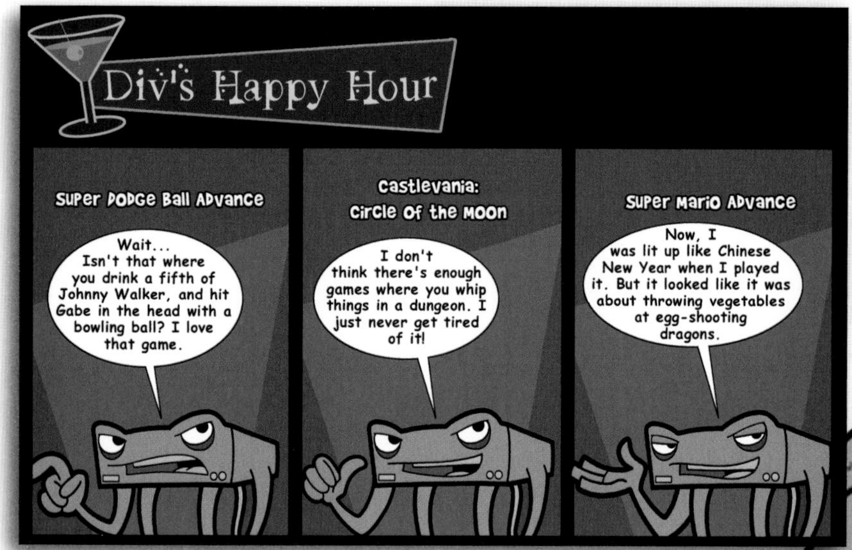
Div's Happy Hour
Super Dodge Ball Advance
Wait... Isn't that where you drink a fifth of Johnny Walker, and hit Gabe in the head with a bowling ball? I love that game.
Castlevania: Circle of the Moon
I don't think there's enough games where you whip things in a dungeon. I just never get tired of it!
Super Mario Advance
Now, I was lit up like Chinese New Year when I played it. But it looked like it was about throwing vegetables at egg-shooting dragons.

Based on the defunct DVD competitor DIVX from Circuit City—a company that is now itself defunct—Div provided a villain local to the apartment. We used him to say things neither of us were comfortable saying ourselves. These days, the things he says are so foul that he rarely makes it into the strip anymore.

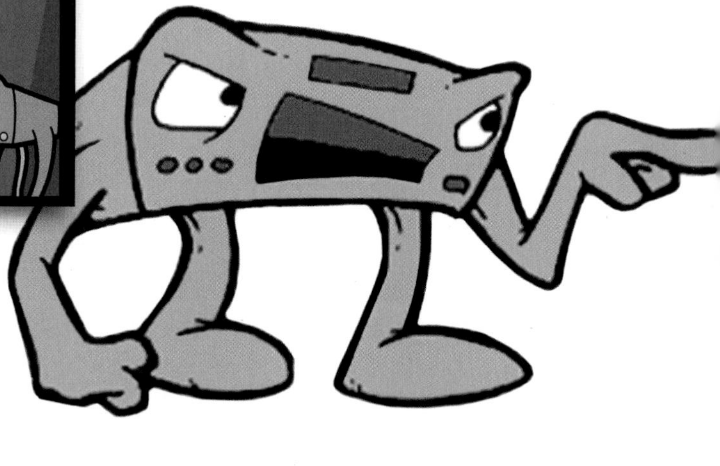

TIME LINE

2001 (March) — The eFront scandal hits the airwaves as the ICQ logs of CEO Sam Jain are made public. Sam flees the country (and at the time of this writing is still at large), eFront goes bankrupt, and the rights to *Penny Arcade* default back to Mike and Jerry. And all is right in the universe.

Frank

Frank

Frank, we've had some complaints from customers.
I haven't heard any.
Really? Not even from the customers you tie up in front of the store like scarecrows?
FRANK
Help us! Oh God!
Please, somebody!
Oh, them.
Sometimes they complain, yeah.
FRANK

An amalgam of every meddling, psychotic, impersonal district manager ever, professional tormentor Frank makes certain that those around him feel constant anguish. He's made several appearances in various contexts, usually to the detriment of other organisms. He also seems to collect *pants,* a habit even we don't completely understand.

Charles

Originally created to sear coworkers who were Apple devotees, "Chuck" was always a creature of pity and disdain. As time wore on, and as the Internet grew to be a focus for personal computing, the religious arguments against the platform began to taste like old gum. A lot has changed since then—I'm writing this on a Mac, for example. He saw a makeover in June 2000 that reflected our changing attitudes at the time, complete with awesome goggles and an engorged snark gland.

Let's just.. Let's stop off at the Apple Store real quick. It's right here.
Whoa, whoa. These guys aren't hip enough to be in here.
It's cool. We'll kinda muss up their hair a little bit.
That's not good enough. You can tie 'em up outside, like the others.

Randy

In a surprising move this week, Soviet copy protection vendor slash *crime syndicate* StarForce began actively promoting piracy of Stardock's Galactic Civilizations 2.
Randy Pinkwood
Channel 2
When asked for comment, the reasonable people of the world called their behavior "extortion."
I've never been to Russia, but I did have sex with a girl who said she was a *communist.*
Randy Pinkwood
Channel 2
I don't know if she was serious or not, but she certainly "seized the means of production," if you know what I'm talking about.
And I think you know what I'm talking about.
I'm talking about *my penis.*
Randy Pinkwood
Channel 2

Gabe and Tycho aren't always the best vehicle to recite straight information, like a newscaster would—they need dialogue that "bounces" back and forth. As a result, we invented the on-air pervert Randy Pinkwood to deliver this sort of material. He was a filthy creature from his very inception, nasty even—Mike would like to see substantially more Randy Pinkwood in the strip. I resist him at every turn. Pinkwood material rides a very fine edge that I find especially challenging.

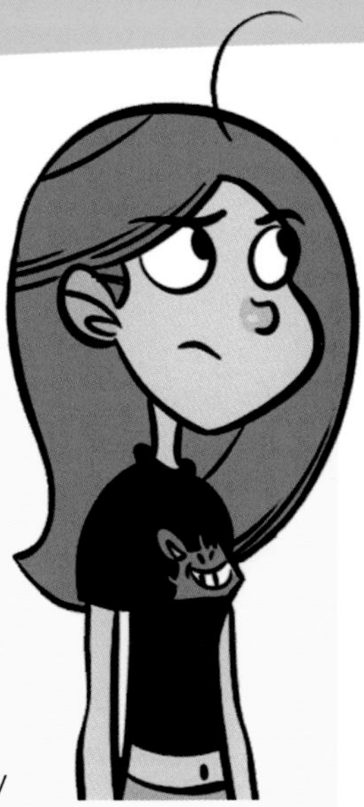

Annarchy

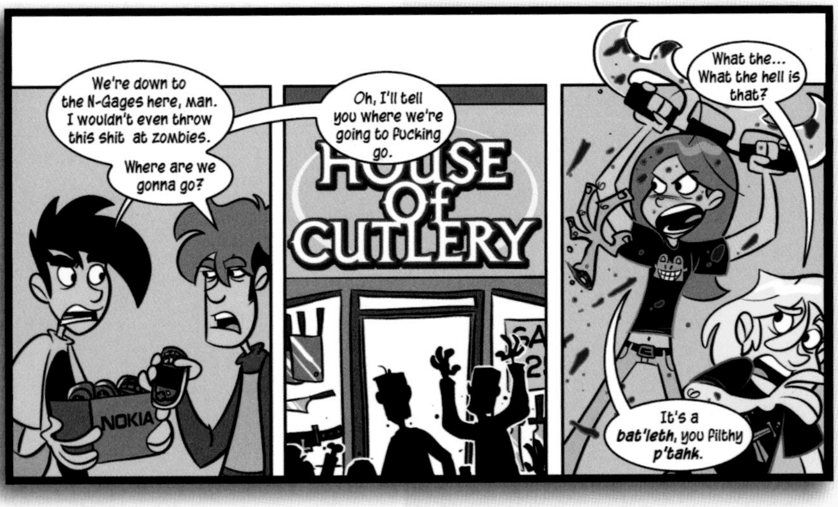
We're down to the N-Gages here, man. I wouldn't even throw this shit at zombies.
Where are we gonna go?
Oh, I'll tell you where we're going to fucking go.
HOUSE OF CUTLERY
NOKIA
What the... What the hell is that?
It's a bat'leth, you filthy p'tahk.

A combination of nieces, associates, and other tough, smart girls, Anne has an extraordinary effect on anyone she shares a comic panel with. The comfortable and established roles are completely subverted: Twisted, egomaniacal Tycho becomes a devoted guardian. Brutal attack dog Gabriel is consistently on his best behavior. She also got a lot of screen time in the video game On the Rain-Slick Precipice of Darkness, in the guise of Anne-Claire Forthwith.

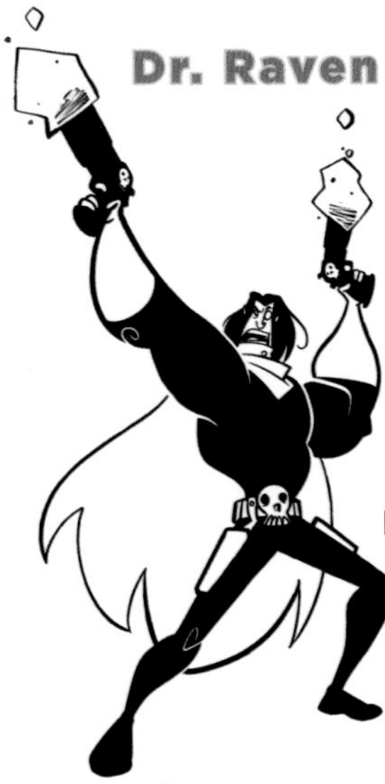

Dr. Raven Darktalon Blood

A pretend character made up by Mike's alter ego, he represents every grasping excess of comics and marketing. We ran a series of strips where Dr. Blood actually *was* licensed by a third party, Universal or something, but we had to stop it when people thought we were being serious. That people would believe this for even a *second* is a gruesome indictment of the entertainment industry.

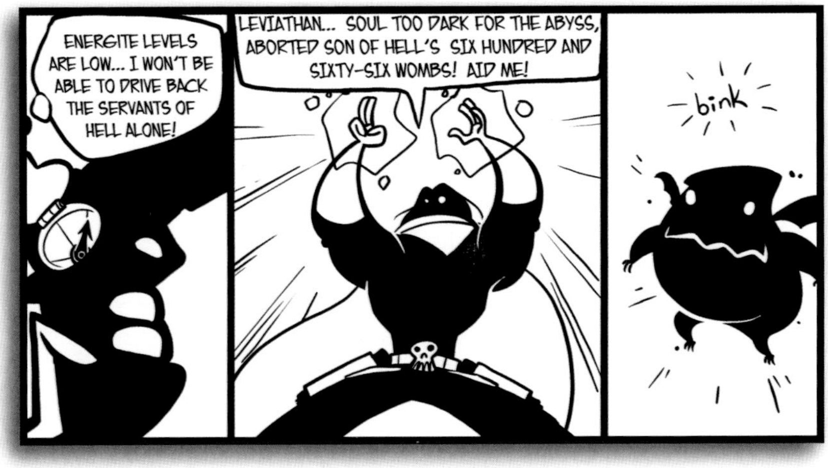
ENERGITE LEVELS ARE LOW... I WON'T BE ABLE TO DRIVE BACK THE SERVANTS OF HELL ALONE!
LEVIATHAN... SOUL TOO DARK FOR THE ABYSS, ABORTED SON OF HELL'S SIX HUNDRED AND SIXTY-SIX WOMBS! AID ME!
bink

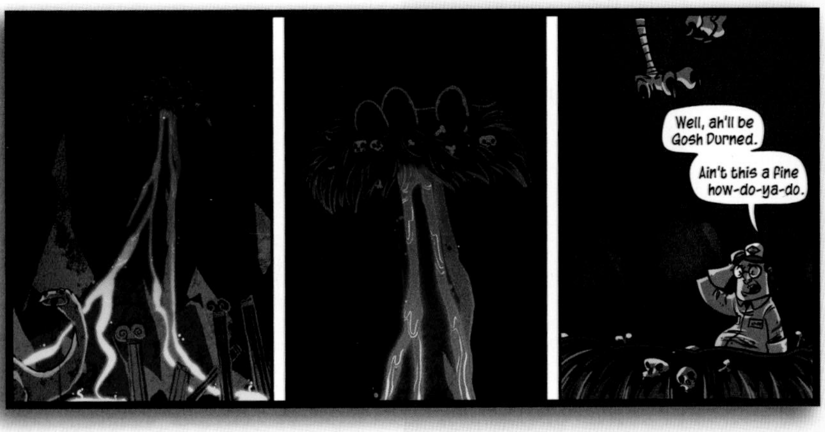
Well, ah'll be Gosh Durned.
Ain't this a fine how-do-ya-do.

Deep Crow (and Carl)

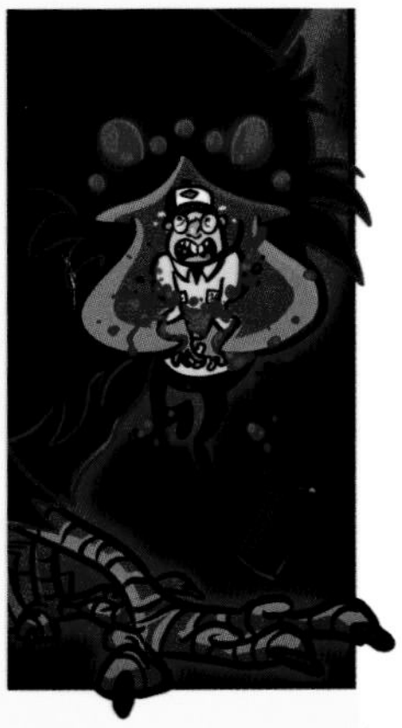

A throwaway joke in a comic about subterranean real estate somehow morphed into an avian insect that people seem to have a lot of affection for. Carl, an exterminator who seems to know far too much about the dark places of the earth, has a strange relationship with the bird thing—and presumably other things that dwell where there is no light. They're a lot of fun to write.

Jim, the Third Roommate

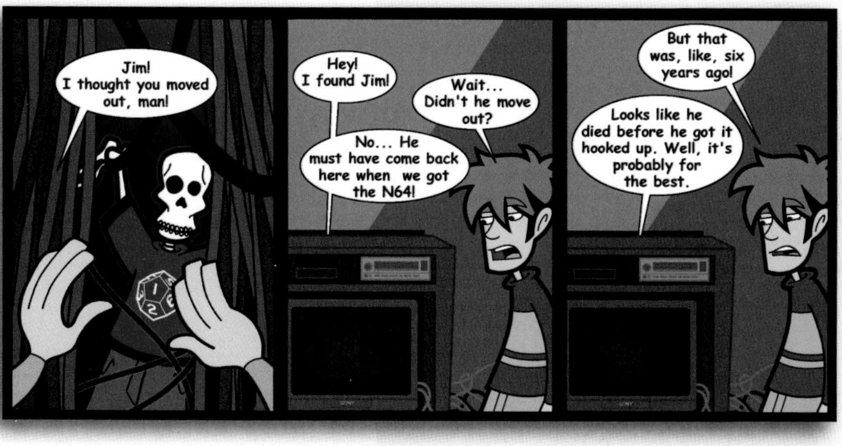
Jim! I thought you moved out, man!
Hey! I found Jim!
Wait... Didn't he move out?
No... He must have come back here when we got the N64!
But that was, like, six years ago!
Looks like he died before he got it hooked up. Well, it's probably for the best.

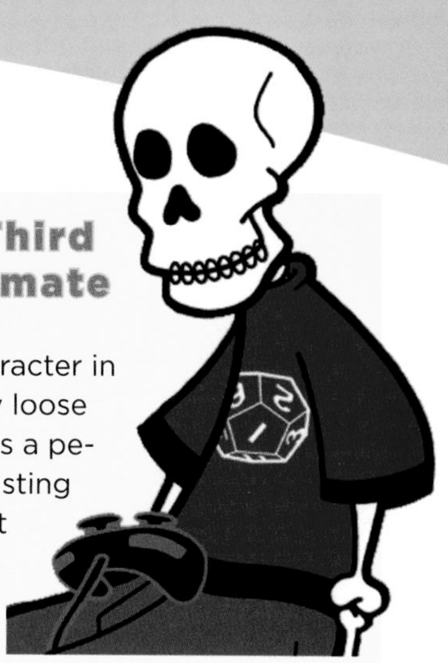

A kind of secret character in the strip's extremely loose continuity, he implies a period "before" the existing comic. Dead of thirst and starvation in a matted warren of audio/video cable, Jim represents everything the comic is not: fair, reasoned, and congenial. These things died with him.

Thomas Kemper

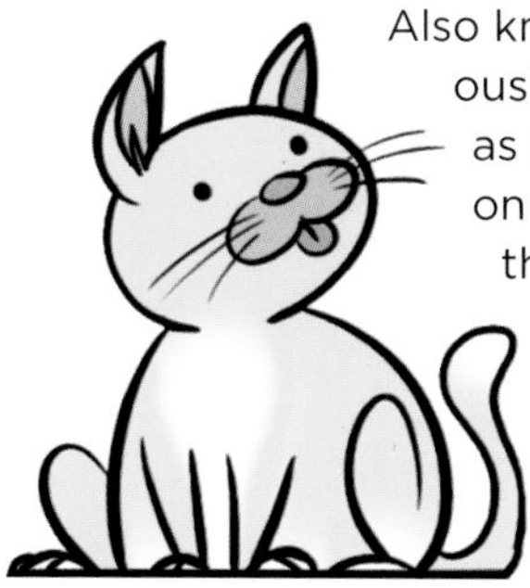

Also known unceremoniously as "the cat," Thomas Kemper was based on the actual creature that lived with us in Apartment 26. We eventually had to take it to a shelter. The drive to that shelter, stroking the terrified cat in the backseat, ranks as one of the worst moments of our lives. As a result, he rarely appears in the strip anymore.

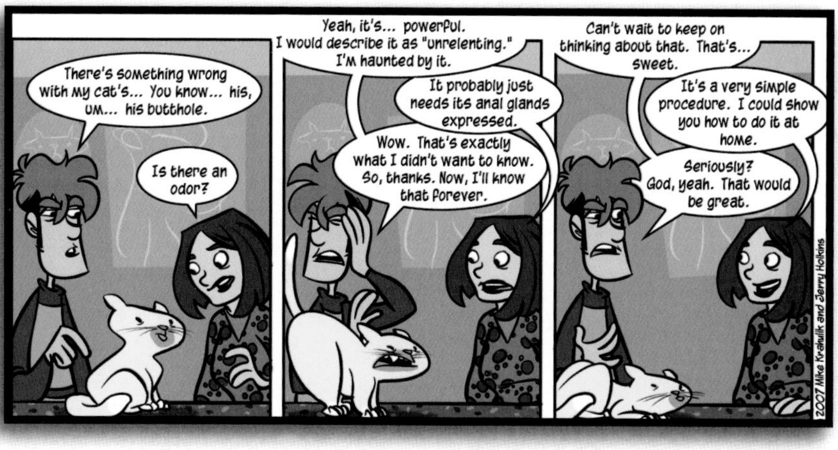
There's something wrong with my cat's... You know... his, um... his butthole.
Is there an odor?
Yeah, it's... powerful. I would describe it as "unrelenting." I'm haunted by it.
It probably just needs its anal glands expressed.
Wow. That's exactly what I didn't want to know. So, thanks. Now, I'll know that forever.
Can't wait to keep on thinking about that. That's... sweet.
It's a very simple procedure. I could show you how to do it at home.
Seriously? God, yeah. That would be great.
2007 Mike Krahulik and Jerry Holkins

Mr. Tails

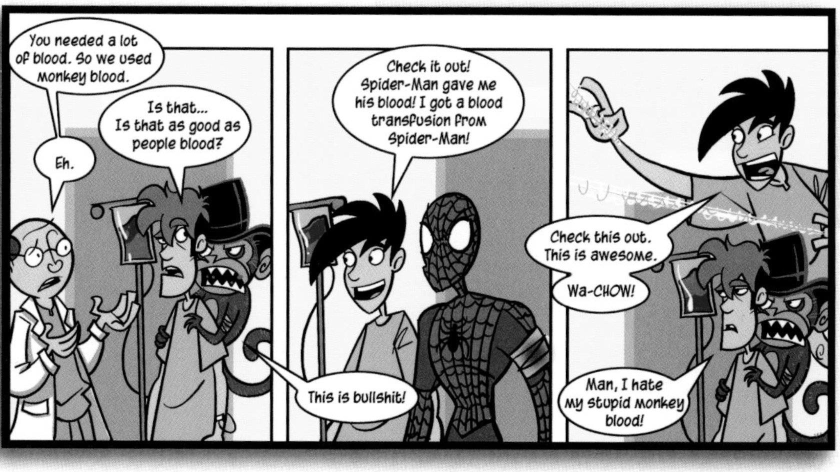
You needed a lot of blood. So we used monkey blood.
Is that... Is that as good as people blood?
Eh.
Check it out! Spider-Man gave me his blood! I got a blood transfusion from Spider-Man!
This is bullshit!
Check this out. This is awesome.
Wa-CHOW!
Man, I hate my stupid monkey blood!

We thought there should be a monkey in the strip—one that bit people on the head. I'm sorry. I wish there was more to it.

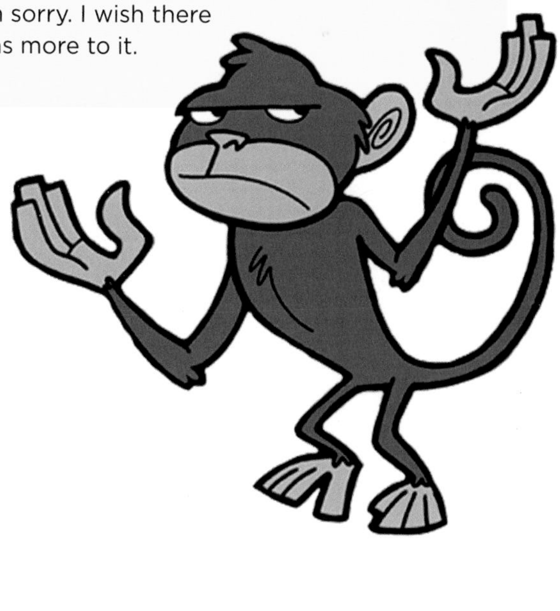

TIME LINE **2001 (April) —** Mike is let go from GameSpy.com. Penny Arcade is now his full-time job.

MAKING JPEGS: A PRIMER

Every week, we publish three comics. Occasionally, we record the writing process and release it as a podcast. What follows is a transcription of that (often very strange) process.

Jerry: I'm a mama's boy, I gotta have sensitive conversations all the time.

Mike: [yawn] Testing. Testing one.

J: You are trying to figure out if you should say one, two, three?

M: Should we just go right to the headlines?

J: Sure.

M: I'm not coming in with anything today.

J: You got no product?

M: Nothing.

J: Beatles Rock Band features unreleased material. Hmm, I was interested to see the versus modes for Resident Evil are going to be DLC. That's interesting to me. People are super mad. They really don't like it when you announce DLC before the game is delivered.

M: Well that kind of shows—

J: It seems callous.

M: It does, yeah. If it's done, why don't you just give it to me?

J: Well, I'm not sure it was done. We know though, because we had the disc. That game had been done. The version we had was a reviewable copy and sometimes that means it's kinda raw, but that was not raw.

M: No, that was solid.

J: If I had purchased that reviewable copy in the store I would not have had any problem with it. I would have felt like that was a real game. So it's been gold for...When did we get that thing? When did we play it? We've been done with it for almost a month right?

M: Yeah, I think so.

J: So it was done. And think about how long it took to get to us, so it's been done forever. But I'm not sure the versus

SKETCH

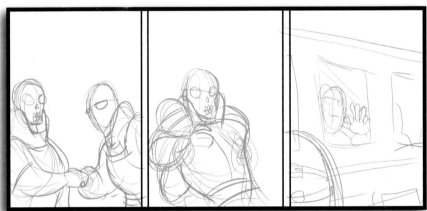

INKS

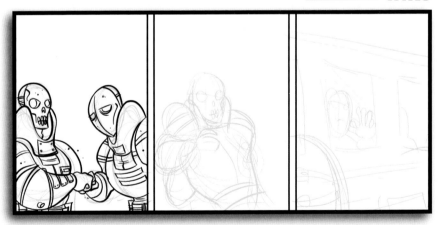

DLC was actually complete at the time. I don't really believe that. On the other hand, I am definitely, I'm very interested in playing it. I really liked it, although I'm not sure I can do the campaign again.

M: I was trying to think if I could do the campaign again with someone. Maybe.

J: In co-op you probably could. I don't remember because it was so long ago when we turned it on, but I don't know if there's a way to turn the difficulty up. Or maybe in co-op mode with another person there is some automatic scaling. But I really liked it. I really liked the experience. At the very least I would want to get that Mercenaries mode unlocked so you could play through those challenges, and that patch is free, I'm not sure if that was done either, but apparently it is ready to go. If we turned on the dev kit we would see it.

M: ...

J: Blu-ray will always be a part of PS3. Was that ever not on the table at some point?

M: I don't know.

J: Let's see...there's a new Army of Two.

M: Fist Bump.

J: You ready? *Y'all ready?*

M: No.

J: It's really bummed me out. I was playing the multiplayer for a while. I found someone to play the multi with and it was actually a lot of fun but for some reason there was no fist bumping. Like the one time I *wanted* to bump fists.

M: You can't fist bump in multi?

J: It was too expensive. They're like "This feature would cost $20 million to implement." I'll be very curious to see what they think they did wrong.

INKS

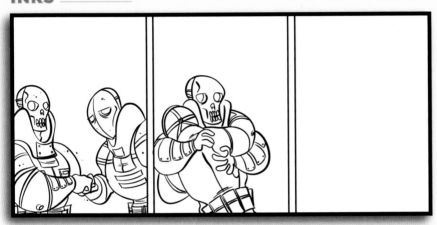

COLOR

M: What I'm curious to see is if they are going to take it down the route of parody. If they realize that people thought it was...

J: ...Funny...

M: ...Stupid.

J: ...For the wrong reason.

M: Yeah, for the wrong reasons. And if they are going to go over the top and make it sort of ridiculous.

J: Yeah, it could have been way more Hollywood, like Bay levels of overwrought power.

M: Jumping up and banging chests...They should have a button where they just kiss.

J: You have to hold it.

M: You have to hold it and you kiss the other guy and he sort of staggers back like he's surprised by it, but he's okay with it.

J: Yeah!

M: But it's not gay.

J: It's not weird.

M: You just killed a bunch of guys. You're just celebrating.

J: There are no questions. Could you have done all this stuff if you weren't a rad dude?

M: No.

J: Obviously not.

M: *Obviously not.*

J: See the corpses before you?

M: Yeah?

J: I mean this is clearly a deeply masculine... hetero event.

M: It goes from the fist pump to the man hug, which is like the hard slap on the back. You got him in the embrace but it can't be tender. It's got to still be violent.

J: It's still an aggressive act.

M: It's like, "slap slap" on the back but then the hug lingers a *little too long*.

J: So maybe it's like one tap is the bump, but if you hold it the animation continues. But your co-op partner isn't able to break out of the animation, so as soon as a person is committed to these acts they have to go to their conclusion.

M: Yeah, so then the hug sort of stays for a little bit, and then maybe he just rests his head on your shoulder.

J: A little.

M: Just a little bit.

J: But he's looking over at the camera, and it's one of these skull masks with fire on it.

M: Yeah.

J: I don't know. I think I wrote about it at the time.

M: You found some fun to have there.

J: After I played through it and I had seen every nasty piece of dialogue, and I had sort of been exposed to it, I was immune. It was like an inoculation.

M: "Ladies lift your shirts."

J: Yeah. Ladies would lift their shirts and it did not faze me, or they'd be exhorted to lift their shirts. Eventually it was like playing Phantasy Star Online, where I was just going through and trying to satisfy all the objectives and nail all these guys so I could earn money and level up. After the stupid story stuff could hurt me no longer, it moved into a place where I was able to actually enjoy it just as a game without some of the stuff they had glommed on. And then they released a free pack that basically changed the game in a serious way. They added a whole other level that was easily the match of anything that was in the campaign, and then they added a new ending. It was almost like an apology in some ways. The work at the end was of a very high caliber. They had all new animations. It was at a high level. If they could tone down some of that stuff, but maybe that's...no. Nobody will like that. I'm not even going to entertain a universe where people like that shit. They either have to go much farther—

M: ...And make it a parody.

J: ...and make it ridiculous, or reel it back to the point where it is not injurious to people of intellect.

M: Yeah.

J: They could have a fun product that has good action and a light RPG element. Anyway, I'm not disgusted at the prospect of another Army of Two, but I am curious to see what they think the franchise needs.

M: Yeah, what it is?

J: Yeah, even "what it is" is a good way of putting it... "Are the features and functions of Army of Two in there?"

M: In three panels you could show the "from fist bump to hug to kiss."

J: It could almost be something from the manual. Press A. Hold A.

M: Yeah. It would help it work if it was all in the context of the manual.

J: Either the manual or just, "these are the buttons," "these are the animations that someone put in," and "it's all mo-capped."

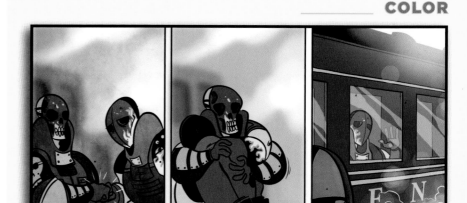

COLOR

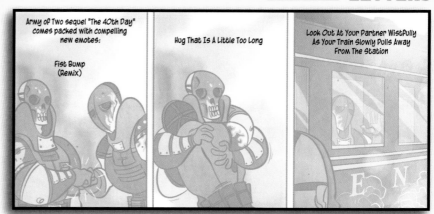

LETTERS

Army of Two sequel "The 40th Day" comes packed with compelling new emotes:

Fist Bump (Remix)

Hug That Is A Little Too Long

Look Out At Your Partner WistPully As Your Train Slowly Pulls Away From The Station

M: It could be the in-game tutorial where you see the button come up when you're supposed to do the action.

J: It's an in-game event, but its men kissing instead of a knife fight or some shit.

M: Let's hang onto that one.

J: Okay I'll drop it in the file.

M: Is there anything else good in the file?

J: Um, we've suggested that Tycho getting drunk on tequila is called the "Patronus Charm." I guess that's possible. We've also suggested that there might be an aggressive interstellar race called the Scrotus, but I'm not sure if...

M: ...If those are comic-ready.

J: ...Are ready for prime time. Lets see a couple more headlines.

J: Army of Two the 40th day..."Gamecube era depressed even Miyamoto." Okay, "Hollywood Executive expects streaming movies/TV on the Wii this year." I would doubt that. There's that first page. "Namco-Bandai registers Excalibur trademark."

2001 (April) — With no hosting and no income, Mike and Jerry ask the readers for donations to run the site via Club PA. Their goal each month? Groceries and rent.

M: There's Madworld.

J: There is Madworld, but I don't know how to feel about that.

M: Yeah.

J: I don't know how to feel about that game, and I don't want to say anything yet because I don't have anything of value. I just didn't understand why you would play it for very long. Maybe it gets more interesting later, but each area that I saw...I love the art, and I like the voice acting and often the announcing stuff really works for me. The Black Baron is very funny.

M: He is funny. The announcers were funny.

J: I like him and his bloodbath challenge. I like the cut scenes, but this is sort of the problem with the Wii. Although I guess it's true enough in games for the PlayStation or the 360. But when I'm playing those games it's true enough that I'm pushing buttons, and the buttons are doing different things in each game. But maybe if you were to look at the raw inputs coming through the USB, I am more or less doing very similar things.

M: Yeah.

J: But in those scenarios like say Hawx or Gears, I'm not really thinking about that controller any more because the movements are so slight in general. Even in something like Flower or Flow. Even those motion-controlled movements are

FINAL

Army of Two sequel "The 40th Day" comes packed with compelling new emotes:

Fist Bump (Remix)

Hug That Is A Little Too Long

Look Out At Your Partner WistPully As Your Train Slowly Pulls Away From The Station

slight. They're gentle. Virtually every Wii game I play has me going *wrararararar*.

M: Jumping around.

J: Yeah, and the inputs feel more or less identical. My gameplay experience on Wii games is identical virtually every time. The input portion of my interaction is me going *wuga wuga* with the thing. I don't know if I want more sophistication or what.

M: Well to me, the pinnacle was Metroid 3. That was something that felt, motion-control wise, like, "Wow, this is what they can do." Everything since then I have just felt the same. I just shake them. I shake over here and shake them over there.

J: I'll be interested to see the Conduit if they're able to bring something cool. I definitely like that developer. I love looking at it, and playing it is fine. After I had put the guys on the spike, through the asshole, I then grabbed another guy. There were diminishing returns. The second asshole I put on the spike was less engaging than the initial asshole.

M: I can see that.

J: I went over and was smashing the guy on the spike. Seriously, it wasn't like I was desensitized to the violence or something. I was holding the guy, and I was like "Ehh, the spikes are all the way over there." You know what I'm saying? I'm just going to punch him.

M: Yeah.

J: It didn't really seize me. I guess there's a story that develops eventually. I don't feel too bad saying this stuff, because eventually I will feel guilty and I'll have to play it all the way through to see if I was wrong. *In the night.*

M: Yeah.

J: Eventually I just got up. Checking my email seemed more engaging to me at that time.

M: I found it hard to watch. I thought the visuals were really sloppy.

J: Really? Maybe you would be better at discerning that.

M: I am.

J: Know this. I've seen a lot of Red Faction Guerrilla. I've seen as much. There's a weapons and vehicles trailer I might look at, at some point—that and Ben 10 Alien Force. When we were at New York City Comic Con sitting there for two or three days, I saw a *lot* of Ben 10, and I saw a lot of Red Faction, and occasionally I wanted to get up and play Red Faction.

M: Yeah.

J: But we were not able to get up. We were in our cage.

M: The cage made of our own fans.

J: And tables and merchandise. "Mad World Hoodie." "Capcom brings The Darkside Chronicles: Resident Evil Classics to Wii." "New Donkey Kong Jungle Beat." I really liked Jungle Beat!

M: I know you did.

J: But I liked it because of the drums. There's no way I am going to hold the Wii controllers and bong bong. I'm not going to do that. No, sir. The drum is what made it fun. I have four, they're still here. I still have the four drum controls up on the shelf in there. Someone made a 360 into a bong. Awesome. "Arcade Explodes." "Is Xbox Live Down for You."

M: That's a headline? That sounds like a tweet.

J: Yeah, this is definitely 140-character-limit type stuff. "John Woo Apparently Not Directing John Woo's Stranglehold."

M: That's too bad.

J: There's a secret costume for Sheva in Resident Evil 5. Yeah, that's gonna help.

M: Looked pretty good. She's an incredible model anyway. That character is one of the few video game characters where I said, "Wow, that's actually a really attractive woman."

J: And when that stuff happens for the amazing ones they usually have a real model. They do a scan or they base it on a person's face. This is an original character that looks like a real person.

M: Yeah.

J: "Arkham Asylum Box Art." "Japan Getting Lifesize Gundam." Did you see the Samus cosplay?

M: MM-mmm.

J: It's off the chain. The costume itself is made out of molded plates and jammed with LEDs. It looks slick.

M: Send me a link.

J: "German Gunman Linked with Gaming." I imagine he was also linked with guns. That's just my guess. Official says "Guns Involved in School Shooting." I mean, you never see that headline, because that's a crazy thing to say. And the long version of the story is even worse. "Firearms were found near the scene of..." Now it's all dumb crap. Or at any rate it is crap that we've already seen.

M: I had a hard time trying to avoid people's opinions on *Watchmen*.

J: I'll bet.

M: It's tough. I'm finally seeing it tomorrow night. They started talking about it last night during our raid, and I had to make them stop.

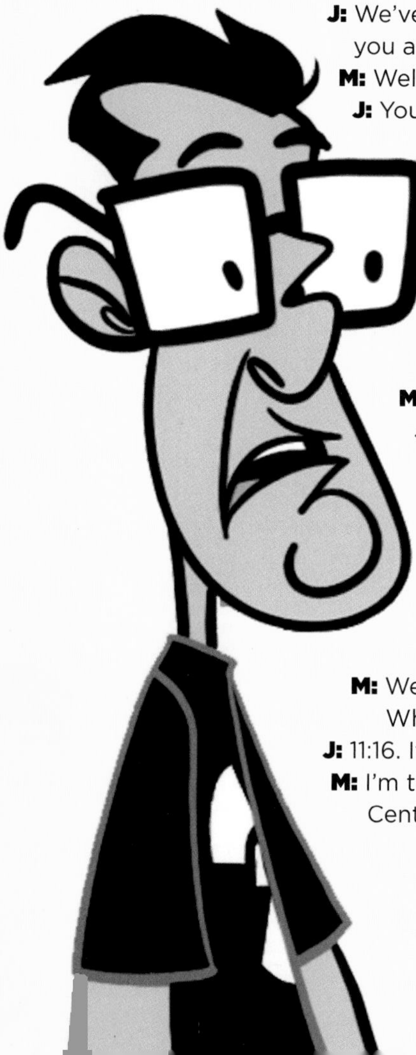

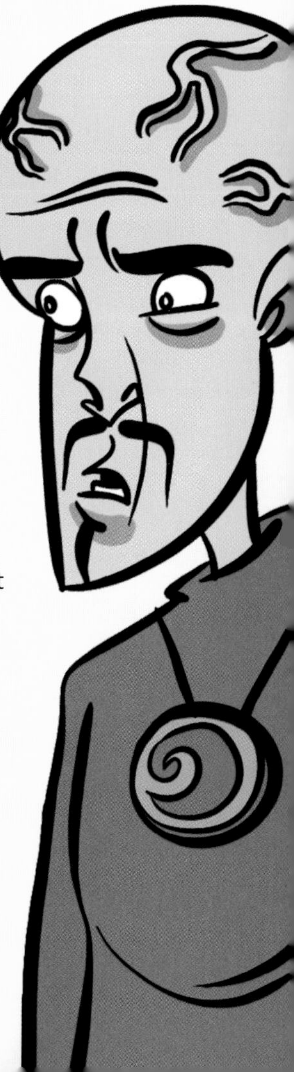

J: We've done comics that are similar, but he's talking to Tycho at the time. But you are actually living in a world where it's impossible.

M: Well, its not so much spoilers.

J: You read the comic. You can't be spoiled.

M: But I'm talking about opinions. I asked you what you thought of it because I usually don't care. What you think of the movie. I'm just sort of curious.

J: It's not going to wreck it. I think we're at the same juncture. I think we both want to know what the other person thinks.

M: Yeah.

J: Which is why I didn't go into any detail. I hope to receive a text message upon your exit of the theater. I am not expecting much.

M: Okay, a yeah or nay.

J: Or a "hmmm."

M: Or a "hmmm."

J: Or a "whaaa."

M: Boogadawah?

J: Boogadawoogadawah. I mean boogadawoogadawah would fit. That would be okay. I would like to know.

M: Well, it seems like the Army of Two thing is solid.

J: We have to fail at it.

M: We'll have to see. It feels like there's three panels there. My gut says there is. What time is it?

J: 11:16. It's all right. We're in a good position. We can take it to the hoop.

M: I'm thinking even if we do the Army of Two one today, I might draw the 50 Cent one for tomorrow.

J: That was always going to happen. It would never happen another way. That would be great because if we put this podcast up—

M: We can't. This podcast is for the book.

J: It is?

M: We gotta do it quick. They're on us for this book podcast.

J: Oh, okay.

M: Are you sad now?

J: No, that's fine. In my head I had already apportioned out the time to edit the files on Monday morning when I came in, so I'm rejiggering my view of the world right now.

M: I mean, I think we should just give it to them and be done with it.

J: New emotes? It's a sequel, so is a regular fist pump even gonna be sufficient? Everything needs to be bigger in the sequel.

M: In my head it was the idea that the fist pump, in the sequel, can be tweaked.

J: Tweaked. It's like in Tony Hawk or something. The way you can express masculine affection has all these different interpretations.

M: Because that is what Army of Two is really about. Showing heterosexual love.

J: Love.

M: For another man.

J: Exactly.

M: But not in a gay way.

J: Because it's not gay.

M: Yeah.

J: *Rwaarrrr*. There should be an emote where if you hold B and A you look out at your partner from a train that is slowly receding from the station. You hold those down and you're reaching out but they have the masks. I think that is kind of funny.

M: That is funny.

J: So you have fist bumps in the first panel.

M: But they've added more.

J: More bumps you think?

M: No. I'm saying "they've added" in the next two panels.

J: Yeah, and B is something else, tap B, hold B, or A whatever it is. I forget because it had a fist pump button and a "ladies lift your shirts" button.

M: "Ladies lift your shirts."

J: Yeah, we really just need a frame two. It is mild. Give a gift or something. You compare something.

M: Like what?

J: A 401(k), I don't know?

M: Maybe it's just sort of an awkwardly long hug.

J: "Hug that is a little too long."

M: His head resting on his shoulder.

J: The idea that "hug that is a little too long" is there, somewhere in the manual. No, I think that's good.

M: And what's the last frame?

J: "Look out wistfully at your partner from a train as it slowly pulls away from the station."

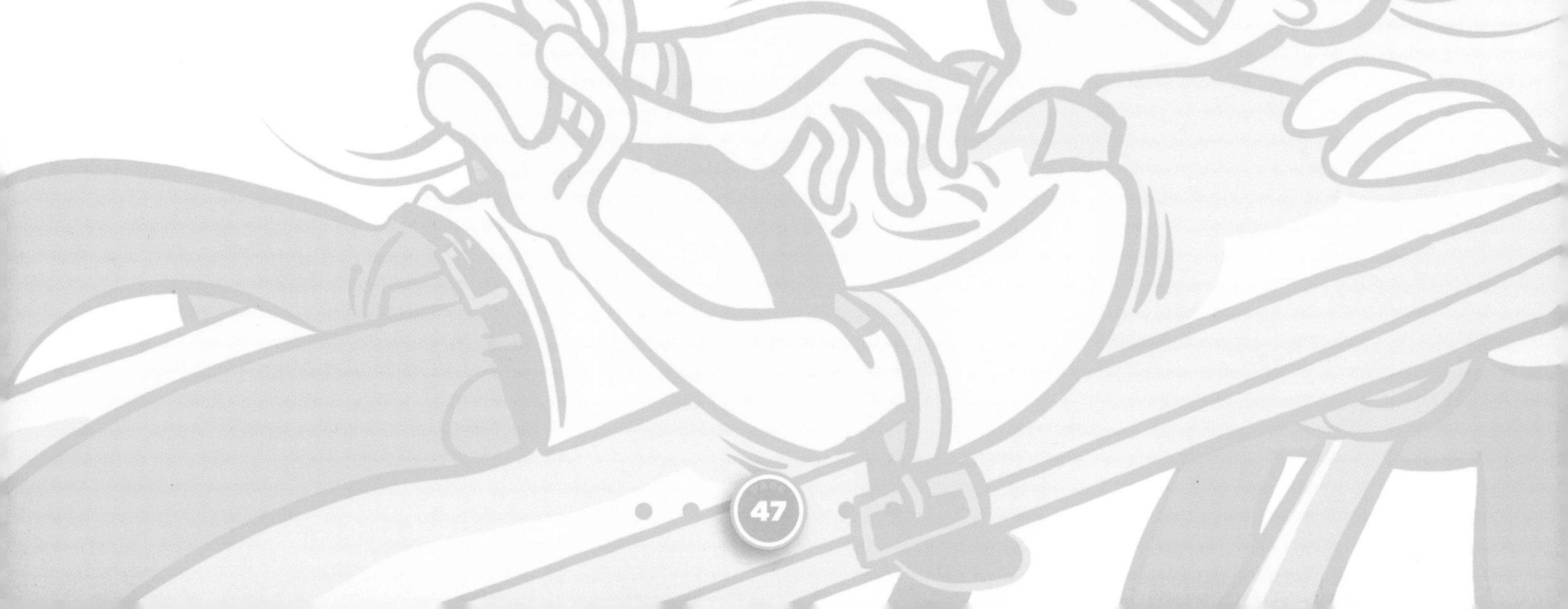

TWISP AND CATSBY

by Jerry Holkins

As their first appearance clearly shows, Twisp and Catsby were essentially a non sequitur:

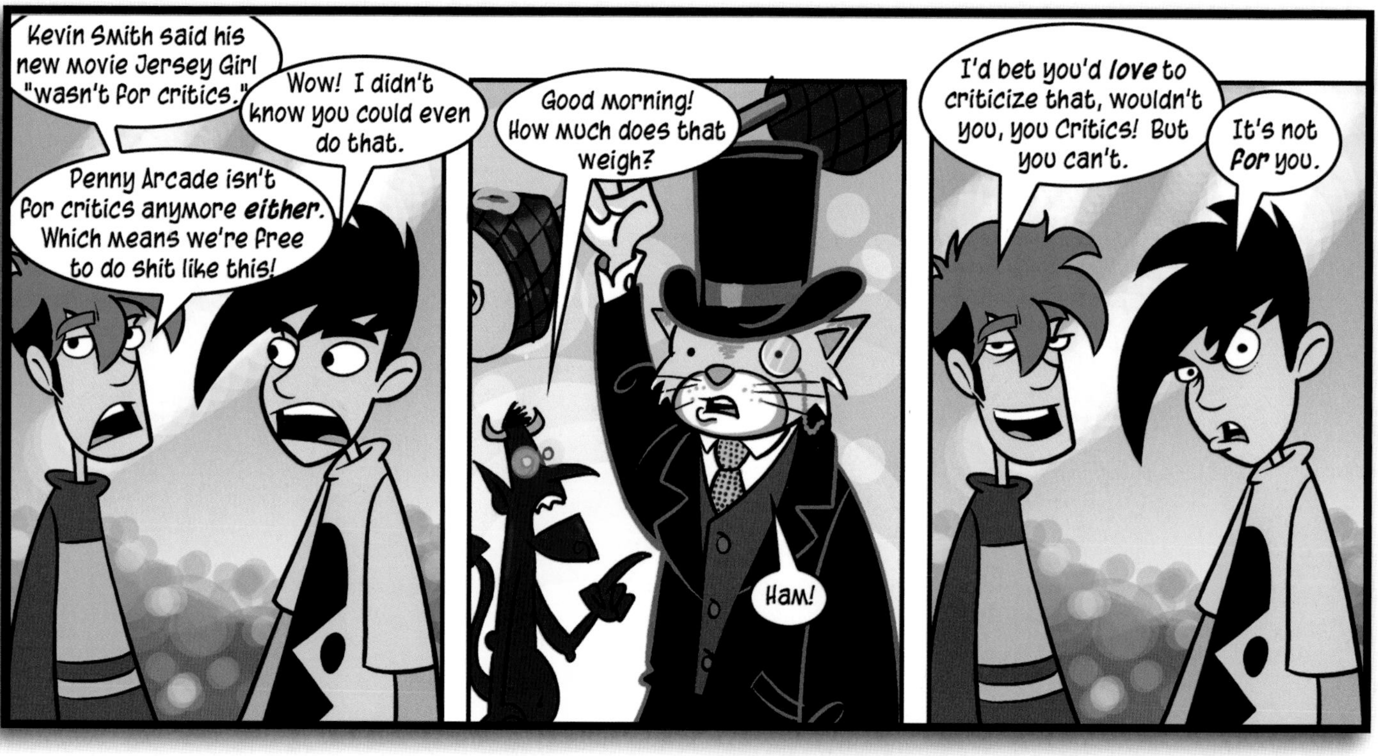
Kevin Smith said his new movie Jersey Girl "wasn't for critics."
Wow! I didn't know you could even do that.
Penny Arcade isn't for critics anymore *either*. Which means we're free to do shit like this!
Good Morning! How much does that weigh?
Ham!
I'd bet you'd *love* to criticize that, wouldn't you, you Critics! But you can't.
It's not *for* you.

Their entire purpose was to represent an act of brutal aggression against the reader. That should have been it, but I made a terrible mistake: I named them.

When I label something, the act creates an enduring realm for it in my mind. When I check back on some old idea, I often find that it has continued to evolve in my absence. So these strange ham-lifting cats and their demonic accomplices began to dwell in yellowed Victorian prints, ordered their luncheon from frogs, and so forth. The strips they occupy are usually a heavily encoded version of some real event. Sometimes it's fairly clear what that event is. Other times it is, um...*less* clear.

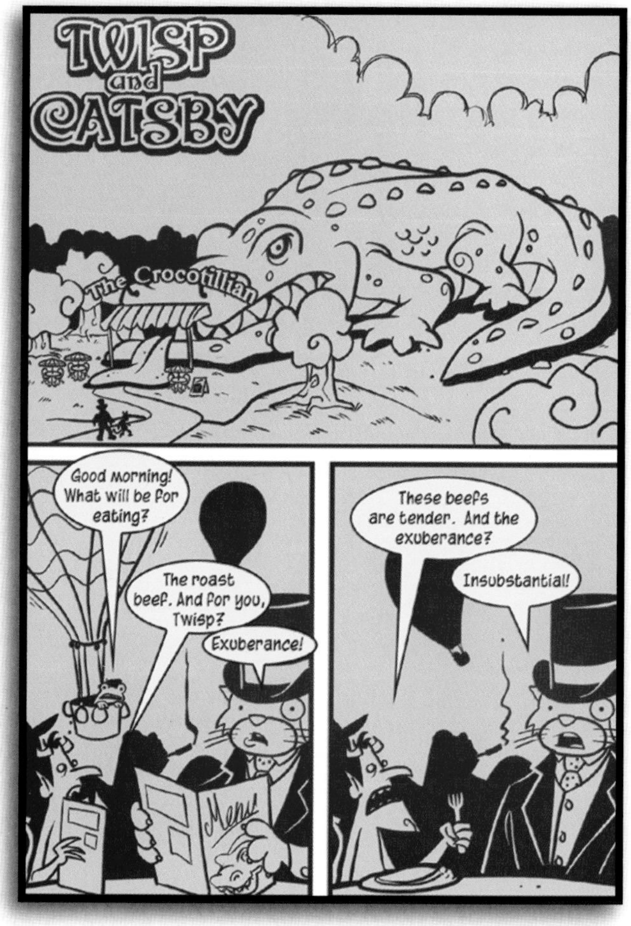
TWISP and CATSBY
The Crocotillian
Good Morning! What will be for eating?
The roast beef. And for you, Twisp?
Exuberance!
Menu
These beefs are tender. And the exuberance?
Insubstantial!

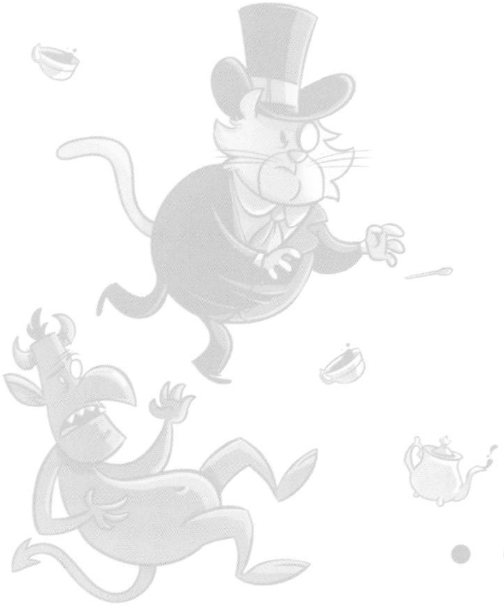

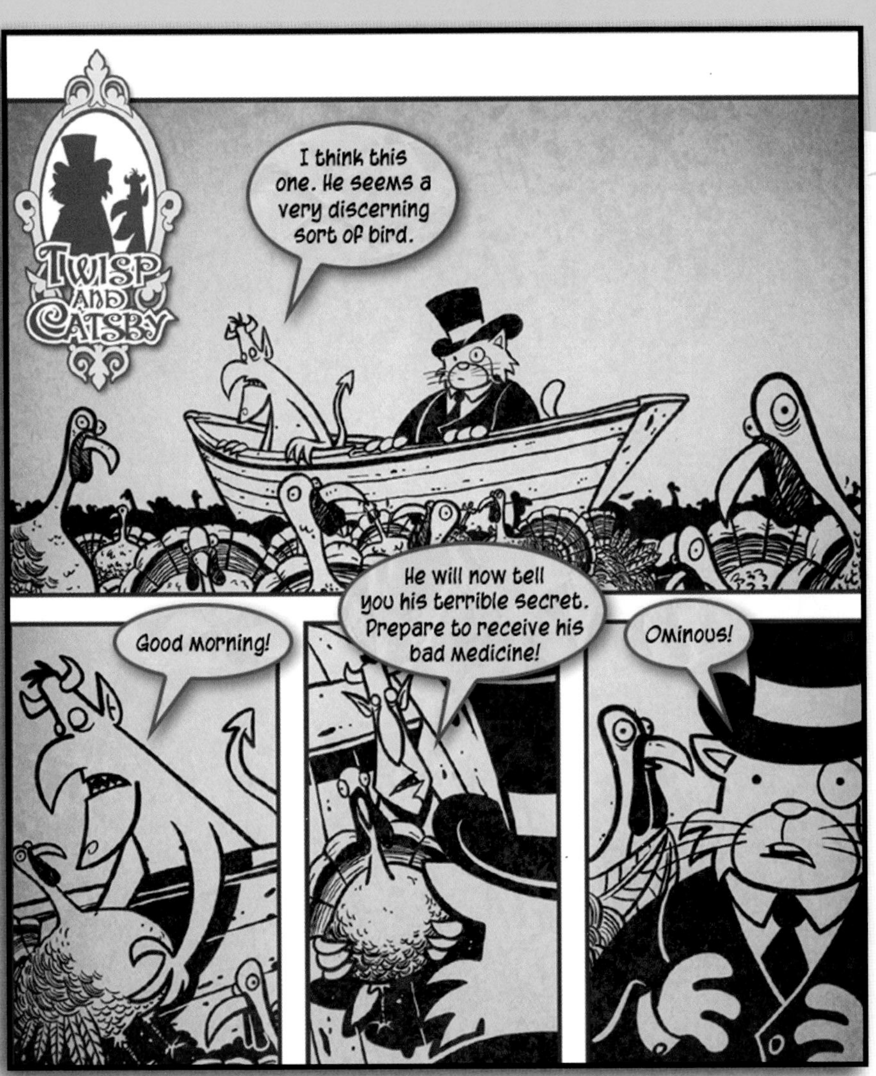
Twisp and Catsby
I think this one. He seems a very discerning sort of bird.
Good Morning!
He will now tell you his terrible secret. Prepare to receive his bad medicine!
Ominous!

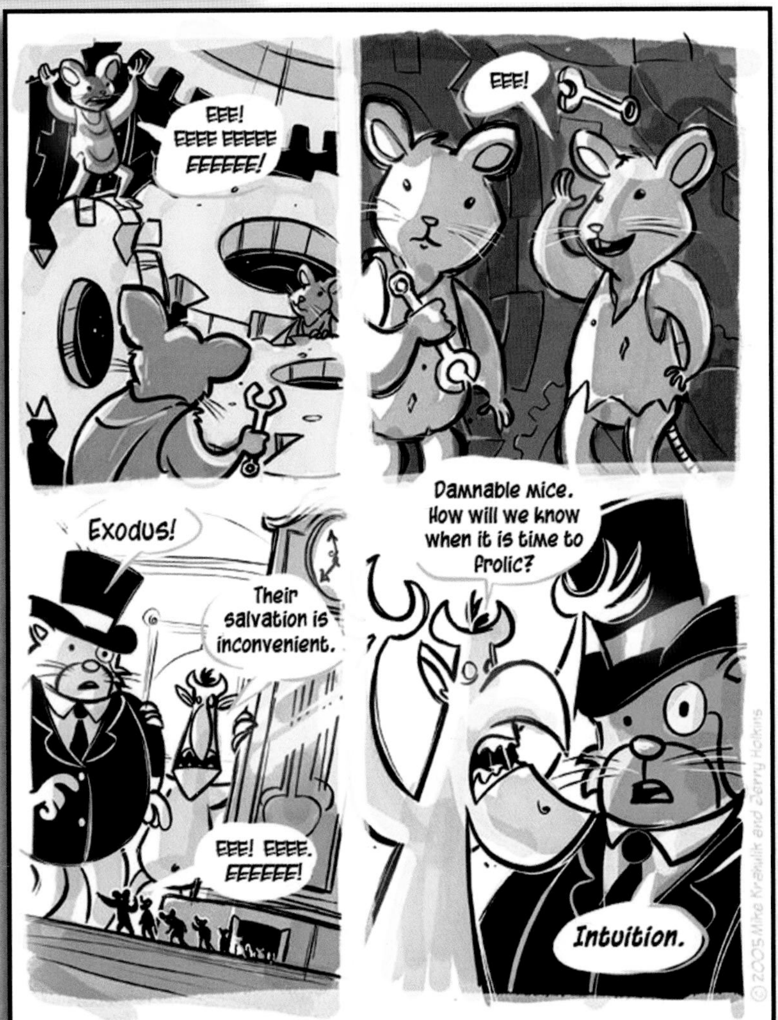
EEE! EEEE EEEEE EEEEEE!
EEE!
Exodus!
Their salvation is inconvenient.
EEE! EEEE. EEEEEE!
Damnable mice. How will we know when it is time to frolic?
Intuition.
©2005 Mike Krahulik and Jerry Holkins

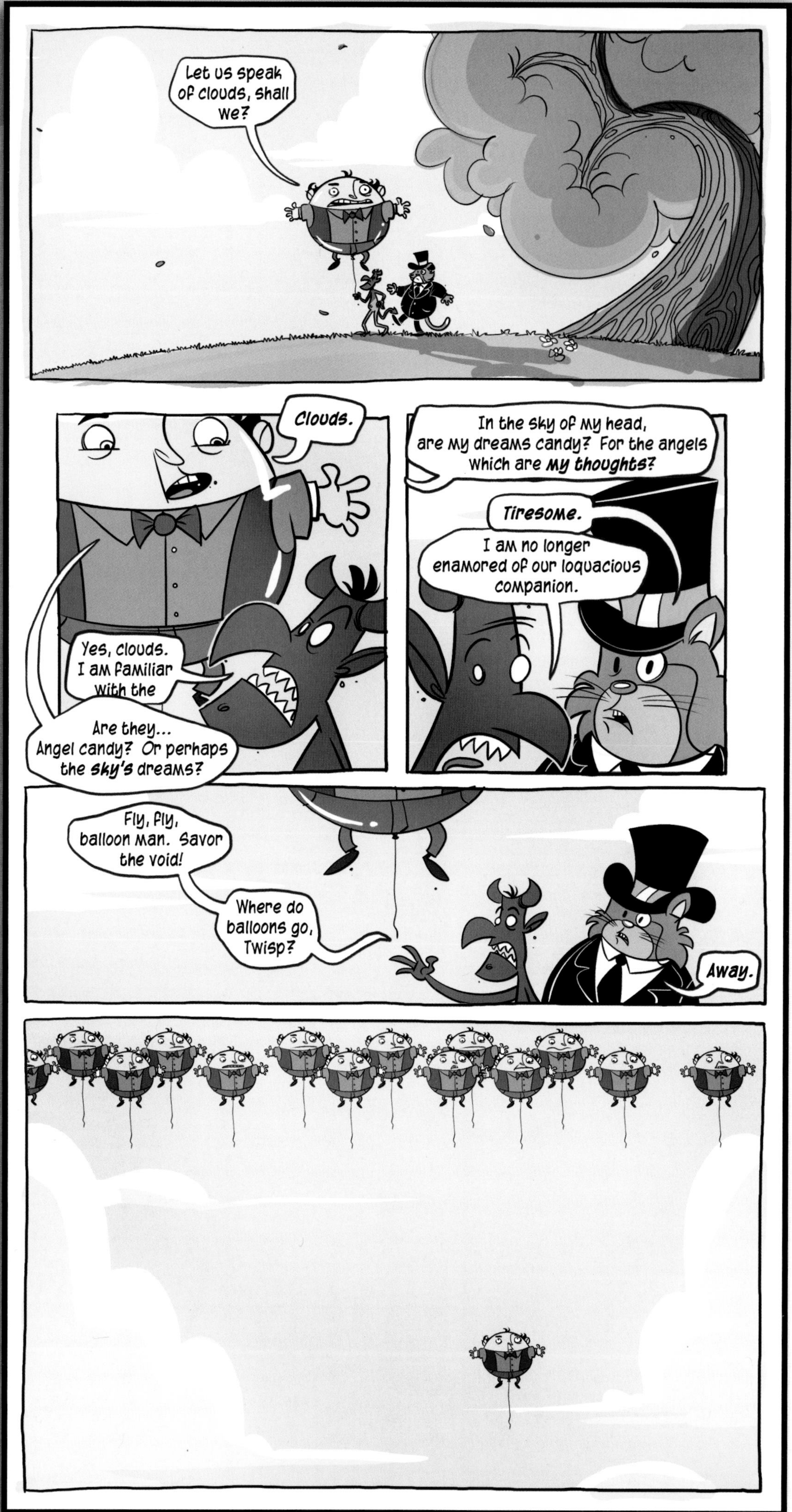
Let us speak of clouds, shall we?
Clouds.
Yes, clouds. I am familiar with the
Are they... Angel candy? Or perhaps the ***sky's*** dreams?
In the sky of my head, are my dreams candy? For the angels which are ***my thoughts?***
Tiresome.
I am no longer enamored of our loquacious companion.
Fly, fly, balloon man. Savor the void!
Where do balloons go, Twisp?
Away.

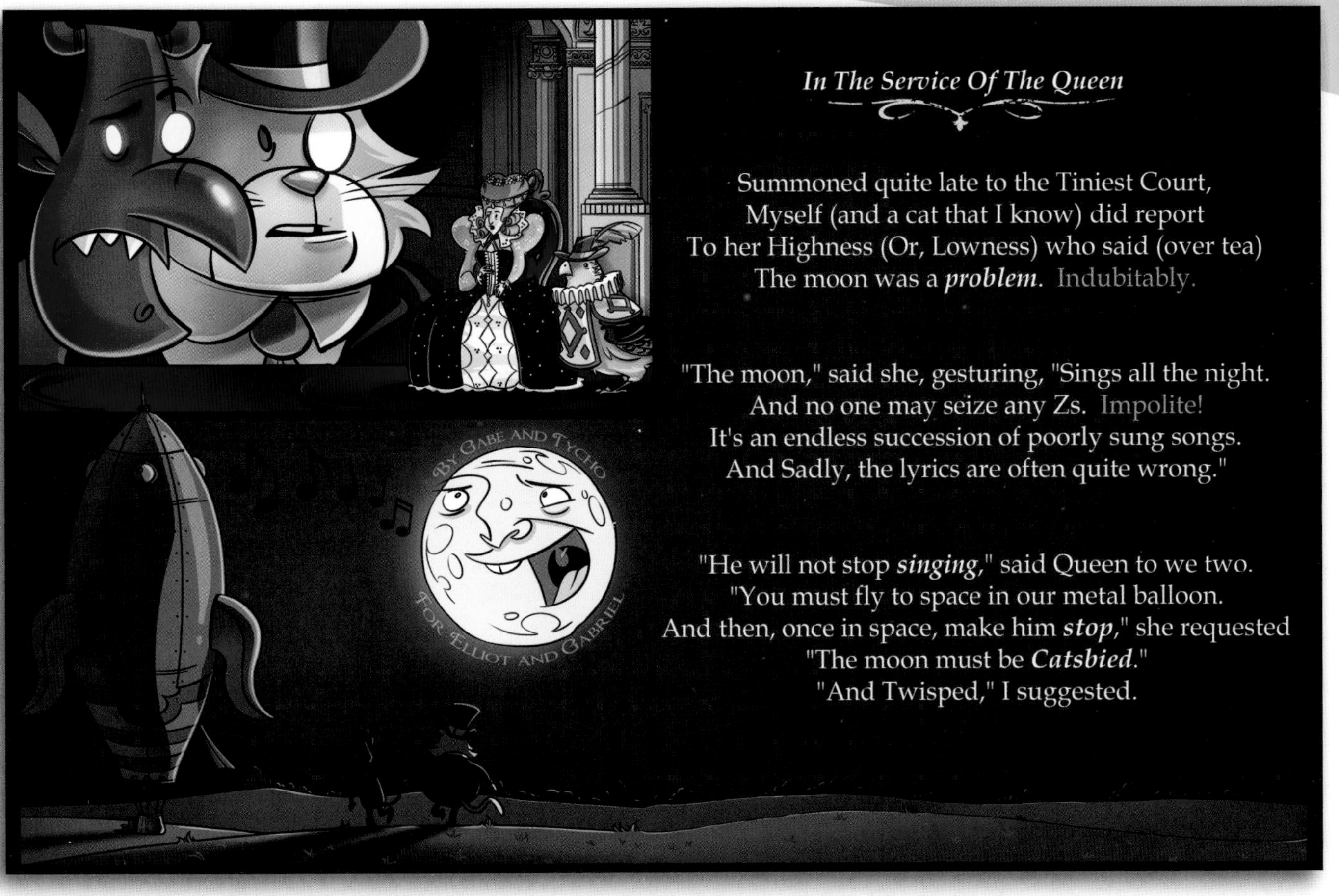
In The Service Of The Queen
By Gabe and Tycho
For Elliot and Gabriel
Summoned quite late to the Tiniest Court,
Myself (and a cat that I know) did report
To her Highness (Or, Lowness) who said (over tea)
The moon was a ***problem***. Indubitably.
"The moon," said she, gesturing, "Sings all the night.
And no one may seize any Zs. Impolite!
It's an endless succession of poorly sung songs.
And Sadly, the lyrics are often quite wrong."
"He will not stop ***singing***," said Queen to we two.
"You must fly to space in our metal balloon.
And then, once in space, make him ***stop***," she requested
"The moon must be ***Catsbied***."
"And Twisped," I suggested.

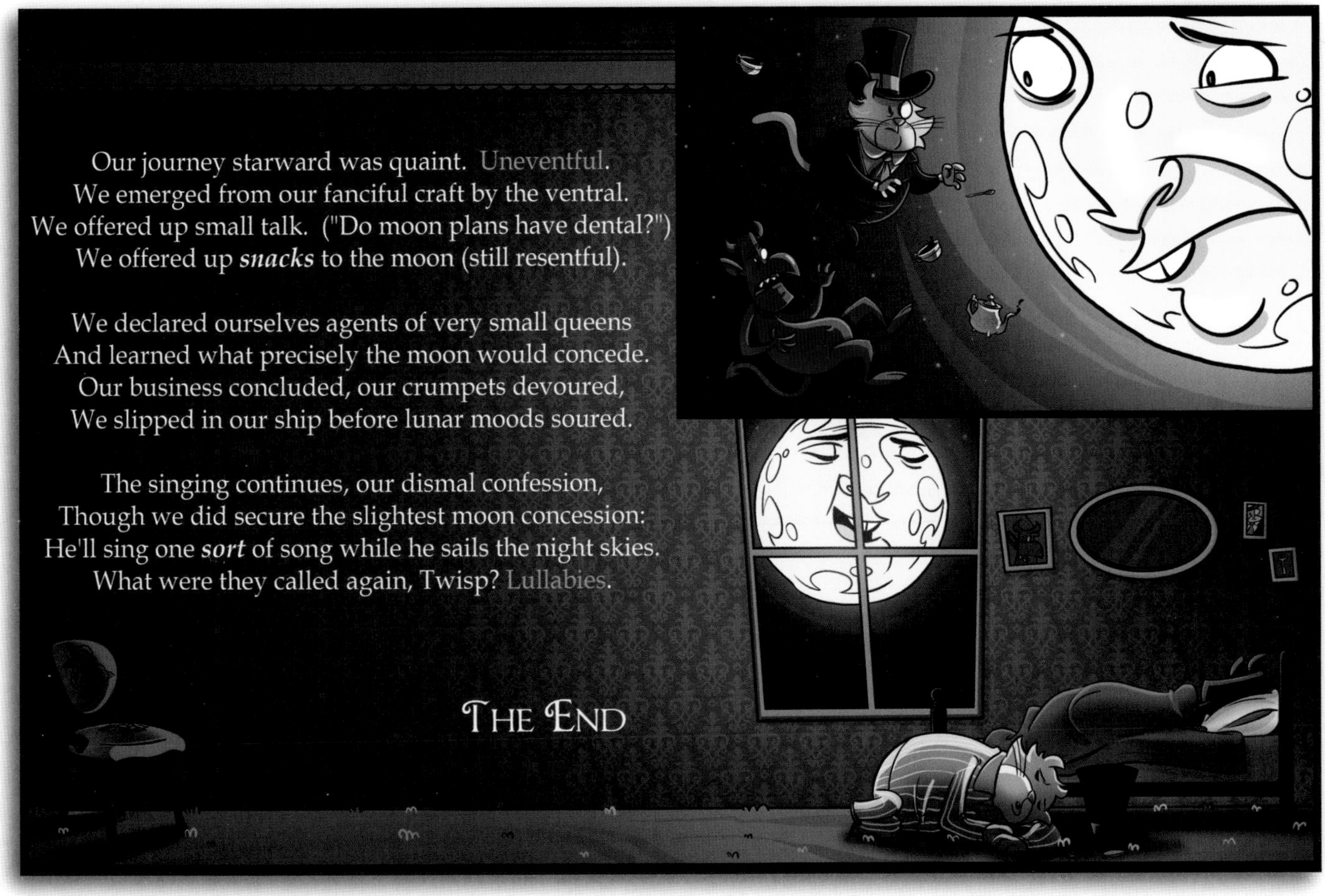
Our journey starward was quaint. Uneventful.
We emerged from our fanciful craft by the ventral.
We offered up small talk. ("Do moon plans have dental?")
We offered up ***snacks*** to the moon (still resentful).
We declared ourselves agents of very small queens
And learned what precisely the moon would concede.
Our business concluded, our crumpets devoured,
We slipped in our ship before lunar moods soured.
The singing continues, our dismal confession,
Though we did secure the slightest moon concession:
He'll sing one ***sort*** of song while he sails the night skies.
What were they called again, Twisp? Lullabies.
The End

TIME LINE **2001 (August) —** The unofficial *Penny Arcade* fan convention, the Necrowombicon, is held in Seattle.

IN THE HOUSE OF PENNY ARCADE

by Jerry Holkins

Mike and Jerry's Desks

These are the desks where we do things. That's mine on the left, and there is Mike's on the right. I'd love to have a psychologist look at this picture and tell me what it means.

Mike and Jerry's Couch

Gaze upon it, O public relations firms, and weep. This is the black altar upon which we sacrifice the products of the electronic entertainment industry.

The Conference Room

The conference table was made by a cadre of mad geniuses called Because We Can, which more or less describes their design aesthetic. It can split into two separate table surfaces, and disguises its heat signature through the use of an advanced polymer.

The Ping-Pong Arena

Because we had some say in how the office was laid out, we chose to dedicate a substantial portion of one side to a table-tennis arena. Things change very quickly around here, though—we'll see if there's room for something like this when Child's Play rolls around.

The Entrance

Solid Snake is positioned in such a way as to say, "Just try to get in here, motherfucker. I DARE YOU."

TIME LINE

2001 (October) — Mike moves from Spokane to Seattle.

ON SORCELATION

by Jerry Holkins

Within the confines of *Penny Arcade*, there are two warring fantasy franchises:

The first is *Epic Legends of The Hierarchs: The Elemenstor Saga*—Tycho's overwrought medieval garbage. Based on a mercenary swords 'n' sorcery brand that has spawned countless card games, board games, novels, novellas, cycles, and at *least* one chronicle, it's bad, certainly. But not awful.

No, awful is what you can expect from L. H. Franzibald, author of the competing (and considerably more successful) *Song of the Sorcelator.* For some reason, we enjoy writing this second one better. You'd think it would be easier to write something that was supposed to be bad, but it's not. It has to be bad in exactly the *right way.*

I cranked up a wiki for *The Elemenstor Saga,* thinking that people would have just as much fun as we did making up the worst possible crap, and contributions to it exploded overnight. It was joined later by a wiki focused on "Franzibald's" work, and the two sites share a lively (if wholly imaginary) rivalry.

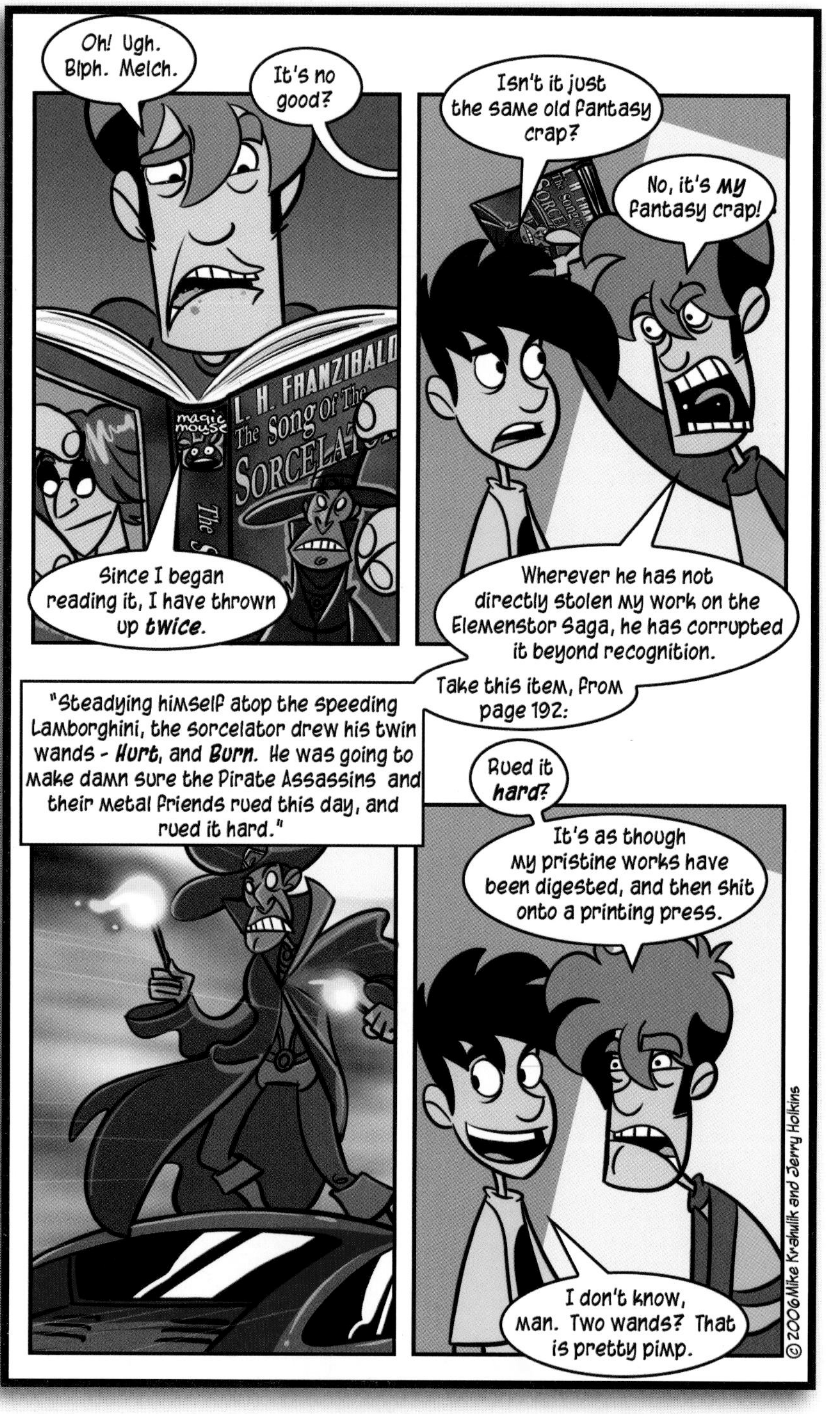
Oh! Ugh. Blph. Melch.
It's no good?
L. H. Franzibald The Song of The Sorcelator
Since I began reading it, I have thrown up *twice*.
Isn't it just the same old fantasy crap?
No, it's *my* fantasy crap!
Wherever he has not directly stolen my work on the Elemenstor Saga, he has corrupted it beyond recognition.
Take this item, from page 192:
"Steadying himself atop the speeding Lamborghini, the sorcelator drew his twin wands - *Hurt*, and *Burn*. He was going to make damn sure the Pirate Assassins and their metal friends rued this day, and rued it hard."
Rued it *hard?*
It's as though my pristine works have been digested, and then shit onto a printing press.
I don't know, man. Two wands? That is pretty pimp.
©2006 Mike Krahulik and Jerry Holkins

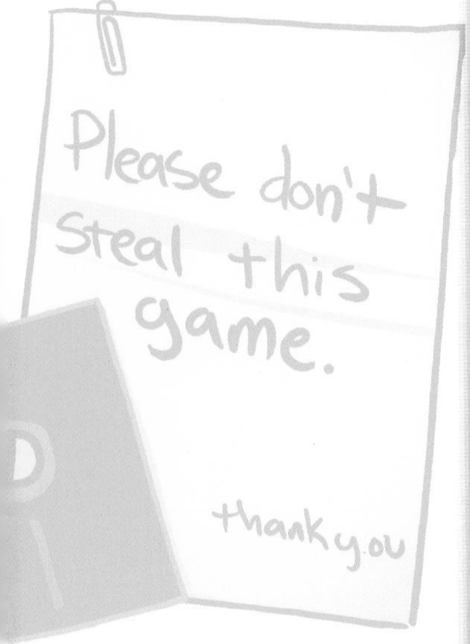
Please don't steal this game.
thank you

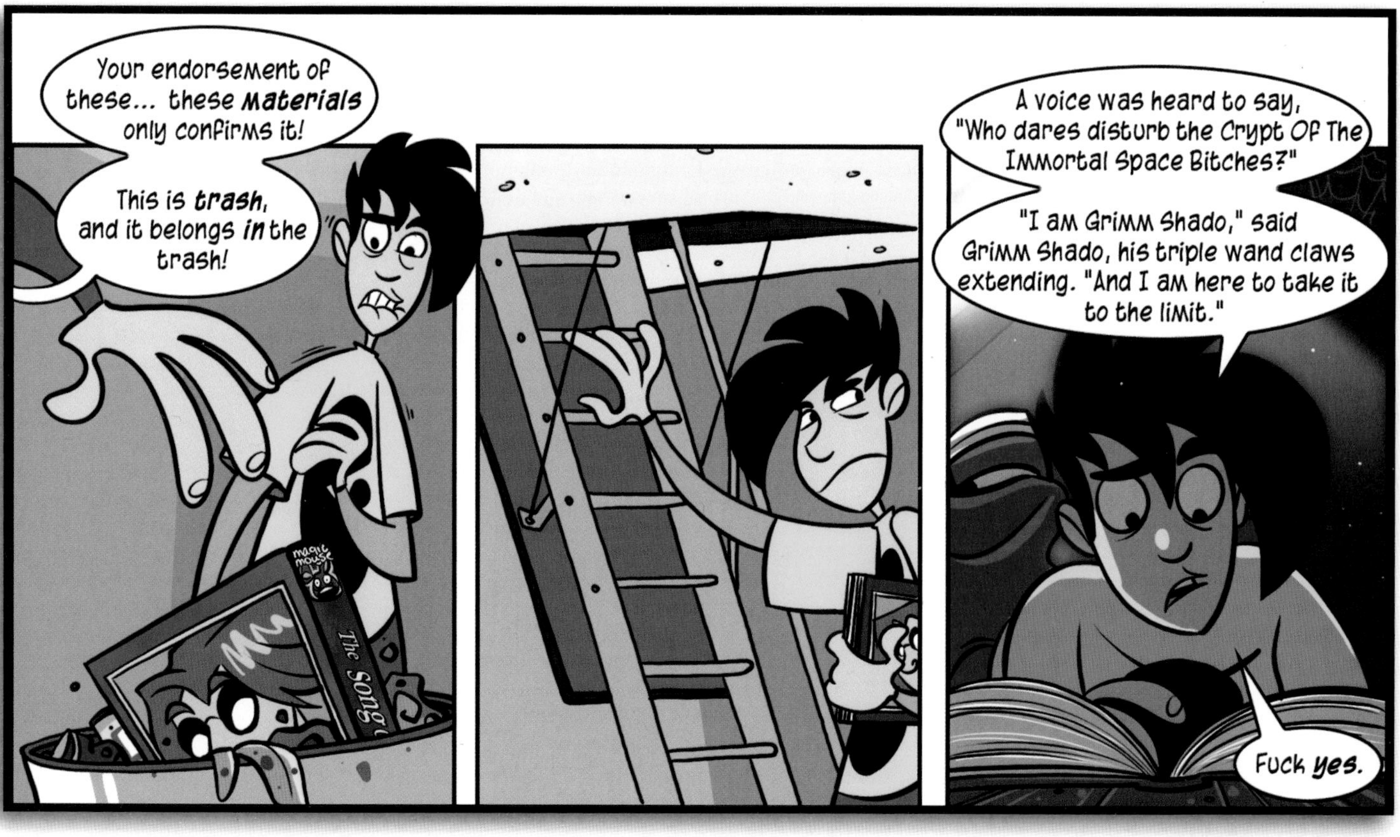
Your endorsement of these... these *materials* only confirms it!
This is *trash*, and it belongs *in* the trash!
A voice was heard to say, "Who dares disturb the Crypt Of The Immortal Space Bitches?"
"I am Grimm Shado," said Grimm Shado, his triple wand claws extending. "And I am here to take it to the limit."
Fuck *yes*.

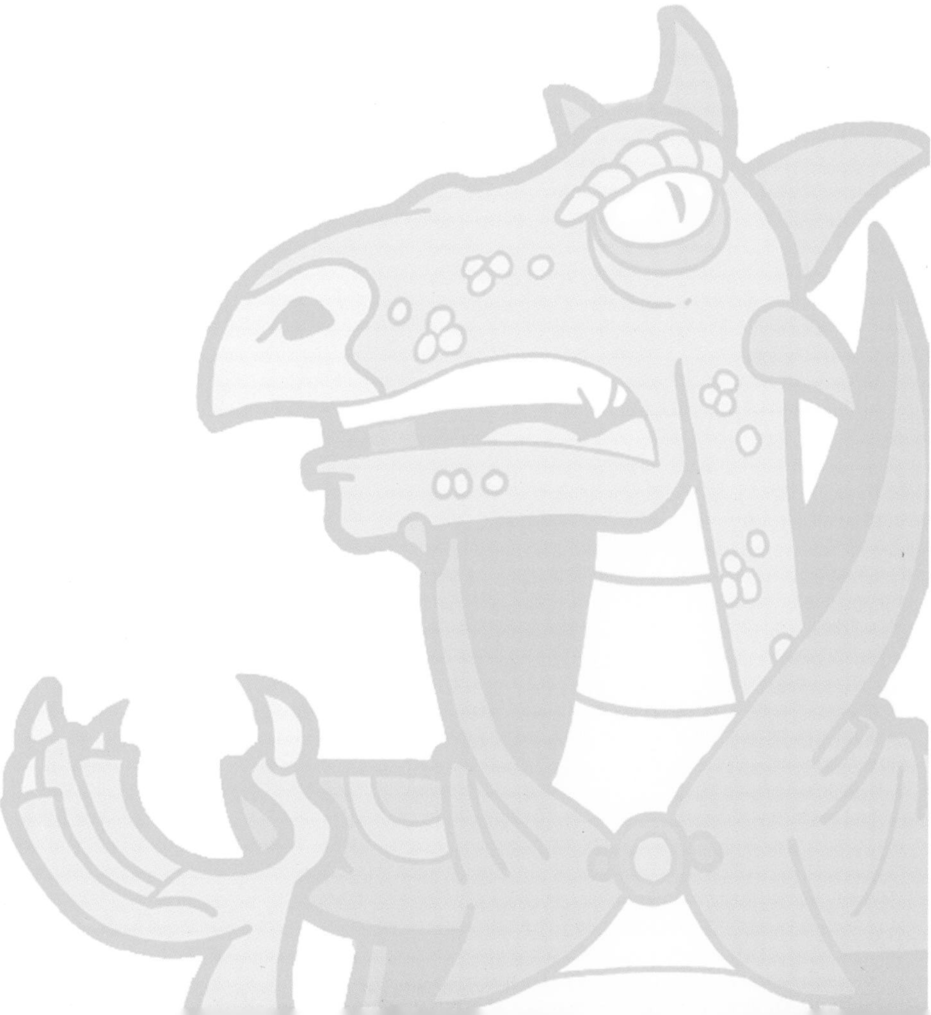

TIME LINE

2002 (May) — First advertiser on *PA* (Meridian 59).

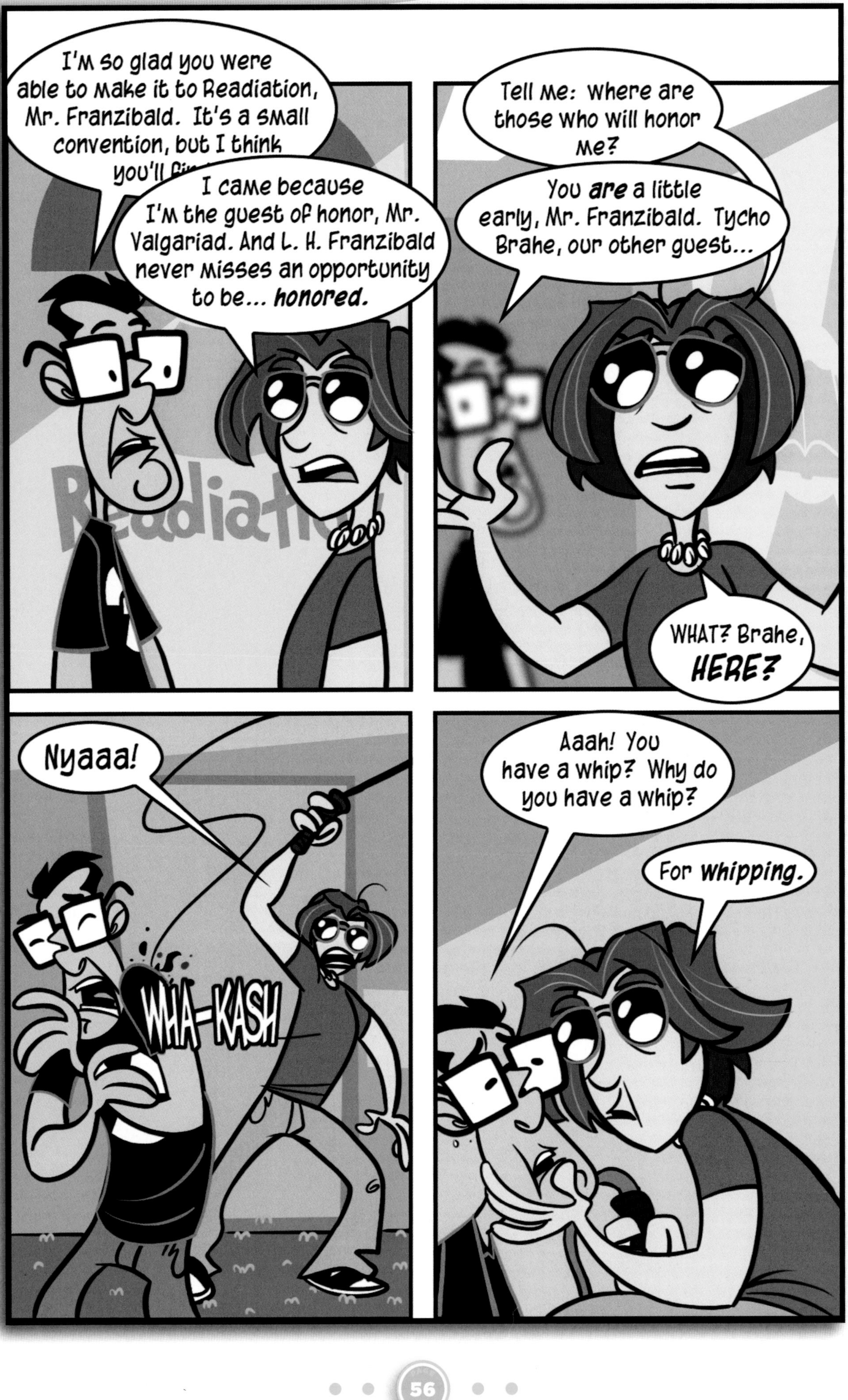
I'm so glad you were able to make it to Readiation, Mr. Franzibald. It's a small convention, but I think you'll fi
I came because I'm the guest of honor, Mr. Valgariad. And L. H. Franzibald never misses an opportunity to be... honored.
Readiation
Tell me: where are those who will honor me?
You are a little early, Mr. Franzibald. Tycho Brahe, our other guest...
WHAT? Brahe, HERE?
Nyaaa!
WHA-KASH
Aaah! You have a whip? Why do you have a whip?
For whipping.

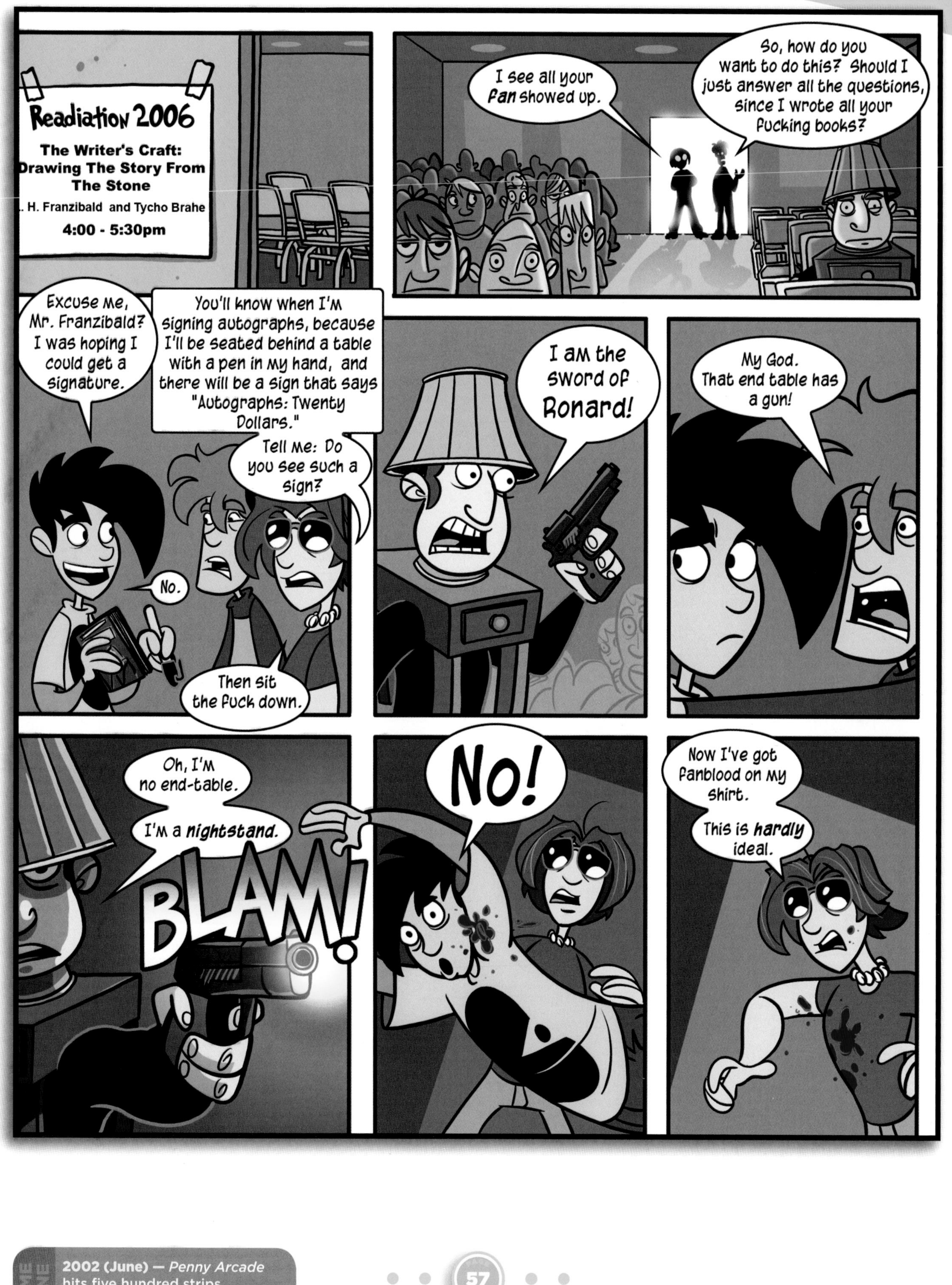
Readiation 2006
The Writer's Craft: Drawing The Story From The Stone
. H. Franzibald and Tycho Brahe
4:00 - 5:30pm
I see all your fan showed up.
So, how do you want to do this? Should I just answer all the questions, since I wrote all your fucking books?
Excuse me, Mr. Franzibald? I was hoping I could get a signature.
You'll know when I'm signing autographs, because I'll be seated behind a table with a pen in my hand, and there will be a sign that says "Autographs: Twenty Dollars."
Tell me: Do you see such a sign?
No.
Then sit the fuck down.
I am the sword of Ronard!
My God. That end table has a gun!
Oh, I'm no end-table.
I'm a nightstand.
BLAM!
No!
Now I've got fanblood on my shirt.
This is hardly ideal.

TIME LINE **2002 (June) —** *Penny Arcade* hits five hundred strips.

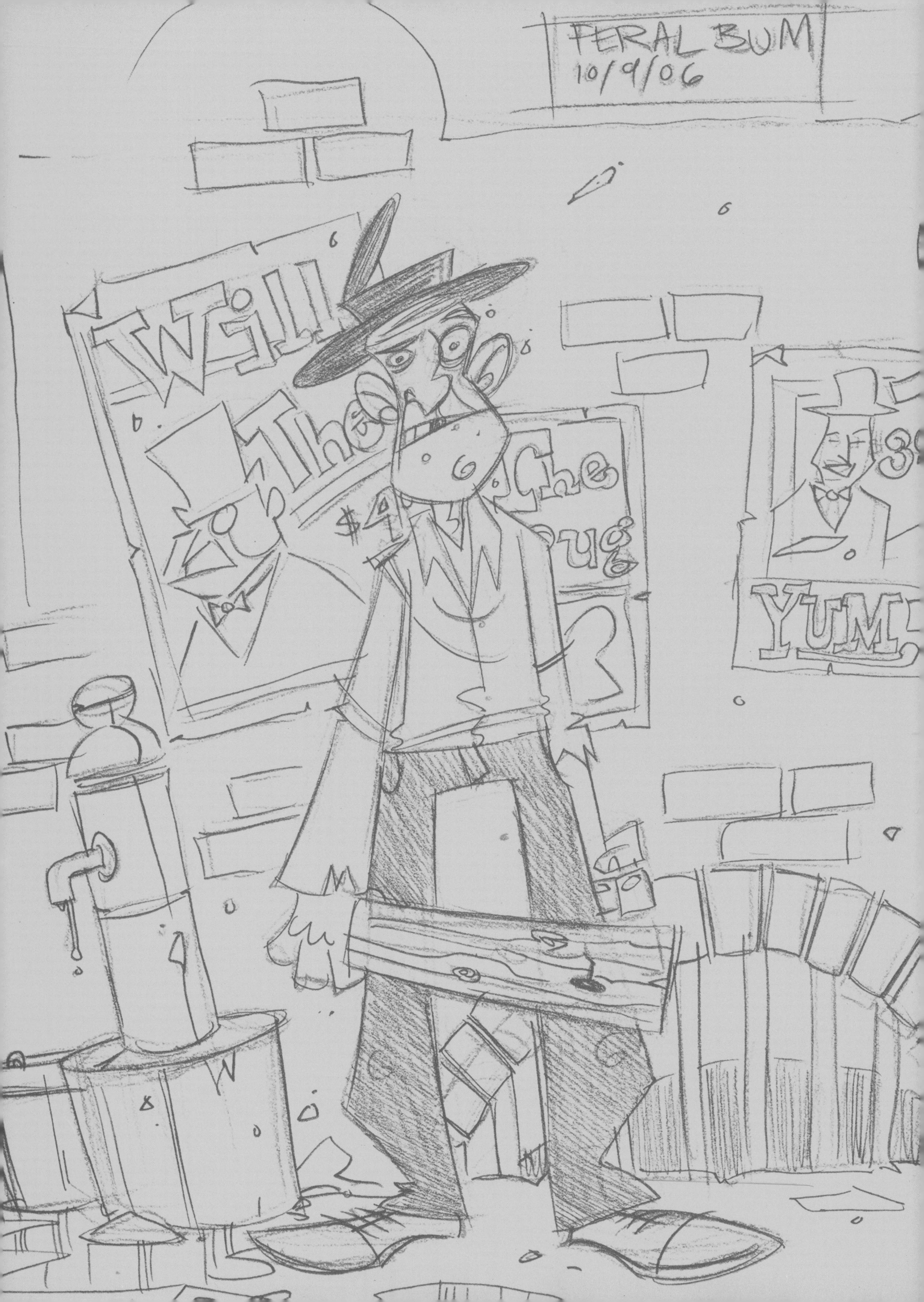

FERAL BUM
10/9/06
Will
The
Che
$4
YUM

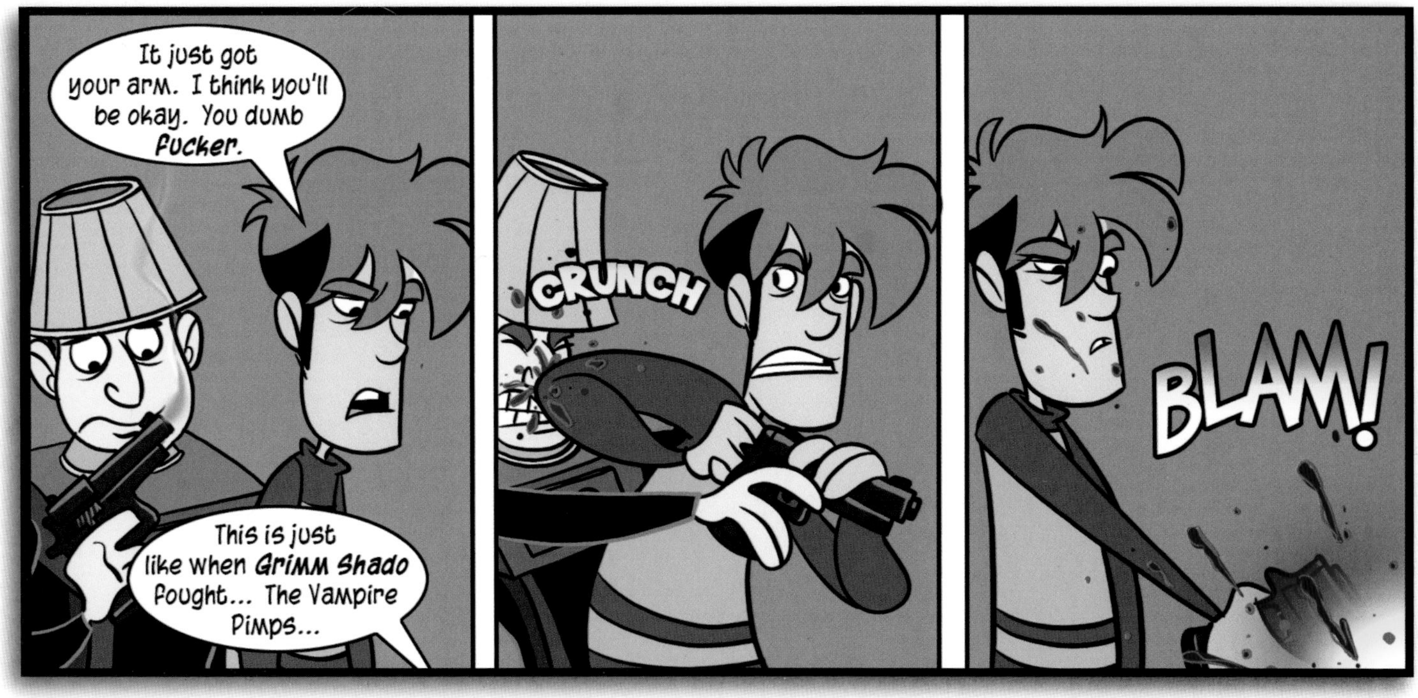
It just got your arm. I think you'll be okay. You dumb fucker.
This is just like when Grimm Shado fought... The Vampire Pimps...
CRUNCH
BLAM!

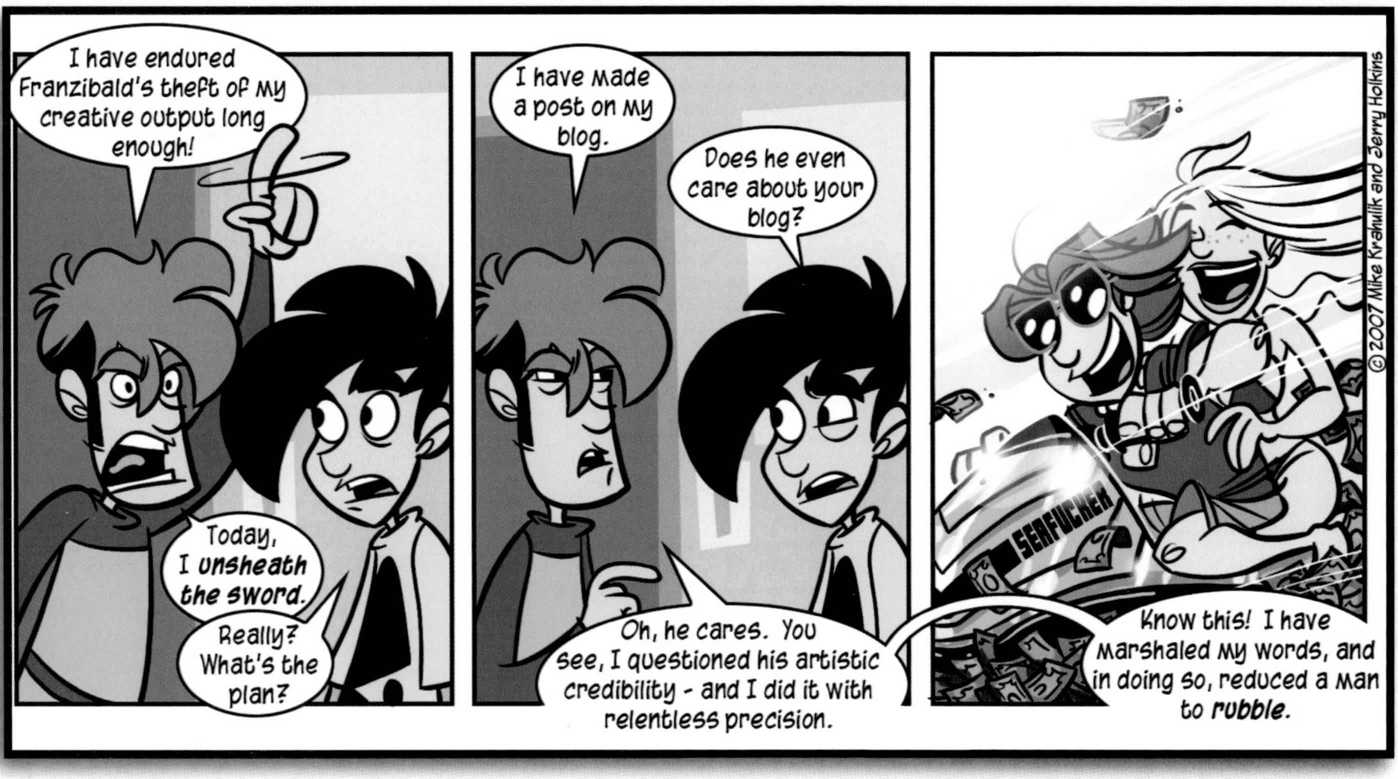
I have endured Franzibald's theft of my creative output long enough!
Today, I unsheath the sword.
Really? What's the plan?
I have made a post on my blog.
Does he even care about your blog?
Oh, he cares. You see, I questioned his artistic credibility - and I did it with relentless precision.
Know this! I have marshaled my words, and in doing so, reduced a man to rubble.
SERFUCKER
© 2007 Mike Krahulik and Jerry Holkins

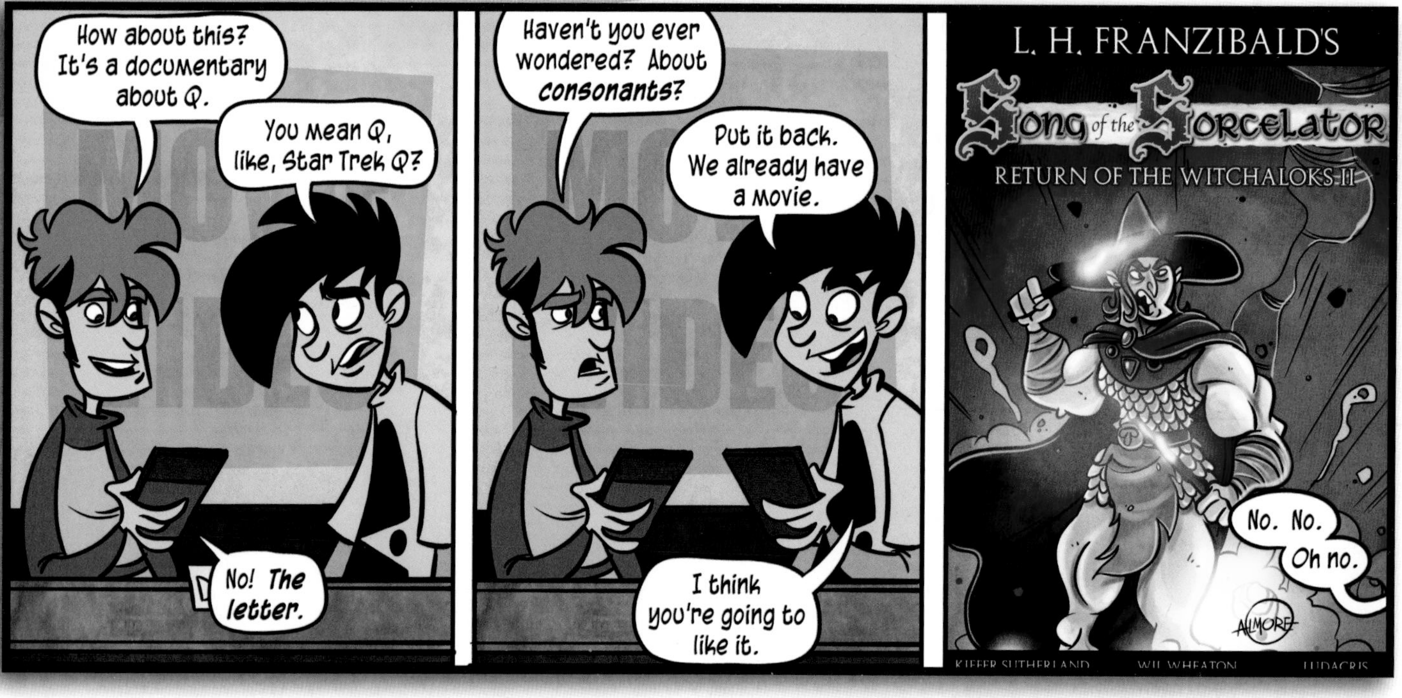
How about this? It's a documentary about Q.
You mean Q, like, Star Trek Q?
No! The letter.
Haven't you ever wondered? About consonants?
Put it back. We already have a movie.
I think you're going to like it.
L. H. FRANZIBALD'S
Song of the Sorcelator
RETURN OF THE WITCHALOKS II
No. No. Oh no.
KIEFER SUTHERLAND
WIL WHEATON
LUDACRIS

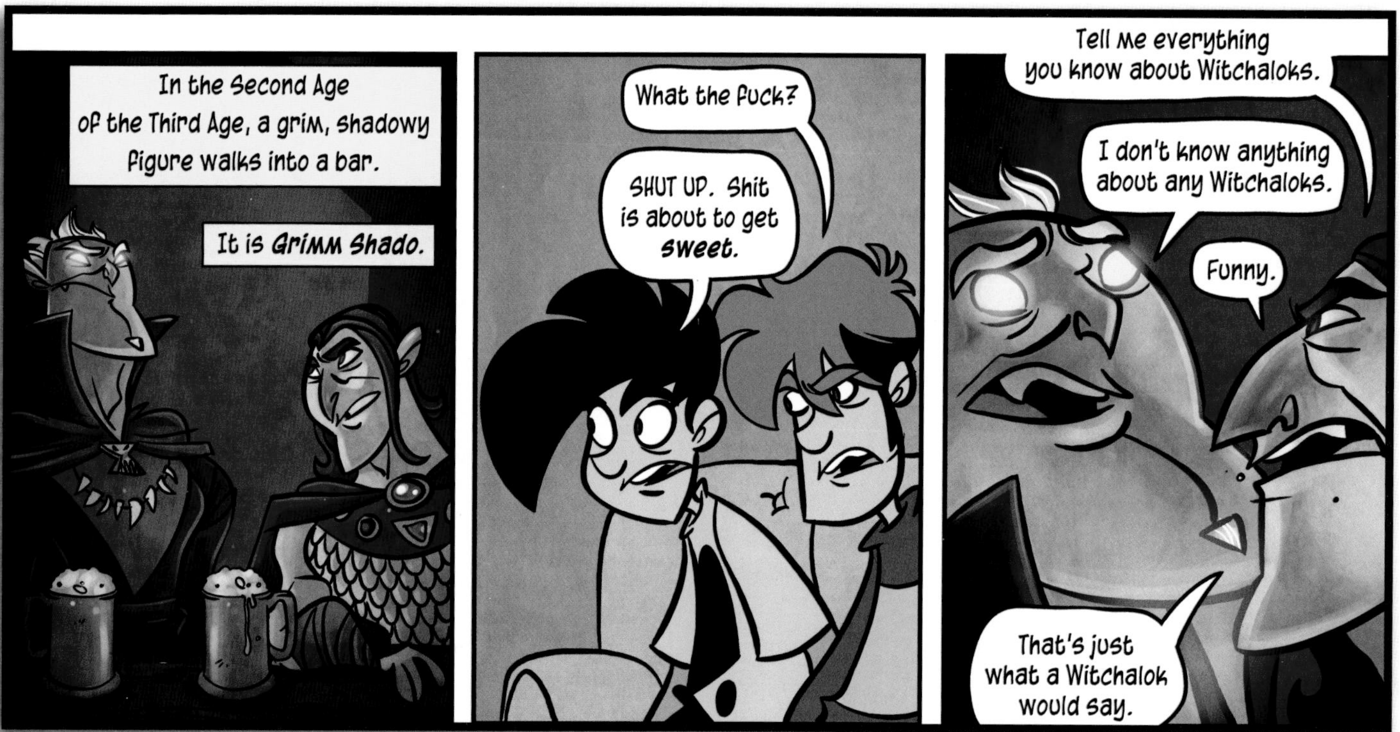
In the Second Age of the Third Age, a grim, shadowy figure walks into a bar.
It is Grimm Shado.
What the fuck?
SHUT UP. Shit is about to get sweet.
Tell me everything you know about Witchaloks.
I don't know anything about any Witchaloks.
Funny.
That's just what a Witchalok would say.

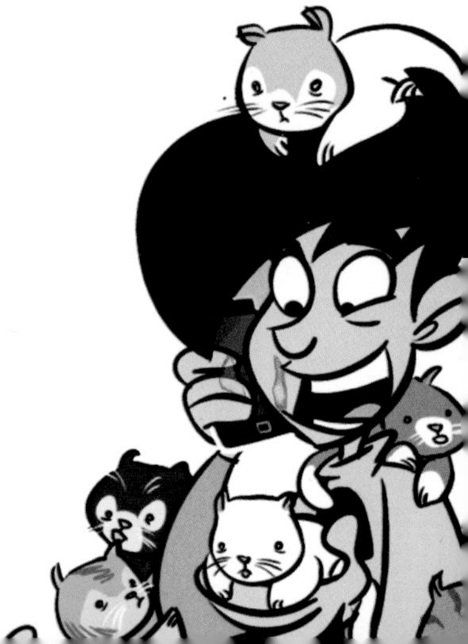

TIME LINE **2002 (July) —** For the very first time, Mike and Jerry have lunch with Robert Khoo.

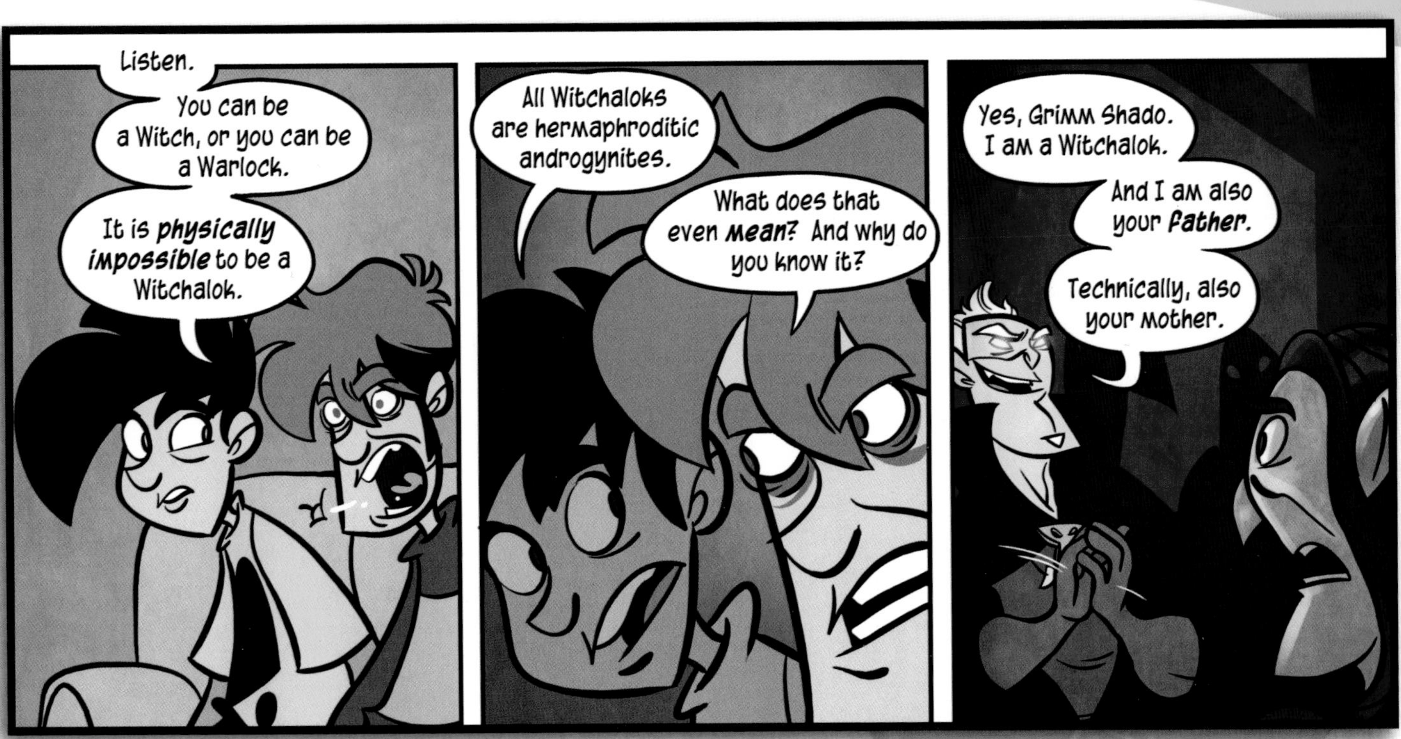
Listen.
You can be a Witch, or you can be a Warlock.
It is ***physically impossible*** to be a Witchalok.
All Witchaloks are hermaphroditic androgynites.
What does that even ***mean***? And why do you know it?
Yes, Grimm Shado. I am a Witchalok.
And I am also your ***father***.
Technically, also your mother.

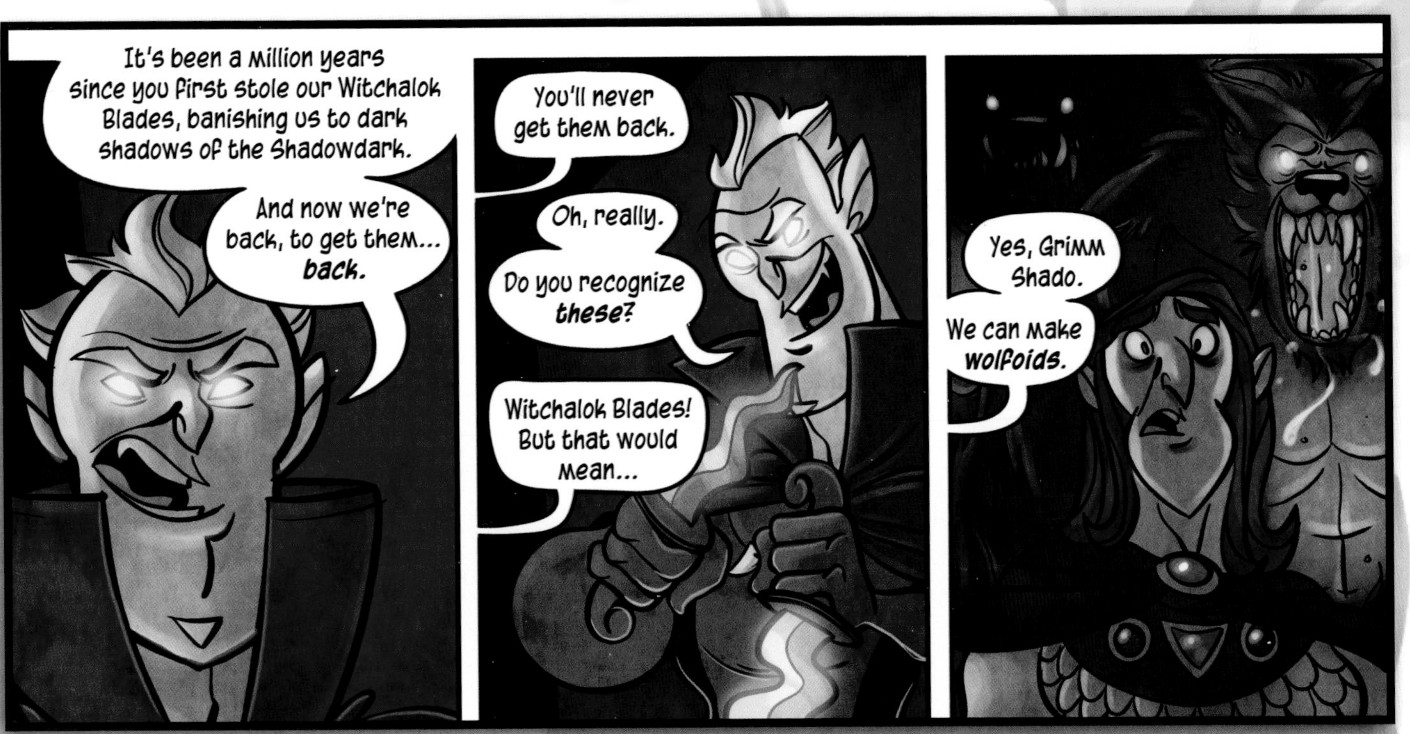
It's been a million years since you first stole our Witchalok Blades, banishing us to dark shadows of the Shadowdark.
And now we're back, to get them... ***back***.
You'll never get them back.
Oh, really.
Do you recognize ***these***?
Witchalok Blades! But that would mean...
Yes, Grimm Shado.
We can make ***wolfoids***.

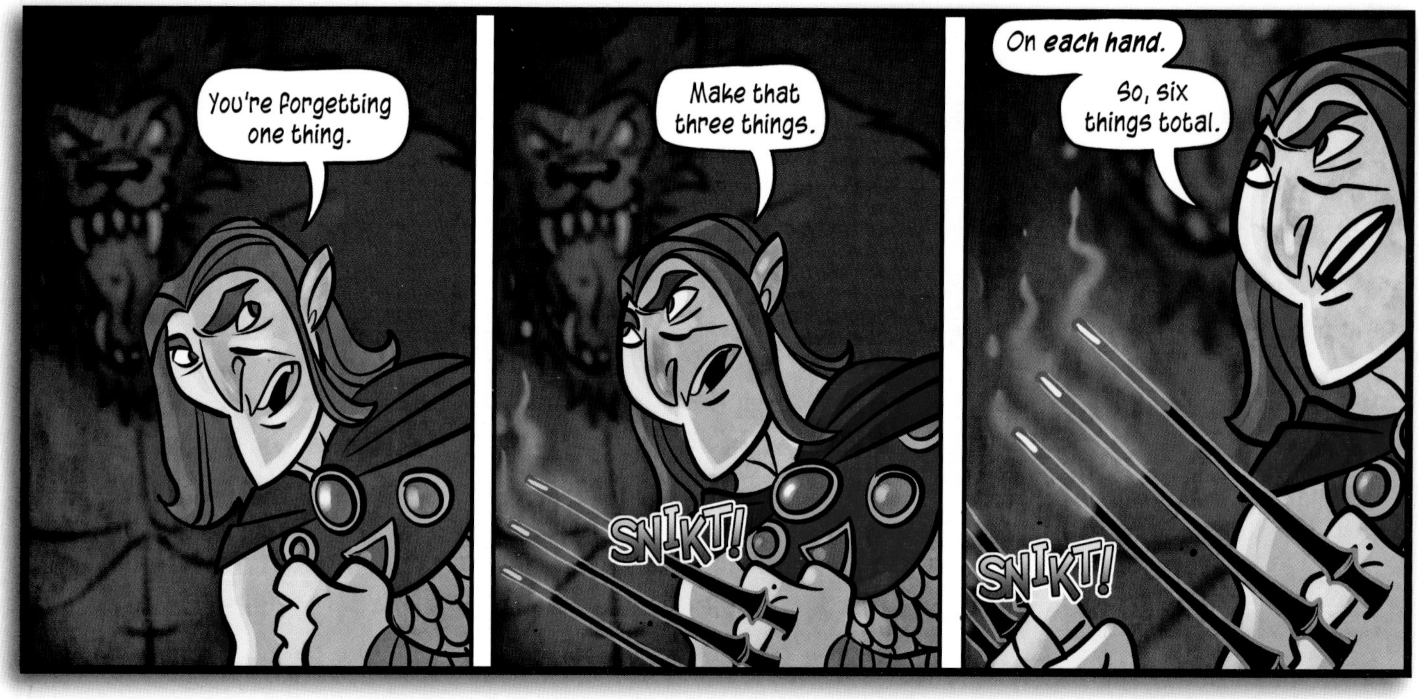
You're forgetting one thing.
Make that three things.
SNIKT!
On each hand.
So, six things total.
SNIKT!

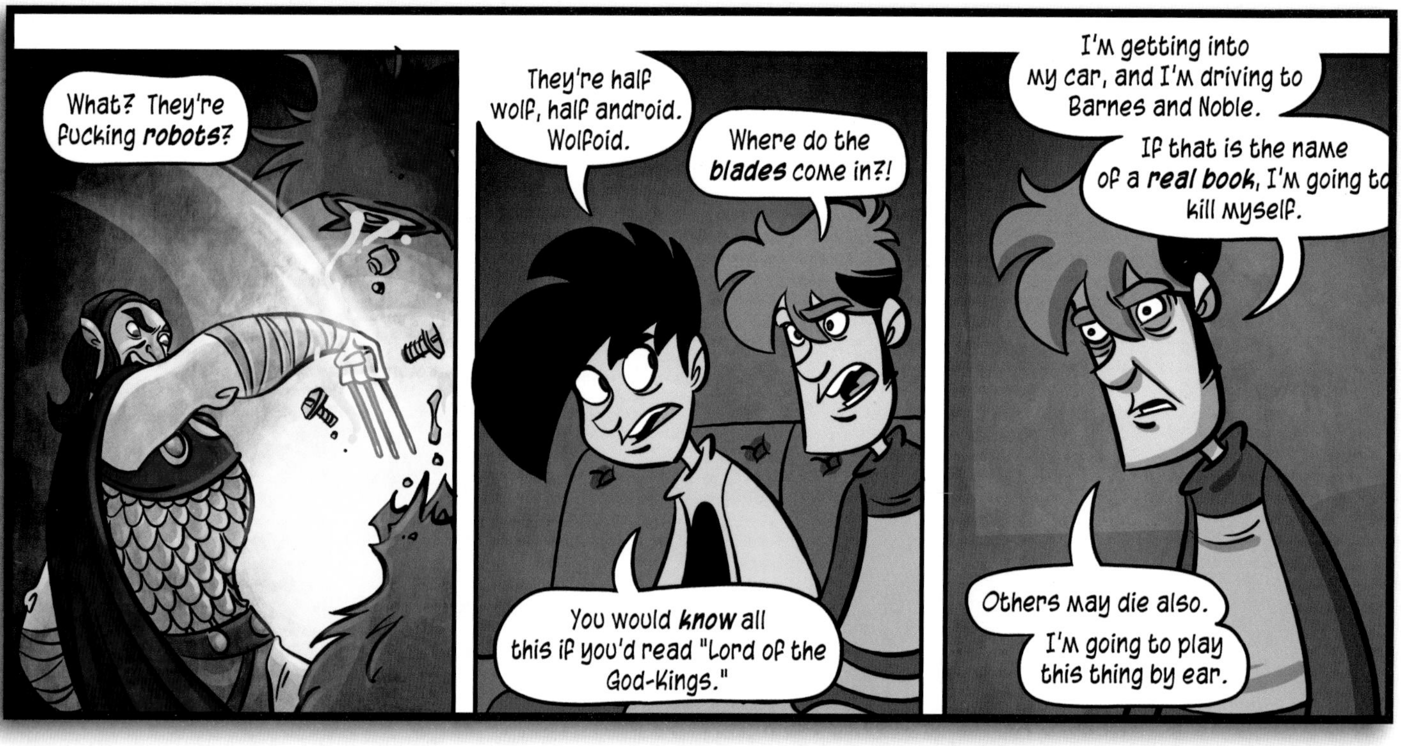
What? They're fucking robots?
They're half wolf, half android. Wolfoid.
Where do the blades come in?!
You would know all this if you'd read "Lord of the God-Kings."
I'm getting into my car, and I'm driving to Barnes and Noble.
If that is the name of a real book, I'm going to kill myself.
Others may die also.
I'm going to play this thing by ear.

TIME LINE **2002 (July) —** Kiko Villaseñor from Gameskins.com invites Mike and Jerry to share his booth at San Diego Comic-Con. Everyone is a little terrified by the line.

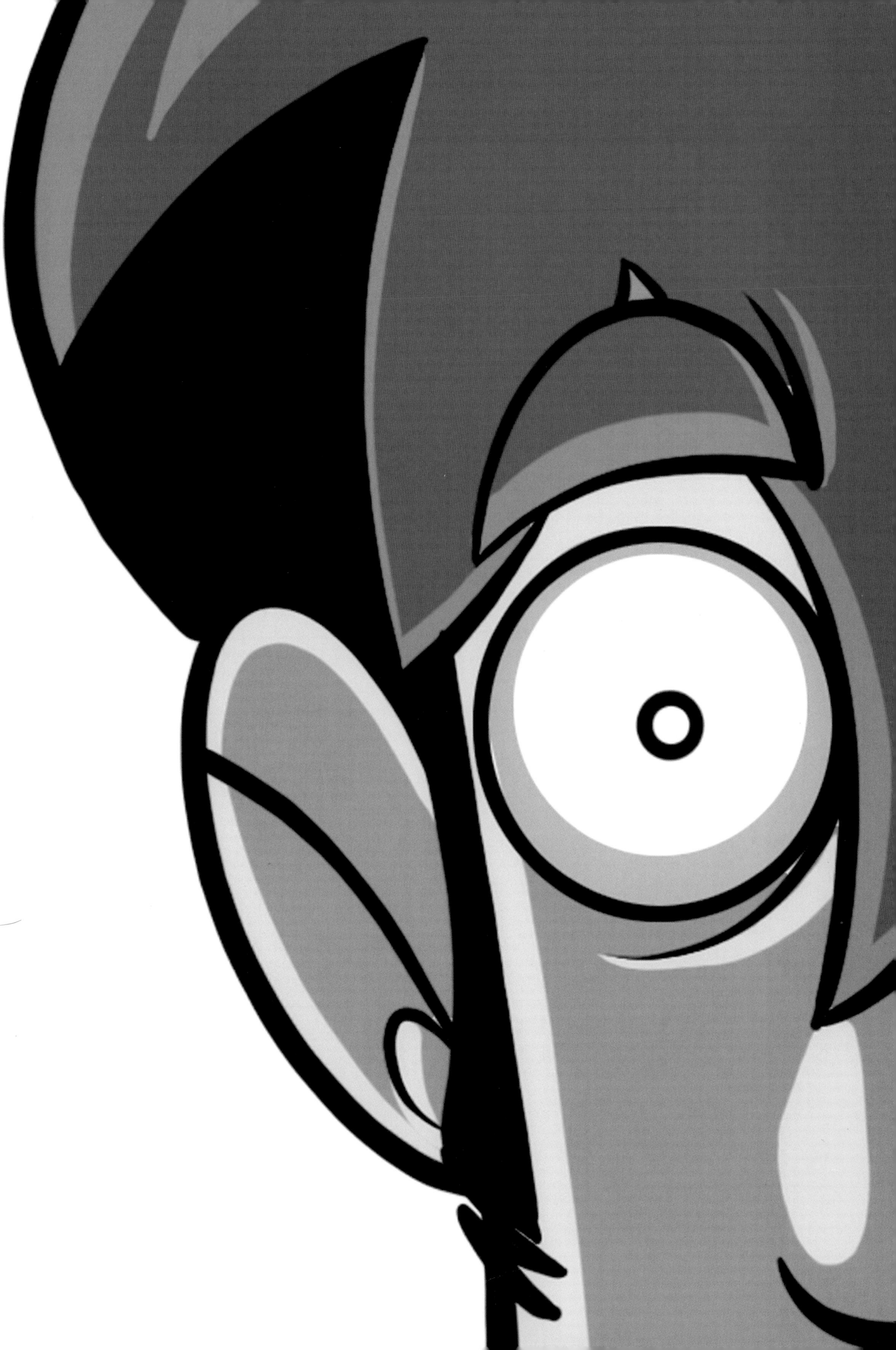

CHILD'S PLAY

by Kristen Lindsay

Origins

Gamers Give Back
Child's Play
www.childsplaycharity.org

In late 2003 an article by writer and child advocate Bill France appeared in the Everett, Washington, HeraldNet. Carrying a familiar tune to those in the game industry, the piece titled "Violent Video Games Are Training Children to Kill" was designed to inform concerned parents everywhere of the *fact* that video games *created killers* and that those who enjoyed them were *horrible people.*

Mike linked to the article on *Penny Arcade* and commented, "The media seem intent on perpetuating the myth that gamers are ticking time bombs just waiting to go off. I know for a fact that gamers are good people." Collectively, gamers had read these articles in frustration for years, but challenging the mainstream media and their speculations was an uphill battle. So instead of trying to debunk the negative news about gamers, Mike and Jerry realized it might be more productive to focus on the more *positive* aspects of the game community.

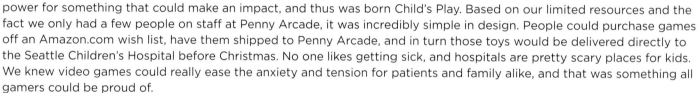

Knowing that a link on the *Penny Arcade* site would destroy any site with a flood of traffic, Mike and Jerry realized they could harness that power for something that could make an impact, and thus was born Child's Play. Based on our limited resources and the fact we only had a few people on staff at Penny Arcade, it was incredibly simple in design. People could purchase games off an Amazon.com wish list, have them shipped to Penny Arcade, and in turn those toys would be delivered directly to the Seattle Children's Hospital before Christmas. No one likes getting sick, and hospitals are pretty scary places for kids. We knew video games could really ease the anxiety and tension for patients and family alike, and that was something all gamers could be proud of.

Initial plans called for Mike's garage to be the "warehouse" until the end of the toy drive, but after a few days we all got phone calls "asking for a little help," followed by emails of "the UPS guy is really mad at me," and then "my apartment complex has filed a complaint about the three dumpsters of cardboard." To call the response "overwhelming" doesn't do it justice, as Mike's garage, living room, and spare bedroom had become completely overrun with toys and a public call for additional space was made. A volunteer truck driver and warehouse space from Amaze Entertainment were the two pieces we needed. When the drive closed at the end of December, twenty volunteers and the Penny Arcade staff delivered $250,000 worth of toys to the Seattle Children's Hospital.

I officially joined the Penny Arcade family in 2004 to help organize the first PAX as the volunteer coordinator. Robert asked me afterward if I wanted to take the lead on organizing Child's Play, and after seeing what happened that first year the answer was a no-brainer. The floodgates had been opened and some very intimidating expectations were set, but being a part of that was something you couldn't say no to.

With the previous year under our belts and the increased demand from readers, Child's Play expanded as our reach grew to four additional hospitals in Oakland, San Diego, Houston, and Washington, DC. "Key learnings" prompted the logistical change of having donations shipped directly to our partner hospitals, rather than repeating the storage and space snafu from 2003. It was a huge improvement in our operation, and being able to ship directly to their hospital of choice really appealed to donors. In the short

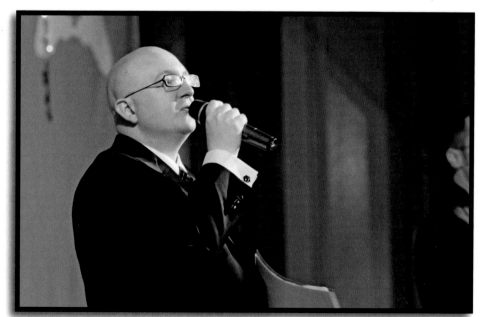

two-month push in 2004, more than $310,000 worth of toys, books, and games was collected, including an increase in support from the industry as we secured nearly forty corporate sponsors including Nintendo, Midway, and THQ.

Also in 2004, Mike and Jerry decided that a centerpiece event for the drive could not only raise money but also be a lot of fun, ultimately settling on a formal dinner auction. Mike announced the event in late November:

Every big charity always has a fancy dinner and auction. We figure that just because we're gamers doesn't mean we can't get dressed up for one night and act like we're a bunch of fancy high society types. So with that in mind I'd like to invite you to the Child's Play 2004 charity dinner and auction— December 9th in Bellevue, Washington.

Tickets sold out almost immediately, and the pressure was suddenly on to not only stage a formal banquet and auction but also to do so in a way that wasn't stuffy and, quite frankly, lame. Luckily, local industry giants jumped in and offered some really awesome items for bidding, including studio tours, lifetime subscriptions, and original artwork. Mike and Jerry personally contributed *Penny Arcade* prints, T-shirts, and the now legendary "Appearance in a *Penny Arcade* Strip." But to top it off, Mike and Jerry also agreed to emcee the evening, making the dinner a...*unique* charity event and fan experience. I quietly asked Robert if it might be more effective to bring in a professional auctioneer, but he replied, "Can you imagine watching them try to run a live auction? They have no idea what they're doing. It'll be *awesome.*"

In no time, we found ourselves standing in the Meydenbauer Center in Bellevue, which at the time was the home of the first PAX held three months earlier. We scrambled, hanging our own Christmas decorations around the room and trying to make it look "formal festive." I had even brought my personal collection of Christmas nutcrackers, which I remember because Mike tripped over a waist-high model on stage and immediately announced, "I was just hit in the junk by a nutcracker. How ironic is *that*?" It was clear that, despite our tuxedos, this wasn't your run-of-the-mill charity dinner.

For Child's Play, there was no looking back. For the next few years, I relied largely on *Penny Arcade* fans and the gaming community to get their local children's hospitals involved, but soon the Child's Play's profile grew to the point that we now have hospitals seeking us out for support. It's one of the ways I know we're really having an impact. In only four years we grew to over sixty partner facilities worldwide, and we broke the million-dollar mark in annual donations for the first time in the winter of 2006. It's a story we're all incredibly proud of and one we don't mind seeing on a headline.

Community Outreach

Child's Play is unique because it remains, at its heart, a community initiative. The bulk of its support still comes from activism by individual gamers across the globe as each year, game clubs, clans, and guilds hold their own niche fund-raisers. Game marathons, tournaments, donation collections, and other events unite these communities under the Child's Play banner.

Some of these community-run events have become cornerstones of the Child's Play season. Fünde

2002 (October) — Khoo quits his job as a management consultant to work at Penny Arcade for free.

TIME LINE

● ● ● 65 ● ● ●

Razor, a Rock Band and Guitar Hero party fund-raiser started in Brooklyn in 2006, now takes place concurrently in three cities across the United States. Desert Bus for Hope, an annual marathon session of what is widely considered to be the most boring video game of all time, is staged by a very brave (or totally crazy?) comedy sketch troupe based in British Columbia, Canada. Their most recent year raised more than seventy thousand dollars as they gamed for 125 hours straight. Efforts like these make us realize that Child's Play is so much larger than some webcomic throwing together a fund-raising drive. Child's Play represents the collective statement of millions of gamers worldwide that our lifestyle and community can make a difference.

Research

In addition to the positive emotional, psychological, and social benefits of video games, we've received reports and studies regarding the use of video gaming equipment for physical therapy and rehabilitation for spinal cord and other motor injuries. Wiis, in particular, have been very popular for encouraging patients of all ages to be active in a hospital setting, and redevelop balance and muscle tone after injuries.

We've also explored the therapeutic role of video games by supporting initiatives such as projectHOPE (Hospital-based Online Pediatric Environment), a network of pediatric patients across the country that allows children undergoing dialysis treatments to play games with other patients. Most people know that being hooked up to a dialysis machine for a few hours a week is painful and a nuisance, as it cuts into a person's free time, but what people don't know is that missing more than one treatment a month shortens the life span of a person by ten years. We were all very excited when projectHOPE started to come back with encouraging results as kids were less depressed, reported a better quality of life in the hospital, and even requested less pain medication while playing games. But the most compelling piece of data was the fact kids began *looking forward* to their treatment sessions. Child's Play was helping to make these things possible!

Impact

I will always recall the year we brought the brand-new Children's Cancer Hospital of Cairo on board as a Child's Play partner. We had collected cash donations for them, and I emailed our contact to let her know that we would be sending them a fairly substantial check, and as we always do, I specified that this donation be used directly for the kids as opposed to general hospital funds. I received a hesitant reply: "Would it be okay if we used some of the money to buy paint?" The walls at the Cairo hospital weren't even painted yet! The children were receiving chemotherapy in rooms that looked like bunkers, and I can't imagine how intimidating that must have been. Every day I hear personal stories of courage, of hope, of love, and of gratitude. We try to put some of these on the website; there you can read some of the letters we receive, such as this one from the aunt of a pediatric hospital patient:

> Words cannot accurately express how I feel. This message seems wholly insufficient to convey my gratitude to those who give to Child's Play. Their contributions bring important, joyful changes in children's lives. Your work is truly a blessing and I thank you from the bottom of my heart.

These emails are addressed to me, but they are really intended for you. For everyone who has ever supported Child's Play, whether it be through donating, printing off a flyer and putting it on a bulletin board, or writing an article about us for your campus paper, thank you. As we continue to come together and throw our support behind this charity, Child's Play will continue to be a voice of the video game community. When gamers give back, it makes a difference.

Kristin Lindsay has been with Penny Arcade since 2003 and is the project manager for Child's Play. She collects and directs donations, fund-raises, and arranges the annual Child's Play auction event. She also organizes the Enforcers who volunteer at PAX each year.

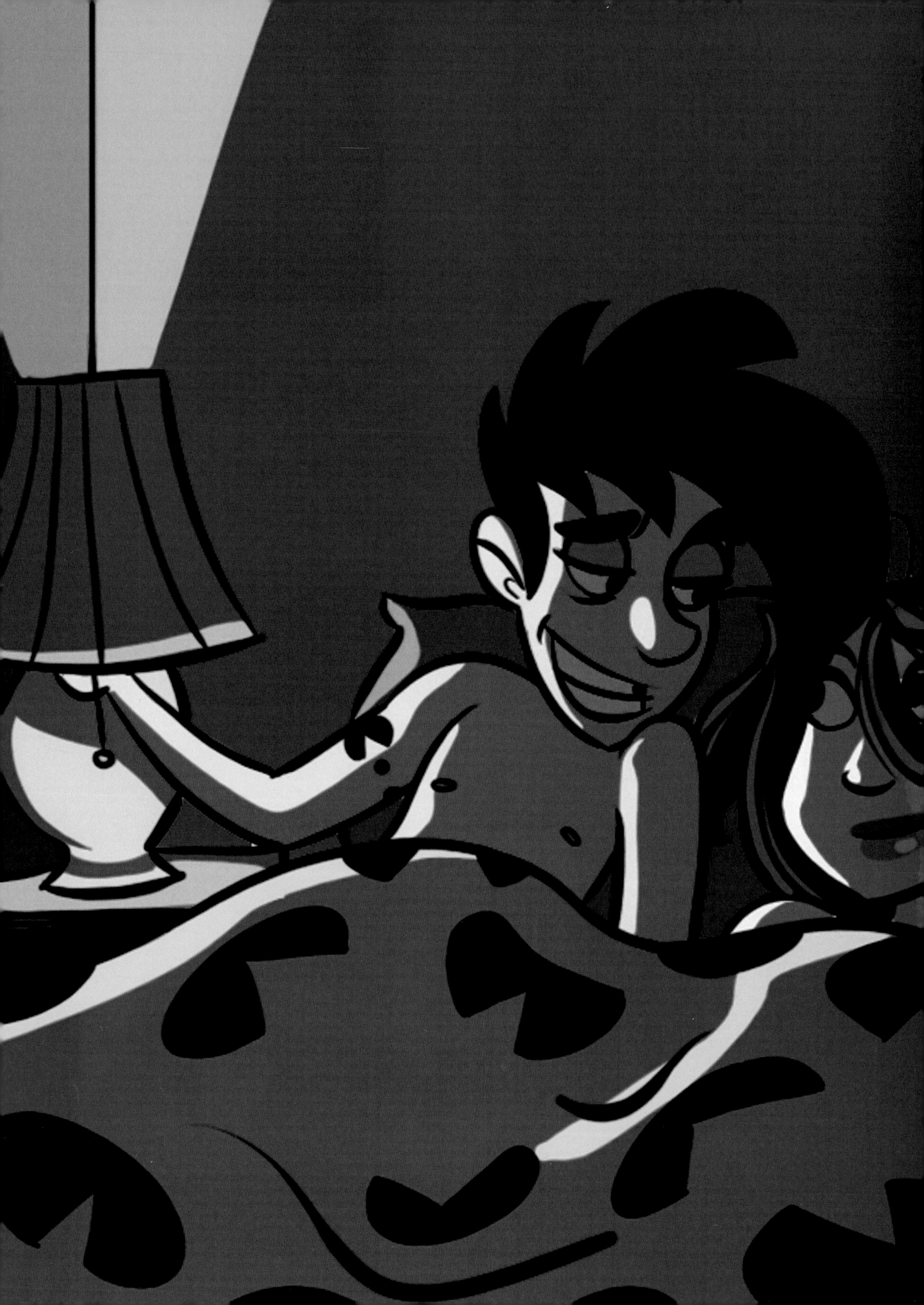

ARMADEADDON

by Jerry Holkins

Zombies figure prominently in this story line, though it isn't really about zombies at all. We were curious about what a feature devoted entirely to fanservice would look like, mining the archive for *Penny Arcade* artifacts to sprinkle liberally throughout. We started packing the ancient references in tight, like Mayan stonework.

Reading back, I wonder if the ancient references aren't packed *too* tight. I wonder if a new reader would even be able to penetrate it. That's all right with me, of course. After all, it's not *for* them (see page 48)

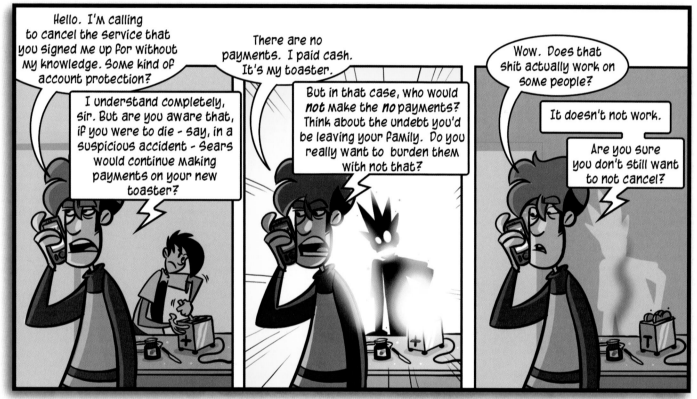

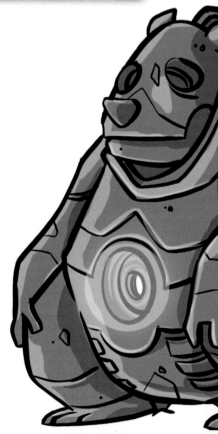

Hello. I'm calling to cancel the service that you signed me up for without my knowledge. Some kind of account protection?
I understand completely, sir. But are you aware that, if you were to die - say, in a suspicious accident - Sears would continue making payments on your new toaster?
There are no payments. I paid cash. It's my toaster.
But in that case, who would **not** make the **no** payments? Think about the undebt you'd be leaving your family. Do you really want to burden them with not that?
Wow. Does that shit actually work on some people?
It doesn't not work.
Are you sure you don't still want to not cancel?

TIME LINE **2002 (December) —** After two months and no traction, Khoo closes an advertising deal with Microsoft for the game MechAssault. The model works!

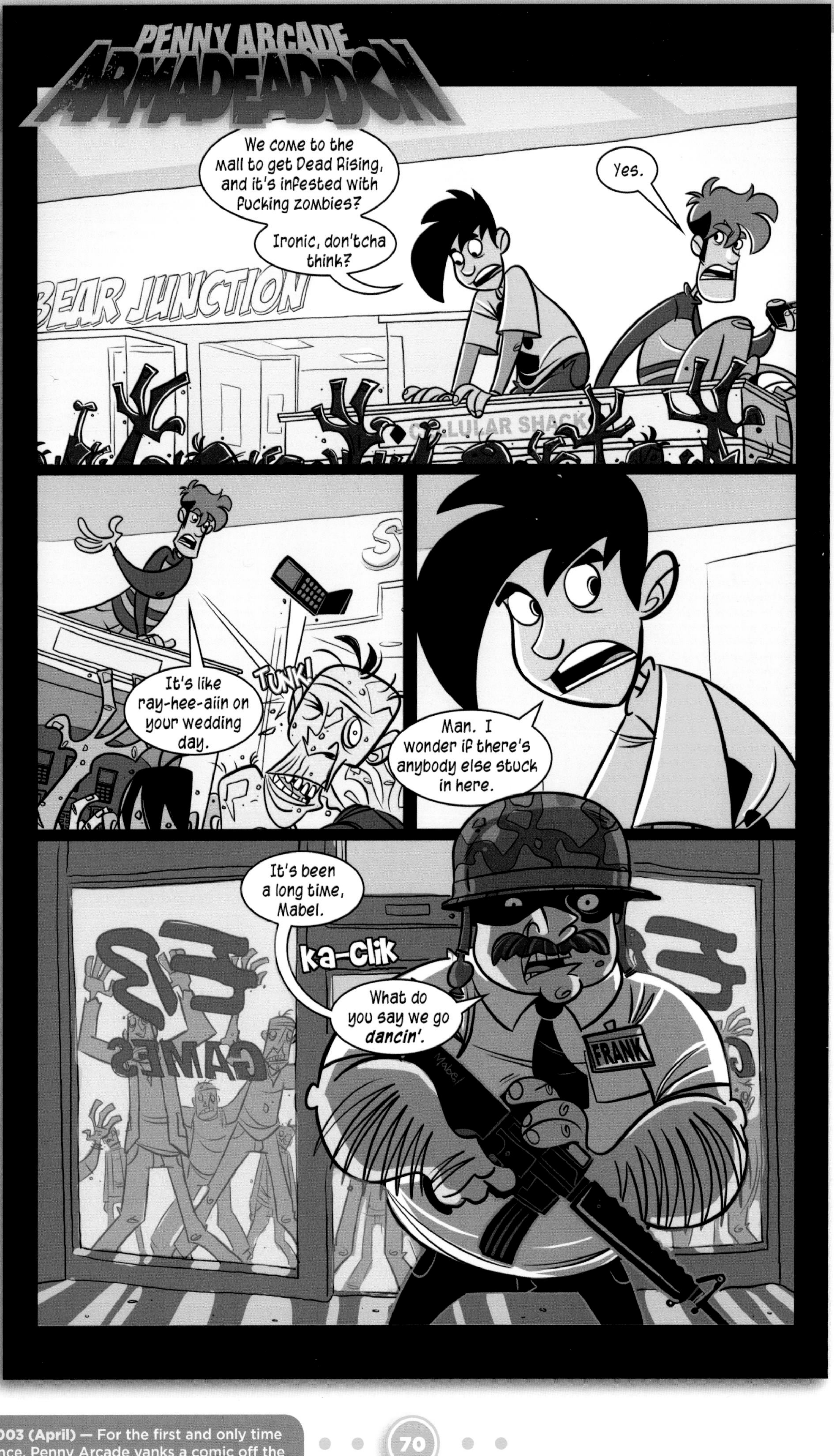
PENNY ARCADE
ARMADEADDON
We come to the mall to get Dead Rising, and it's infested with fucking zombies?
Ironic, don'tcha think?
Yes.
BEAR JUNCTION
CELLULAR SHACK
It's like ray-hee-aiin on your wedding day.
TUNK!
Man. I wonder if there's anybody else stuck in here.
It's been a long time, Mabel.
ka-clik
What do you say we go dancin'.
FRANK
GAMES

TIME LINE

2003 (April) — For the first and only time since, Penny Arcade yanks a comic off the site because of legal action (see page 86).

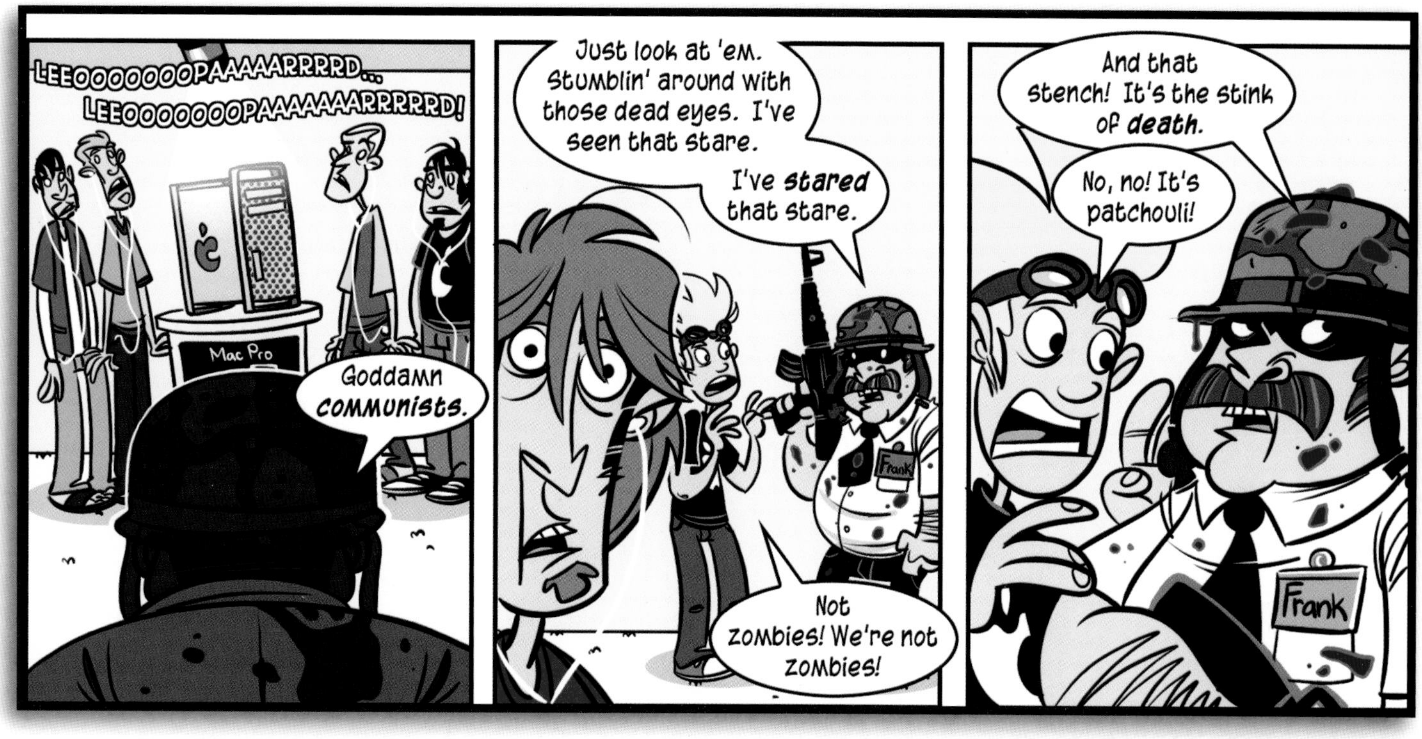
LEEOOOOOOOPAAAAARRRRD...
LEEOOOOOOOPAAAAAAARRRRRRD!
Mac Pro
Goddamn communists.
Just look at 'em. Stumblin' around with those dead eyes. I've seen that stare.
I've stared that stare.
Frank
Not zombies! We're not zombies!
And that stench! It's the stink of death.
No, no! It's patchouli!
Frank

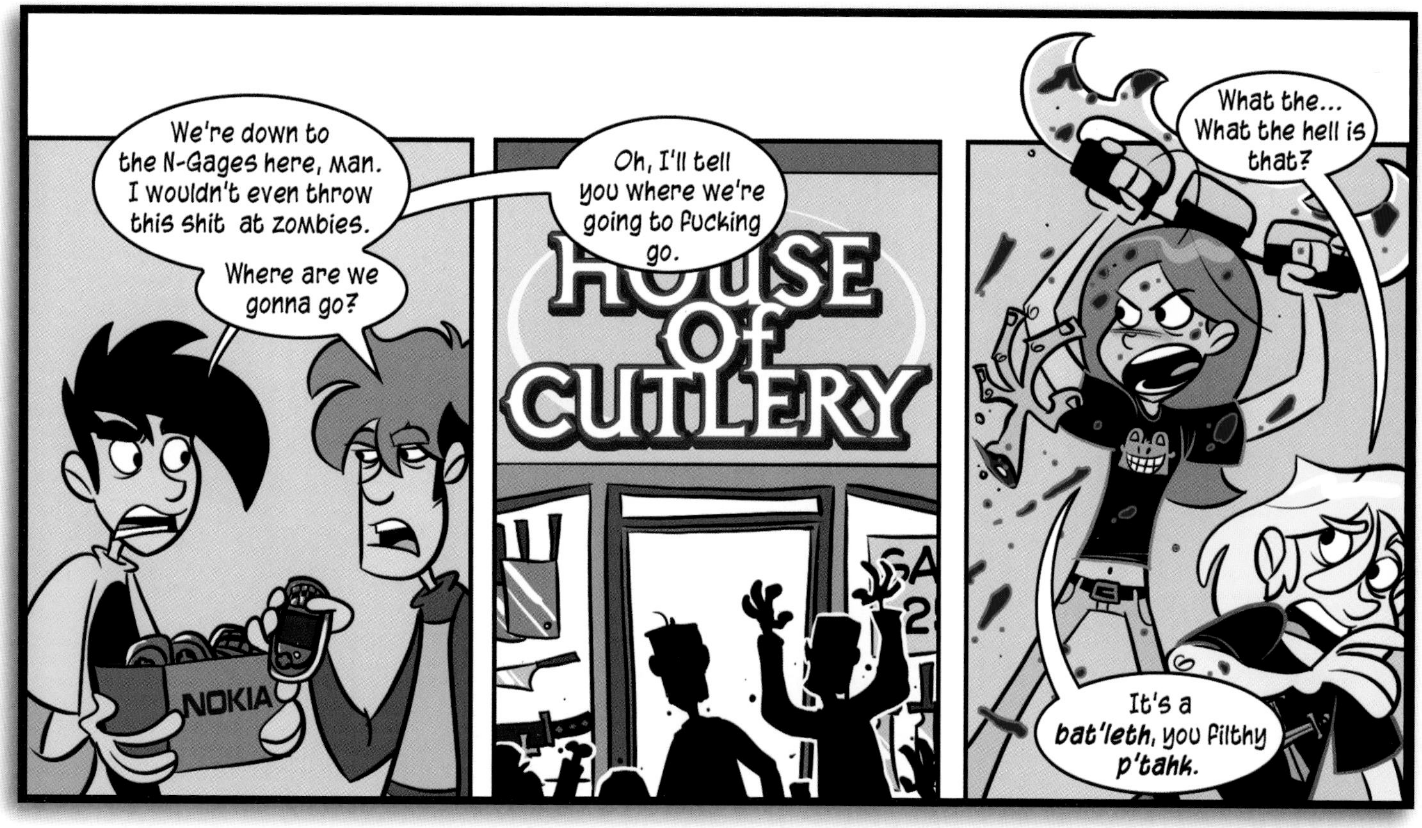
We're down to the N-Gages here, man. I wouldn't even throw this shit at zombies.
Where are we gonna go?
NOKIA
Oh, I'll tell you where we're going to fucking go.
HOUSE of CUTLERY
What the... What the hell is that?
It's a bat'leth, you filthy p'tahk.

2003 (October) — Mike and Jerry, feeling the advertising model is going well, tell readers that donations are no longer being taken.

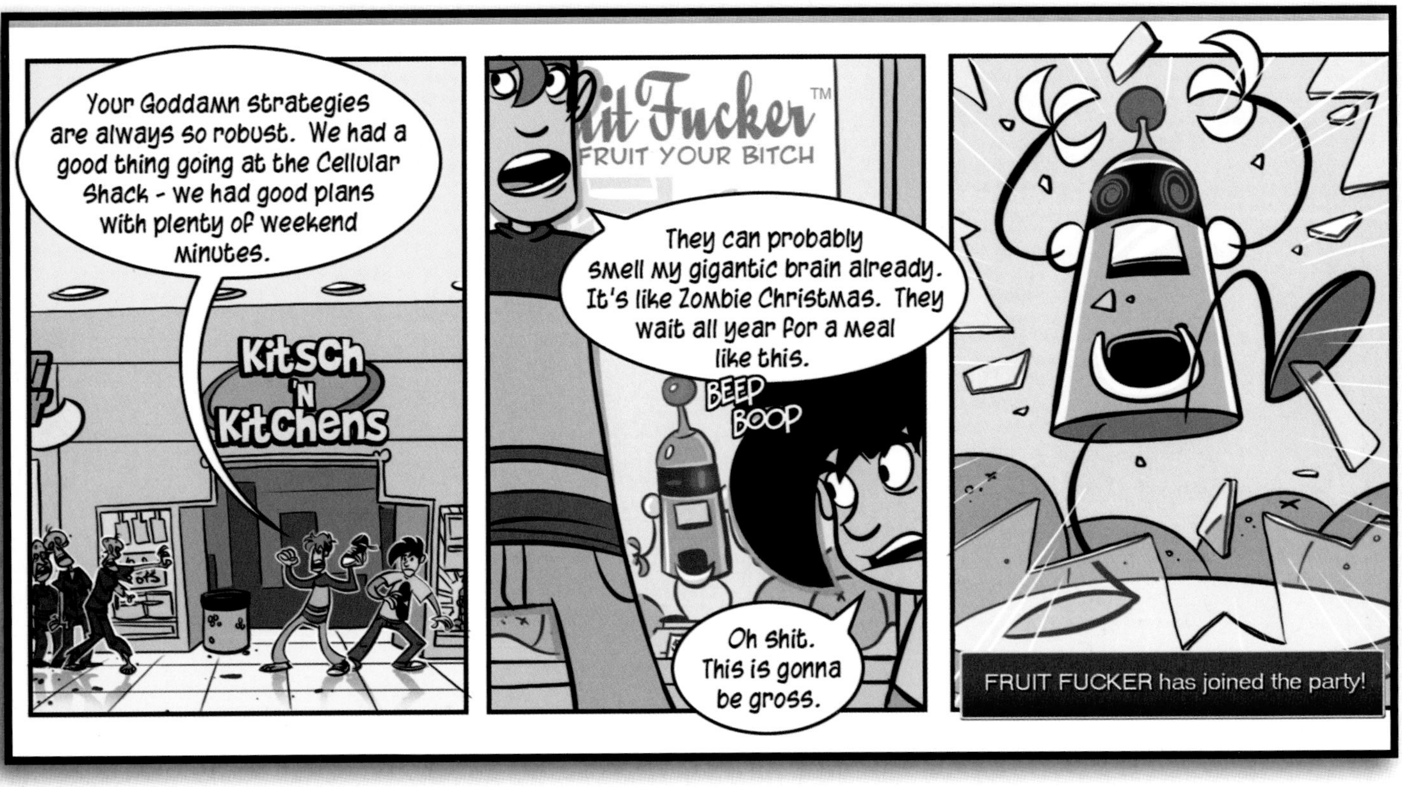
Your Goddamn strategies are always so robust. We had a good thing going at the Cellular Shack - we had good plans with plenty of weekend minutes.
Kitsch 'N Kitchens
FRUIT YOUR BITCH
They can probably smell my gigantic brain already. It's like Zombie Christmas. They wait all year for a meal like this.
BEEP
BOOP
Oh shit. This is gonna be gross.
FRUIT FUCKER has joined the party!

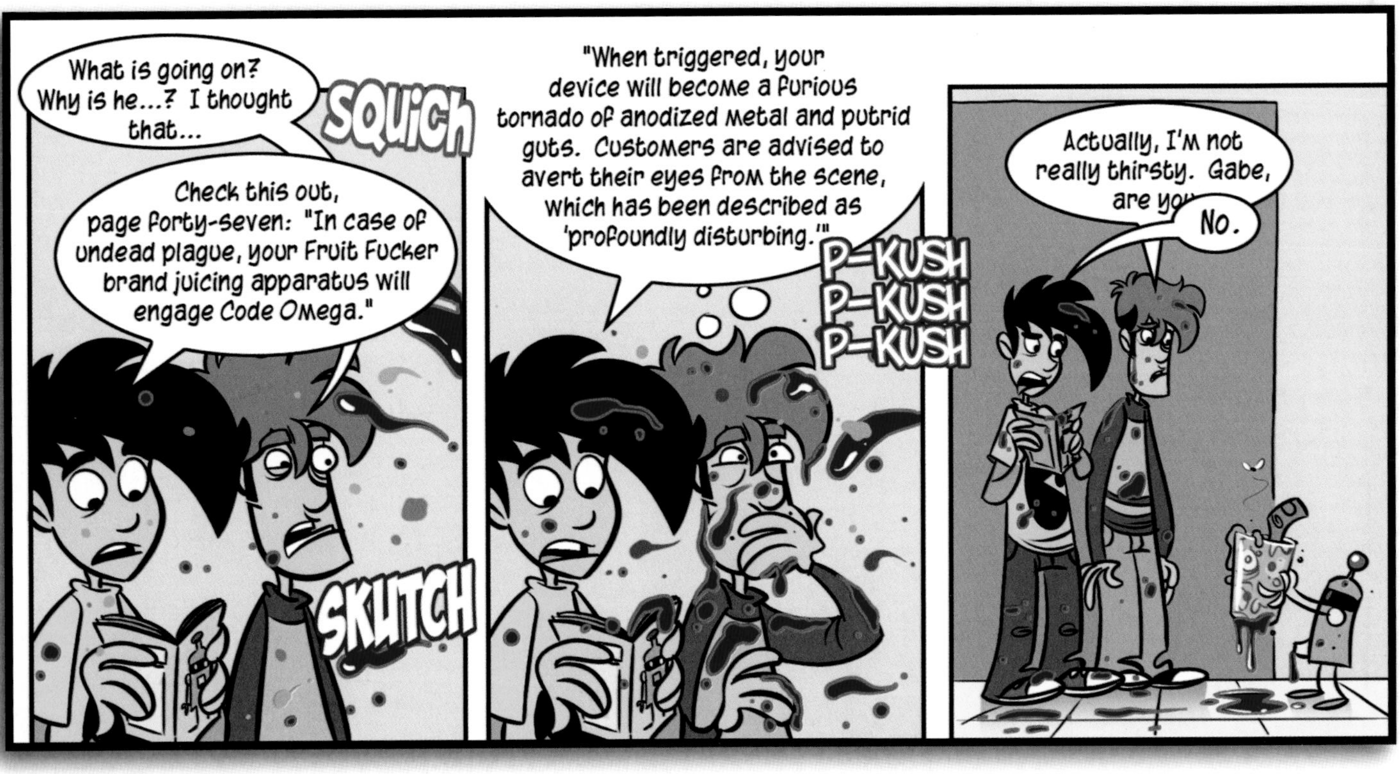
What is going on? Why is he...? I thought that...
SQUICH
Check this out, page forty-seven: "In case of undead plague, your Fruit Fucker brand juicing apparatus will engage Code Omega."
SKUTCH
"When triggered, your device will become a furious tornado of anodized metal and putrid guts. Customers are advised to avert their eyes from the scene, which has been described as 'profoundly disturbing.'"
P-KUSH
P-KUSH
P-KUSH
Actually, I'm not really thirsty. Gabe, are yo
No.

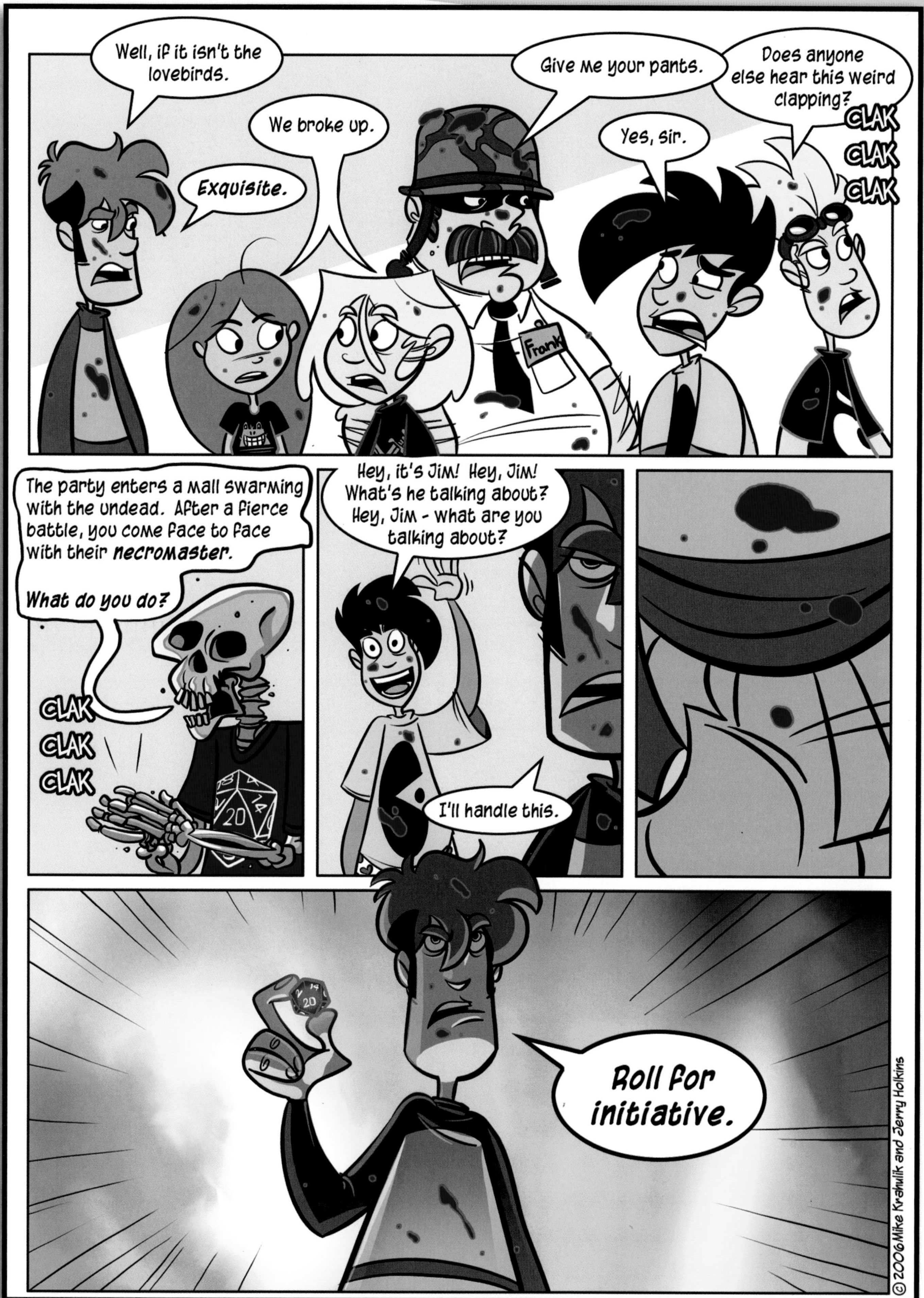
Well, if it isn't the lovebirds.
Exquisite.
We broke up.
Give me your pants.
Yes, sir.
Does anyone else hear this weird clapping?
CLAK
CLAK
CLAK
Frank
The party enters a mall swarming with the undead. After a fierce battle, you come face to face with their necromaster.
What do you do?
CLAK
CLAK
CLAK
Hey, it's Jim! Hey, Jim! What's he talking about? Hey, Jim - what are you talking about?
I'll handle this.
Roll for initiative.
© 2006 Mike Krahulik and Jerry Holkins

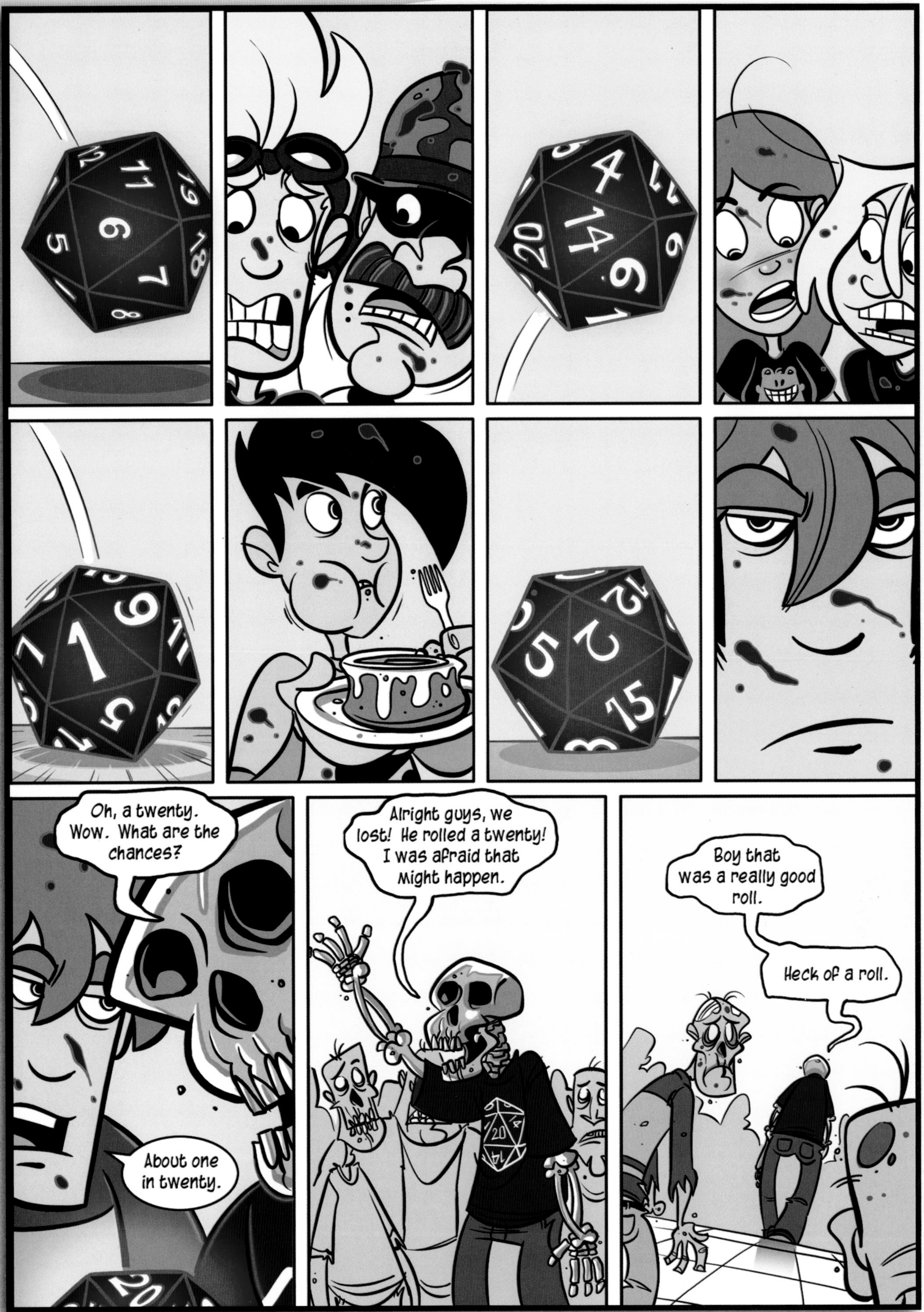
Oh, a twenty. Wow. What are the chances?
About one in twenty.
Alright guys, we lost! He rolled a twenty! I was afraid that might happen.
Boy that was a really good roll.
Heck of a roll.

TIME LINE

2003 (November) — From an innocent editorial piece to the largest game community charity in the world, Child's Play is conceived, generating over $250,000 in toys, games, and cash in less than four weeks.

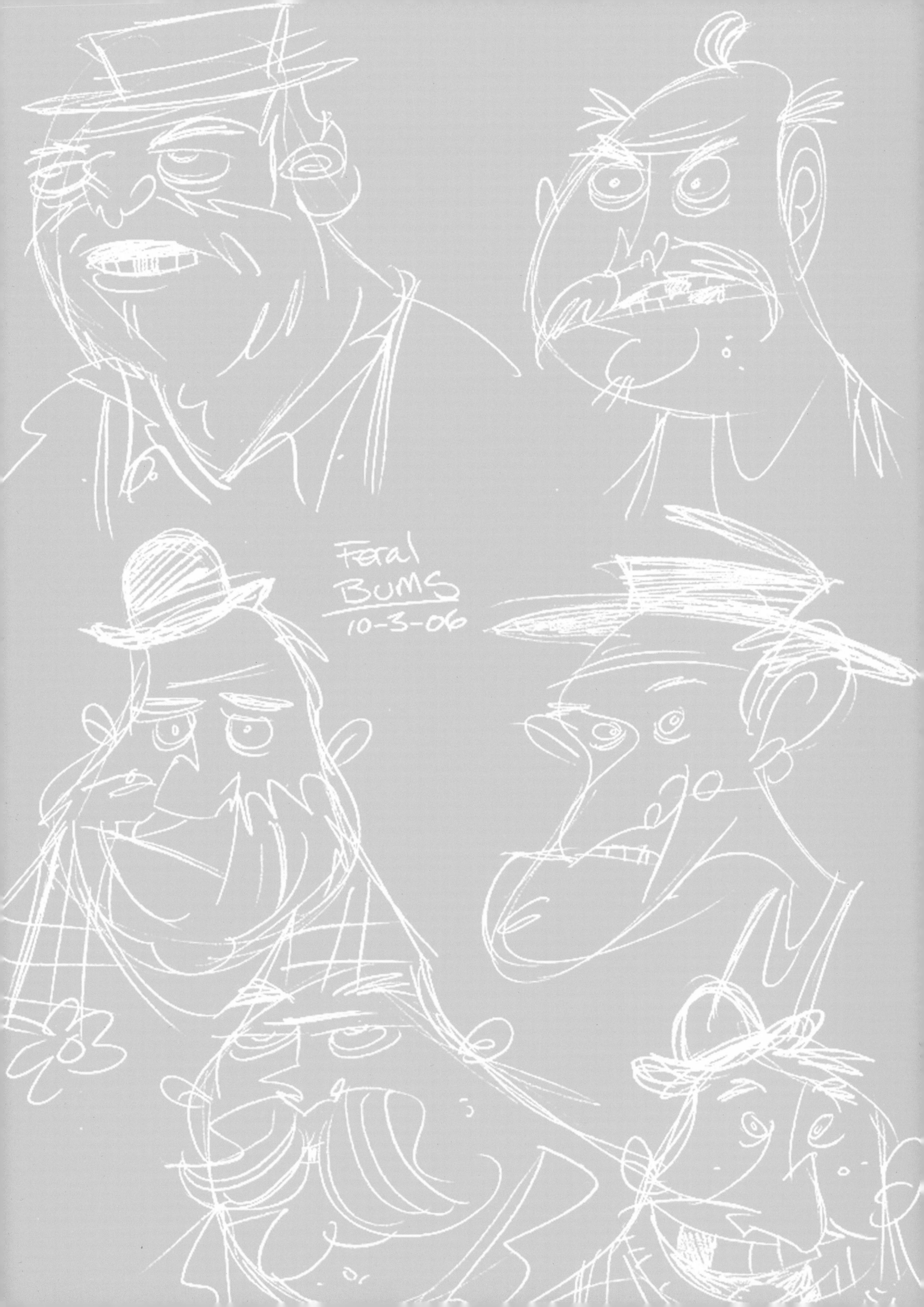
Feral
BUMS
10-3-06

by Robert Khoo

It's common knowledge at this point that in 2002 I approached Mike and Jerry with a business plan. In it, I provided a road map for the operations side of the "company," which wasn't really anything you could call a company yet. Between advertising, merchandising, and creative services, the three-pillared strategy was pretty basic and—in my mind—completely achievable. What wasn't in that plan was to pool all our resources into a high-risk, completely unproven, historically unsuccessful model, almost drive the company into bankruptcy by doing so...and ultimately create the largest gaming festival in North America.

Only idiots would do that.

It started in February 2004, when the three of us were at a small event called UberCon, which was considered a "catchall" convention for all things geek. You'd see anime booths, video game setups, and panels on comic book culture all mashed into one hotel. Honestly, it seemed to really work for them. Two things clicked for us while we were at the event: First, one of the registration volunteers let us know on opening day that of all the people he had checked in, almost three-quarters of them said Penny Arcade was the reason they were there. Second, throughout the show Mike and Jerry both wondered why there wasn't something like this focused exclusively on gaming.

We continued to flesh out the idea throughout the weekend, as they laid out their vision for the event and I tried to make that fit into some kind of coherent business model. It would be based on the three main types of gaming, with content built around that core. Tournaments, industry panels, an exhibit hall, rock concerts, a LAN, and a freeplay area—all the staples to the show today were conceived in an afternoon between autographs and T-shirt sales. We didn't quite understand that the combination of these had never really been done before, but at that point we didn't really care. All our decisions were based on one premise, which was: "If we attended the show, what would *we* want to do?"

Keep in mind that collectively we had absolutely zero experience in planning events. I'd put together parties here and there, but entertaining seventy-five to a hundred people was a bit different from our best guess of around a thousand attendees. We needed help. On the last day of UberCon, I approached the people running the show. It was literally a two-minute meeting.

Me: "We want to do a show that's about gaming and gaming *only* in Seattle. Tabletop. PC. Console. Do you want to help?"

UberCon: "Yes!"

Me: "Excellent. We'll talk next week."

Sadly, the partnership got off to a rocky start, beginning with the most basic element of the show.

Keep in mind that one of Jerry's superpowers is his ability to name things. I picture his brain as some giant tagging engine that relates every single word in the dictionary with every single emotion and situation possible, and doing so in a way that isn't as horribly chaotic as my metaphor implies. It's both beautiful and incredibly frustrating to witness, as he will make you realize how stupid you are with your frail grasp of the English language. So if Jerry names something, I have a tremendous amount of faith that it's the right call.

The three of us were walking through Costco a few days after returning to Seattle, trying to find comfortable chairs for the freeplay area, when I answered a call from the UberCon folk.

"Hey have you thought about a name for the show?" they asked.

"Hold on for a second." I placed my hand over the phone. "Hey, Jerry—we need a name for the show."

2003 (December) — Penny Arcade moves from a "work-from-home" operation to a small two-room 180-square-foot office in North Seattle.

TIME LINE

76

Without missing a beat, he said "PAX." I repeated it to our potential partners.

"PAX? That...that doesn't sound...right."

"What do you mean?" I asked.

"What about...UberPAX?"

"That sounds stupid."

"Well, what about PAX, presented by UberCon?"

"Look—I understand what you're trying to do, but I can say that this isn't about UberCon. This is about a new show, and we're asking for your *operational* expertise. But I'll tell you what—you're coming into town next week. Let's discuss it then."

After ending the conversation, I began to have tiny pangs of doubt about the potential for a partner, but felt we could resolve the name issue. The situation only became worse during their visit the following week.

Sitting in our conference room, we couldn't seem to agree on anything, from the name, to the business terms, to where the show would actually be. The breaking point, however, came from a discussion of the cover to the program, of all things.

"So we can use Mike to draw the cover, right?"

Mike nodded as I said, "Sure, that seems reasonable."

"Perfect! Well, here's what we're thinking. We can have a giant LAN room with PCs as far as the eye can see, and sitting up front playing the computer is Vlad the Dragon [the UberCon mascot]! What do you think?"

Mike, Jerry, and I looked at one another, puzzled, as Mike addressed what we were all thinking. "What about...you know...Gabe and Tycho?"

"Oh! Of course!" He paused for a second in thought. "Well, you can have them in the background if you want. Can you draw that?"

At that point I knew the deal was dead in the water, and I was pissed. "Mike, you don't have to answer that. You guys can go back to your offices." As Mike and Jerry left the room, I stood up and continued. "I'm sorry for wasting your time, guys. This conversation's over."

It turns out when you fly across the country for what ends up being a fifteen-minute meeting that results in you getting kicked out of someone's office and a deal turning stone-cold dead in a matter of seconds, you become agitated. Perhaps *pissed off* is a better term for it. I'll never forget what they screamed as they walked out.

"This is the biggest fucking mistake you'll ever make."

Maybe he was right. We had this great idea for a show, but no one to actually run it. I knew we couldn't plan it ourselves, and Penny Arcade really didn't have the financial resources to put on an event. To me, the concept was dead.

However, a month later, Mike and Jerry came knocking on my door, asking for "an update on PAX."

"What are you talking about? PAX? That show that isn't happening?"

"Yes!"

"But you were there! Don't you remember? Vlad? UberPAX?

Taking on the Black

Besides Mike, Jerry, and Robert, there's a significant operational back end with Amber, Mike, Kristin, Kiko, Jeff, Josh, Dave, Brian, and Erik. But it's no secret that the show would be impossible with just the Penny Arcade staff. In addition to the full-timers are the popular and celebrated Enforcers. They represent our volunteer corps that tirelessly gives a week of their year and at times literal blood and tears to make the show happen. Originally numbering thirty-five in 2004, by 2009 the number has skyrocketed to more than five hundred individuals. Throughout the year, not only does this group help with our charity, Child's Play, but they also keep in touch with community events and PAX planning. Every facility we work with says they're one of the most amazing volunteer groups they've ever seen, so if you're looking for help at PAX, there's an Enforcer nearby!

Did you not see the show DIE BEFORE YOUR VERY EYES? Besides, we don't even have the financial resources to pull it off."

They stood there, in my doorway, looking at me, confused, as if I had just given them some kind of math problem.

They broke the silence with, "We should still do it."

I looked at them, irritated but not shocked, shook my head, and said, "Fine."

Within twelve hours I was touring facilities, figuring out the scheduling, and laying out the business plan. I was in completely over my head, but I was determined to figure out how to make PAX work. After pinning down the show

date a mere 150 days away, "learning on the job" became the concept we would live and die by. August 28 became a self-set time bomb, and the pressure mounted as the stakes and investment in both support and finances were higher than any endeavor Penny Arcade had ever been a part of. The show became an obsession for all of us, and we worked tirelessly as the date drew closer. I was working 140-hour weeks for three months straight as we recruited enforcers, organized tournaments, planned panels, acquired talent for concerts, sold sponsorships, mapped out the organizational logistics, and, of course, got the word out.

Financially we'd try to eke out cost savings wherever we could. Whether that meant getting all our AV equipment from furniture rental stores or renting consoles at Blockbuster Video, every penny counted. Four of us spent seven hours one night hand-crimping three thousand feet of ethernet cable for the LAN. I was able to get donated computers from a local LAN facility, and all of our consoles were 100 percent donated for the weekend by friends and volunteers. I have to reiterate that, realistically, we could not afford to put this show on. The business side of Penny Arcade was still very much in its infancy, so frankly the show was made to work through five credit cards and the sacrifice of time. If we could save twenty dollars by doing something ourselves for ten hours, we would.

Planning was arduous and mistakes were made and learned from, but the collective "show" began to come together either through solid planning or sheer dumb luck. Even fundamentals that today seem core to PAX serendipitously fell into place. For instance, a single post was made on the front page asking for volunteers to the show, and *poof*, the Enforcer Corps was created. A giant collection of every PS2 game ever made arrived, unsolicited, from a gamer who wanted to quit his gaming habits. Even though it was one of the coolest things to ever arrive at the office, our desire to find a good home for it birthed the first Omega Collection and ultimately the Omegathon. Bungie, a company the guys had previously skewered over and over on the main site, decided to surprise us by making the first publicly playable build of Halo 2 available at the show. Musical performers like the Minibosses and MC Frontalot all enthusiastically accepted invites to the show, despite not knowing exactly what PAX was.

Even the community initiatives we all see today devel-

Top 10 Mistakes at the Inaugural PAX

1. The show was thirty-nine hours straight. Please try to imagine the aroma.

2. Twenty minutes before the doors opened, we realized we forgot to arrange moderators for the panels. Robert and Jerry covered all of them.

3. Instead of badges, we decided to hand-stamp each person who walked in and paid. All thirty-five hundred of them. We had three hand stamps.

4. Pong was selected as the secret finale for the first Omegathon, but we had a tough time tracking down the machine. It wasn't until an hour before the final round that a friend brought one in from home.

5. Since the Omegathon wasn't really announced until the last minute, no one knew what it was. Nearly everyone who was randomly called to participate turned it down!

6. An hour before showtime, it came to our attention our twenty-four Xboxes had exactly twelve controllers.

7. One of our banners (the infamous "Gabe grabbing Tycho's junk") was stolen before our eyes and we were stupid enough to try and chase the guy down the street at 3 AM, pitchforks and all.

8. With the underestimation of attendance, we were severely short-staffed—PAX 2004 had fewer than thirty-five Enforcers.

9. We believed the packaging on our radios when they said twenty-two hours of talk time. All of them were dead by noon.

10. For move-in, we neglected to rent a truck of any kind, so we brought everything in our cars.

2004 (May) — Penny Arcade, after being on a merchandising hiatus, partners with ThinkGeek.com to handle the merchandise.

TIME LINE

78

oped organically. The annual Cross Country Supertrips were created when a few attendees from Phoenix decided to make the drive and didn't want to do so alone. The now annual hotel parties were being planned on the forums months prior to PAX.

The pre-registration number of 1,337 even appeared to fate the show to its eventual success as little by little, slowly learning and executing, we turned PAX from a potential train wreck into something that just might not completely fail.

Five months, thousands of planning hours, and fourteen "all-nighters" later, 10 AM on August 28, 2004, arrived. The doors to the inaugural PAX swung open, and the line, extending four city blocks and holding more than three thousand people, poured into the Meydenbauer Center.

It was absolutely one of the most terrifying experiences of my life. Right before unlocking the doors, we took a hard count of the growing line outside and realized our thousand-person expectation was going to be blown away. Could the building hold that many people? Did we have enough content to actually entertain that many folks? Would people be super-angry about waiting in line for so long? Was our registration system built to handle that number of transactions? We had so many questions and the only response we had was *fear*. The adrenaline from those first fifteen minutes carried us for the remaining thirty-eight hours (see the sidebar "Top 10 Mistakes at the Inaugural PAX").

A frantic manhunt for a banner thief, impromptu nap shifts for staff, and an obscene amount of BAWLS later, the first winner of the Omegathon was crowned and PAX 2004 was over. In retrospect, so many things could have gone wrong. No one could have showed up, killing the show. *Too many* people could have arrived, causing us to shut down the show. Bands could have flaked. Exhibitors could have been unprepared. The home-brew AV and power setups could have failed. All of our equipment could have been stolen. But none of that stuff happened. It all just worked out, and we were lucky to have not only a very talented group of core volunteers who could adapt to whatever *did* come up but also some incredibly patient fans who understood it was our first go at this thing.

And we survived.

What attendees don't realize is that 95 percent of the show is planned months before the doors open. What we try to do is survive the weekend as those plans unfold, because once those first people walk through that door the show's on

rails and there's nothing you can do to stop it. It's a nonstop job of putting out fires (sometimes literal fires), quelling concerns, and making sure everyone is having a good time. It's a party, and we're the hosts.

The show was considered a runaway success by both fans and media alike, and most organizers would be celebrating and communicating with the media after the doors closed, jockeying for coverage and doing interviews about how amazing the show was. Us? We crawled into a hole and wanted to die. The show took everything we had to give and wore it down to a nub. I personally needed three full days of sleep after it ended, and I'm sure everyone else had a similar routine. I didn't even want to *hear* the word *PAX* until the spring-

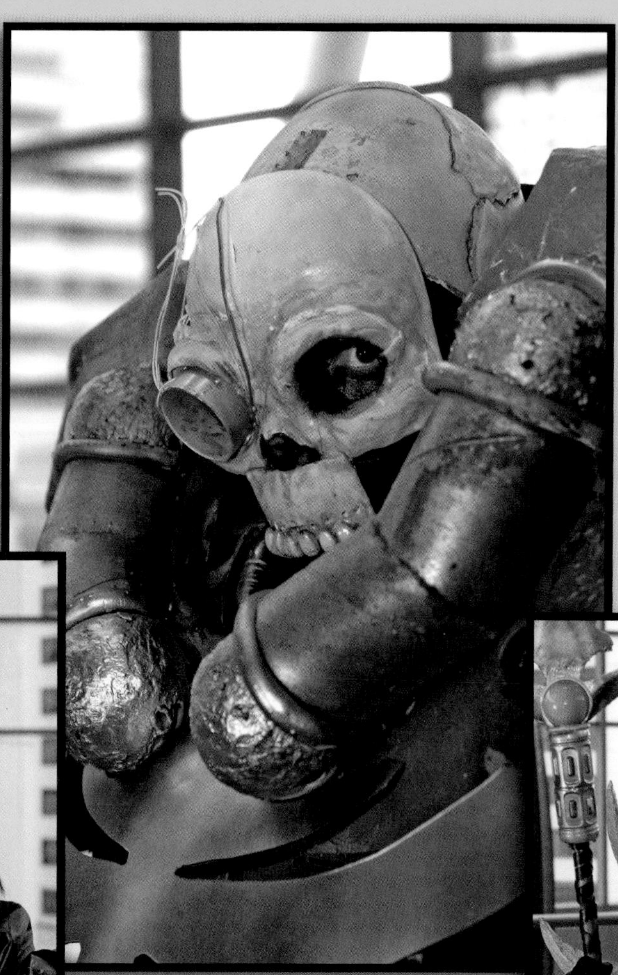

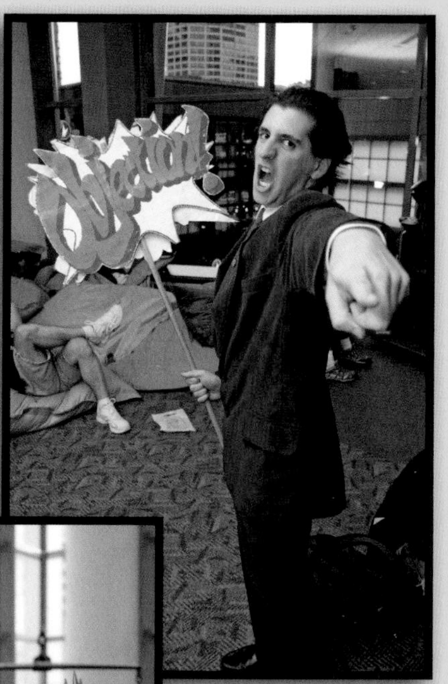
Objection!

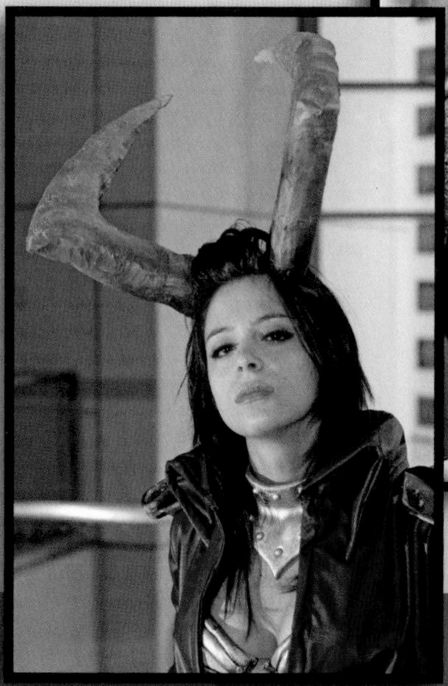

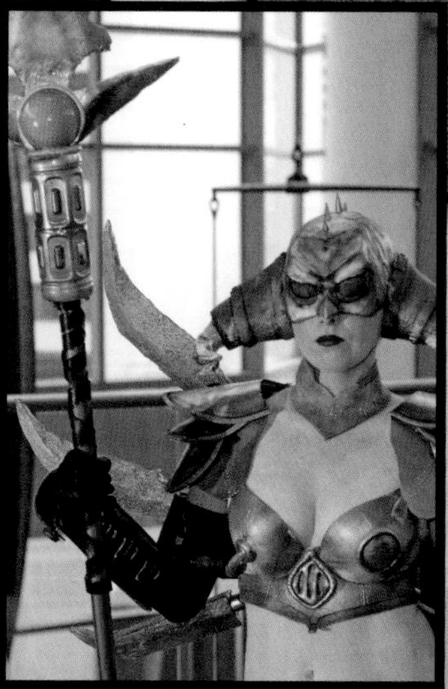

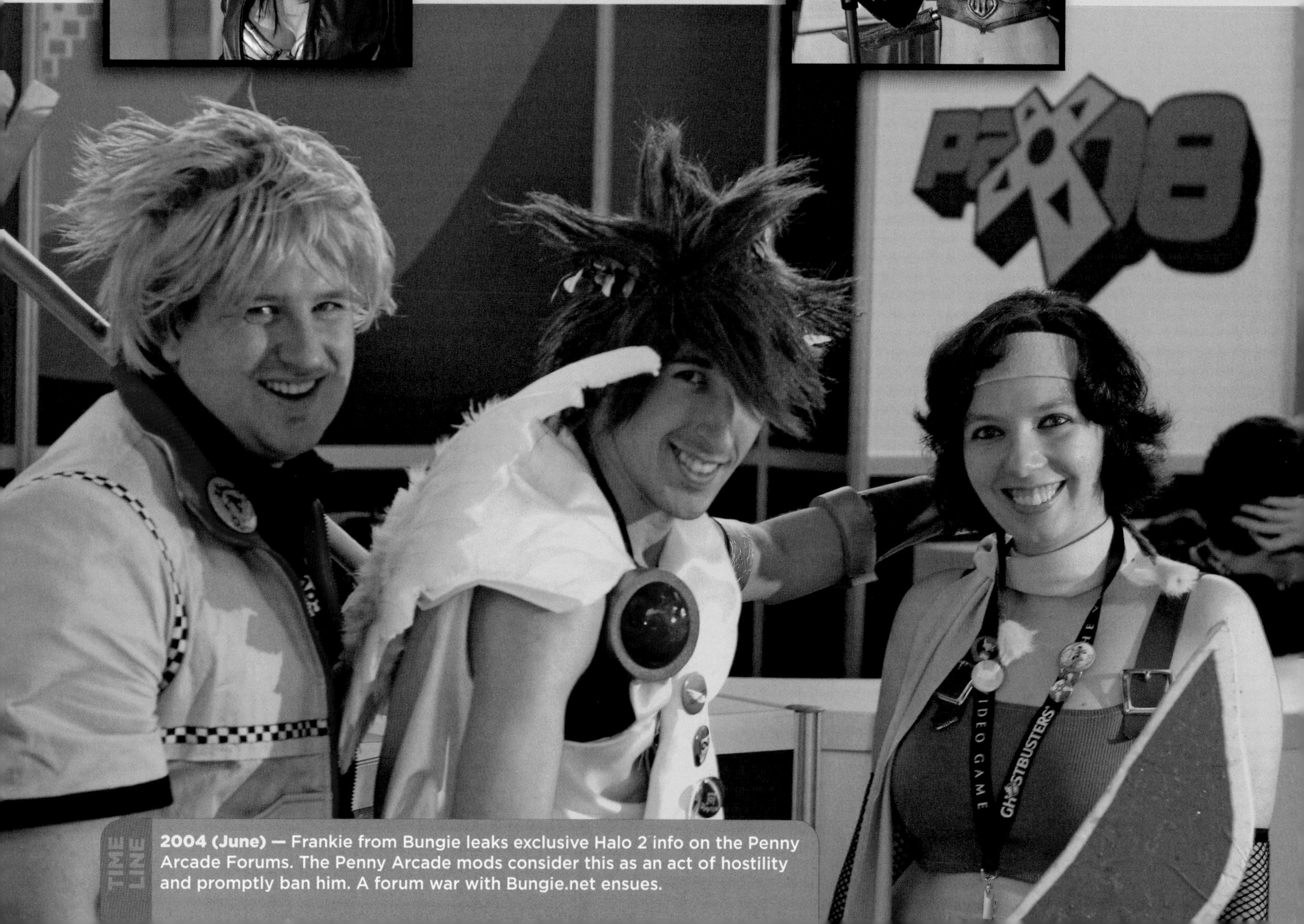
GHOSTBUSTERS
VIDEO GAME

TIME LINE

2004 (June) — Frankie from Bungie leaks exclusive Halo 2 info on the Penny Arcade Forums. The Penny Arcade mods consider this as an act of hostility and promptly ban him. A forum war with Bungie.net ensues.

time, but much to my dismay when you do something well, the people who experienced it not only want it again, but they've just gone and told all their friends about it. And so that was it. We were trapped, for all of eternity, to run this beast.

Since 2004, the show has been on a runaway growth curve, doubling the number of attendees each year, attracting nearly every major game publisher as an annual exhibitor, and occupying the largest venue in the state of Washington. Now PAX is considered *the* show to attend and exhibit at, but honestly it didn't become that way until what I consider a "perfect storm" of events hit.

First, inaugural events for IGN Live and GameSpot's G.A.M.E. both tanked in 2005. I'm not talking about "a slow start" sort of setback. I'm talking about massive commercial and critical failures so catastrophic that they couldn't recover to do another show. I had the opportunity to attend both, and the differences from PAX were both stark and incredibly satisfying. From that experience I realized if we kept true to our original goal of "creating a show for us," we'd be fine and they would flail in desperation. So that immediately took out two of the potentially largest competitors out there. Six months later the ESA announced that E3 would be downsized to a more intimate event, effectively turning all media and exhibitor attention to PAX. And then, last but not least, we had another colossal year at PAX 2006 with nearly twenty thousand attendees. These were all gifts to us—we didn't ask for them, but no one at Penny Arcade was complaining.

Three years later and we're at the size of the old, pre-downsized E3. The demand has even spawned a second show dubbed PAX East Coast to be held in Boston each spring. I look at what we've done, from those small intimate conversations in a ten-by-ten-foot booth in New Jersey that spawned what essentially was a fan convention to what we have now, which is a straight-up cultural event. PAX is so much larger than some webcomic—it's evolved to represent this incredible community of gaming enthusiasts. People who love games don't have many outlets to celebrate that lifestyle and culture, and honestly, we're honored that they choose to call PAX their home.

Robert Khoo is the president of operations and business development at Penny Arcade, building the business and operational model of Penny Arcade from the ground up since 2002. Khoo also acts as the show director for PAX, and is the co-founder and chairman for the Child's Play Charity.

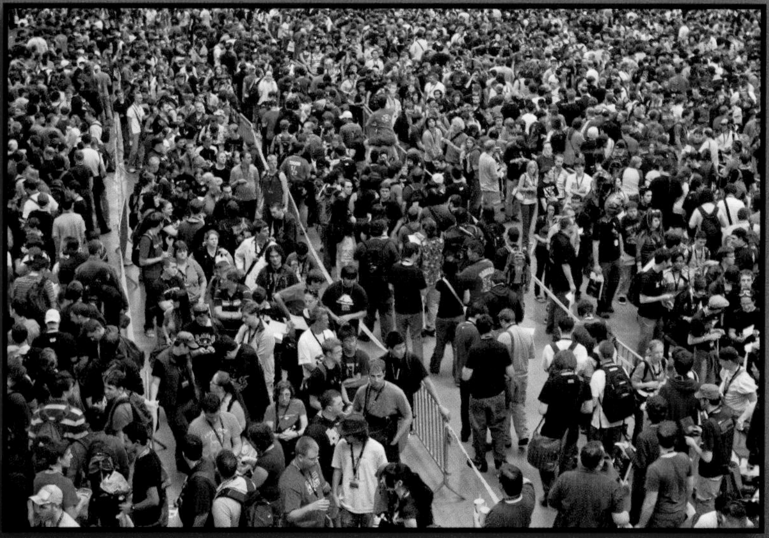

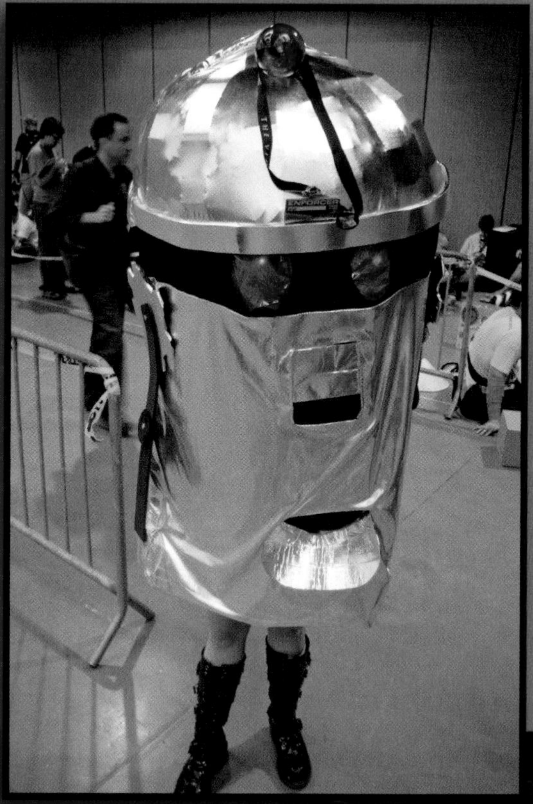

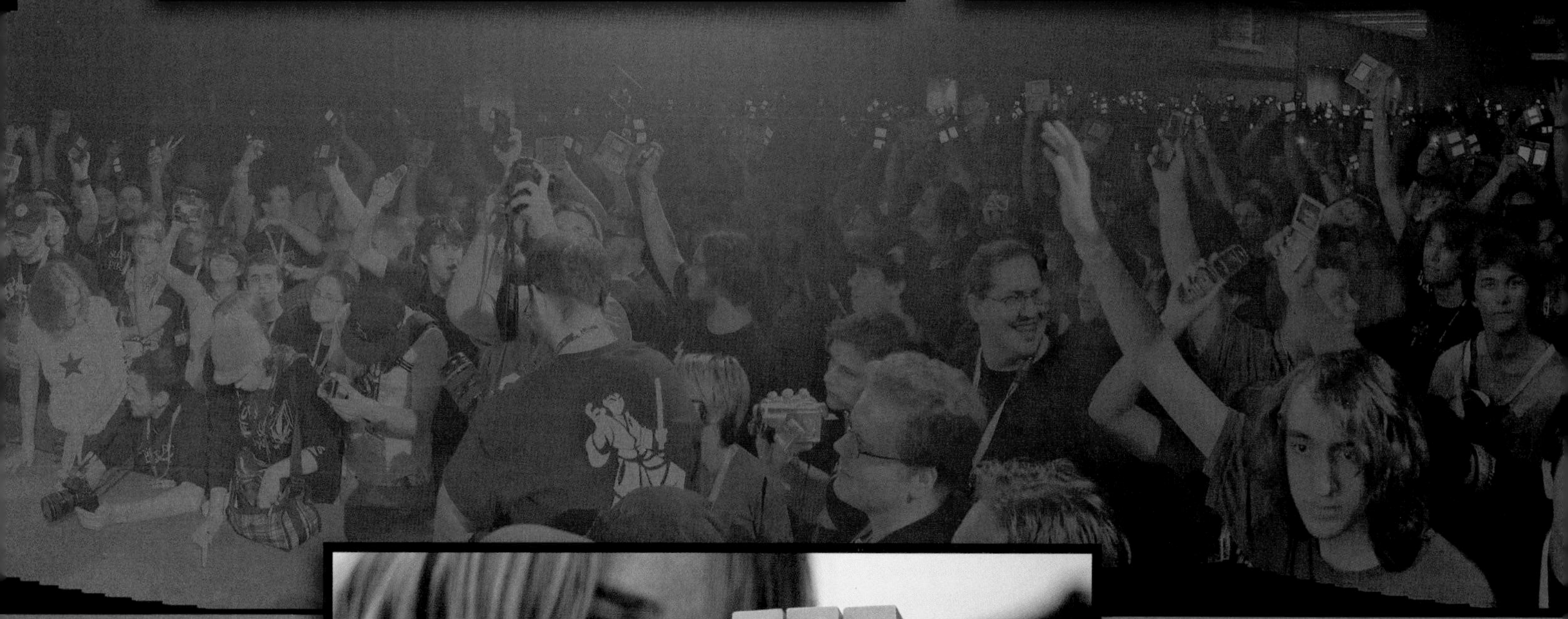

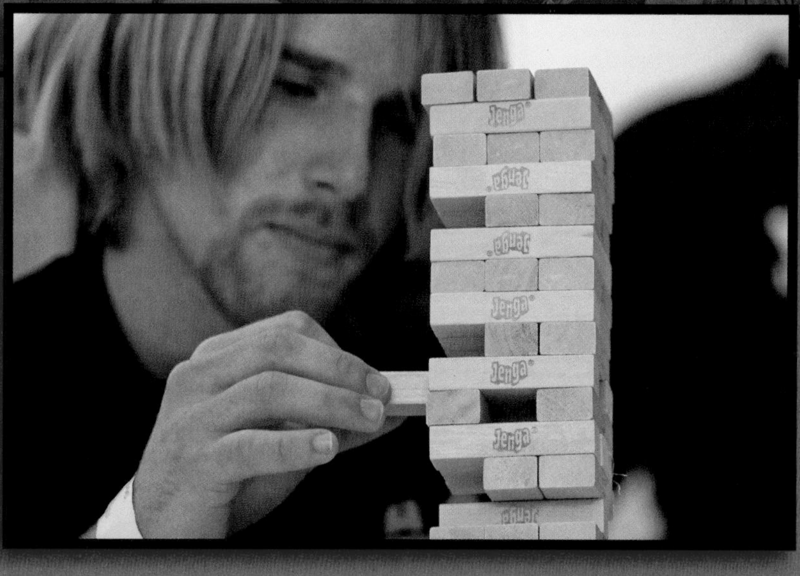
Jenga

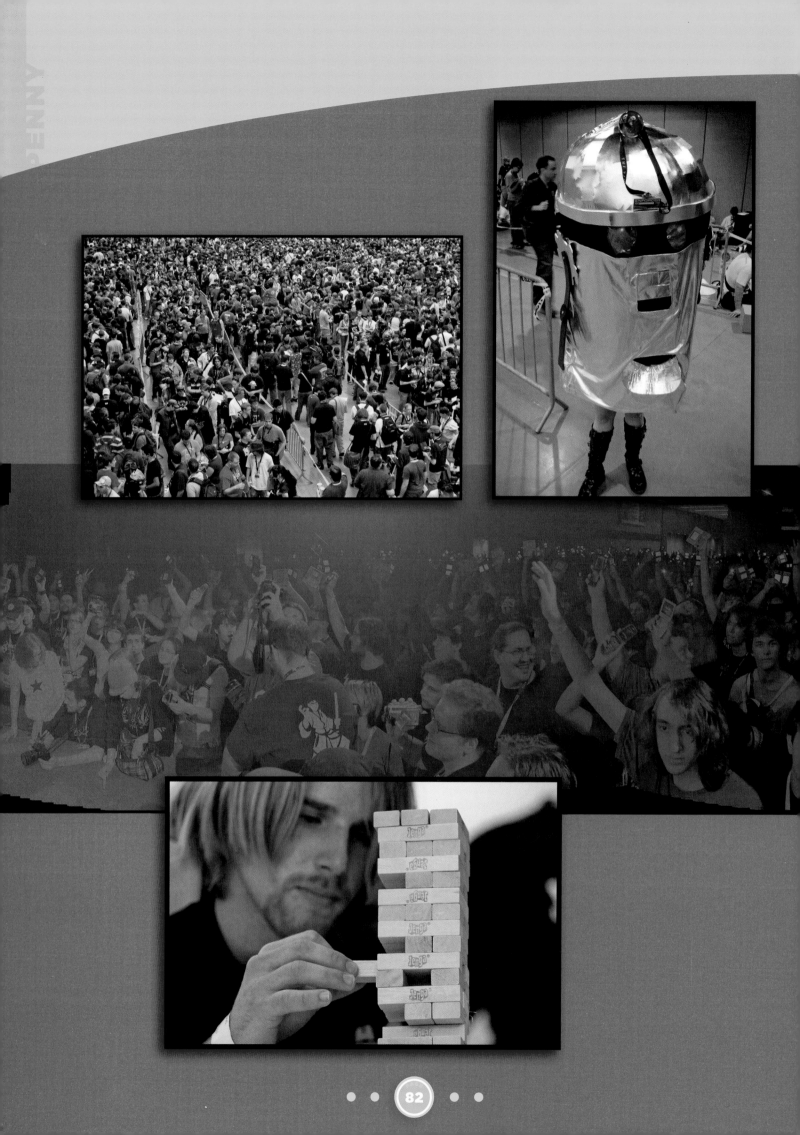

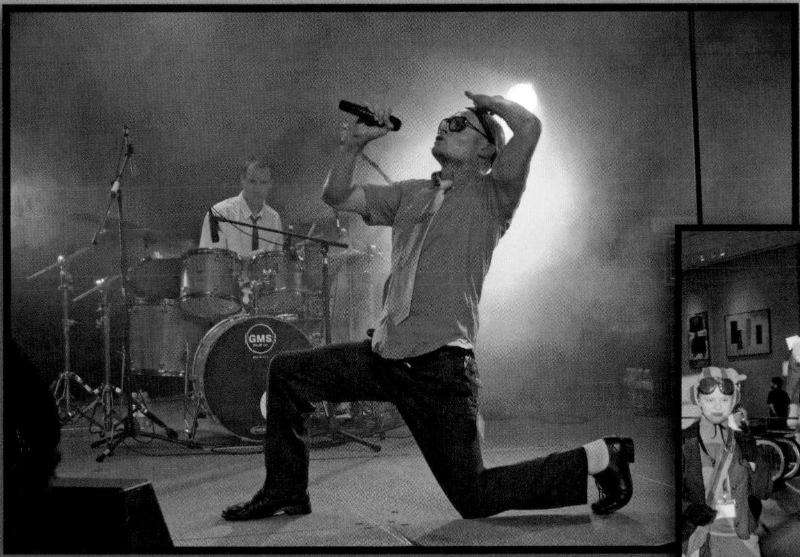

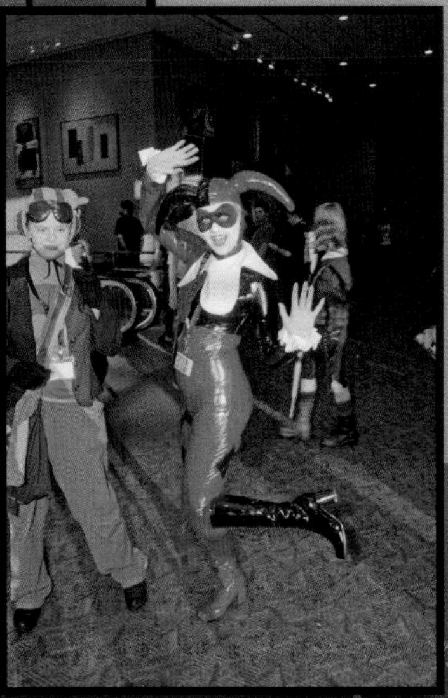

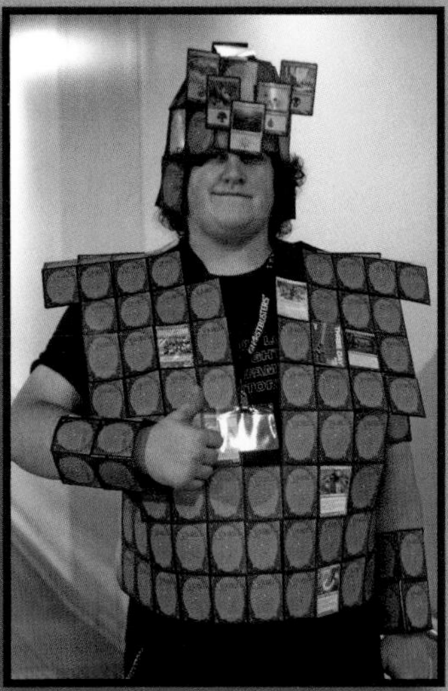

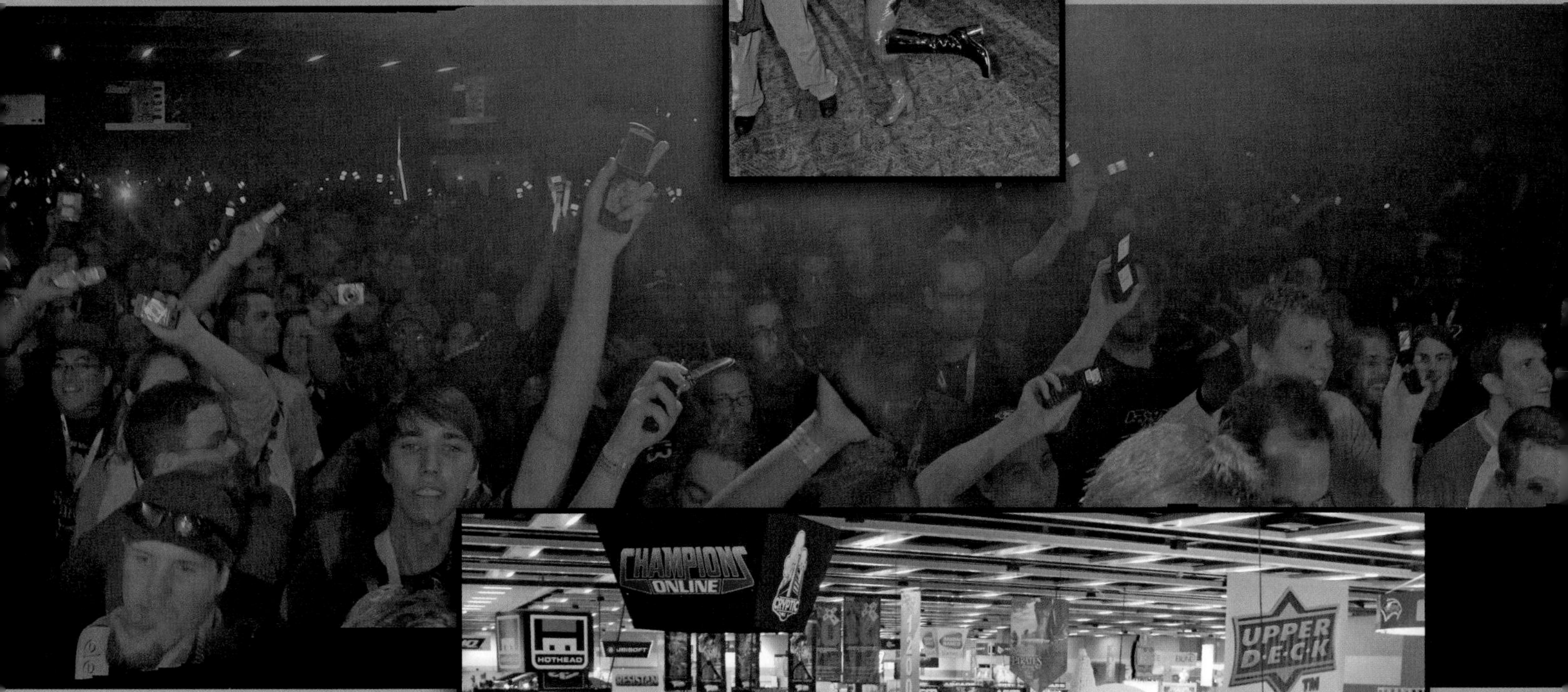

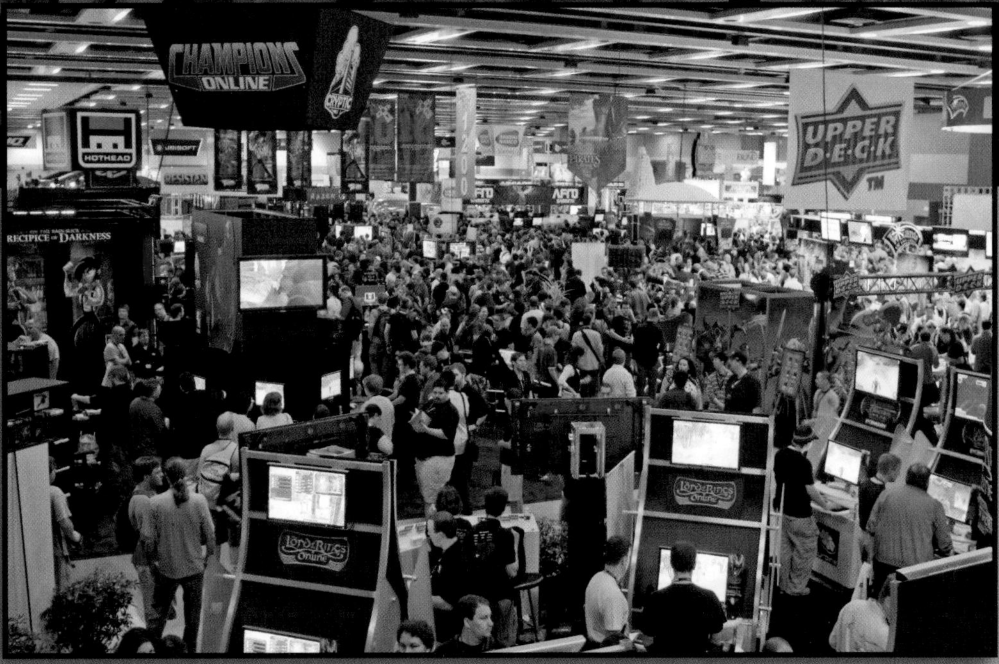
CHAMPIONS ONLINE
UPPER DECK
HOTHEAD

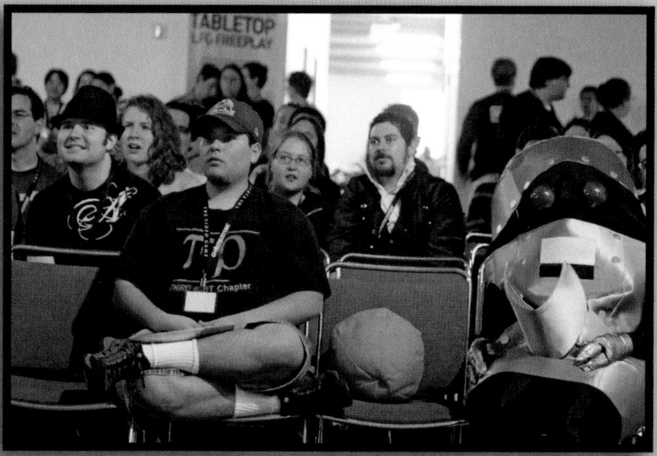
TABLETOP

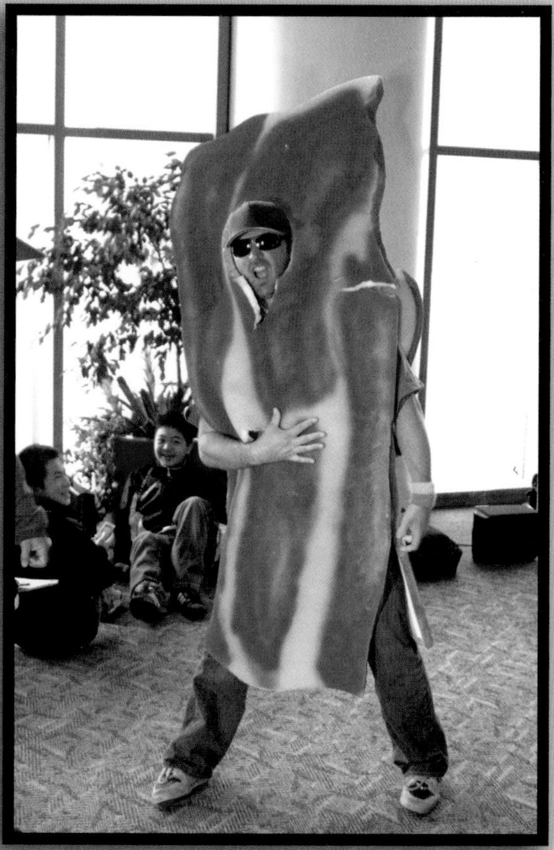

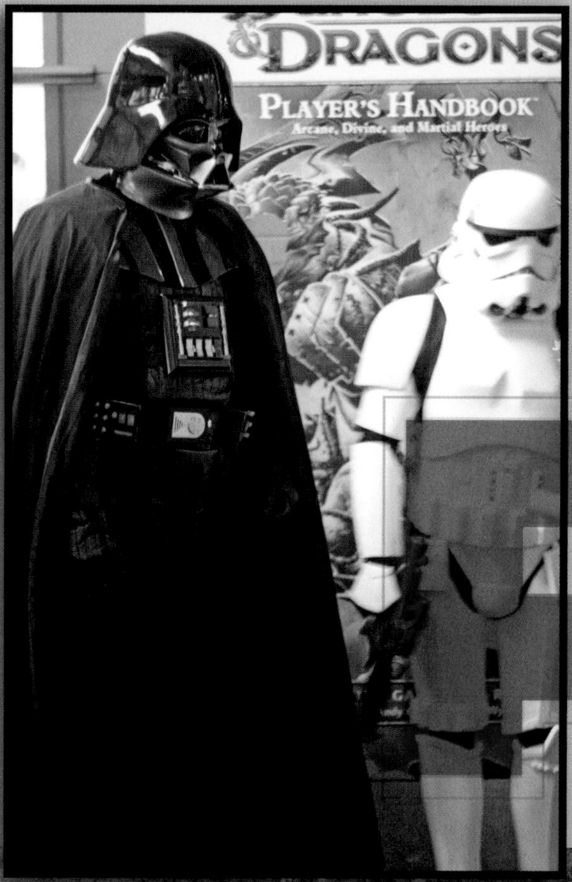
&DRAGONS
PLAYER'S HANDBOOK
Arcane, Divine, and Martial Heroes

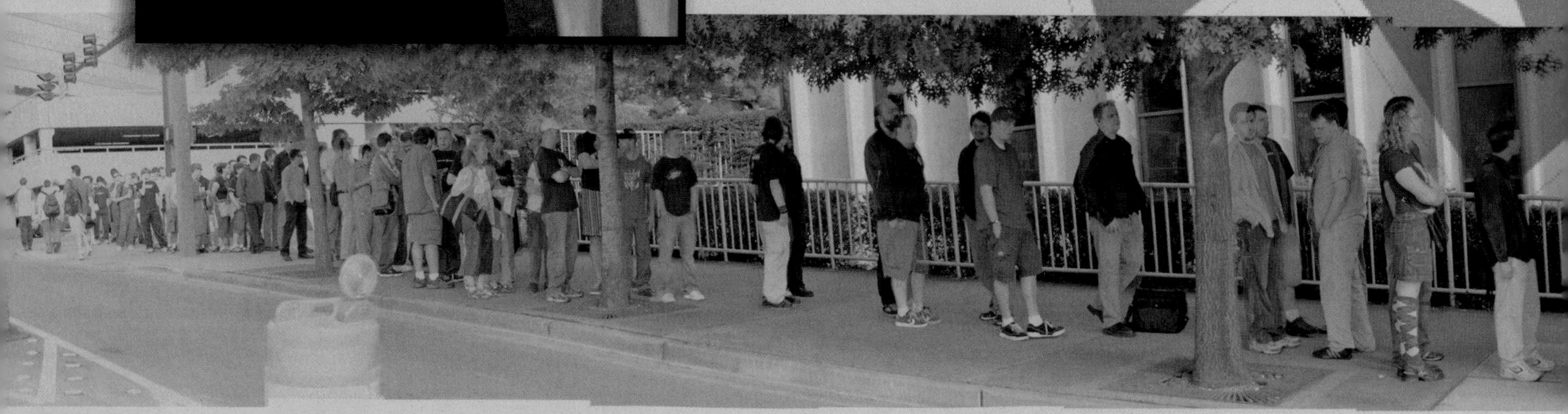

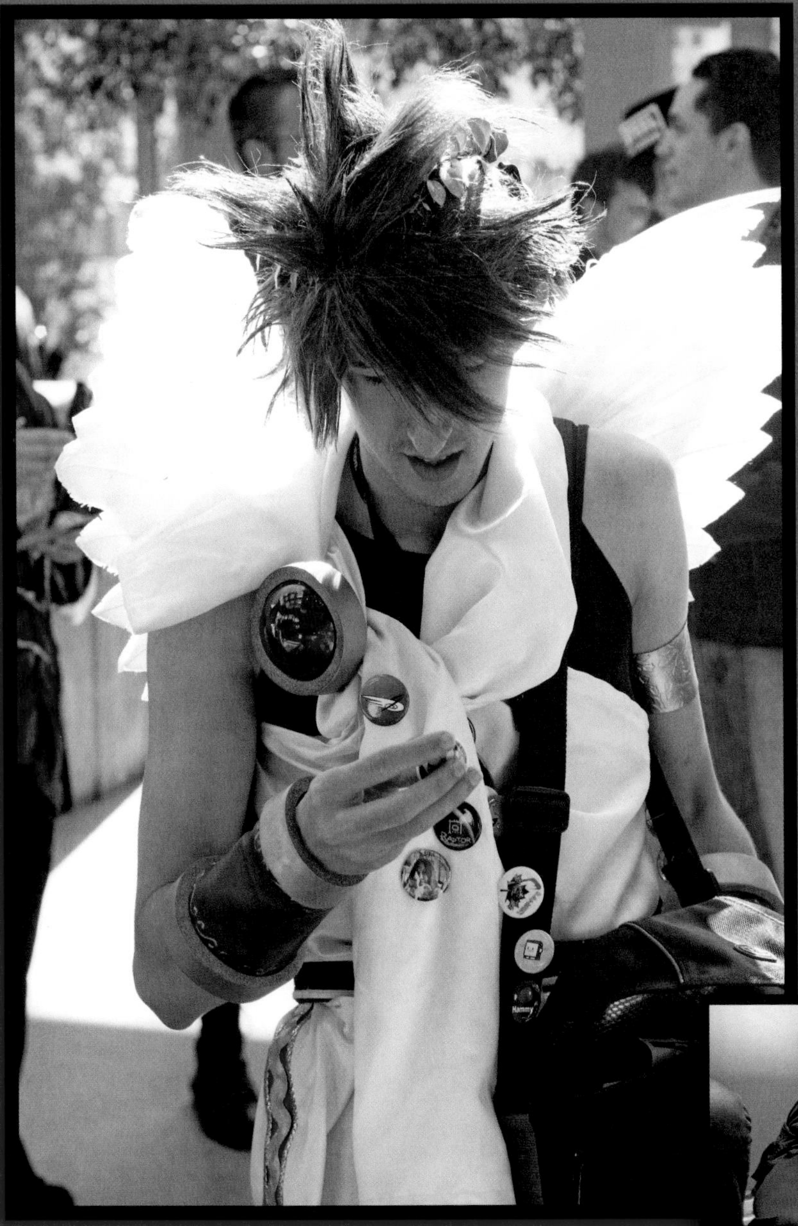

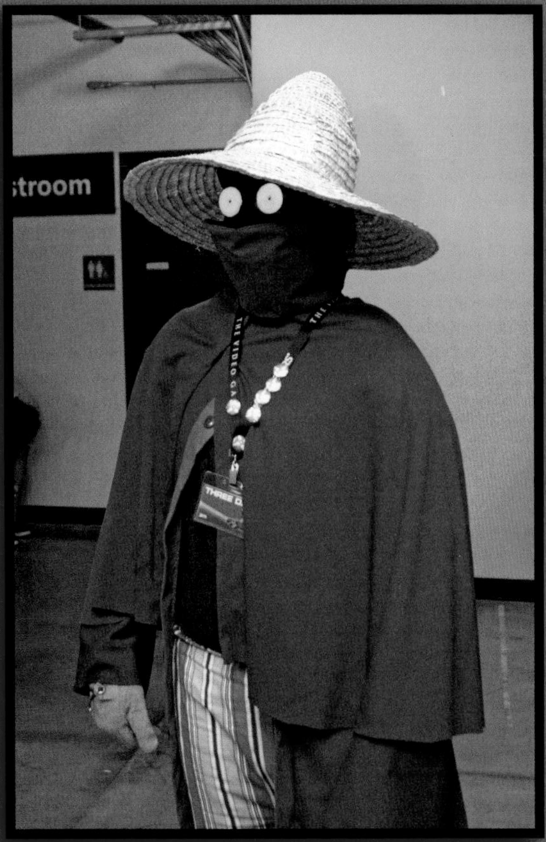
stroom

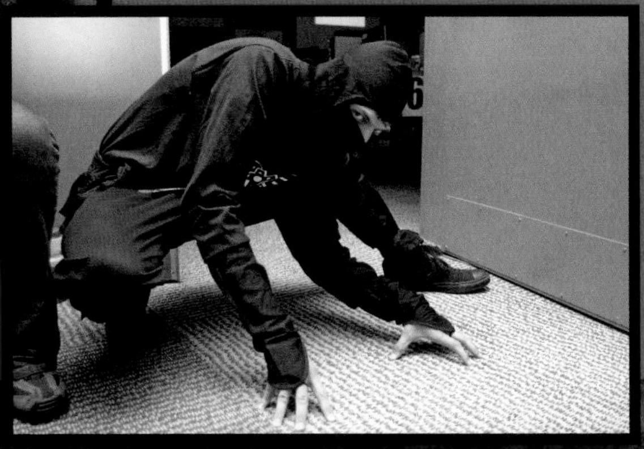

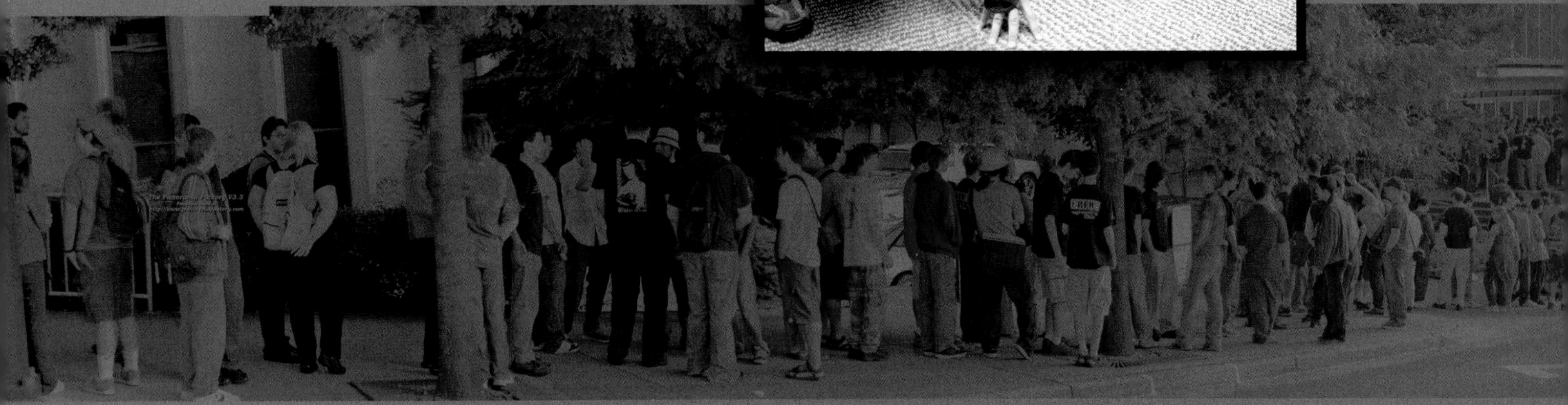

BREAKING THE LAW

by Robert Khoo

It's no secret that Mike and Jerry don't shy away from confrontation, and if they have something to say about an individual, a game, or an international megacorporation, they will do so. Occasionally feelings get hurt or some executives need to flex their muscles with a document that includes scary terms like *defamation of character* and *cease and desist.* I'm not complaining, by any means. If they weren't completely crazy, I wouldn't have a job.

Sometimes they'll ask me for advice on certain situations, but I tend to limit myself to a purely advisory role. What I would do in a given situation doesn't really matter. My role is to let them know of the possible, likely, or *imminent* ramifications their choices will have for the company. Sometimes the assessment is as simple as "Don't worry about it," or "Pack your bags and leave for Mexico, tonight"; other times it's as complicated as "Nothing that you're saying is illegal, but they'll still threaten to sue us, exactly like the last time you tried to pull this kind of shit."

Most of the time I don't know what they did until a lawyer calls.

Although these conversations happen fairly often and aren't always associated with a legal scuffle, every now and then something significantly "big" breaks through. Three such cases are included here, but I could probably fill a whole book with things like this and still have a few left over.

Penny Arcade Versus American Greetings

April 14, 2003

After game designer American McGee announced his serious, dark, brooding take on *Alice's Adventures in Wonderland* to follow up his serious, dark, brooding take on *The Wizard of Oz,* the guys realized this was sort of his "thing" and created the promotional poster for a fictional game, American McGee Presents Strawberry Shortcake. It depicted Ms. Shortcake as a dominatrix in pink lace, whipping the bare ass of her submissive "friend" Plum Pudding. Subtitles read "She's a sweet girl with a taste for pain," and "Taste her in 2005."

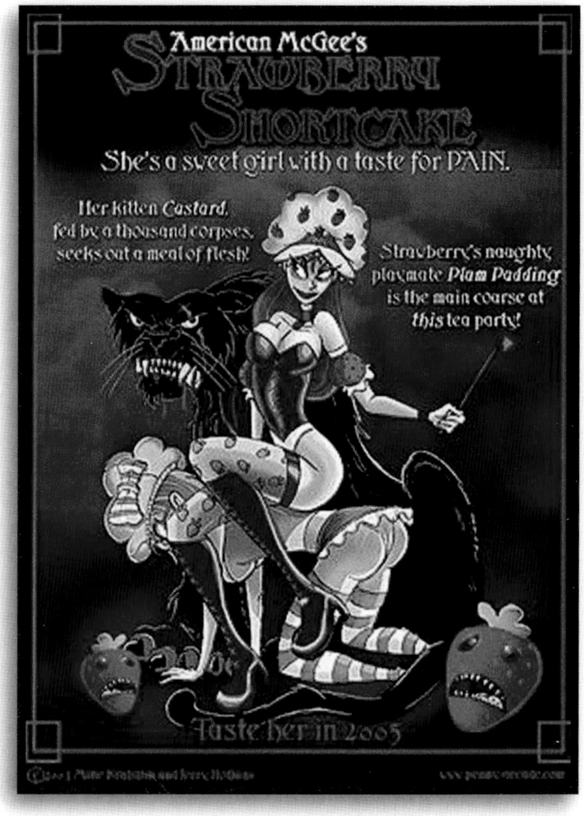
American McGee's
Strawberry Shortcake
She's a sweet girl with a taste for PAIN.
Her kitten Custard, fed by a thousand corpses, seeks out a meal of flesh!
Strawberry's naughty playmate Plum Pudding is the main course at this tea party!
Taste her in 2005

It was only a few hours before emails and calls began to pour in. We couldn't have known it at the time, but American Greetings was preparing to do a massive global launch of the brand. Although "free speech," "satire," and "parody" were our obvious knee-jerk reactions, it soon became apparent none of these actually applied. We weren't parodying or satirizing Strawberry Shortcake at all. We were making fun of American McGee and had appropriated Strawberry Shortcake—an American Greetings brand—to do so.

Oops.

To this day it's the first and only strip to ever be "depublished" on the site, not to say you can't find it with a simple Google search. The image itself was replaced with text helpfully explaining the situation, asserting that readers should contact American Greetings attorney Linda Vas if they had any questions. Mike and Jerry kindly included her email address in the image, which she didn't appreciate, but what do you do. Although our readers' accusations of "witchcraft" and suggestions that she develop cancer may have been unsportsmanlike, they are not outside the laws of this country.

Linda no longer works at American Greetings.

TIME LINE

2004 (August) — Residents of Bellevue, Washington, hide in their homes as nearly four thousand attendees descend onto the first PAX ever. The number of pre-registrants? Thirteen hundred thirty-seven.

Penny Arcade Versus Jack Thompson

October 10, 2005

Does Jack Thompson need an introduction? He's this ex-lawyer guy "on a mission from God" to preserve conservative Christian Moral Values™ and protect children and the public from what he considers to be obscene and immoral content. We think he is crazy. Our feud with him is long.

October 10, 2005

Thompson sends an open letter to the creators and publishers of electronic entertainment, titled "A Modest Video Game Proposal." In it, he challenges said industry to create a game following the story of a character he has invented called "Osaki Kim." Kim's son is murdered by a rampaging gamer, which causes Mr. Kim to set off on a rampage of his own, killing the CEO of the game maker, his family, the lawyers of said game maker, game retailer employees, and every other executive in the game industry. Oh, and then urinating on their bodies. If the challenge was met, Thompson vowed to donate ten thousand dollars to the charity of Paul Eibler's choice. Paul Eibler was the CEO of Take-Two Interactive at the time. Take-Two Interactive was the publisher of Grand Theft Auto. *Crazy.*

October 12, 2005

Mike emails Jack the following:

> *10 grand is pretty weak man. Through our charity* www.childsplaycharity.org *gamers have given over half a million dollars in toys and cash to children's hospitals all over the country.*

In less than half an hour Thompson was screaming on the phone with Mike, threatening him with lawsuits and further chest puffing. Mike tried to appeal to him with a conversation later in the day, but as the strip accurately transcribed, Jack was less than receptive.

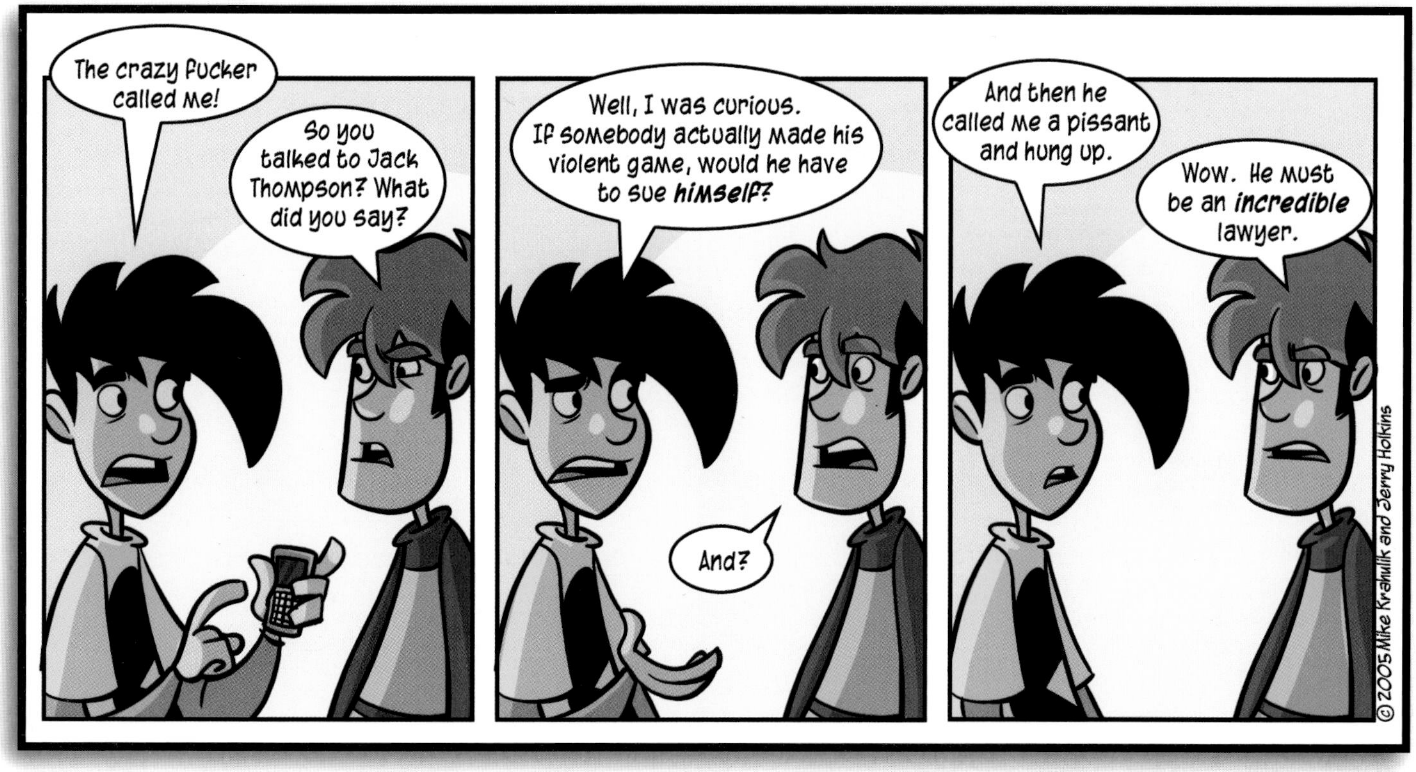
The crazy fucker called me!
So you talked to Jack Thompson? What did you say?
Well, I was curious. If somebody actually made his violent game, would he have to sue *himself?*
And?
And then he called me a pissant and hung up.
Wow. He must be an *incredible* lawyer.
©2005 Mike Krahulik and Jerry Holkins

October 14, 2005

Jerry recalls the "Jack Experience" in the newspost:

Gabe turned to look at me, not just with his head but his whole body, a single motion that had a mechanical look. He asked if it was really Jack Thompson, and it was at this point I knew he had done something wrong. I don't doubt that his adventures, both online and off, are a source of amusement for a percentage of the readership. Secretly, I delight in them—but he must not be allowed to know. His glee in these endeavors is already a kinetic force.

Conversation one is where Jack Thompson asks Gabe if Gabe has ever donated to charity. Of course, we have—it's usually a couple Game Boys a year for Child's Play, but the "take" from the distributed gamer metamind is over five hundred thousand dollars in two years. This answer did not satisfy him. He suggested that if Gabe mailed him again, he would be sued so fast that his head would "spin," and that he, Jack Thompson, had given more to charity than Gabe could even imagine. Gabe isn't very good at math, so he may have a point. I'm told that numbers larger than ten give him a headache. What's more, his donations were more valuable, because he wasn't some flush-with-cash game company. Which I guess is relevant to us, because...Well, I guess it's not relevant.

Then he hung up.

Usually when a person threatens us with a lawsuit we don't really pay attention. The fact of the matter is that rude people and idiots often try to threaten people by gesturing wildly at the edifice of the legal system. But this man is actually a lawyer, and also demonstrably crazy, and he apparently has time to call random people who mail him on the phone so maybe he's looking for something to do. In any case, we aren't a flush-with-cash game company, so at the very least my cohort wanted to excise this erroneous statement from the record.

This next mail elicited a second call, which we have detailed in the strip. Gabe's own voice rose triumphantly throughout this phase, I thought perhaps he was just getting into the rhetorical spirit of the thing, but the reality is that Jack screamed at him the entire time. The point he submitted went without answer: if a company made his reprehensible game, he would literally have to sue himself and talk about what a bastard he was on national television. Of course, he's not serious. Machination is too glorified a word for what he's doing. Ruse would make it seem debonair. He's essentially holding money hostage from charity, and if someone did make it, even as a joke, he would say that it didn't conform to his "design." This sort of thing is usually called a shell-game. The song license itself he mentions—Lawyers In Love—would probably run anywhere from ten to fifteen thousand by itself.

This vile "challenge" Jack Thompson has put to the supposedly monolithic "game industry" is like a topographical map of the twisted fantasy realm he inhabits. I could excerpt it, but I don't want to be accused of selective editing. The reality is that what he suggests is grotesque. I mean that it is literally disgusting. Of course, the violent acts he's cobbled together here from other games are robbed of a narrative context in which they make sense. Killing GameStop and EB employees, though? That's not metaphor. He's not being metaphorical. He is batshit fucking loco insane.

Oct 18 05 05:13a John Thompson 305-666-4366 p.1

John B. Thompson, Attorney at Law

[redacted]

October 18, 2005

Chief R. Gil Kerlikowske
Chief of Police
Seattle Police Department
610 Fifth Avenue
Seattle, Washington Via Fax

Dear Chief Kerlikowske:

A Seattle business by the name of Penny Arcade, whose phone number is [redacted], employs certain personnel who have decided to commence and orchestrate criminal harassment of me by various means.

This company has done this because I dared to go on CBS's *60 Minutes* in March and again in July to explain a wrongful death lawsuit I have brought on behalf of two police officers and a police dispatcher in Fayette, Alabama, who were shot in the head and killed by Devin Moore who obsessively trained on *Grand Theft Auto: Vice City* to kill them.

As you may know, this incredibly violent Rockstar Games product is actually a "cop-killing" murder simulator. There are a bunch of computer geeks out there who think that the video game industry has a constitutional right to paint a bullseye on your back and on your officers' backs but that I do not have a constitutional right to point out on *60 Minutes* or anywhere else that they do not have that "constitutional right."

That is what this criminal harassment of me by Penny Arcade is all about. They're even selling an "I Hate Jack Thompson" t-shirt, but that is just the tip of the iceberg. These idiots have been so careless as to post on their www.pennyarcade.com web site what they are doing regarding the harassment of me.

I look forward to working with your fine Police Department to shut this little extortion factory down and/or arrest some of its employees.

Regards, Jack Thompson

1

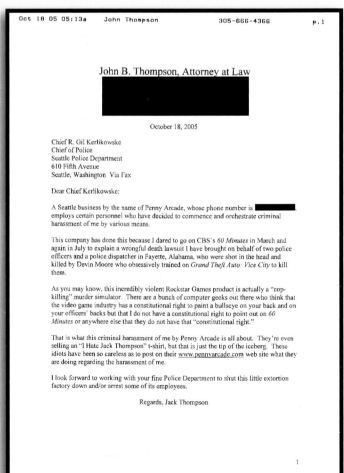

October 17, 2005

Developers respond to Thompson's "Modest Proposal" with many, many versions of the game, up and running within the week. Jack backs down from his promise and claims the entire ruse was merely "satire" and that no ten-thousand-dollar donation will be made. Penny Arcade decides to donate ten thousand in his name to the ESA Foundation. Jack immediately threatens to sue us, for what exactly we're not sure. Jack sends Mike mean emails, which Mike responds to with form letters:

*****This is an automated response*****

Thank you for contacting Penny Arcade. I'm sorry but I am simply not able to respond to all my fan mail. I want you to know that I'm glad you enjoy the comic strip and I appreciate you taking the time to mail me.

Thompson's response can only be described as "typical."

After speaking with the Seattle PD and them realizing fairly quickly this was a "civil matter" as opposed to a criminal one, they left us alone. Thompson, not easily deterred, contacted the FBI. In the end, no one came to arrest us, no agency we spoke with was unreasonable, and—most importantly—nobody outside the game industry was taking Jack seriously.

Since our interaction, Jack has been disbarred from practicing because of inappropriate behavior, among other things. So, we won. Basically.

Penny Arcade Versus Some Dude Who Ran Away to Alaska with All of Our Money

Before I came along, Mike and Jerry managed to accidentally sell the publishing rights for their books—something I had considered to be a priority in getting back. Although it was by no means as bad as selling the entire company unknowingly, something they also did, getting the rights back was quite an ordeal. It's difficult to summarize what exactly happened, but I believe the following seven-step list can be a true inspiration to all entrepreneurial publishing houses out there.

1. Mike and Jerry sign deal with PUBLISHER X.
2. PUBLISHER X takes all the preorder money to print books.
3. PUBLISHER X runs out of money and asks Mike and Jerry for additional funding.
4. PUBLISHER X is six months late on delivering said books.
5. PUBLISHER X asks Mike and Jerry for manuscript for second book.
6. Mike and Jerry ask when they will get paid for the first book.
7. PUBLISHER X runs away to Alaska.

I still look back on the experience and can't decide whether the legal system defended the good guys or was a complete failure to us. We can't go too much into detail on it, but hundreds of thousands of dollars in legal fees later, we ultimately were able to secure the rights. So, we won, sort of, if losing two years of my life along with a wheelbarrow full of money can be called "winning."

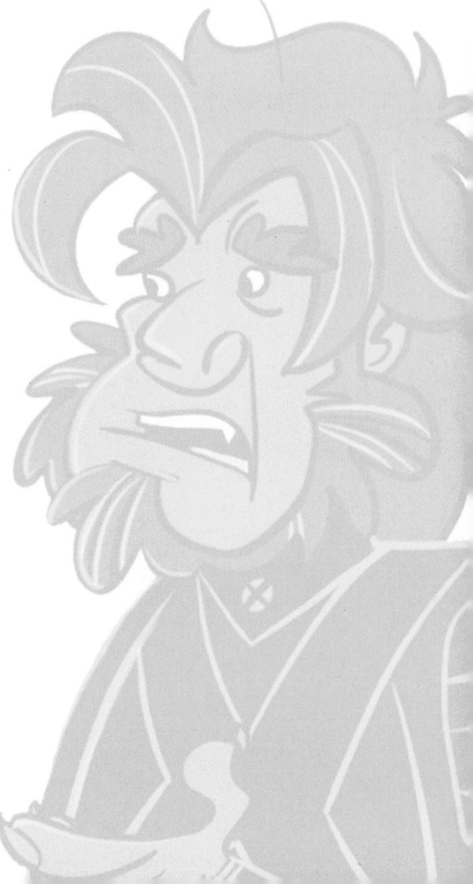

TIME LINE **2004 (September) —** Headcount at Penny Arcade Megacorp has officially doubled in size with the addition of Mike Fehlauer, tabletop gaming guru.

PAINT THE LINE

by Jerry Holkins

There's a strong case for the assertion that *Penny Arcade* is a "journal comic" in disguise. Every comic is just a congealed version of some conversation we've had. To the extent that it is a "video game comic," it only *covers* games because they're something we're obsessed with. Everything we like (also: everything we hate) ends up in the strips eventually. With Ping-Pong, it was only a matter of time.

We'd been wanting to do this story for a while, but never had the time. The fantasy was that we would be able to make a full-sized comic, and a soundtrack, and potentially a line of men's fashions. It began to dawn on us that we'd specced out a project that we could never actually complete.

We decided to try creating it in parts, delivering them according to the site's regular update schedule. Also, for some reason, we decided to do the *sequel* to our original story. The end result was sufficiently ridiculous.

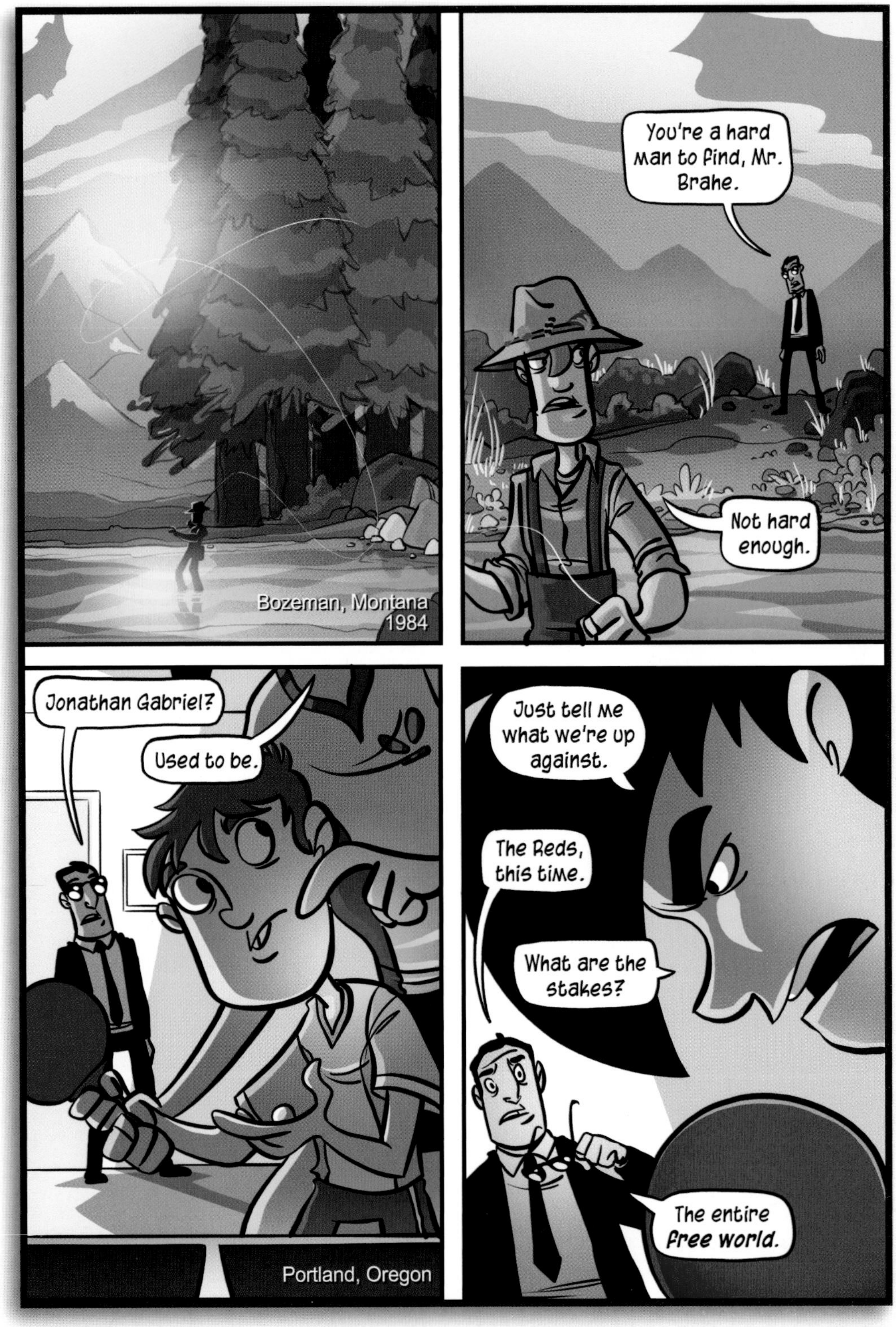
Bozeman, Montana
1984
You're a hard man to find, Mr. Brahe.
Not hard enough.
Jonathan Gabriel?
Used to be.
Portland, Oregon
Just tell me what we're up against.
The Reds, this time.
What are the stakes?
The entire free world.

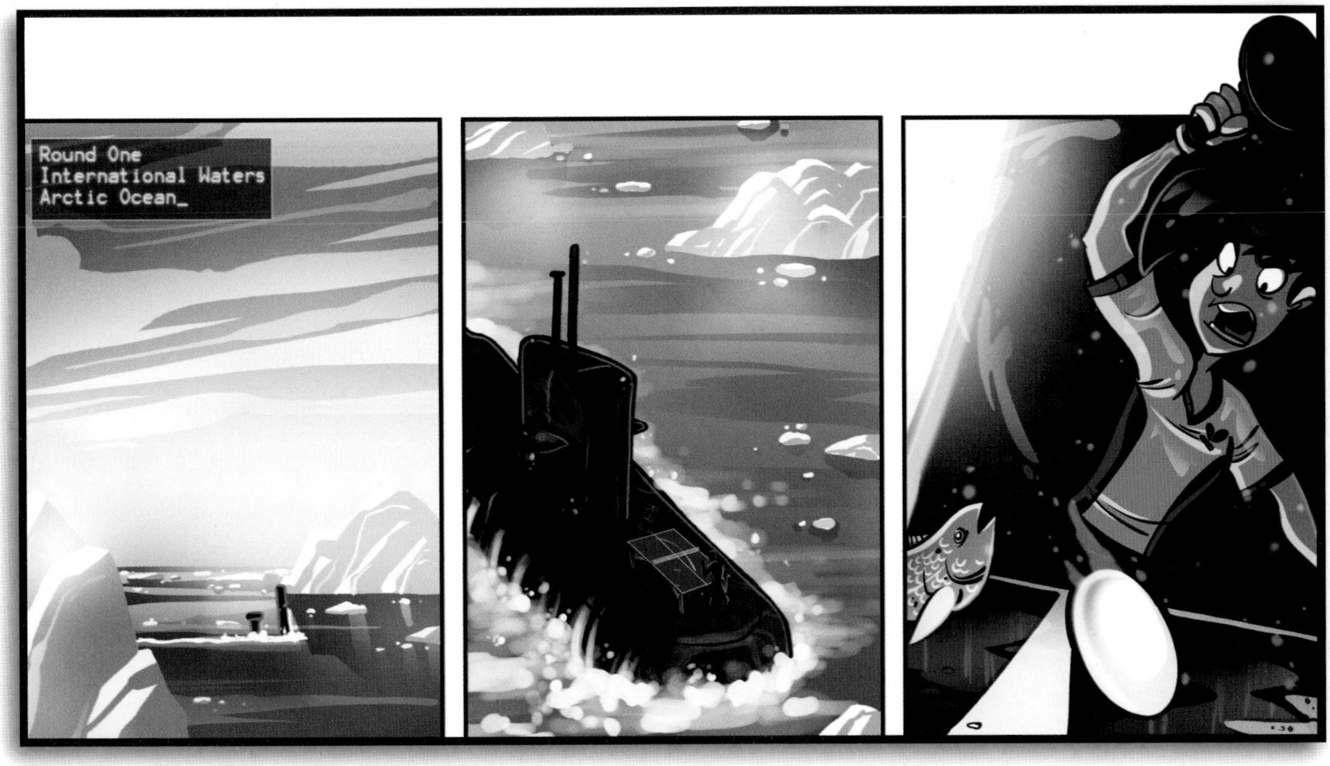
Round One
International Waters
Arctic Ocean_

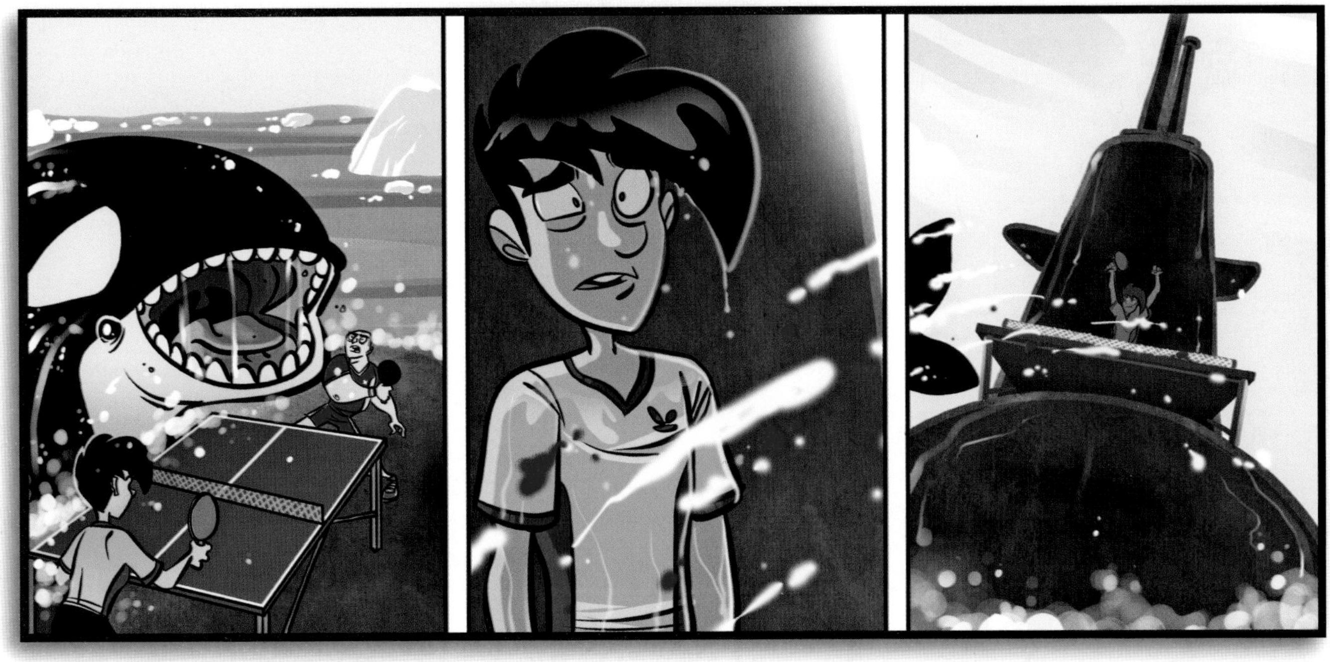

2004 (December) — The inaugural Child's Play Charity Dinner is held with Mike and Jerry as emcees.

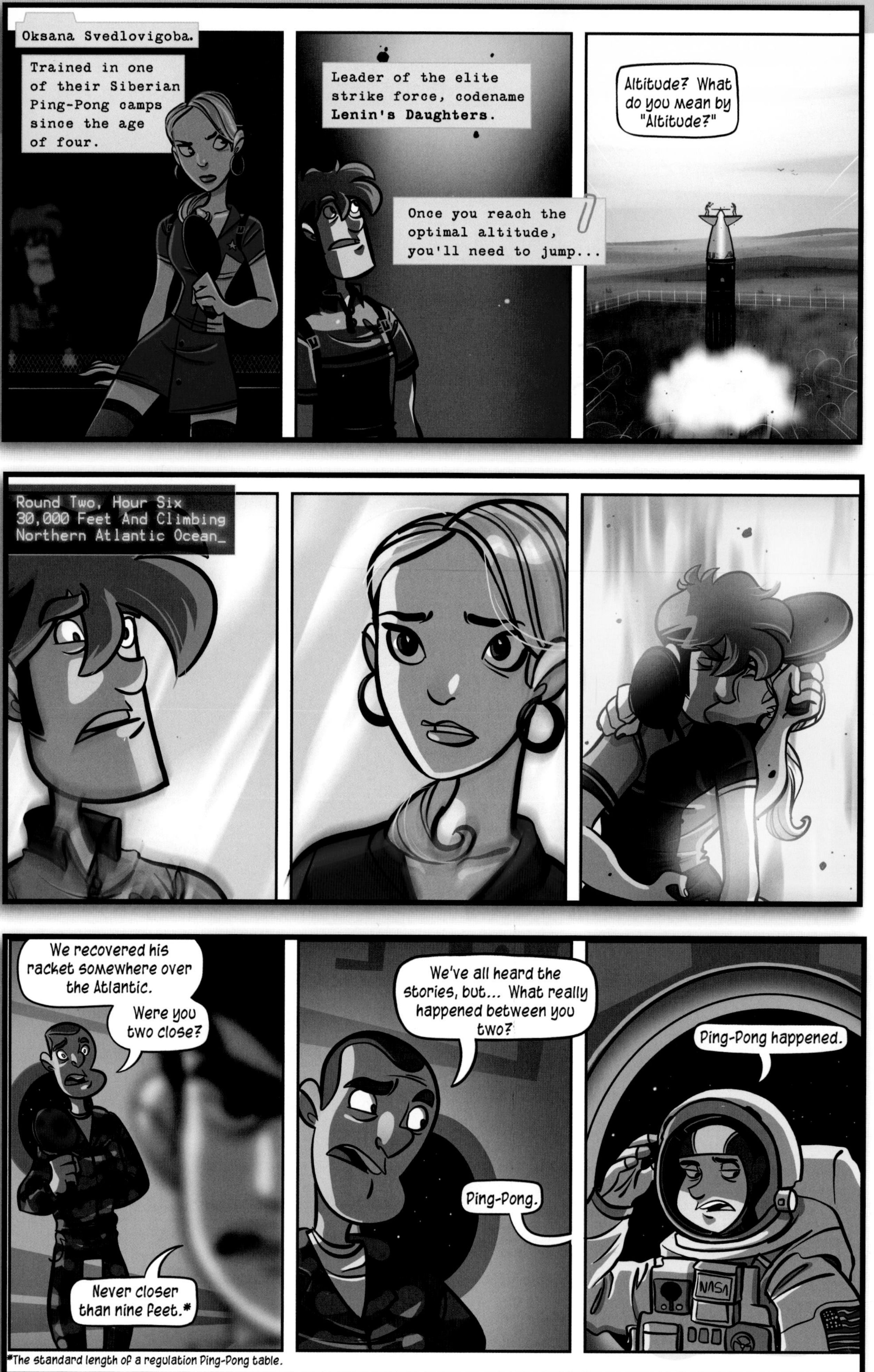
Oksana Svedlovigoba.
Trained in one of their Siberian Ping-Pong camps since the age of four.
Leader of the elite strike force, codename **Lenin's Daughters**.
Once you reach the optimal altitude, you'll need to jump...
Altitude? What do you mean by "Altitude?"
Round Two, Hour Six
30,000 Feet And Climbing
Northern Atlantic Ocean_
We recovered his racket somewhere over the Atlantic.
Were you two close?
Never closer than nine feet.*
We've all heard the stories, but... What really happened between you two?
Ping-Pong.
Ping-Pong happened.
NASA

*The standard length of a regulation Ping-Pong table.

Round Three
Geosynchronous Orbit
Omega Station_

Your final match is a doubles match.

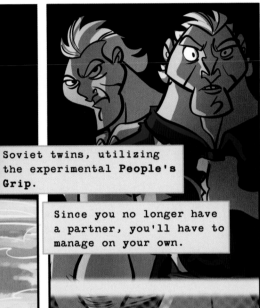

Soviet twins, utilizing the experimental **People's Grip.**

Since you no longer have a partner, you'll have to manage on your own.

This ain't really fair, now, is it?

I mean... There's only two of 'em.

We received one final transmission from the missile, before it broke the atmosphere.

It was short, only three words. Unencoded. And it was directed at you, specifically.

What did it say?

Sir, he said...

he said to "Paint The Line."

2005 (January) — After four long years, Penny Arcade once again owns the rights to their books.

LYRICS

by Jerry Holkins

My Belruel

'Twas the Twelving Day of Everfair
When fell my maid of raven hair
Beneath her cloven standard of the Wren
And damn that roiling goblin horde
We'd almost slain the overlord
But I could never roll an elf again

The Queen of Bells and Battle-downs
She wore the title like a crown
In foes so deep a man would drown
But she still stood alone
A princess and a duchess both
And sworn to nine prestigious oaths
These duties they would take her
To that twisting spire of stone

Against his tower a silhouette
She called out like a coronet
And the green sea of his armies
Burst from warrens far below
The pacts he made with demonkind
Had rent his thin and tattered mind
And hellish princedoms occupied
The arrow he let go

They took her through the crowded square
And laid her at the temple stair
The sorcelled barb of Arudair
Beyond their healing arts
There stands a circlet on her brow
That turns the blades of men around
But if Belruel could hear me now
This song would pierce her heart

'Twas the Twelving Day of Everfair
When fell my maid of raven hair
Beneath her cloven standard of the Wren
And damn that roiling goblin horde
We'd almost slain the overlord
But I could never roll an elf again

Soldier's Lullaby

I've taught kings their manners, child,
Wrangled the thanes.
I've sheathed all the bitter blades
West of the Crane.
I beg of you, child, as the wheat begs the rain,
to sleep.

I've parleyed with centaurs, child,
Knelt at the feet
Of leaf-laden forest kings
Thick with deceit
I beg of you, child, while the rain falls in sheets,
to sleep.

Are You Really a Woman

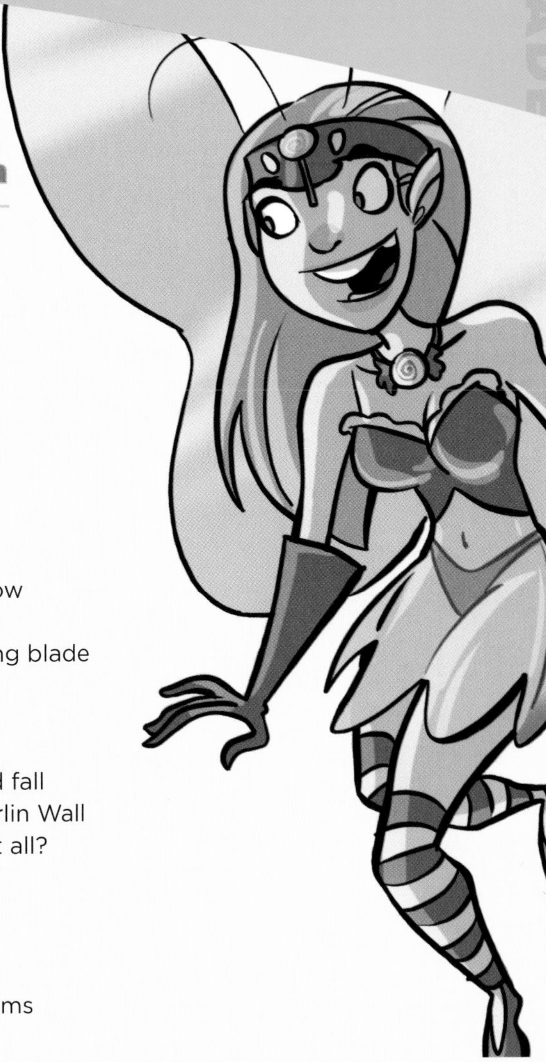

Lady-O
You hear me rocking on the radio
You got me thinking 'bout fellatio
If you're really a woman

Give us a little kiss
I cock my weapon and I never miss
Do you want to hear my serpent hiss?
Are you really a woman?

Bridge:
I'm only askin' cause I really want to know
Will I find Eden or the Snake
Is there something that can sheathe this aching blade
Or is something more at stake?

Chorus:
My thrust, Vesuvius, and then Pompeii did fall
I swung my dammerung, brought low the Berlin Wall
Are you receiving, am I getting through at all?
Are you really a woman?

Do you know what I mean?
If we can keep it out the magazines,
Then I can haunt you with my Devil Dreams
That is, if you're a woman

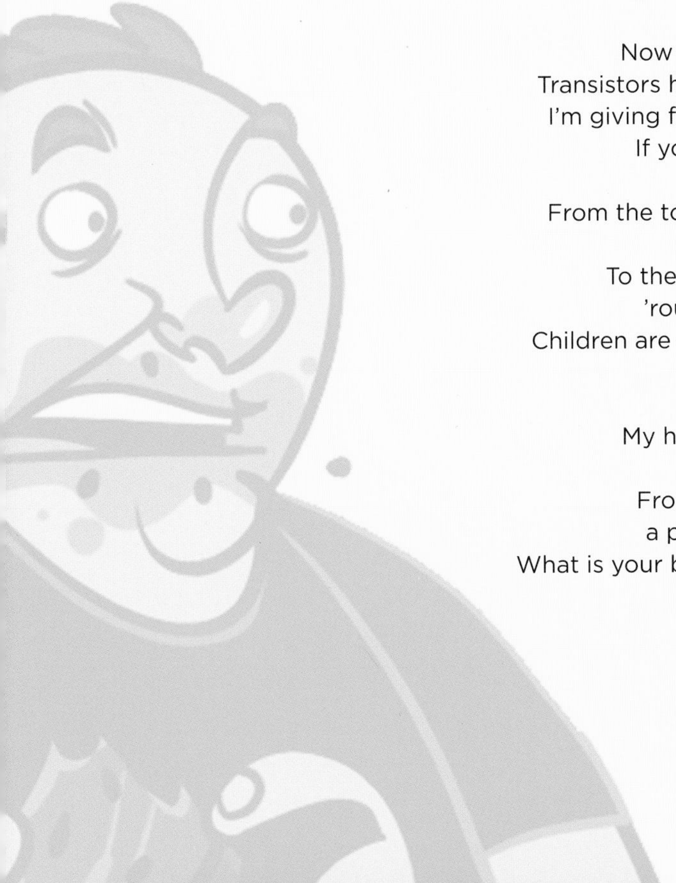

Now it's the witching hour
Transistors humming with a ready power
I'm giving free tours of the Eiffel Tower
If you're really a woman

From the tooth of that mountain, child,
All of the way
To the reefs that lie, reaching
'round Tourmaline Bay
Children are doing what their parents say:
to sleep!

My horses are weary, child
I'm weary, too
From making this world
a place worthy of you.
What is your bidding, child? What must I do
to sleep?

TIME LINE

2005 (March) — After numerous complaints from other tenants (storing Child's Play materials in the lobby, having one hundred Enforcers over at once, cooking chicken in the hallways), Penny Arcade is forced to expand their office space to eleven hundred square feet. It feels like a real company.

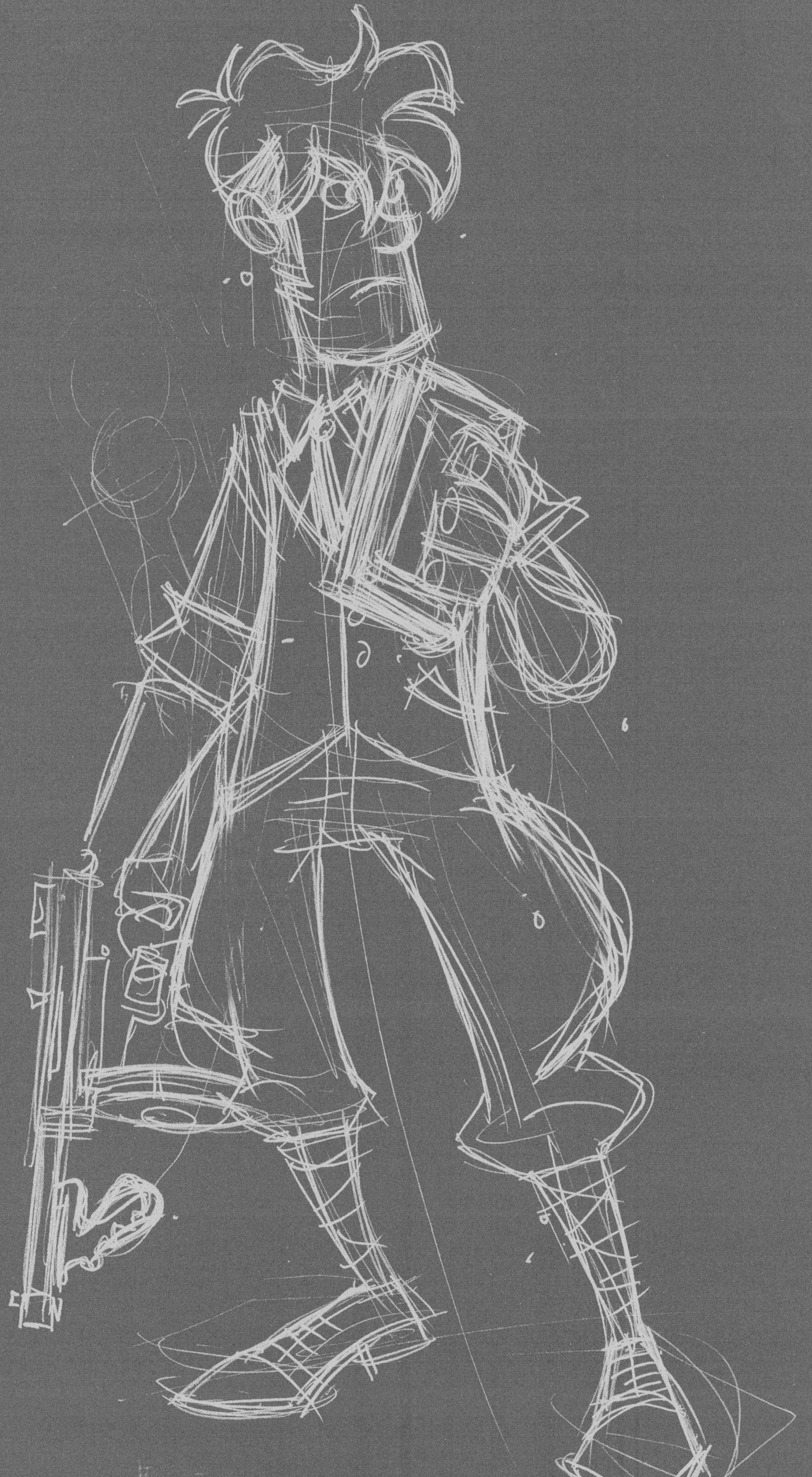

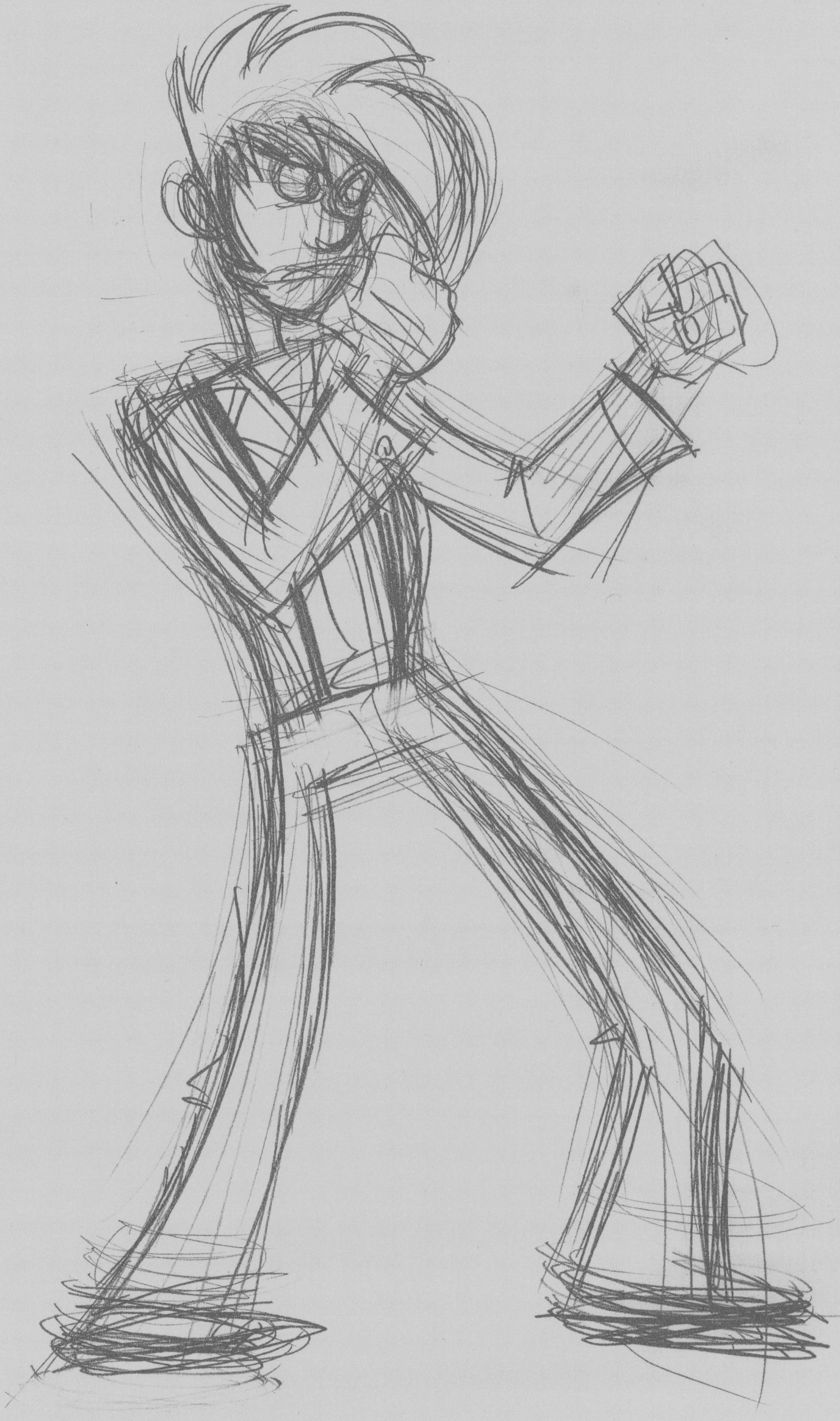

Q&A SECTION

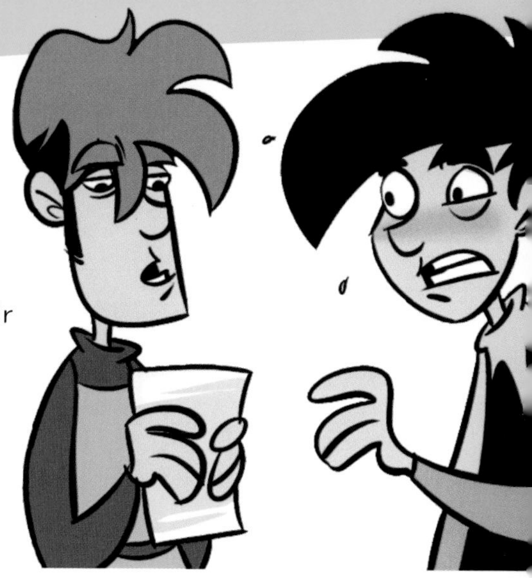

Starting from over five hundred reader-submitted questions, the pool was culled to the following fifty-five that cut the widest swath through common themes. Mike and Jerry talked through their answers, and what follows is the unedited transcript.

What would you both be doing now if you had never met each other?

Mike: Oooh, that's interesting!

Jerry: I am certain that I would have continued in technology services. I had a good job...that I could endure.

M: Sure.

J: ...And probably could have endured for a long time...It drove me nuts. But I could do it.

M: I want to believe that I would have continued pushing on and I would be a comic book artist, maybe? Drawing something at Marvel or DC maybe.

J: You would have kept up with it. It would have happened exactly the same way. You would have continued to make art. At the very least it would have been in the margin of your life, you would have made time for it.

M: Yeah.

J: And then you would have been putting stuff up. You would have probably made a comic by yourself.

M: Maybe.

J: I don't know that *I* would have.

M: Yeah, I had decided already by the time we met...that that's what I was going to do with my life. So I don't think that I would have gone into cartooning, though. I think it would be into comic *books.* Because that was the path I was on. So I think that's where I would have ended up.

Are there any strips you regret writing/drawing?

J: I know that for my part I don't, because even if there's a strip that I look at now and say, "That is not incredible work," [laughs] I know, at the very least, if nothing else, I know not to make that comic again. *I know that I'll only make that bad comic one time.*

M: Yeah, I don't regret making any of them. We've had to make a comic three times a week for ten years, [laughs] the fact that I think we've done that one is good. I'm not going to go back and nitpick.

J: Well, I'm happy to nitpick, but even a strip that didn't succeed on *any* level is still a learning experience.

M: I think they all succeed on some level, even if the level is "we put up a comic that day."

J: [laughs] "We saved it out as a jpeg."

Are you optimistic about the direction of video games (and/or webcomics) as a medium and an industry?

J: That's a weird comment. That's a weird question.

M: It's two very different questions.

J: I don't think of video games and webcomics being very similar.

M: No.

J: So maybe we should answer it as two different questions.

M: Okay. And what was the first part?

J: Well, are we optimistic about the direction of video games? Um, and/or webcomics.

M: Uh...I am. Yeah.

J: Me too!

M: I think games just keep getting better. [laughs]

J: Yeah, and there's this huge middle area of games that aren't incredible, history-making games that would be remembered for all time, but there is a very wide middle of very decent, fun-to-play games.

M: A casual market.

J: Well, casual's one thing. I mean are we talking about like POP3 or are we talking about just in general? Casual means more than just people who wanna play Bejeweled. There's interesting things happening virtually at every level of development. For instance, people leaving big companies and making tiny companies and making interesting games that will influence the games that are being made at the big companies they left. There's a lot of cross-pollination right now. As being able to download games becomes an authentically viable channel, we're just going to see *more,* and it's going to be more interesting. As far as webcomics as a medium in the industry, I mean it's just a *medium.* I guess I don't really know what direction webcomics are taking.

M: Well, we don't spend a lot of time thinking about "webcomics."

J: Well, not webcomics as a concept. I think a lot about comics in general, and webcomics are just comics that happen to be on the Internet.

M: Yeah.

J: [laughs] I mean, you know what I'm saying—that distinction might have meant a lot more when regular comics were a huge force.

M: I'm definitely optimistic about it just in the fact I think that more and more people will start being able to make a living off their webcomic.

J: The reality is that every regular comic will eventually become a webcomic. That's just the direction of publishing. So yes.

M: I am optimistic about it.

J: [laughs] I guess in that respect we can say that things are good.

Aside from the apparent visual changes, how would you describe the evolution of *Penny Arcade* from its inception to today? What's changed and what has remained the same?

M: Aside from the art?

J: They're saying aside from the *apparent* visual changes...So that doesn't necessarily mean all of the art.

M: So what's changed, first?

J: Yeah. Well, I guess we're making them inside an office...where employees work.

M: Our environment has changed, sure.

J: Yeah, it seems to me the comic is the thing we try to keep the same.

M: Our lives sort of change around it. Well, but we've added a lot more stuff with the kids and the wives, as we became fathers.

J: True, true. But we still try not to let those things overrun the strip in any way. We try to keep them on the periphery.

M: No no, I mean it hasn't become *For Better or for Worse* or something.

J: Although our version of *For Better or for Worse* might be pretty sweet.

M: Might be funny actually.

J: The evolution of *Penny Arcade.*

M: I think there's less violence. I think violence as a punch line happens less now.

J: Yeah. Eventually you run out of ways to...

M: ...kill or murder or dismember someone...

J: ...with the available items.

M: I think that what stayed the same is the—

J: Hard hitting...

M: No, the relationship between Gabe and Tycho.

J: Yeah.

M: We don't really have story lines but we have—

J: Character.

M: The characters have been consistent I think for all ten years.

J: Everything else in the strip, in and out, just moves around those poles.

At what point did you know that *Penny Arcade* had become a Big Deal?

M: Hmm.

J: I don't know that I would ever say it with those words, because I have a...an almost... superstition about it. Saying things like that out loud. *In fact we're already in danger.*

M: [laughs] It is a big deal.

J: That's as may be, but saying that it is a big deal—

M: I guess it depends on the *size* of the deal.

J: Yeah yeah yeah! It's relative to *what other deals?*

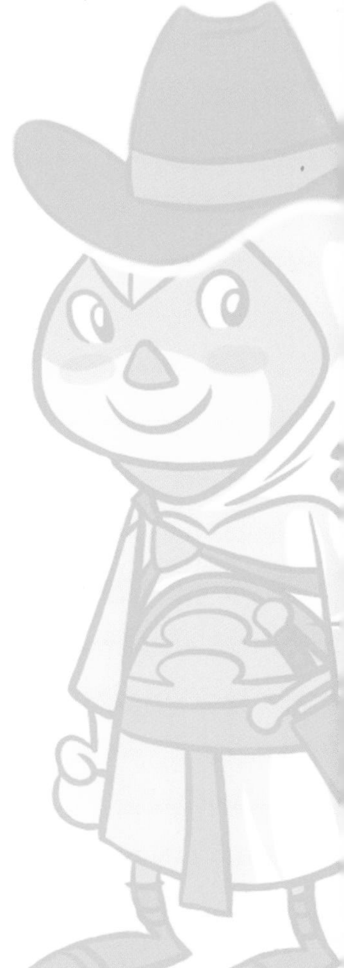

TIME LINE

2005 (September) — Mike and Jerry are invited to MIT as guest lecturers. Not knowing exactly what they were looking for, Mike begins by drawing the Jonathan Gabriel's Greater Internet Fuckwad Theory on the chalkboard.

M: When we quit our jobs, I definitely felt it was a big deal.

J: It had graduated.

M: When we had the very first Necrowombicon and people actually came. Even though it wasn't that many.

J: And it was in a food court.

M: It was in the food court at the mall. I thought, *Wow, that's a big deal.*

J: I guess it's just always in the process of.

M: When they opened the doors for the first PAX and that line that wrapped around the building...just poured in...

J: I would say that it was the first PAX.

M: Yeah, the first PAX was the real big one.

J: It was always interesting and watching that sort of shit change was interesting, but I would say that *that,* with the people pouring in the doors when they were opened. That...that was different.

M: Yeah, that was a new level.

Do either of you have any "guilty pleasure" games?

M: Guilty pleasure *games*...like games that aren't very good that you like?

J: Yeah. Essentially a game that you know is not good, but you still stick it out. The thing is that I have a hard time playing games that don't have some virtue, you know what I'm saying? So I always just latch on to whatever I think are virtues, but there tend to be games that we like that no one else likes. I would say the biggest one is probably the first Crystal Chronicles.

M: Oh, maybe that's true.

J: We are *it.* Nobody else likes that. And the virtue it had was that it let us all play together in an RPG.

M: When I think back about the games I've liked, I think all of them are good. That's why I played them.

J: [laughs] Exactly! Why would you play a game that wasn't good? But the only way we have to determine this is by looking outside our circle.

M: Well, I guess Assassin's Creed, I loved Assassin's Creed, but the reviews for that were not great.

J: But again, that's another special case, just like Crystal Chronicles. It's a game that *we* love, and we loved it I think in large part because we played it together.

M: Yeah.

J: You know what I'm saying. We used Assassin's Creed, and I mean all these missions that people didn't like or whatever—we used it to make little parkour videos. We had a different relationship to that, and I think partly because we were playing it together.

M: Hmm.

J: So I think having this kind of scenario could help you get a lot out of games. A *lot* of the games that came out for the Genesis were not very good.

M: That's true. Yeah, and playing games with someone else definitely helps.

J: Right.

Do you ever see *Penny Arcade* branching out in a spin-off comic?

M: Spin-off comic...

J: Well, 'cause that would imply...that would imply more work.

M: Yeah no, nuh-uh.

J: That would imply more comics. That was the original idea, but that was back when we only did one strip a week. We wanted to do comics that were based on work. "Retails" I believe was the name.

M: "Retails," yeah. I can see *Twisp and Catsby* spinning off into a children's book or an animated show, and I could see an *Acquisitions Incorporated* comic or cartoon even.

J: Yeah. Those make sense.

M: I think there's parts of *Penny Arcade* that could spin-off.

J: There's a bunch of little ideas that sort of exist *in Penny Arcade* that might warrant further investigation.

Do you ever think of breaking into media outside of video games? For instance, write a comic book that isn't *Penny Arcade* or write a novel that isn't *Penny Arcade* related?

J: Absolutely, of course.
M: Yeah, all the time.
J: It's just that *Penny Arcade* takes us a lot of time.
M: [laughs] Yeah.
J: I have maybe two-fifths of an album written. I have a novel idea that I think is going to be really great. But I really don't have a lot of time.
M: Yeah, we have that children's book idea.
J: *Which one?*
M: Yeah, which one, really.
J: There are a *ton* of ideas that we would love to investigate and it may be that that's something we have to look at later...Right now we *like* giving our time to *Penny Arcade.*
M: Yeah, it's still fun.

Do you find yourselves ever struggling to go into the "office"?

J: I don't actually.
M: No. I don't.
J: No, I have a three-year-old at home...
M: [laughs]
J: So the office is sort of like—
M: A *sanctuary.*
J: My fortress...my Fortress of Solitude.
M: No, it's great to come here and play games and make comic strips.
J: And answer questions.
M: Yeah!

Do you have, and, if so, would you be willing to flesh out for us, a philosophy of game criticism? A set of axes on which you rate games and a method (even if it's rough-and-ready) for weighting those ratings?

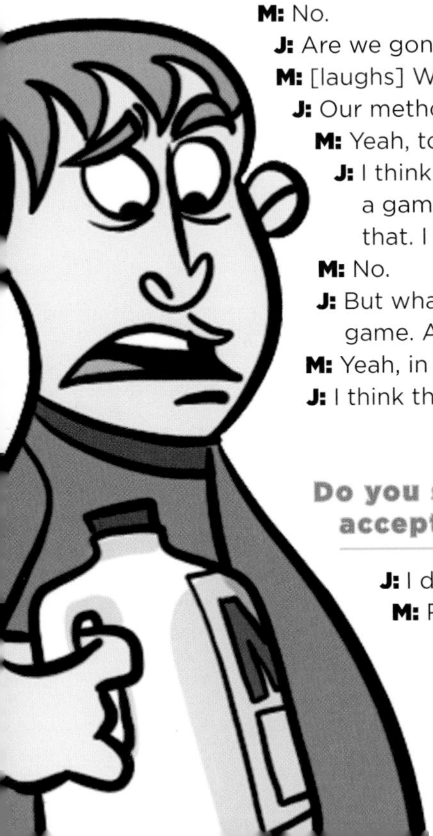

M: No.
J: Are we gonna remove that question?
M: [laughs] We don't have any of those.
J: Our method, if you can call it that, is mostly intuitive.
M: Yeah, to play a game and see if we like it.
J: I think that those rules are mostly sort of subliminal for us. There are people who can dismantle a game from an artistic perspective, right? They can look at the different systems and stuff like that. I don't think that mathematically we have those chops.
M: No.
J: But what we *can* do is we can give someone a very strong idea of what it *feels* like to play a game. And I don't think that's without value.
M: Yeah, in fact I'd say that has more value sometimes than giving it a, you know, 6.258.
J: I think that both are important.

Do you see the success of *Penny Arcade* as indicative of a greater acceptance of geek/gamer culture by the mainstream?

J: I don't think so. Our enthusiasts are people who like video games, right?
M: Right.

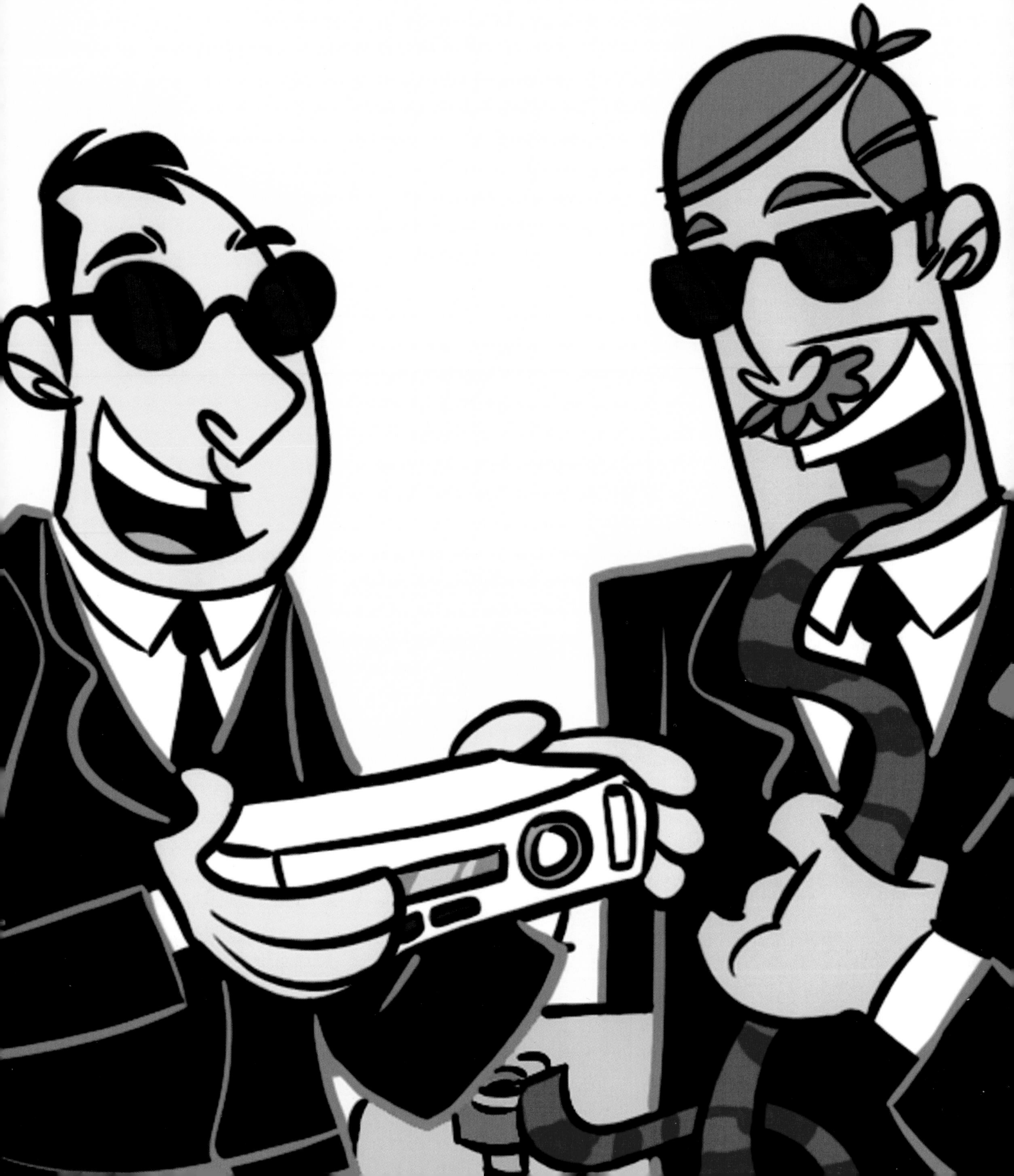

J: They're geeks or people who like games, and so I don't see how success within the subculture that we crave is indicative of greater mainstream acceptance.

M: I think they're saying that if there's more gamers, doesn't that just mean there are more people to like *Penny Arcade* now? I think that is probably true.

J: Yeah?

M: Yeah.

Do you segregate video game playing into hours "for work" and "for fun"?

J: I don't.

M: No, I don't.

J: I guess it's because it would be taking place at the office...

M: ...for work or for fun. Every time I sit down to play a game I hope to have fun.

J: Yeah yeah yeah. There we don't turn a light on that is like our analytical light.

M: Yeah.

J: Playing games for us is a form of recreation, even if we're doing it for *Penny Arcade.*

M: There are definitely times where a game we had no intention of buying will come to the office. Someone will send us a copy and we'll put it in.

J: Sure, but we're still curious and our process hasn't shifted.

Everyone has a few all-time favorite movies that somehow define him or her in an intimate way. What are your soul-mate movies?

M: Movies? Hmm. Movies...I'm used to answering this question for games.

J: Yeah right, then they flipped the script.

M: [laughs] I don't think about movies that often. I like to *watch* movies.

J: It may be that the type of entertainment they are is not something you use as a landmark internally.

M: No.

J: For me, definitely, I would say *Falling Down.* You ever seen that movie?

M: Oh yeah.

J: For some reason *Falling Down* is a really important movie to me.

M: *Falling Down* made a big impact on me.

J: *Falling Down, The Mosquito Coast,* and *Hurlyburly* are probably my three favorite movies. *Falling Down* is right in the middle there in terms of the dialogue. *The Mosquito Coast* is just a big idea. *Falling Down* is a big idea that is written in a very interesting way, and *Hurlyburly* is almost entirely just an excuse for people to talk to one another. The way that that dialogue is written just feels very true to me. It's something I like to approach.

M: Yeah, I guess I would put *Falling Down* on my list, but the original *Star Wars* trilogy.

J: Yeah, just a huge idea.

M: It's a big idea and was very important in my early years. I guess it still is. [laughs]

J: [laughs] I guess that hasn't gone anywhere.

For Jerry: Did writing for your own two games change any of your notions about how words, sentences, or narratives operate in a video game context?

J: No, because the dark secret is that I was really just writing a book! I wasn't really trying to write a game necessarily, I was just trying to write a book that the reader progressed through at their pace. So Hothead handled all the obstructions to my book, and the player navigated it in much the same way as a choose-your-own adventure. So I was really just writing a book, I wasn't trying to write a game at all.

2005 (October) — Video game critic Jack Thompson writes an open letter to the industry titled "A Modest Video Game Proposal" challenging the industry to create a game where you can kill game developers. If done, he would donate ten thousand dollars to charity. When the challenge is met, Jack refuses to donate the money, so Penny Arcade does so in Thompson's name to the ESA Foundation.

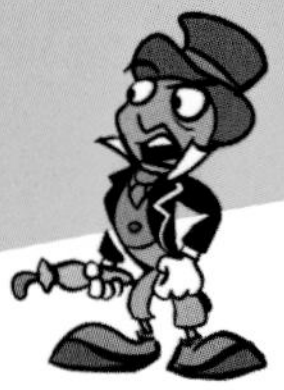

For Jerry: Do you write anything that isn't explicitly related to *Penny Arcade* or video games—stories, poems, et cetera—and if so, how seriously do you take that writing as a craft or discipline?

J: I take my writing on *Penny Arcade* very seriously as a craft and discipline, so I guess I don't know how to take that. But, yes, I absolutely do write. I write songs, which is essentially a poem and music together.

M: Even those have a video game, sort of, vibe to them, though.

J: Yeah, I guess that's true. It's based around the idea of a video game or the idea of a character just as a generalized theme.

M: But do you write anything completely separate from gaming and *Penny Arcade*?

J: Let's see...Not yet, but I will.

For Mike: What haven't you done artistically that you still want to?

M: I would like to....I would definitely like to have a gallery show at some point of physical work like paintings and maybe sculpture. Doing *Penny Arcade* is cool but there is something about the physicality of the paintings I've been doing recently that is really exciting. I would like to have someplace that is full of those, and people could walk around them and look at them.

J: [laughs] So something like a gallery show.

M: Yeah.

For Mike: Who or what was your biggest influence on your art style?

M: My biggest influence was Stephen Silver. He drew *Kim Possible* and the *Clerks* animated show, and I think more recently he did a lot of the designs for the *Madagascar* cartoon on Nick.

J: It's a cartoon now?

M: Yeah. But just his work in general has really inspired me.

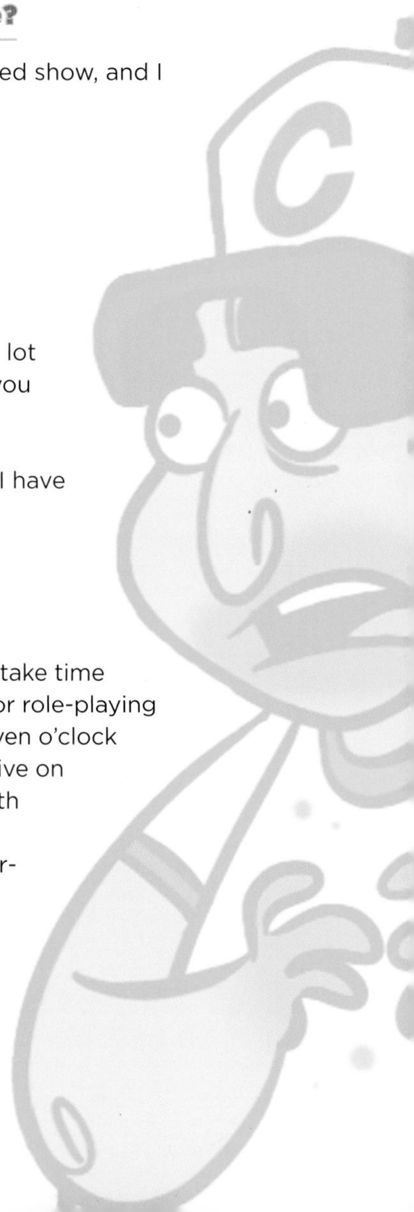

Has having a child changed your perspective on the gaming industry or on gaming in general?

M: One thing I can definitely say it's done is make me appreciate the time I play games a lot more. We've talked about this among ourselves, but you realize just how much time you wasted once you have a kid.

J: Yeah, you fucked off a lot.

M: Before you had a kid you really just fucked around for a long time. And so now when I have two hours...

J: You hurl yourself into it.

M: To sit down and play a game—I *really* enjoy those two hours.

J: For me being married was a bigger change than having a kid.

M: Yeah.

J: Once I was married you have sort of this structure, and you need to figure out when to take time for yourself inside that structure. "My time" is almost invariably spent on video games or role-playing games, but it's recreation time and it was always at night. Now Elliot goes to bed at seven o'clock and there's a lot of time left in the evening. But that hasn't really changed my perspective on the gaming industry. I think it probably helps when people our age, who are familiar with the medium, have kids and some of the media exposés. I think that we know perfectly well that a young person shouldn't be playing certain kinds of games, it is not any different from movies or anything else.

M: Yeah.

J: Their cultural experience needs to be metered by their parents, that's not weird.

TIME LINE

2005 (October) — Jack Thompson reports Penny Arcade to the Seattle Police Department and the FBI for criminal harassment, extortion, and terrorist activities.

Have you ever considered expanding your team to more writers/artists?

M: Not on a full-time basis.

J: I guess you've worked with colorists.

M: Yeah, I've worked with colorists before. I've worked with Scott Kurtz on some stuff like the D&D project. I definitely like collaborating with other artists, but as far as another full-time artist...I really like drawing *Penny Arcade!* [laughs]

J: Yeah, and I think that our process is sort of insular, you know what I'm saying?

M: Yeah.

J: There may be another process and maybe another comic or another product, but this process is very based on us.

Have you ever considered making an animated movie?

M: I have definitely had ideas about a *Penny Arcade* cartoon or animated show.

J: It seems like *Twisp and Catsby* could make for a nice cartoon.

M: I think *Acquisitions Inc.* would make a really funny Saturday-morning cartoon.

J: Yeah, in that style?

M: In that style, yeah.

J: I even think that *Cardboard Tube Samurai* could make a great cartoon. I think that there's a lot of those sub-ideas in there that could probably stand on their own in some cool ways.

Have you ever considered retiring or pursuing other projects?

J: Sure.

M: Yeah, at some point we'll stop and do something else.

J: At some point we won't be able to endure it anymore. It's like right now, it's hard to find new ways to kill people.

M: Right now I don't know when that would be. I really enjoy making *Penny Arcade* and I want to keep doing it.

J: In no way am I watching the clock or anything.

M: In another twenty years am I still going to want to do it? I don't know.

J: My guess would be no.

M: Yeah, I would guess no.

J: Who knows what we'll be doing then!

Have you had any interesting experiences meeting people in RL after lampooning them in print?

M: Yeah, we have. Oh, what was it? Didn't we meet a guy at some kind of press event? It was at a Nintendo event, wasn't it?

J: No, it was Microsoft, right?

M: It was Microsoft.

J: Michael Wolf?

M: Michael Wolf, yeah. And he was cool.

J: Yeah, he was actually a super-cool dude. But people that we lampoon typically have a while before meeting us so they have time to really interpret it. By then things are usually cool.

M: And John Smedley is cool.

J: Absolutely. Eventually we make friends with almost every person that we make fun of.

M: McCloud.

J: I mean, eventually we make friends with these people. But there was the one dude, I think he was an artist on *Athena Voltaire,* which is a comic book and has been optioned for a movie now. But I said something bad about—

M: Oh yeah, you laid into it.

J: ...I said something bad about him in the post and then I was at San Diego Comic-Con and I was over in a comic booth, like looking for a comic, and this guy came up to me and said, "Are you Jerry Holkins?" And people say that sometimes at San Diego Comic-Con and I said, "Yes," and I thought he worked at the booth so I asked him if he could help me find something, but he was actually there to yell at me, and he seriously yelled at me for like five minutes!

M: Wow! He was pissed.

J: He was really mad. But it had never happened to me, and you know how I get when I get into a super-uncomfortable situation: I'm delighted by it. And so for some reason I actually really enjoyed it, and I think that that only incensed him further.

M: Probably.

J: And eventually we became friends, again. I mean the arc is always the same.

How and why do you keep deadlines? What horrendous torture awaits you if you do miss one one day?

J: I think in large part, at least for me, the deadline is what creates *Penny Arcade.*

M: Yeah.

J: Obviously they were self-imposed at the beginning and now it's just a part of the...like the *beast.*

M: [laughs]

J: Like the beast must be fed three strips a week.

M: Yeah, we just have to keep it going.

J: Right, right, it's just a momentum thing now.

M: Yeah.

J: But at the start we had to say, "This is what's happening." And if it wasn't for that date, even if it was a made-up date...My problem is that I wouldn't know when to stop writing. This is especially true for the posts. If there wasn't a day or a time that I had to turn it in, my guilt about not posting it is what empowers me to write it.

M: Yeah, it's really guilt that keeps us going. I would feel really bad if a comic goes up late or, God forbid, it didn't go up *at all* someday. I would, I would feel bad.

J: We don't even know what would happen.

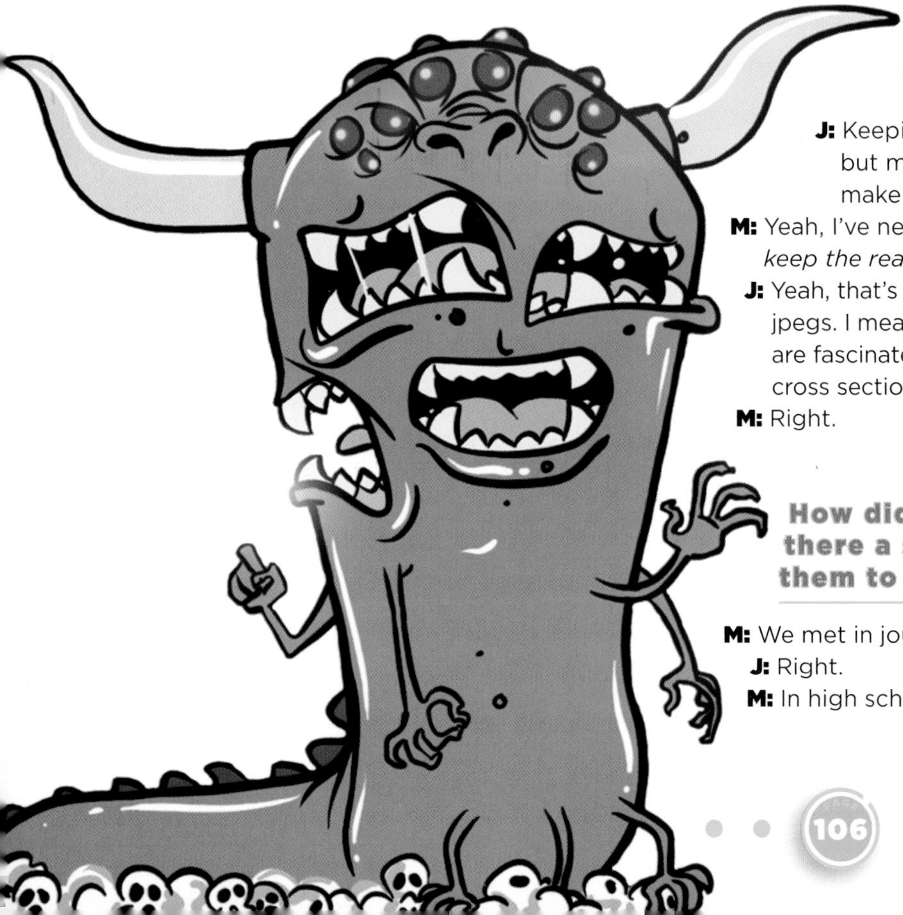

How challenging is it to keep the material fresh enough to keep the readers coming back?

J: Keeping readers coming back is definitely a nice benefit, but mostly we want to create interesting work. We want to make comics that are fun to read.

M: Yeah, I've never once thought, *Will this comic that we just made keep the readers coming back?* [laughs]

J: Yeah, that's a scary, scary way to think about the production of jpegs. I mean, for us it's really trying to create something that we are fascinated by on some level, and that *hopefully* will appeal to a cross section of those readers.

M: Right.

How did Jerry and Mike first meet, and was there a single incident or event that caused them to become such good friends?

M: We met in journalism class.

J: Right.

M: In high school.

J: Right. You could draw.

M: I could draw and you told me you could write.

J: Yeah. [laughs] At that time.

M: At that time I had no proof of it. Yeah, I think you just came over and looked at my sketchbook and you said that you liked my drawings.

J: I knew that this would work.

M: And I, at the time, was hungry for a story. Because that was the...

J: You wanted something to draw.

M: Yeah! Writing was the boring part of making the comics.

J: [laughs]

M: And if I...I thought if I could get someone to do the shit work for me...

J: Yeah, the bullshit?

M: [laughs] Yeah.

J: Let alone someone who actually enjoyed it...

M: Sure.

J: "That person *must* exist!" Yeah, we always got along and had fun. So the answer to that question is over. We always got along and had fun, but I didn't become your best friend, on my side, until you called me the day your brother died.

M: *Oh,* yeah.

J: That's for me. I'm like a vampire.

M: Yeah.

J: Like I can't enter someone's house.

M: [laughs]

J: You know what I'm saying. I have a super-strong sense of place, and I can't go places that I'm not welcome.

M: Yeah.

J: And when you called me then. When you called *me*...I knew that you...I knew that it was...I knew that it was about me...there was something about me in particular.

M: Yeah, no that was probably it. I guess that was probably the...Yeah, I chose to call you because I knew that we could...

J: Yeah.

M: Work it out.

J: Yeah, listen, we had fun. I mean there's no question, we always did. Our time together was well spent, but that's when...and we didn't talk about it. We didn't say a word about it.

M: Yeah.

J: We didn't have to, it wasn't about that.

M: Yeah.

J: I don't know, maybe that would be good for the book after all.

M: Maybe.

How do you cope with criticism?

J: I don't cope with it very well.

M: [laughs] I cope with it poorly.
   [Both laugh.]

M: *"Are you criticizing me?"*

J: [laughs] Yeah.

M: I don't like the tone of that question.

J: Yeah, I know, right? Let's just skip to the next one.

M: [laughs] Uh...

J: No, I think we should leave it.

How do you think gaming will be viewed when your children are your age?

J: So when our children are thirty?

M: Wow.

J: That's fucking *crazy* to think about.

M: Well, I certainly hope they're fuckin' riding around in holographic motorcycles and shit, right? Like *Lawnmower Man.*

J: Right, right. Or reclined, on some kind of *thing.* Plugged in.

M: They need to be in some sort of pod that's filled with some sort of gel. Right?

J: I certainly think that in thirty years' time, that what we think of games...interactive simulations...are going to be a fundamental part of daily life.

M: I think that all movies will be interactive. I don't think there will be anything that is something you just watch passively anymore. I think that if you get a Sherlock Holmes movie you will be Sherlock Holmes.

J: Or at least Watson.

M: [laughs] Yeah, or at least Watson.

J: Maybe when our kids are our age it'll be Watson. It'll get to Holmes eventually.

How is *Penny Arcade* different today from your original vision of the website?

J: Well, our original vision wasn't to have a website.

M: So, that's different.

J: It was just to give someone else a jpeg and then retreat to the shadows.

M: All the stuff that sort of sprung up around it, PAX and Child's Play, I think all of that is different than where I'd ever expected it to go.

J: Why would it? And it wouldn't have without Robert (Penny Arcade's business manager). Those would have remained ideas. And they would have been cool ideas, and maybe we would have posited them and would have achieved some level of formation as community events.

M: But we couldn't have executed them.

J: No, it takes some level of planning intelligence. Robert creates the structures that sustain things like that.

How many times did you come close to just calling it quits, and what made you continue on?

J: I don't know that I ever really came close.

M: Once.

J: When?

M: I remember I called you. I was still living in Spokane and you were here, in Seattle, and I called you because the eFront money had stopped. And I said, "Well, you know, the choice is we either try this donation thing that I just read about or we just quit."

J: Right.

M: And I was pretty close, at that point, to quitting.

J: I guess I didn't think of that. I thought of that as, *Penny Arcade failing as a business entity.* I was more as if I didn't *decide* to quit, and that the decision had been taken from me.

M: Oh, it had just not worked out?

J: Yeah. It had been like the result of an act of God or something. An external force had collapsed it.

M: I see. You weren't quitting.

J: No.

M: The world was quitting you.

J: Exactly. The world was squeezing out the portion that Penny Arcade was contained in.

M: As far as the question is concerned that's the closest we ever came to stopping, I think.

If there is one thing you would have done differently with Penny Arcade, what would it be?

M: It's worked out so good! I wouldn't change *anything.*

J: I would be afraid to retroactively change things at this point.

2005 (November) — Penny Arcade moves out of their building into a larger facility, but it doesn't last long.

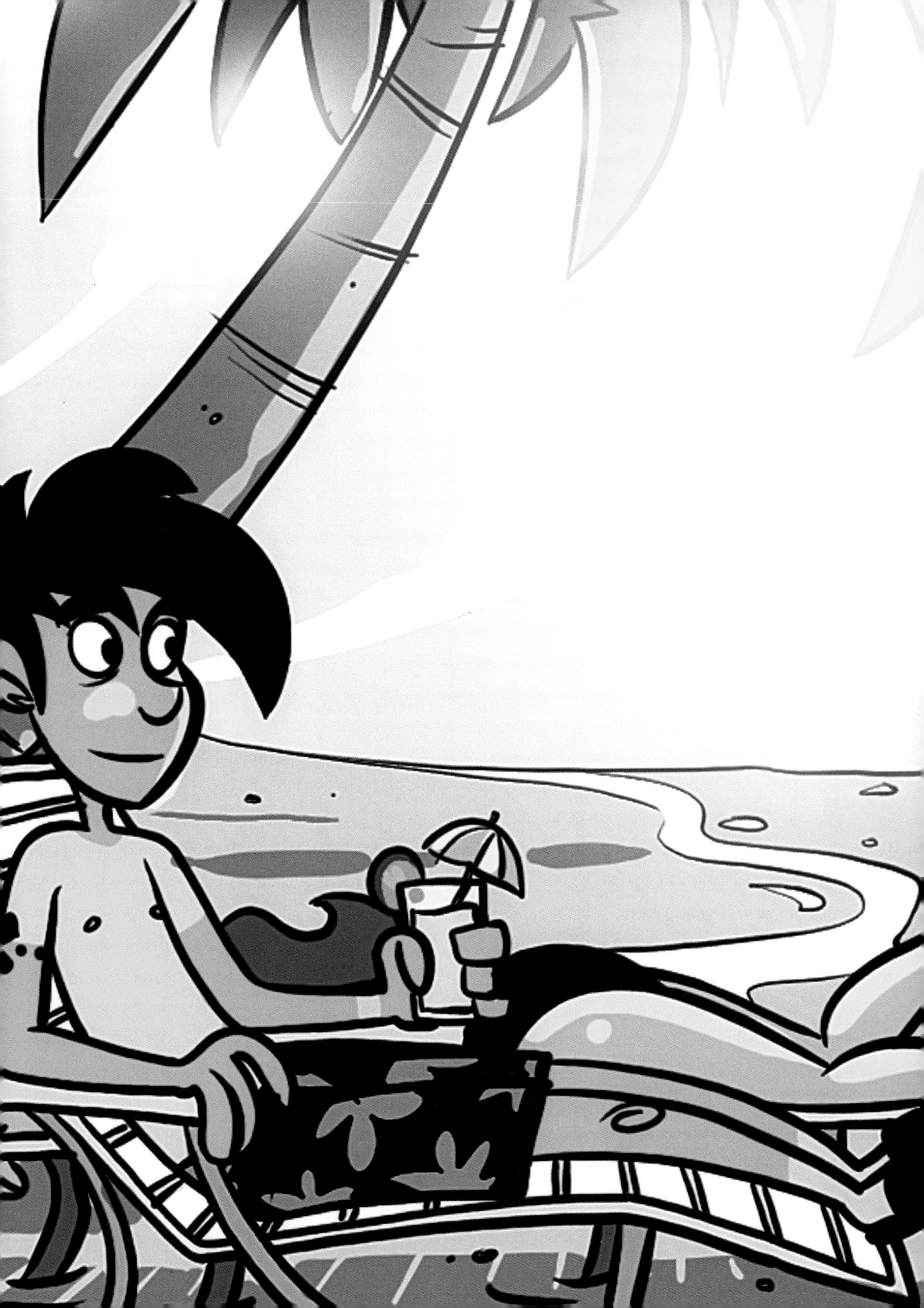

M: Yeah.

J: In general, I think that if we had recognized earlier that we were not—

M: Businesspeople?

J: Businesspeople, yeah. We should have just recognized every time we had to make those calls. Those business calls to do advertising and stuff...

M: Yeah.

J: If we had just recognized that sensation, that tightening of the chest. It was because we weren't those people. If we had recognized that that's what that sensation meant, maybe we would have accelerated the process somewhat. But everything seems to have, more or less, happened at the right time. It may be that PAX becoming what it is largely has E3 to thank. The collapse of the original E3 concept.

M: Yeah right, that was another sort of "right time" sort of moment.

J: The *timing* of these things, in a lot of cases, was correct.

M: Yeah, I wouldn't change a thing.

J: By hook or by crook, by accident it worked.

If you could ask one question of your readers, what would it be?

M: Oooh, that's an interesting one!

J: Yeah it is!

[long pause]

J: I would ask if we had created any language that had been useful to them. I mean, I think of myself as sort of like a tinkerer, right?

M: Yeah.

J: I put together little phrases and things. I just put them out there, and I hope that they use them. My curiosity would be, "Has any of this errant language entered your social circle? Is there anything from *Penny Arcade*, as a language tool, that has been of use?"

M: That was a good one.

J: Well, that's my *only* interest.

M: Yeah. Uh...

J: A/S/L?

M: [laughs] A/S/L. I don't know what I would ask. That question is too much for me.

If you could change one thing about the gaming industry, culture, or gamers, what would it be and why?

M: I would love to change the immaturity of the immature. But they're just young. You can't change that.

J: But you feel like that's a natural force.

M: Every time I look at a Kotaku thread and I see them arguing about the xbots and the gaystation I think, *Wow, that's just... that's too bad that these people are out there—*

J: Existing.

M: But then I think about how I fought the same fight only it was for the Nintendo and the Genesis.

J: Right.

M: *Young people.*

[Both laugh.]

J: The preponderance of youth.

M: Yeah.

J: I think it's officially time to be done with scores.

M: Yeah.

J: I know that this keeps coming up, and I hate to bring that up now, but this is as good a place as any. I think we're done. I think we're done fucking using Fahrenheit to measure *the heat* of a game experience or whatever bullshit. I think that these experiences have graduated beyond that crude metric.

If you could choose one classic '80s or '90s video game to get a modern sequel, what would it be?

M: Hmm!

J: Oooh!

M: MMMM!

J: Yeah!

M: Boy.

J: You know a lot of them *have* gotten sequels. That's the crazy thing.

M: Each time I think of one I think, *No, they did that.*

J: And there's spiritual sequels. Right at the outset I'd say Wasteland, but Fallout's largely considered a spiritual sequel to Wasteland. Man, classic '80s games, huh?

M: Picking one that hasn't been done is the tricky part.

J: Yeah. God, I played a *bunch* of great games in the '90s, too, a bunch of really great—Dungeons and Dragons, back then D&D was the go-to.

M: Yeah, I would have said Panzer Dragoon but they redid that on the Xbox.

J: Orta was *nice.*

M: Orta was nice. Maybe I gotta go back further, like Genesis.

J: Yeah. Vectorman, what do you say?

M: Killer Instinct.

J: There you go, that's what you want.

M: Killer Instinct would be great.

J: I wanna see more D&D beat-'em-ups along the lines of Shadows Over Mystara.

M: Yeah.

J: Capcom style, though—a fresh interpretation of those tropes would just be great.

If you could get somone else to draw/write the strip for you, who would it be and why?

M: Stephen Silver would be awesome to draw it. Or John K. of *Ren and Stimpy* fame.

J: Wow.

M: That would be incredible.

J: That would be nuts. Organic shapes!

M: One of those two guys would probably be my dream... or Tim Biskup! Tim Biskup would be incredible.

J: Oh, is that the style you did for the print?

M: Yeah, he's a painter and sculptor.

J: Let's see.

M: I'd like to see what John Scalzi's *Penny Arcade* would be.

J: I was thinking about that, too. I'd go with either Steven Brust, Neal Stephenson, or Mark Twain. I think [they] would be very cool takes. Mark Twain might be a tough one.

M: Well, if you're going to people who are dead, I'd love to have Mary Blair for *Penny Arcade.*

J: The storybook?

M: Yeah.

2005 (December) — With their publishing rights safely recovered, Penny Arcade publishes *Attack of the Bacon Robots* with Dark Horse books.

TIME LINE

In making your own video game series, did you find yourself making any of the mistakes that you criticized developers for in the past?

M: All the time.

J: Constantly.

M: At every step.

J: At every juncture that ground was treacherous.
[Both laugh.]

J: I'm not sure you can answer it more completely than that.

M: It turns out that people fall into those traps because they're huge fucking traps.

J: They're gigantic.

M: And you don't see them until you're in them.

J: Until you're in the trap. And it turns out there's a trap *inside the trap.*

In the beginning when things where tough, why did you guys keep making the strip?

J: God, that's a great question.

M: I often wondered that myself.

J: I don't know why.

M: You know what was interesting is when Ken was the keynote...

J: Oh, Ken Levine?

M: Yeah, and Ken Levine was backstage at PAX last year and he was talking to us about being a creative person. He said much like himself, we were just too stupid to quit when we should have.

J: Right. You know Scalzi says that, too. Scalzi's wife says that he's the perfect example of a man too stubborn to fail.

M: Yeah, I think that's probably it. So many horrible things happened, and when I look back at them now, I'm like "God, why would we have kept going after *that.*"

J: It's crazy. What's crazy is that sometimes the other things were *so* bad that we actually retreated *into* the production of the comic to escape them.

M: Yeah, that's true.

J: So the comic in some instances was a refuge from how bad those things had gotten.

Is it getting harder to maintain that community feeling as *PA* keeps getting bigger and bigger?

M: Well, we don't see the size of it. I mean that's all imaginary to us.

J: Yeah.

M: Whenever we make a comic or write a newspost we're writing it for one person basically. I don't think of the six million or God knows how many people read it.

J: Yeah, from my part, the community is separate from *Penny Arcade.*

M: Yeah. It happens around the comic.

J: That's right. That's actually not our responsibility. That culture develops organically and it's not something that we police.

Is there anything that you *almost* did that would have forked our time line and resulted in a drastically different *Penny Arcade*?

J: Creating a substrip of *Retails* would have done that.

M: Oh yeah, *Retails* would have done that, definitely.

J: Early on. If when the eFront money had collapsed, and if there had not been two turnkey solutions for donations—which is to say Amazon Honor System and Paypal—if those systems hadn't been readily available...because Amazon had just introduced Honor System.

M: Literally that week almost.

J: It may be that we would have created *Penny Arcade* on the side just as a recreational thing. And *Penny Arcade* may have done well even so. We didn't have kids then, we still had a lot of free time as we've described. It may be that

 2006 (January) — Gameskins.com and designer extraordinaire Kiko Villaseñor get folded into Penny Arcade.

 112

we would have retreated much like we did at the very beginning where *Penny Arcade* would become a refuge from the cares of the world, right?

M: Yeah.

J: And it might have grown well. Robert might still have been enthusiastic about it. There might have been a point where it could have joined back up, but I think that was a very real possibility then.

M: I think you not taking the job at GameSpy, too, was a fork.

J: Yeah, I guess that's true.

M: I think if you had taken that job and we *both* worked at GameSpy, things would have been much different.

J: We would have followed them through that whole thing.

Is writing/drawing comics and playing video games for a living really all it's cracked up to be?

M: Yes.

J: It's nice work if you can get it.

M: Yeah.

J: It is our pleasure to do so.

M: It's as good as you think it would be.

Jerry: You seem like a real music lover. Have your experiences in rock-and-roll shaped your *PA* work?

J: Well, I would say I have done my best at writing *Penny Arcade*, but I think that at some level I consider myself more of a failed musician than a successful writer.

M: [laughs]

J: And I can't stop writing lyrics even though I'm not a lyricist and I'm not composing music. The posts tend to have a really odd—sometimes there's phrases in the posts that have a really odd caste. And that's that sublimated poet trying to poke out.

Twisp or Catsby?

M: Pick one?

J: *Yeah.* Obviously.

M: I like Twisp a lot.

J: Yeah, obviously Twisp. [laughs]

M: Yeah.

J: End of story.

M: I mean, Catsby's the straight man.

J: Exactly. Twisp is the...Twisp is the huge cat, in a suit.

Tycho, what's the best writing you've seen in a game? And by that I mean a game not written by you, of course.

J: The best writing I've seen ever in a game is Planescape: Torment, easily. By a mile. There's so much writing in that game that it seems like philosophical. It was a cool game and you met a lot of interesting people, but it seems like a book, too. I remember the sensation of eye strain, and I was a young man then, but you can get *exhausted* reading the amount of text in that game. There was no filter on it of any kind.

M: What about a modern game?

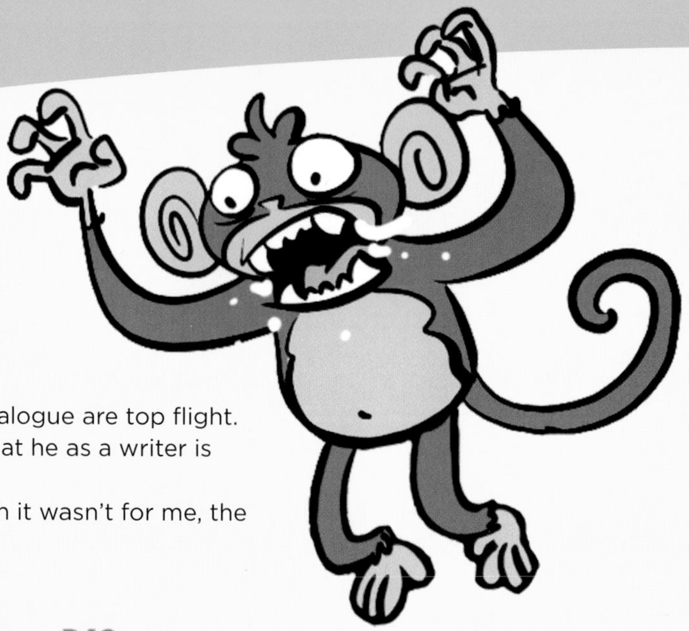

J: Good writing in a modern game? *What are you talking about, Willis?*
M: [laughs] What about BioShock?
J: BioShock. Ken Levine knows his shit.
M: BioShock is pretty great.
J: Exactly. I would say that's correct. His characters and dialogue are top flight. And it's like that in System Shock as well. I would say that he as a writer is great. But Portal was also very good.
M: Portal's hilarious, yeah. Portal probably has, even though it wasn't for me, the best writing I've seen in a long time.

Were there any other projects that failed before *PA*?

J: Absolutely.
M: Oh my gosh, yeah, tons. [laughs]
J: We had...remember we had that *Clan Walrus*...we wanted to make a *Clan Walrus* graphic novel.
M: Yeah, we had that, but we also had Web design.
J: *Walrus Design.*
M: *Walrus Design.*
J: That was yours. That was not me.
M: I guess that's true. No, you helped me with that! You were writing code for it for a little bit.
J: I guess that's true. I did some HTML.
M: You helped me with some tables and stuff. We had *Chickenman* the comic book.
J: *Chickenman,* right.
M: We had the comic book *Sand.*
J: *Scythe.*
M: *Scythe, David and Goliath.*
J: *David and Goliath,* right. *Gen*^{13}.
M: *Gen*^{13} failed. [laughs]
J: No wait, not *Gen*^{13}, it was *G4*!
M: *G4*! But it was basically *Gen*^{13}. God, did we screw anything else up?
J: I think that's it. I think that's all the shit, right? And then we still have projects that we want to do, but don't do.
J: Right.
J: Or because we can't do. *Automata* would have been very cool.
M: *Automata* would have been cool, yeah.

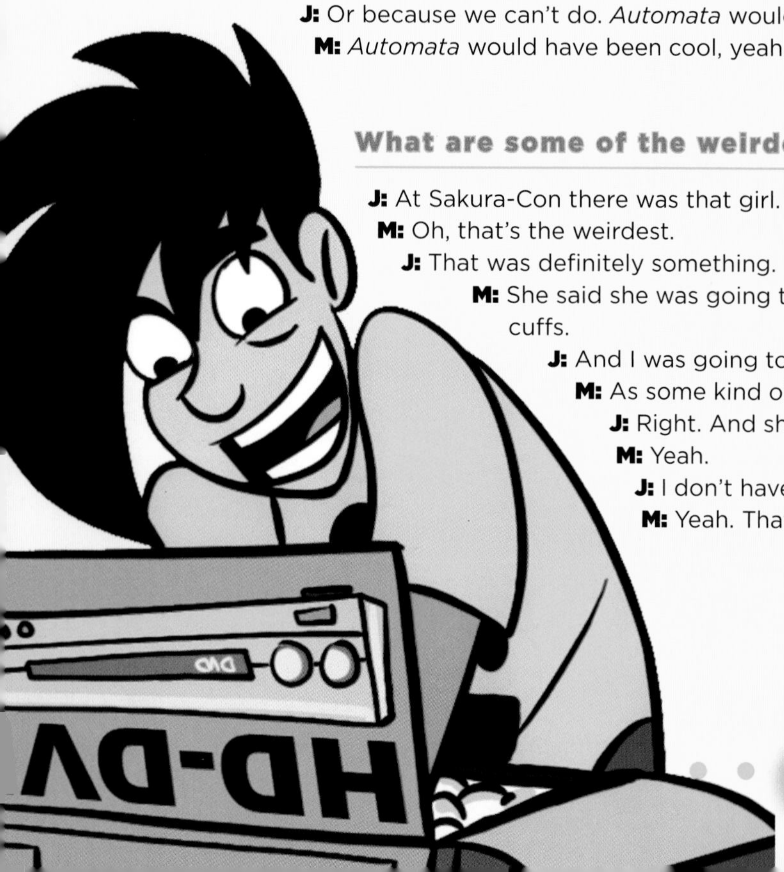

What are some of the weirdest interactions you've had with fans?

J: At Sakura-Con there was that girl.
M: Oh, that's the weirdest.
J: That was definitely something.
M: She said she was going to chain you up in her closet or something? And she had handcuffs.
J: And I was going to live there, in her closet.
M: As some kind of slave.
J: Right. And she claimed to be a transsexual.
M: Yeah.
J: I don't have a problem with that, but that's what she said.
M: Yeah. That was weird.

What did you originally want to be when you grew up?

J: I imagine you're doing something like that.
M: I wanted to be a comic book artist, yeah.
J: I wanted to be an actor. But like the buddy actor. Not the guy who's the focus of the show, but the funny friend.
M: [laughs] Yeah?
J: That was my fantasy. That's more or less come true as well.
M: [laughs]

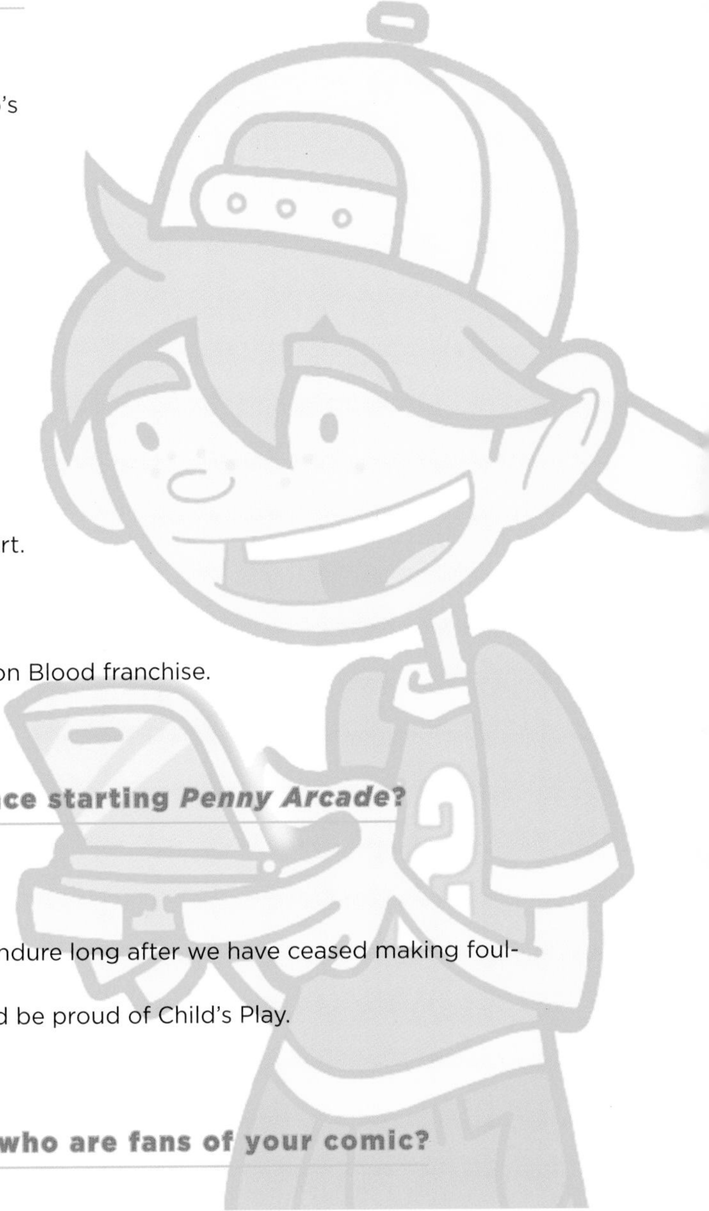

What do Gabe and Tycho do for a living?

J: They don't do anything.
M: Oh, in the comic.
J: Right. I guess maybe they make *Penny Arcade*?
M: Yeah, we've never really been clear about it.
J: That was the idea of *Retails*. It was to investigate what they did.
M: I *think* it's come up a couple times that Tycho does do tech support.
J: I do tech support but I also write bad fantasy novels.
M: You write fiction.
J: Fantasy tie-ins.
M: I think Gabe is independently wealthy off of his Dr. Raven Darktalon Blood franchise.
J: Exactly. So we *have* covered it.

What do you consider your greatest achievement since starting *Penny Arcade*?

M: Child's Play.
J: Oh easily.
M: Yeah.
J: That's the easiest fucking question in the world. Child's Play will endure long after we have ceased making foul-mouthed jpegs.
M: Yeah, when there's no more *Penny Arcade,* I will still look back and be proud of Child's Play.
J: Exactly.

What do you think when you encounter non-gamers who are fans of your comic?

M: I think, *Whaaaaaa?!*
J: If they come or they're there with a friend at a convention and they come up and they're like "I don't even really play games." And I say, "Boogedawaah?"
M: I say, "Really? Then what do you get from it?"
J: Exactly. We always fucking interrogate these people, and what they tend to say is that, if you don't follow games, a lot of that stuff is just like a non sequitur. It just makes it more surreal if you don't understand it.

What do your families think of *Penny Arcade*? Are they involved?

M: They're not involved directly. They're involved in so much, as every human being that we come into contact with is.
J: They're material.
M: They're material.
J: You know my grandma on Brenna's side, Shirley?
M: Grandma Shirley, yeah.
J: We're actually on their link bar on their browser.
M: [laughs]

J: They visit every Monday, Wednesday, and Friday. They probably just shake their heads. Every time I come over she tells me that I don't need to work blue.
M: [laughs]
J: That I'm so much better than that. That Bill Cosby never needed to swear.
M: Yeah, he's pretty awesome. No, my parents are super-proud. I think it really hit my dad at PAX.
J: Yeah?
M: Yeah, he was definitely tearing up.
J: Well, he was probably tearing up because it was such a relief.
M: [laughs]
J: He had watched us fuck this thing up for years.
M: Yeah, that's true.
J: Do you remember the shirt when we were at Moon's Mongolian Grill?
M: We borrowed money to make some shirts.
J: Yeah, and then we made the shirts and they sold really well.
M: They all sold.
J: Exactly, and then he was like, "All right, so did you save some of the money from the shirts to buy more shirts?" And you could hear the fucking "WAH Wah waaaah."
M: [laughs]
J: You could hear like the sad trumpet sound.
M: Yeah, we were a real disappointment for a long time. [laughs]

What is the most rewarding/coolest/most interesting thing that you've ever gotten to do/experience as a result of your work on *Penny Arcade*?

J: I think it's Child's Play.
M: Well, it's rewarding, yeah, definitely Child's Play. But also I'd say the couple times we've gone to teach kids how to make comics has been really rewarding.
J: That's cool, too. That's always fun. I even liked the panel we did at New York Comic Con, even though it was all adults.
M: Yeah.
J: We still taught them as though they were third graders.
M: [laughs] For coolest, I also would say that getting to go see *Saturday Night Live*. The dress rehearsal was cool.
J: That was cool. And also going to Star Trek: The Experience...
M: ...And being treated like a VIP for the whole night.
J: All the different people and all the different characters were fans of the strip and basically gave us the ultimate experience...everybody was totally nailing the Trek vibe.
M: That was pretty cool.
J: We saw Quark's Bar like no one has ever seen Quark's Bar.

What is the greatest story that has happened around "the office"?

M: Wow. So many good things happen here. Exciting tales.
J: Every Friday, Robert buys lunch.
M: We have office lunch, yeah.
J: Family Lunch.
M: Family Lunch.
J: That's *every* Friday.
M: That's every Friday.
J: Let's see...
M: What's a good story that's happened here? The hundred dozen donuts being delivered was pretty crazy. When we did the comic about Sony Online, we said that their new DC

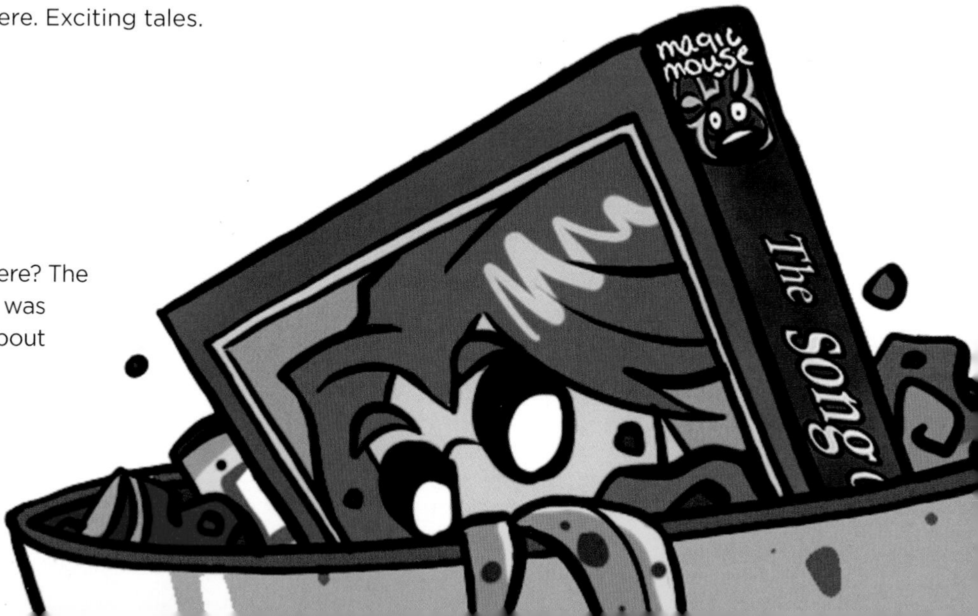
magic mouse
The Song

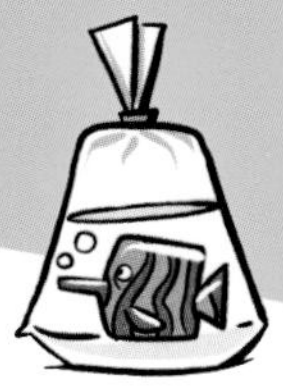

Universe game would be like putting shit in a donut or something like that. And the very next day a Krispy Kreme truck showed up with a hundred dozen donuts, and hauling those things in and finding some way to get rid of them was pretty crazy. We have John Smedley to thank for that.

J: *Sí.*

What one tip would you give to a gamer who is soon to become a dad?

M: Play games now while you still can.
J: Yeah. Absorb them. Because games can actually be absorbed by your liver.
M: Yeah, just play everything you can.
J: Eventually it's not going to be a big deal, and then even further beyond that you'll be able to play games with this creature.
M: Yeah, but for a little while there you won't be doing anything.
J: Except for hosing shit off of yourself.
M: Yeah. And cleaning up puke.
J: In the backyard. And not just regular puke. Spaghetti puke.
M: Yeah.
J: Puke you could never even have fucking imagined before.
M: [laughs]
J: Things get commingled.

What part of game design did you least expect to be difficult?

M: So what was the most difficult thing that we didn't think would be hard?
J: Yeah.
M: A lot of the game design stuff we didn't really do.
J: We didn't manage game design in general, but I would say the biggest thing that was complex for me was that we're sort of spoiled working together.
M: Oh yeah.
J: We sort of understand what the other person is thinking about, and when they phrase it a certain way we more or less understand what they mean and can imagine it in its totality.
M: Yeah.
J: What you find out when you work with large groups of people is that a single or concept means a million different things.
M: That's true.
J: And every person is interpreting it in a different way. So what happens, for instance, is you make a comic. It has three panels. People perceive the passage of time correctly. There's no bugs in that. They know that time goes this way to that way and these are the moments that are being expressed. What happens in a game is that absolutely every item needs to be made exact. And I did not even forsee that. Everything has to be realized. Even small things. None of it. There's no chance in it. It's all a system. And that was a big idea to get my head around.

What was the biggest (most terrifying) leap of faith you took during the formation of Penny Arcade?

J: Yours is probably different from mine.
M: Terrifying leap of faith? Mine would definitely be going into the donation system.
J: Not quitting your job?
M: No, because we had money coming in.
J: I guess it wasn't that weird.
M: I was giving up one paycheck for another one.
J: Yeah.
M: But then when *that one* stopped.

TIME LINE

2006 (March) — "Downloadable Content: The *Penny Arcade* Podcast," a "fly on the wall" recording session of the comic writing process, is launched on iTunes. It ends up being one of the most popular pieces of Penny Arcade content ever.

J: [laughs]

M: And we decided that we would ask our readers to pay us. That was terrifying. I wasn't sure anyone would give us any money.

J: Yeah. It turns out that they will.

M: Yeah, they did for a long time.

J: For me it was definitely moving to Seattle when you were still in Spokane. It was contingent upon my marrying Brenna that we not live in Spokane for the rest of our lives and that we have to move to a big city. Seattle is not a big city in *comparative* terms, but we had to move there. I did not know if that was something that *Penny Arcade* could survive.

M: It would break it, yeah.

J: It was very stressful, but we did manage it.

When you see slash fiction/Rule 34 drawings of you and your characters, is that an honor, a LOL, kind of creepy, or all of the above?

M: What the hell is Rule 34?

J: Let's investigate that. Oh, "Rule 34. If it exists, there is porn of it."

M: Oh, that's funny.

J: I actually think it's kind of awesome.

M: I think it's awesome, yeah.

J: It doesn't bother me at all. And some of it is very tasteful!

M: I am honored that people would like the characters enough to want to see them fuck.

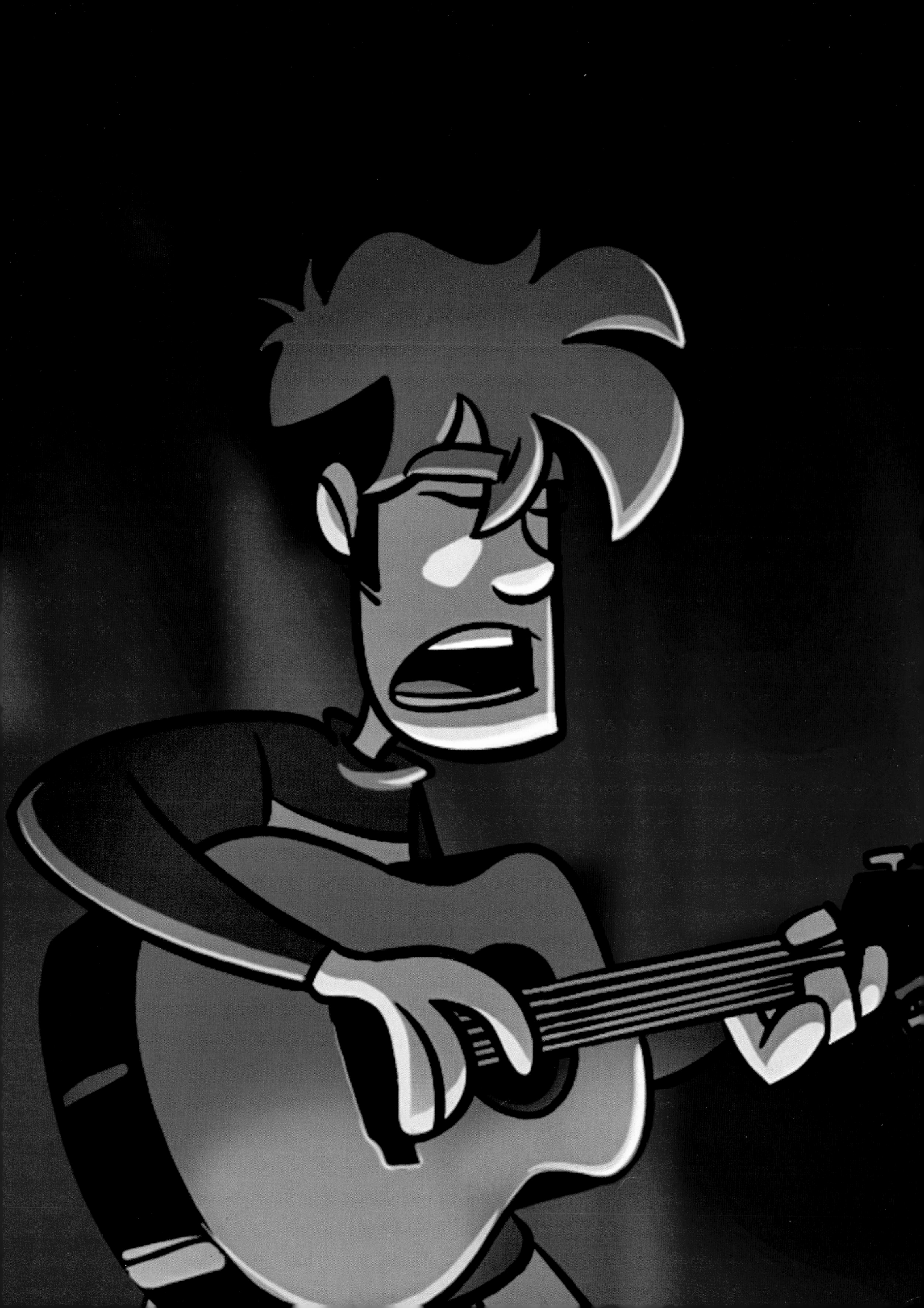

IDLE HANDS

Introduction

It all started when a fan gave us a Play-Doh sculpt of the Fruit Fucker at a convention, but eleven and a half years into this thing, we've amassed an incredible collection. Ranging from apparel, to toys, to *food,* it always seems to be second-string characters in *Penny Arcade* that get the handmade love. What follows is a very limited selection of our treasures.

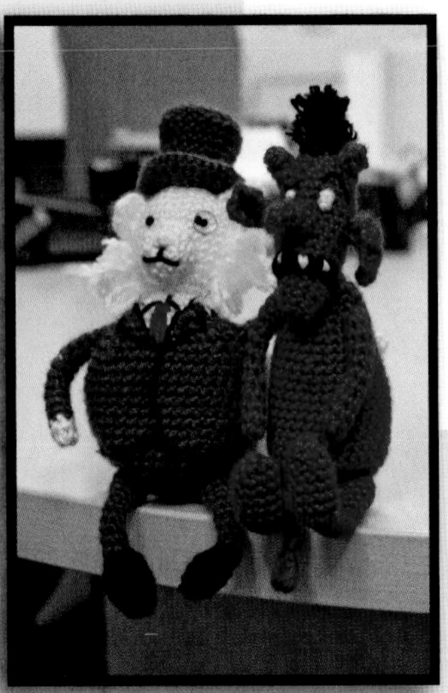

Twisp and Catsby

Hand-delivered during a Q&A session at Seattle-based anime show Sakura-Con, the meticulously constructed cat-and-imp set has always held a special spot in our hearts. Twisp's tiny monocle truly elevates the proceedings.
Materials: Acrylic Yarn, Polyester Batting, Metal
Creator: Aimee Skeers

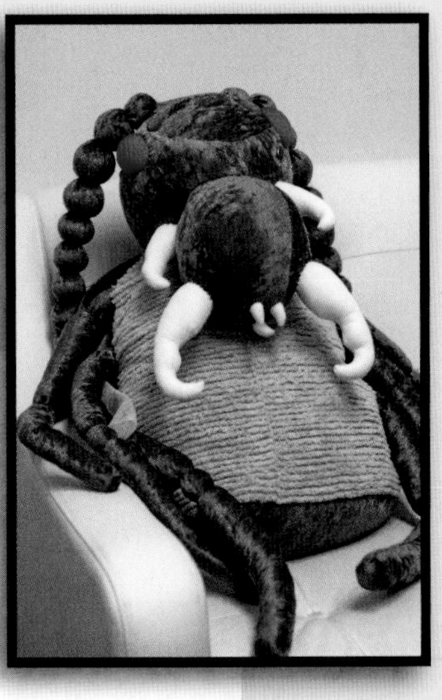

Broodax Plush

That's a full-sized couch he's sitting on, making this a 1:1 re-creation of one of our favorite characters. He clocks in at over fifteen pounds. We assume that a hat, made from Mike's face, is forthcoming. *Materials:* Felt, Cotton, Plastic Gems, Tulle
Creator: Cathy Keeble

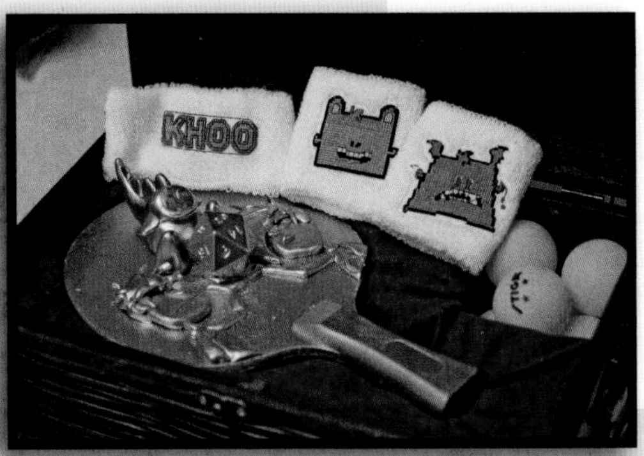
KHOO

Ping-Pong Set

The paddle was the result of the Pink Godzilla (now Pink Gorilla) vs. *Penny Arcade* Ping-Pong match, with the winner taking home this coveted (and custom) golden paddle. The sweatbands and accompanying "table-tennis chest" were a Secret Santa gift from our forums to Robert.
Materials (Paddle): Ping-Pong Paddle, Twenty-Sided Dice, Clay, Gold Paint
Creator (Paddle): Pink Gorilla Games
Materials (Wristbands): Cross-Stitched Wristbands
Creator (Wristbands): Forumer Accualt

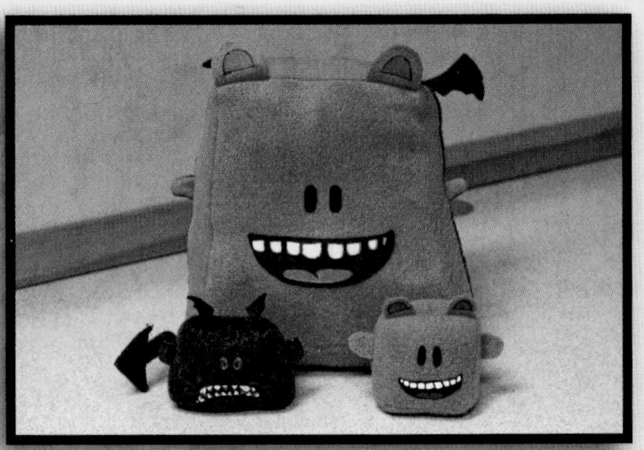

Merch/Fleshreaper with Minis

Another Cathy Keeble classic, the larger plush is actually reversible—a terrifying Fleshreaper waits on the other side. We eventually had no choice but to make a hat based on the same nefarious principle.
Materials: Acrylic Paint, Cotton, Felt, Plastic Gems
Creator: Cathy Keeble

Div and Thomas Kemper

The Thomas Kemper plush is one of our favorites, and the flight goggles just scream *class.* The Div, with its working plug and actual (that is to say *real*) Jack Daniels, guards the entrance to our office.
Materials (Div): Sateen, Acrylic Paint, Cotton, PC Power Cord, Jack Daniels (!)
Materials (Thomas Kemper): Cotton, Yarn, Fuzz, Plastic
Creator: Cathy Keeble

Leviathan

Dr. Raven Darktalon Blood's constant companion, the Leviathan is as adorable as a summoned demon can possibly be. It's hard not to pick him up and make "flap-flap" noises. He must be cuddled constantly, and friends, *we are up to the task.*
Materials: Felt, Cotton, Acrylic Paint, Metal Wire
Creator: Cathy Keeble

Fruit Fucker and Orange

Is the orange wincing? Is that an entry wound? There is no answer from the juicer. Its crocheted stare is alien, and menacing.
Materials: Acrylic Yarn, Cotton Yarn, Polyester Batting, Metal Wire
Creator: Aimee Skeers

Mr. Period (and the Bad Boys of Punctuation)

The characters themselves only seem to exist in the perpetual black-and-white of ancient educational filmstrips, but Cathy reimagined them for today's discerning audiences. Capital Letter seems a little *too* happy. Perhaps disturbingly so.
Materials: Cotton, Felt, Acrylic Paint
Creator: Cathy Keeble

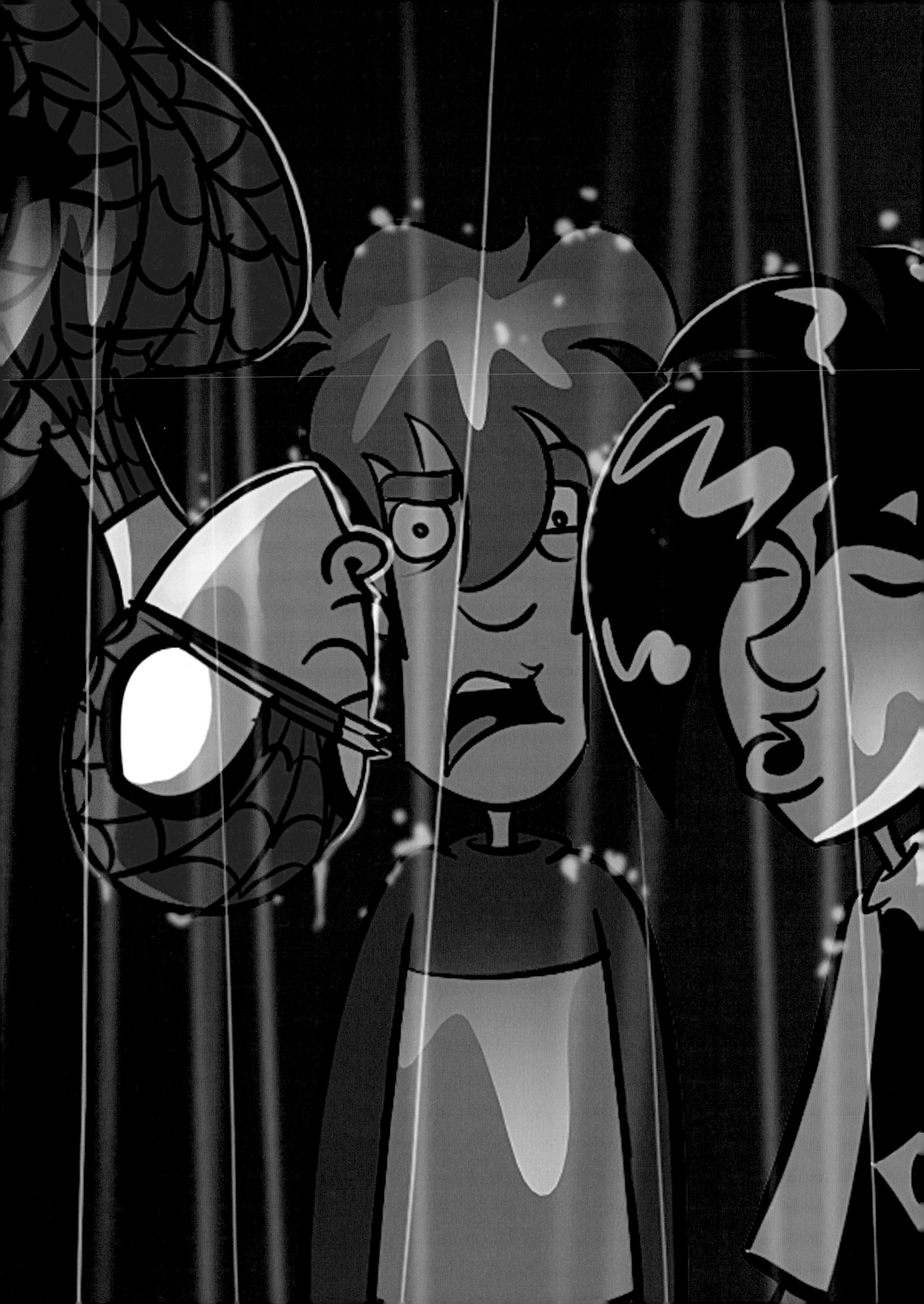

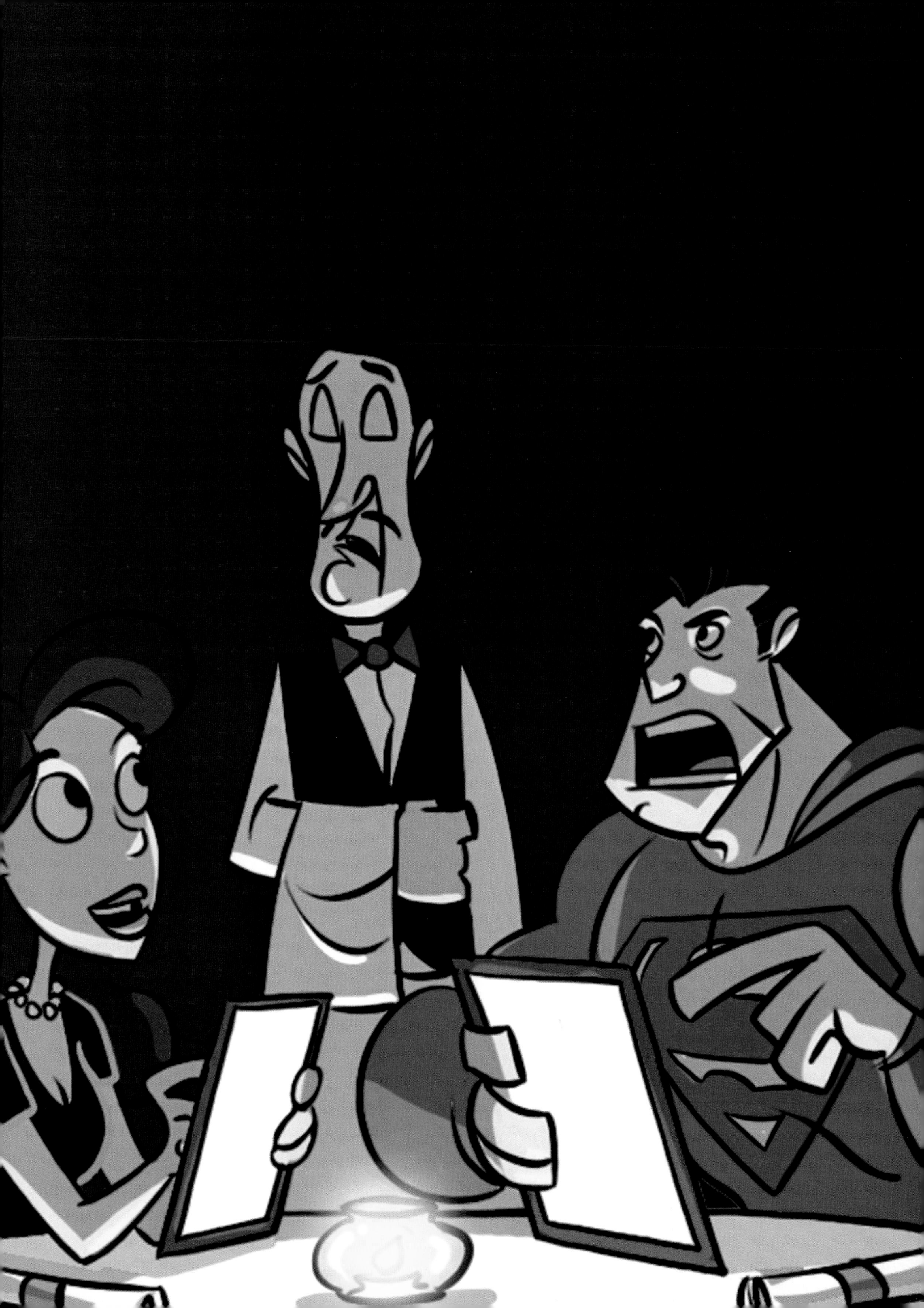

INTERPRETATIONS

Becky Cloonan

Penny Arcade was naturally one of the first comics I came across on the Internet. Not to sound patronizing, but the most striking thing about it was Mike's rapid transformation from a newspaper strip artist into one of the finest cartoonists I've seen. Gabe's clean lines are striking, as are the cartoony and expressive character designs. I struggle to liken his fluid style to anyone else, other than an influence he cited himself, Stephen Silver. I find his work increasingly more emotive and dynamic, with a caricature-like quality comparable to Al Hirschfeld.

Jerry's writing has always kept me coming back, as I considered myself a bit of a gamer. Although I now limit myself to Animal Crossing and Pokémon, his ever-increasing vocabulary and poetic way with words keep me chuckling through the comics even when the game references otherwise fly over my head.

Erika Moen

Penny Arcade is flat-out one of the most amazing, witty things ever created. What I like about it most is that, though the comic is generally addressed to gamers, it doesn't just stay there, but goes beyond it—to what everyday life is. That is what makes it fun and addictive to read. When I first heard about it, I wasn't sure whether it would appeal to me or not (since I don't consider myself much of a gamer), but as I began reading the comics I just couldn't stop. You can identify with so many of the situations or, if not, I'm sure you know someone who could! I know that today *PA* is more than just a comic but, thanks to what? To a pair of creative minds with a passion for games and good humor, and to those three panels drawn back in '98—that's the pillar where everything it is today stands on. I'm glad Mike and Jerry have never forgotten that and still delight us with constant updates. Thank you for making our lives a little more interesting by giving us something to look forward to every day!

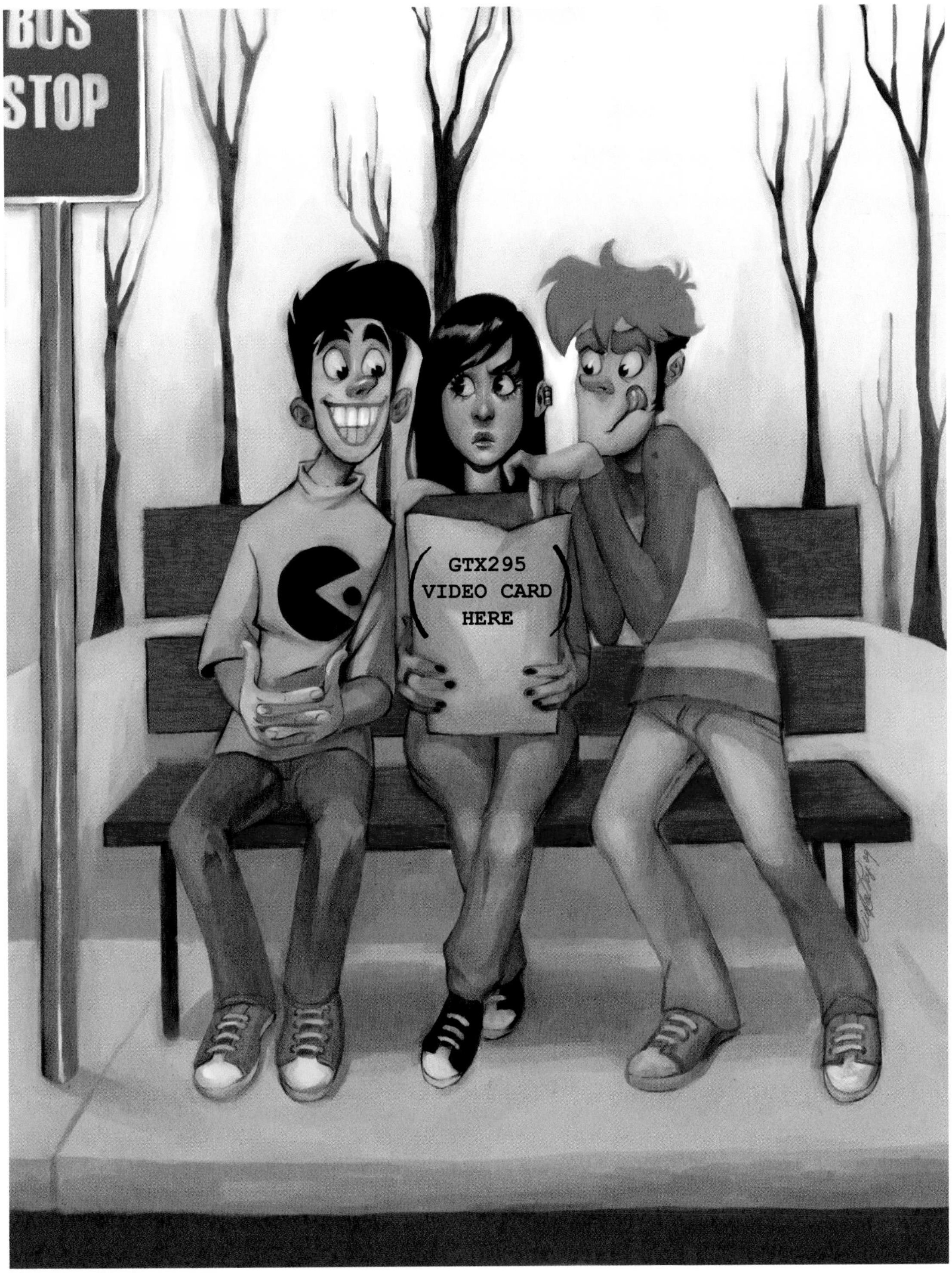
BUS
STOP
GTX295
VIDEO CARD
HERE

Kazu Kibuishi

When I first started reading webcomics, I followed quite a few strips, but I lost interest in most of them over time. Or it was the artists who lost interest in their own work and the comics faded away. *Penny Arcade*, however, has remained a staple part of my Web reading diet, and I still go back to it on a regular basis. For most of my life, I've been influenced by video games, so perhaps I was destined to be a regular reader. But I think the real reason I come back to the site is because I like its creators, Mike and Jerry, not because they produce the best regularly serialized comic on the Web (they do), or because they're funny as hell (they are), but because they're not afraid to tell it like it is, regardless of what others think of their opinion. It's a rare trait among people and a fine gift to their readers. Combine that with their professional attitude, commitment to their community, uncommon generosity, and Robert Khoo, and what you have there is a finely tuned machine designed to make legions of people happy. I'm looking forward to seeing where this happy machine goes in the future. Congrats on an amazing ten years, guys!

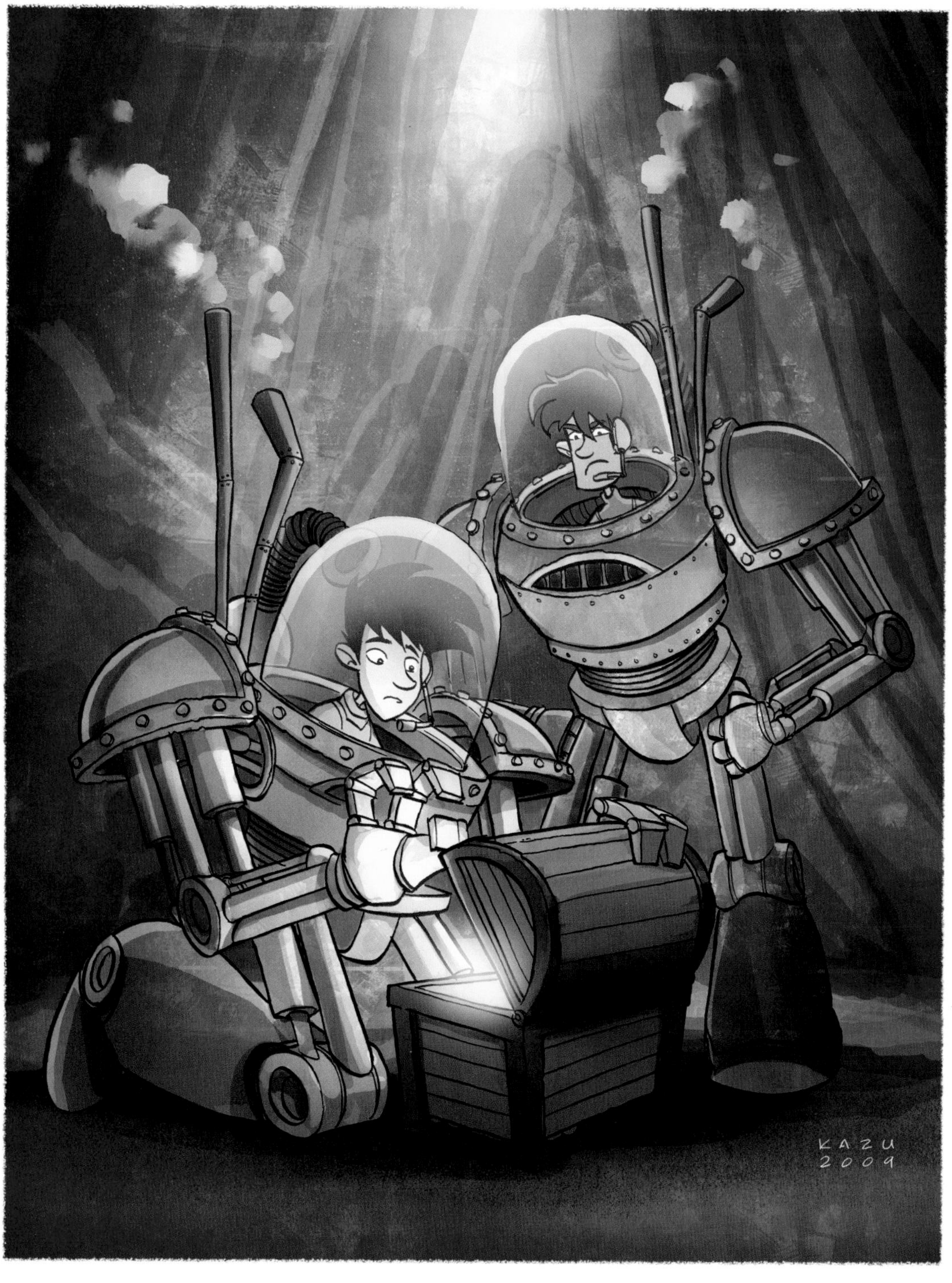
KAZU
2009

Woody (gfball84887)

This is a pixel interpretation of Mike's character the Cardboard Tube Samurai. I've used a couple of modified NES textures, the ledge and the tree, but everything else has come from observing the comic and placing pixels until they looked right. I love this style, as it leaves much to the imagination. I suppose that might be the cause of my infatuation with NES and SNES games.

It was less than two years ago that I was pointed in the direction of *Penny Arcade*. I began reading these comics and commentaries on the gaming scene and soon found myself at home more than I had ever in the past with such media. So articulate, poignant, vitriolic, and well illustrated were the authors ideas and points that I soon found that *Penny Arcade* was part of my daily browsing. Before long, I had scoured all their archived comics and was left waiting with bated breath for new ones to arrive.

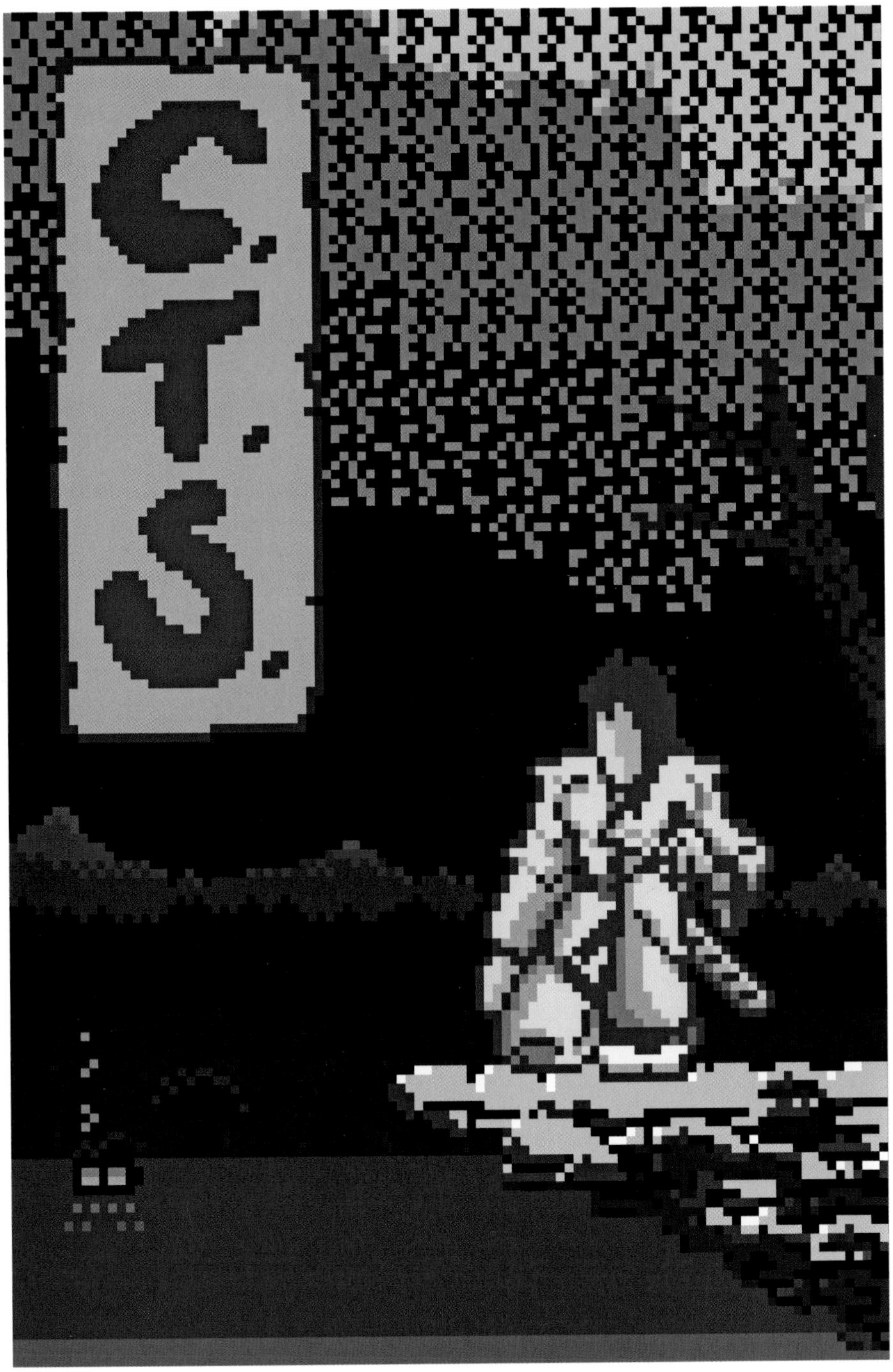
C.T.S.

I must profess my appreciation and admiration for Mike in regard to developing his artistic style. If you go back to the beginning of the comic and read through, you'll see the progression from a simplistic, sharp style to a very smooth, rich, and natural one. Only with years of practice and passion for the art can one achieve such a thing. To not give up. To constantly improve upon.

To care for one's art as if it were a developing organism. These are the elements of his efforts and pursuits that I try to take and apply to myself, so I might achieve something as personally rewarding.

What Mike is artistically, Tycho is in a literary sense. I know of few writers who would have me visiting Dictionary.com with more frequency. I imagine him sitting at his desk, writing updates with a dusty old book filled with archaic and arcane words to implement as land mines for those with unkempt vocabularies. I also enjoy his slights to those who would make accusations and ridiculous assumptions regarding the gaming world (*cough* Jack Thompson). Not to mention that his screen name, Tycho, is a reference to a five-hundred-year-old astronomer and alchemist. I suppose if more people put as much care into their callsigns then I wouldn't find myself being saddened by being one-shotted in Unreal Tournament by YOuRmUM6969 and his ilk.

I take my hat (well, if I'd bothered to buy a hat anyway) off to everyone at Penny Arcade in their efforts with Child's Play and with PAX. It must be one hell of a burden and one unmitigated sense of accomplishment.

Bill Amend

Born of equal parts caffeine-fueled, late-night, devil-dealing deadline panic and affection, our tribute cartoon to *Penny Arcade* may be viewed here. We are told Jason Fox was most excited by the opportunity to co-mingle—nay, *fuse*—with two webcomics legends—*demigods,* if you will. What results is a hybrid of sorts, a *chimera,* and though it strays from the familiar mythology, we hope you will deem it worthy.

Our appreciation of Mike and Jerry's work stretches back to the dawn of the millennium, when the molten art of web-comics was still being forged. To say that this appreciation has grown since is akin to saying that a final-stage Katamari has grown, that is, too insufficient. Too *mere.* As something short of hard-core gamers—though our/played extends back to the original Pong—it is true that much of *PA*'s *oeuvre* transcends our capacity for full understanding, yet strangely, like Pippin and the Palantir, our gaze cannot be averted. We are helplessly transfixed. Thrice each week we are its captives, and we are grateful. Oh, yes, so very, very grateful.

Though we suspect it will take greater minds than ours to divine the true and presumably dark source of this comic's hold over us, a few clues do exist. The artwork has evolved these past ten years at superhuman speed, into something truly magical to behold. The writing is filled with a potent mix of irreverence and confidence that one would accurately describe as downright *testicular.* And the entrepreneurial acumen that has transformed this enterprise from *aspirational* to *dominant,* offers lessons and hope to those of us in similar endeavors. Job well done, gentlemen. Well done, *indeed.*

(FT)BA out.

PennyTrot
by Bill Amend
PREPARE TO BATTLE THE CARDBOARD TUBE SAMURAI!
PREPARE TO BATTLE THE CARDBOARD TUBE JEDI!
A TOILET PAPER TUBE? THAT'S PRETTY LAME.
IT'S MY LIGHT SABER. I JUST HAVE IT SWITCHED OFF.
AMEND
IT'S PROBABLY WORTH MENTIONING THAT I'M REALLY GOOD AT SCIENCE.
HERE. YOU FIGHT HIM.
(CLICK) FZSHHHHHH!

Scott Kurtz

I wanted to show Gabe and Tycho in a quiet moment, checking in on their boys. It's hard for me to read the comic without thinking of Gabe and Tycho as Mike and Jerry. It's like that old Warner Bros cartoon with the sheepdog and the coyote. All this crazy shit goes down during work hours. Then the whistle blows at 5 PM and everything stops down. They punch out, say good night, and turn into these quiet family men who love their wives and kids. That's *Penny Arcade*'s dirtiest secret: Gabe and Tycho are secretly pretty wholesome.

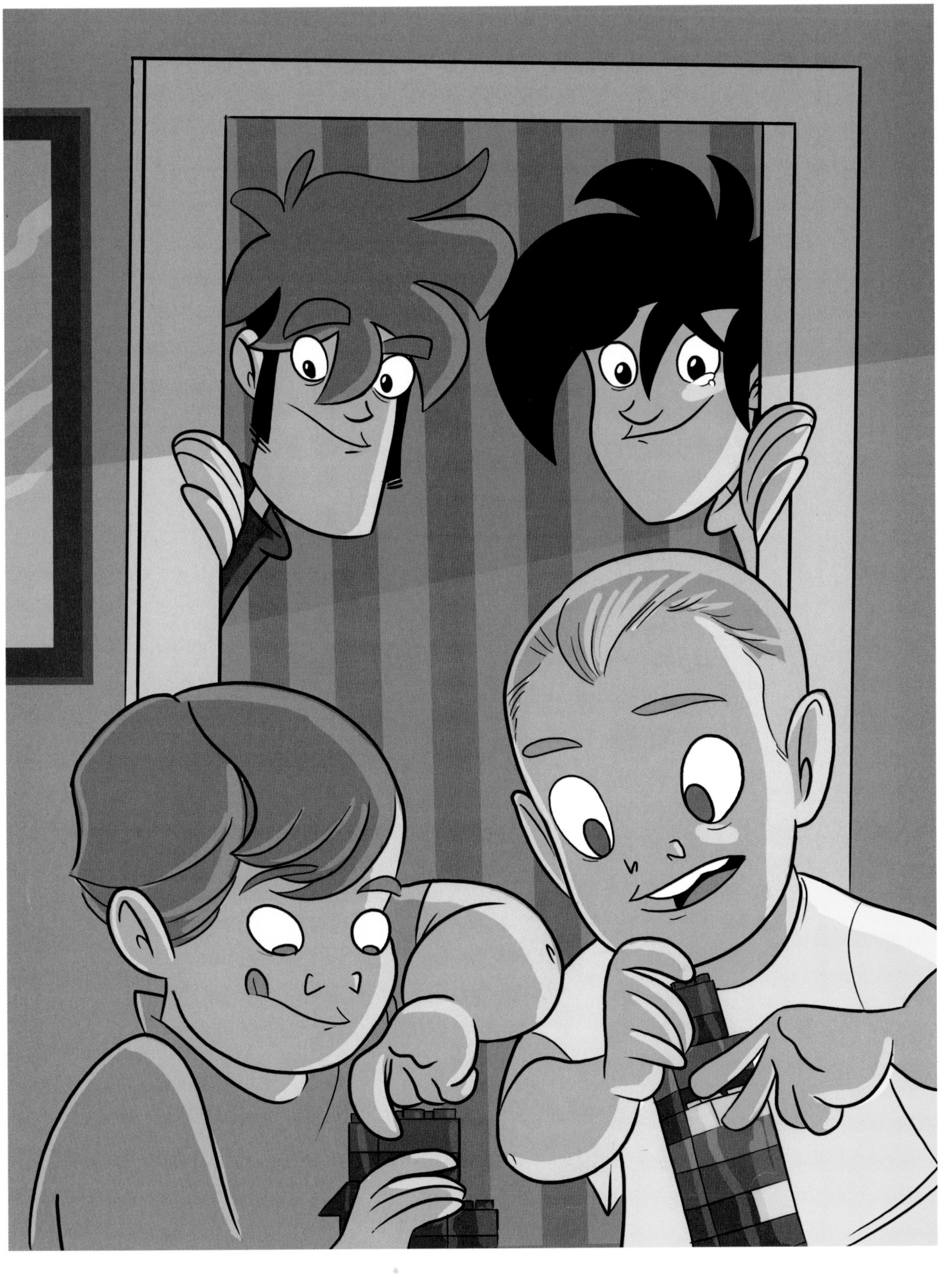

Dirk Erik Schulz

I'm always sad to notice I live under a rock, as I've actually never been a very avid webcomic reader. But when the guys from *Penny Arcade* asked me for an illustration, I was amazed and immediately took a journey through the archives. The development in the style, inside jokes, and characters was a pleasure to witness, so congrats for the fun and success you guys are having. Good luck with the next ten years!

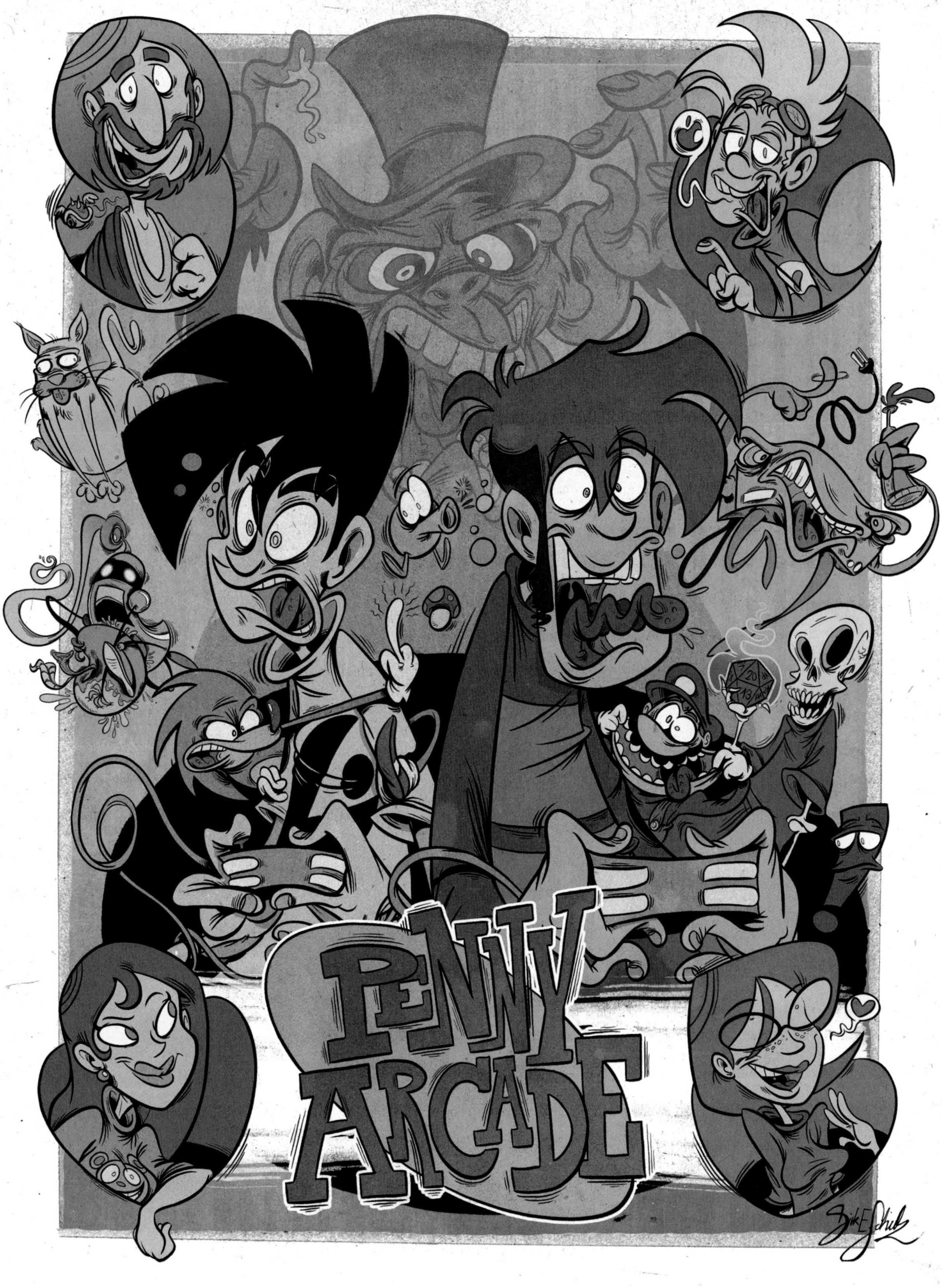
PENNY
ARCADE

Stephen Silver

All I can say is that I love these guys! Not only is the content of the comic great, but I have always been a supporter of doing things independently. It is great to see how fast *Penny Arcade* has grown over the years and watch it breaking new boundaries. In an era when we are starting to see the newspapers fold and comic strips fade away, *Penny Arcade* is innovative, catering to the new generation of comic strip readers. What can I say? I LOVE IT.

Stephen Silver
www.silvertoons.com

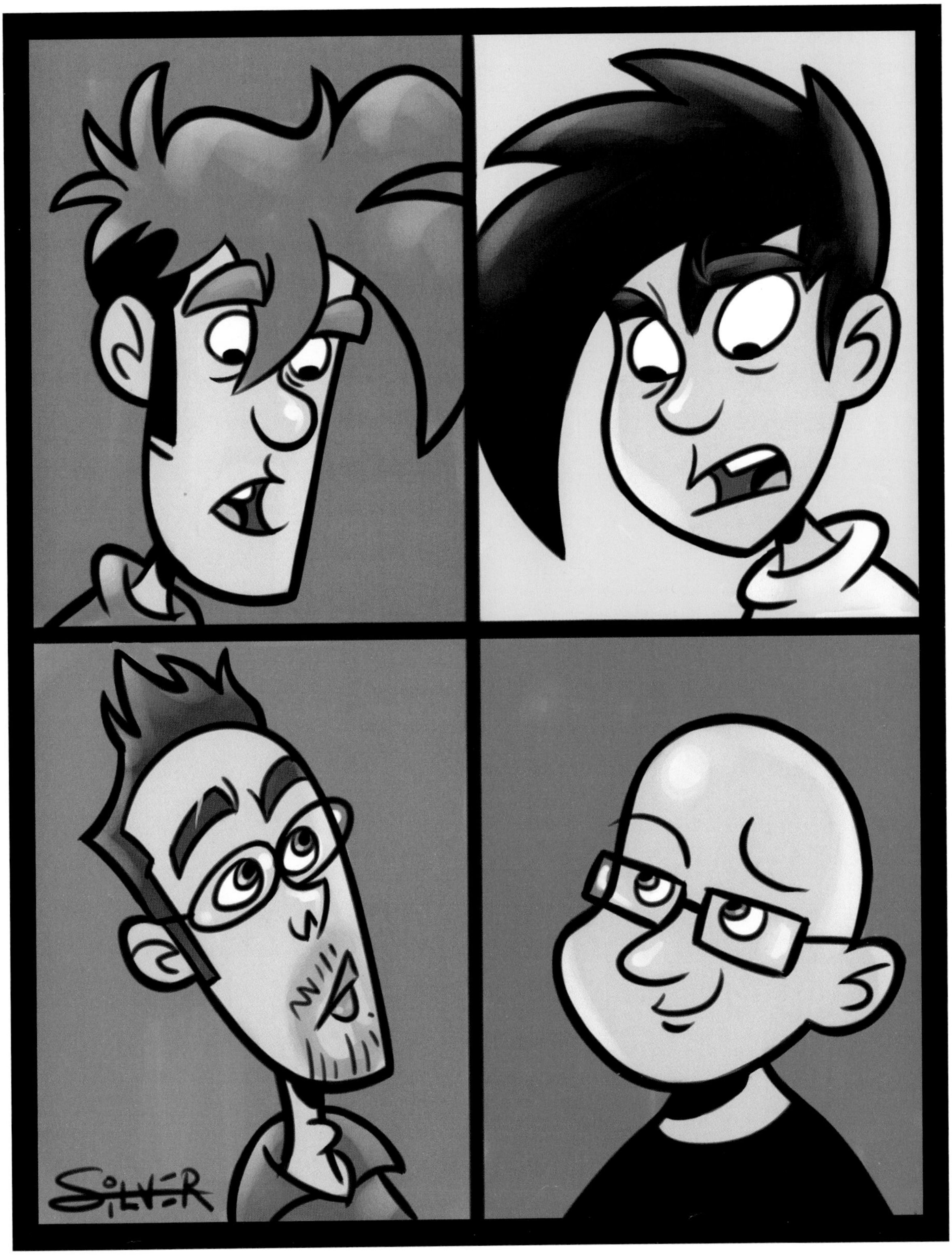
SILVER

Samwise

Some days it is a struggle to roll in to work at the crack of 9:30 or 10 AM, rope-swing across our new lava moat security system, and continue to make game after awesome game. Mouse fingers get cramps, and eating the same steak-and-lobster breakfast burritos from our on-campus cafeteria every morning can really wear down the spirit over the years. Your comics help me through this burden. So, dear readers, please raise a tankard or the hollowed-out drinking skull of your enemy to Gabe and Tycho (or whatever the hell your real names are). Thank you so very much for devoting all these years to making my mornings a bit more bearable. And remember one last thing:
FOR THE FRIGGIN' HORDE YOU ALLIANCE PUKES!!!

Love, Sammy

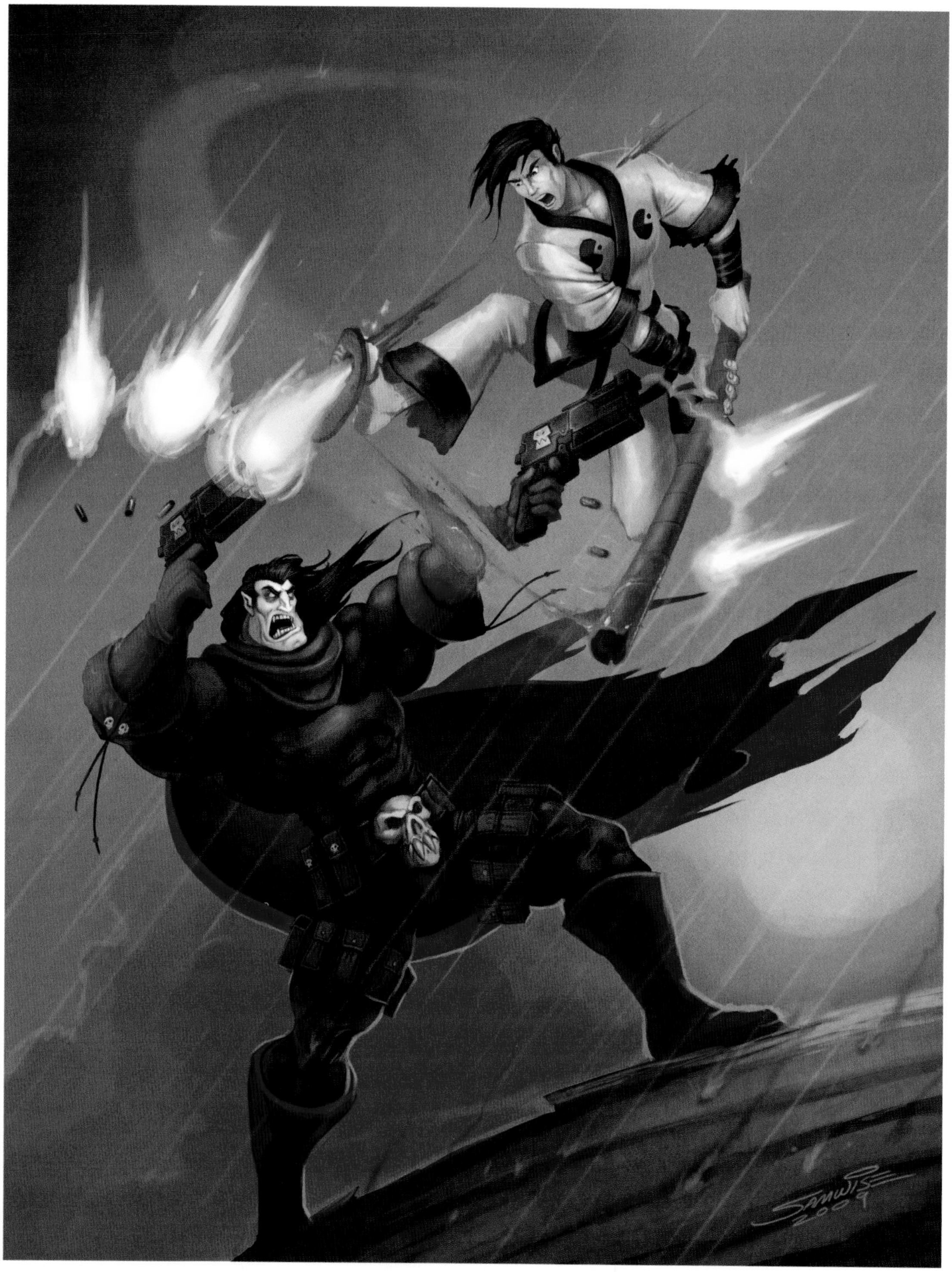
SAMWISE
2009

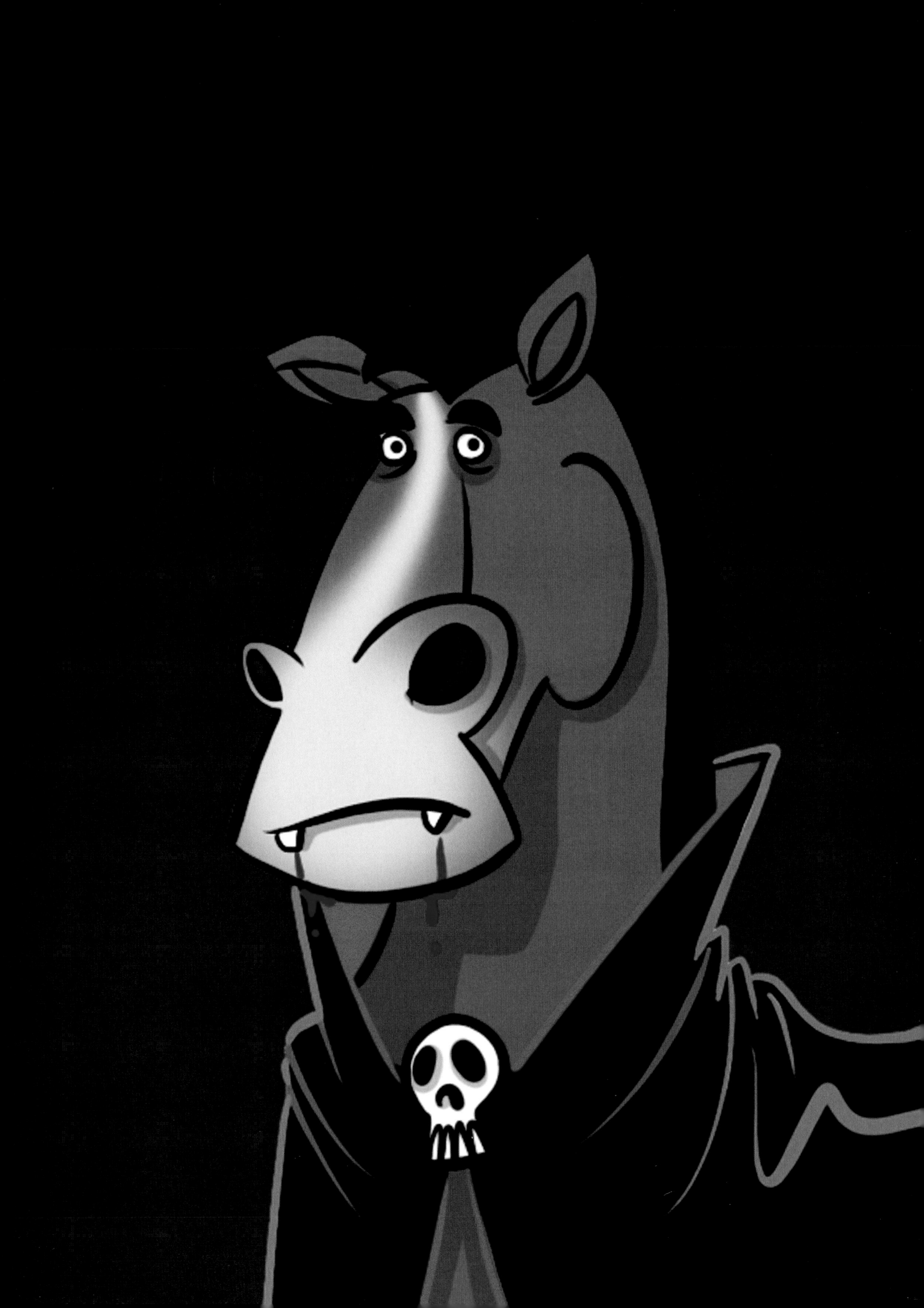

WE LIKE THESE COMICS

Thank you, Lord, for this Requiem: Avenging Angel demo we are about to receive.
Amen.
BLIP!
Was it good for you?
Now I know how my girlfriend feels.

Requiem: AA Strip

This was a really funny comic.

You haven't moved an inch since I left! What the hell have you been doing?
I'm waiting for this Sin level to load.
I've had time to harness my latent pscyhic ability.
Really?
I also knit you this sweater.

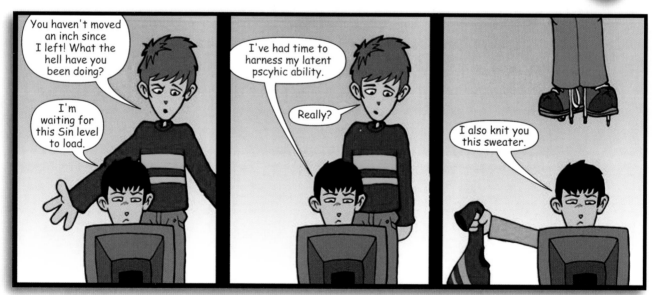

The Sin of Long Load Times

Although not *technically* the first *Penny Arcade* comic, it's close enough.

We had done a few other test comics as entries for a contest. Some of them were "high-concept," which is a nice way of saying "unintelligible." Even so, this was the first strip we made with full knowledge of what it meant: that we were committing to the creation, every week, of work we were going to put in front of people. We were eating dinner when we wrote it, which was difficult because the enormity of this concept was making me physically ill.

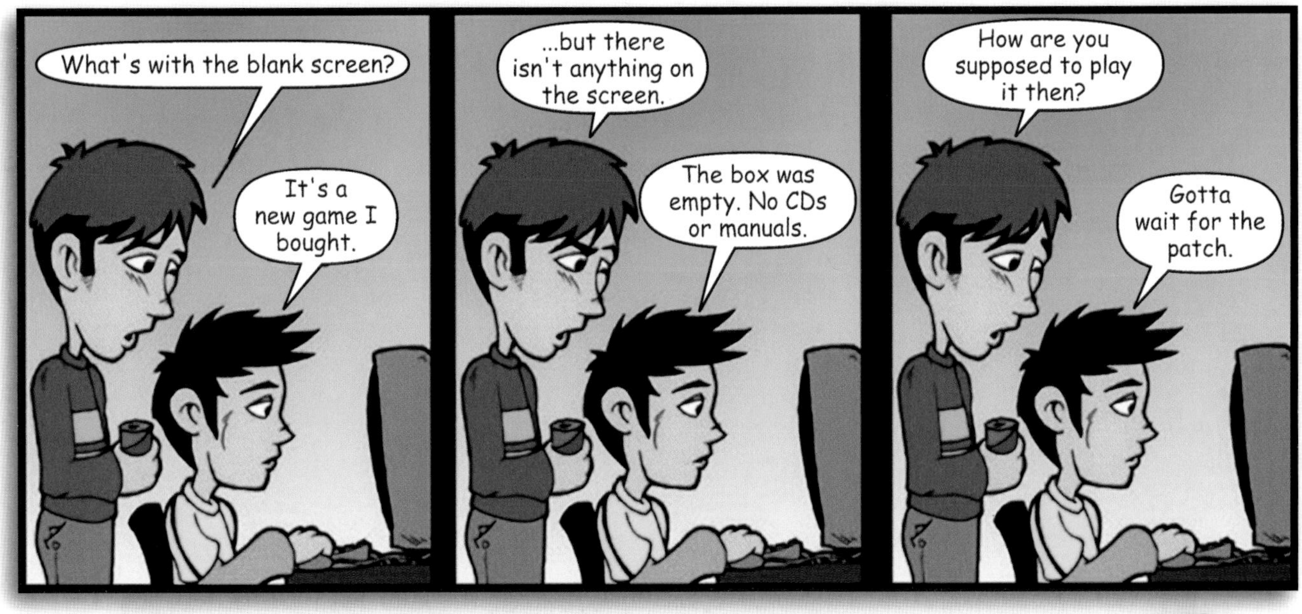
What's with the blank screen?
It's a new game I bought.
...but there isn't anything on the screen.
The box was empty. No CDs or manuals.
How are you supposed to play it then?
Gotta wait for the patch.

The Patch Parade

I like this one a lot.

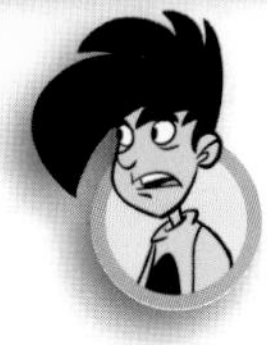

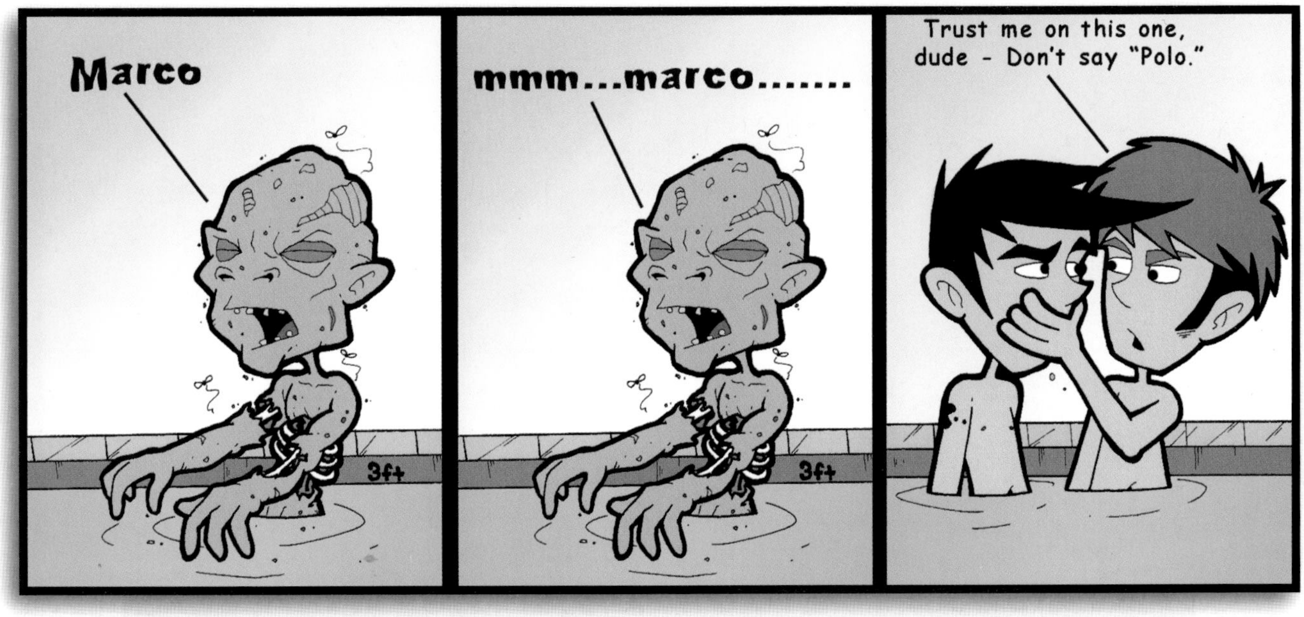
Marco
mmm...marco.......
Trust me on this one, dude - Don't say "Polo."

Don't Say It

Absolutely, zombies are a huge draw. No question. But back then I can remember a lot of hand-wringing about a strip like this because it had no explicit connection to gaming. We weren't as comfortable, then, using the site as a general creative platform. That sensation is less intense now, but I'm not sure it will ever be completely gone.

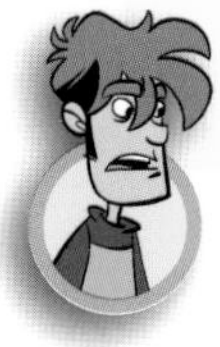

TIME LINE **2006 (August) —** The Annual *Penny Arcade* Scholarship is announced, awarding a ten-thousand-dollar grant to one student every year.

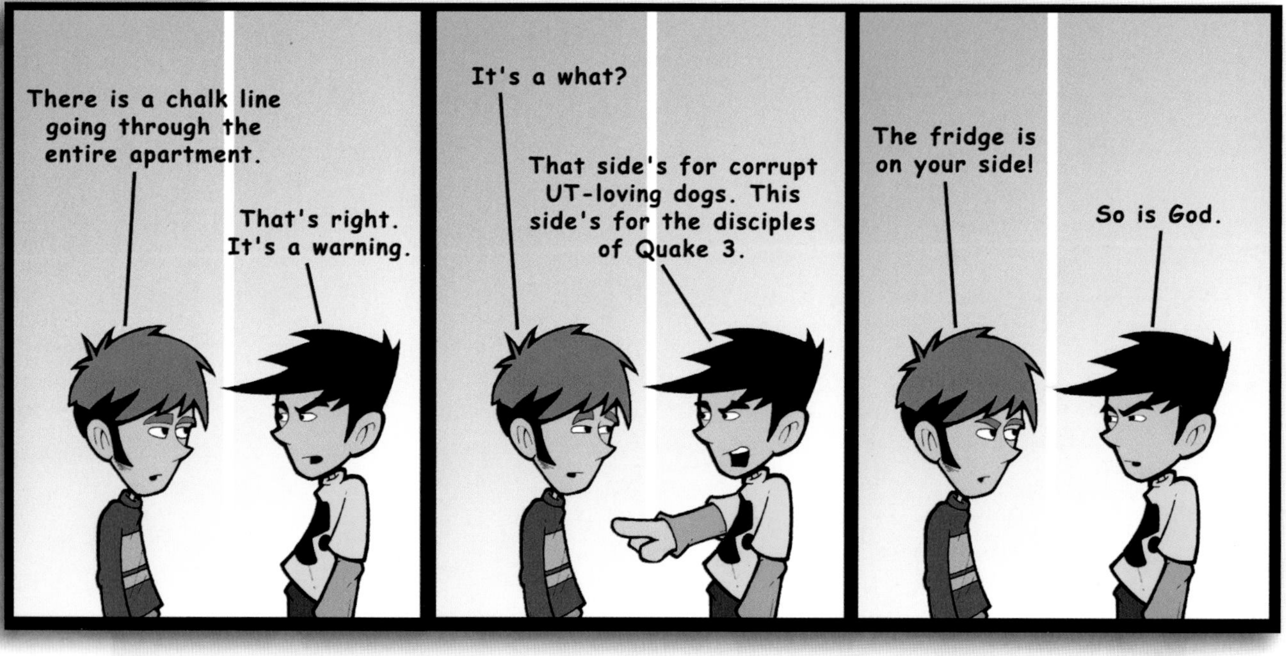
There is a chalk line going through the entire apartment.
That's right. It's a warning.
It's a what?
That side's for corrupt UT-loving dogs. This side's for the disciples of Quake 3.
The fridge is on your side!
So is God.

Infidels

Another funny one.

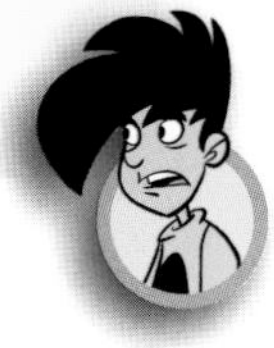

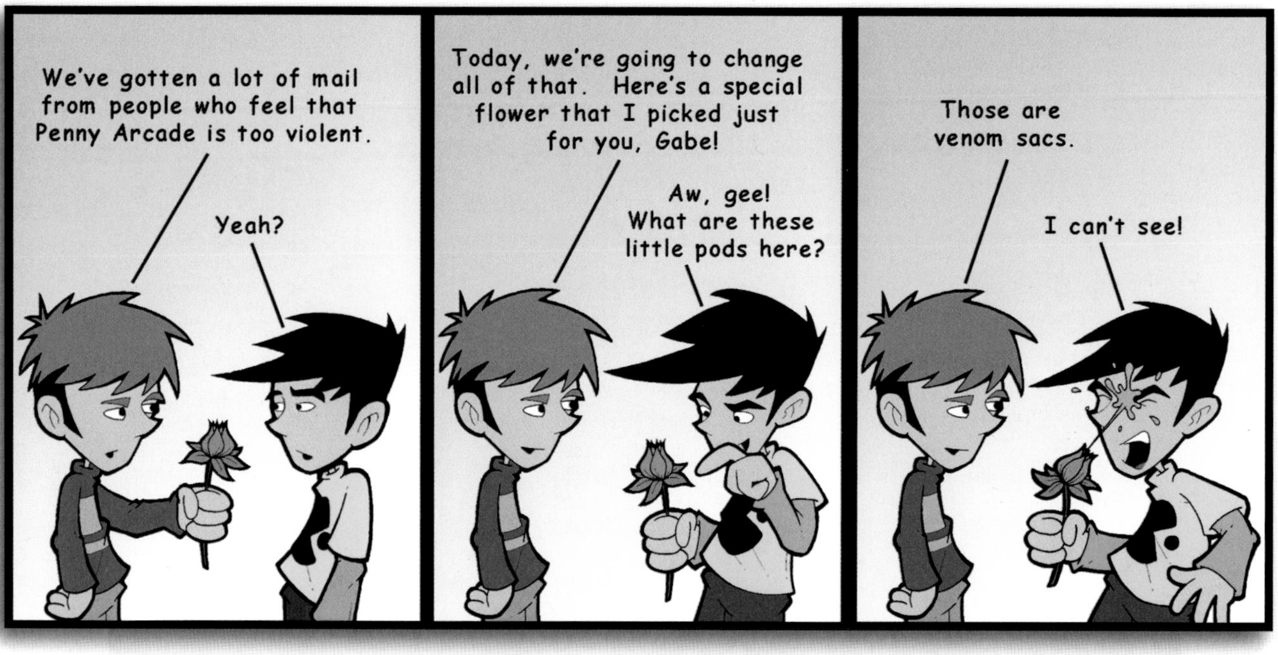
We've gotten a lot of mail from people who feel that Penny Arcade is too violent.
Yeah?
Today, we're going to change all of that. Here's a special flower that I picked just for you, Gabe!
Aw, gee! What are these little pods here?
Those are venom sacs.
I can't see!

He Loves Me Not

It's hard to imagine, but something we thought was the site's greatest virtue—horrendous acts of cartoon violence—was deeply offensive to people, even though we'd always done it that way and are *physically incapable* of kindness. We've always cultivated a mildly adversarial relationship with our readers, and this is a product in that vein.

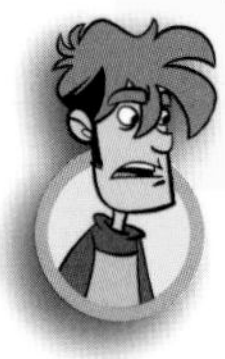

TIME LINE

2006 (October) — Too many people are running amok in the office and PAX is growing too fast. A wall is crushed through with a sledgehammer into the neighboring unit, which happens to be a residential apartment. Penny Arcade, Inc. gains a stove, an oven, and a laundry machine.

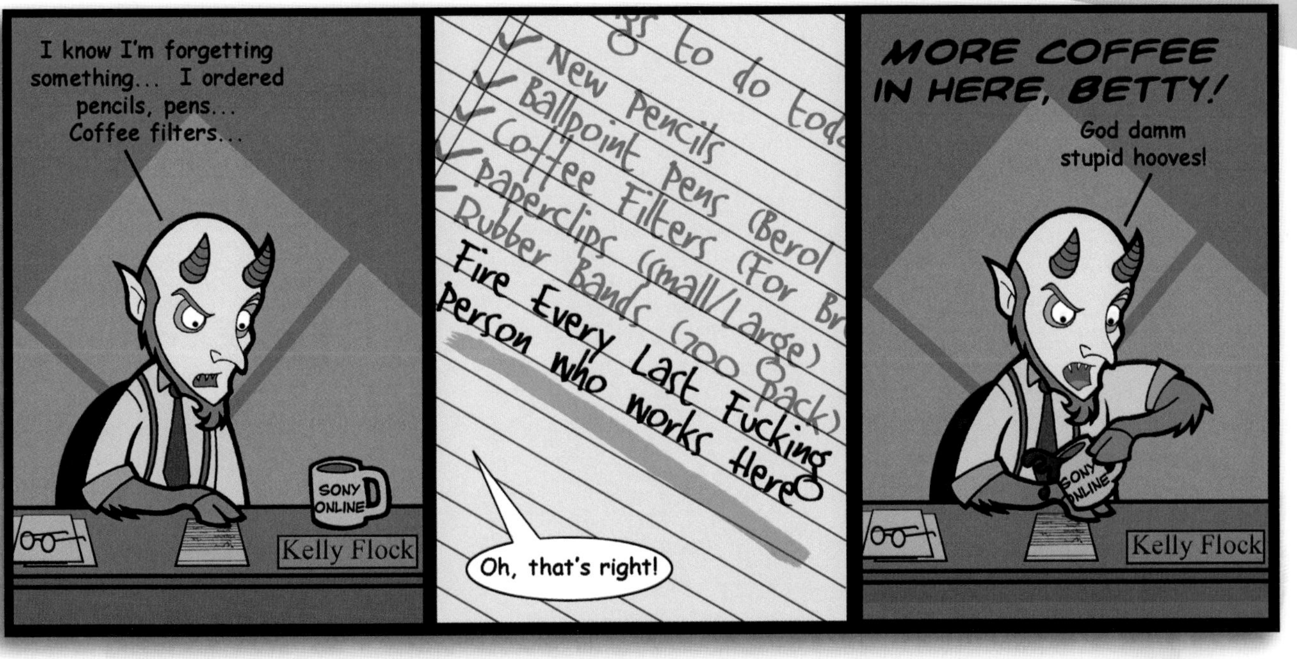
I know I'm forgetting something... I ordered pencils, pens... Coffee filters...
New Pencils
Ballpoint Pens (Berol
Coffee Filters (For Br
paperclips (small/Large)
Rubber Bands (700 Pack)
Fire Every Last Fucking Person who works Here
Oh, that's right!
MORE COFFEE IN HERE, BETTY!
God damm stupid hooves!
SONY ONLINE
Kelly Flock

Betty, Fetch My Pitchfork

Haha, those hooves crack me up.

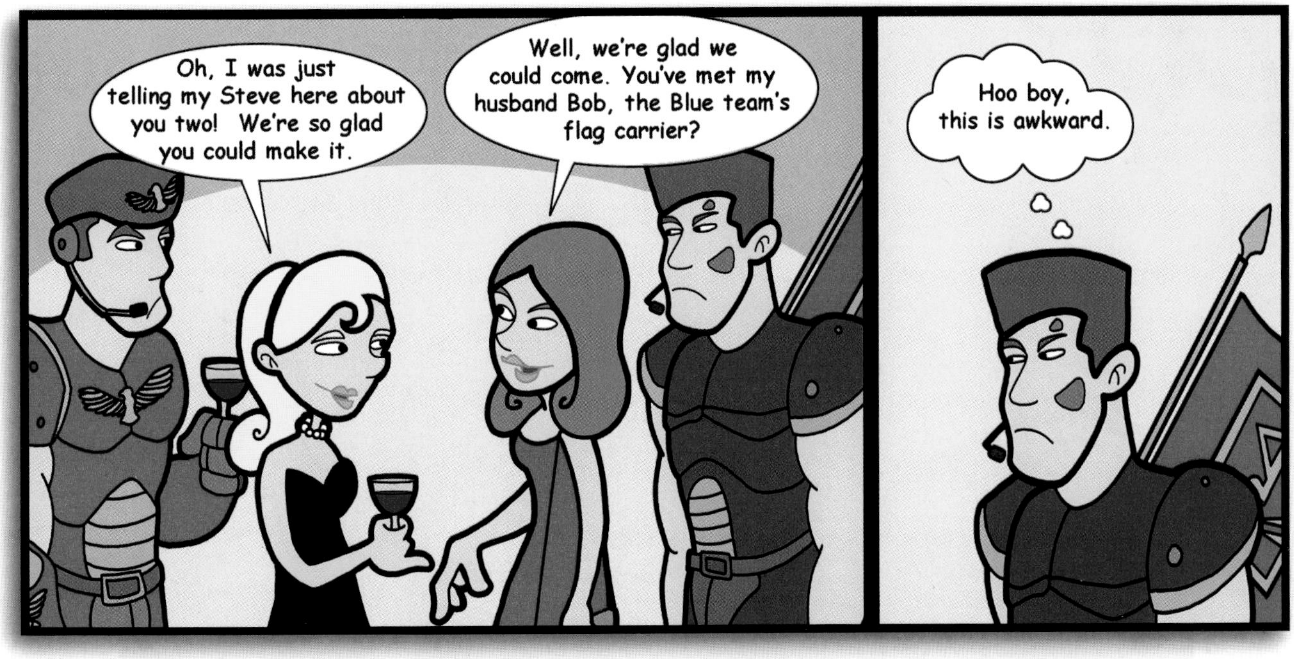
Oh, I was just telling my Steve here about you two! We're so glad you could make it.
Well, we're glad we could come. You've met my husband Bob, the Blue team's flag carrier?
Hoo boy, this is awkward.

Red and Blue In: The Party

A concept I'm convinced still has legs, several of them, several *very long legs,* the war between these colors is something I want to plumb with a blend of determination and extremely sensitive equipment. I'm not sure we could get away with it, though. I think this concept is pretty well owned by Rooster Teeth now.

TIME LINE

2007 (February) — Penny Arcade issues a challenge to the world with the Official Game Industry Ping-Pong League. Team Inferno finds that winning a match is difficult.

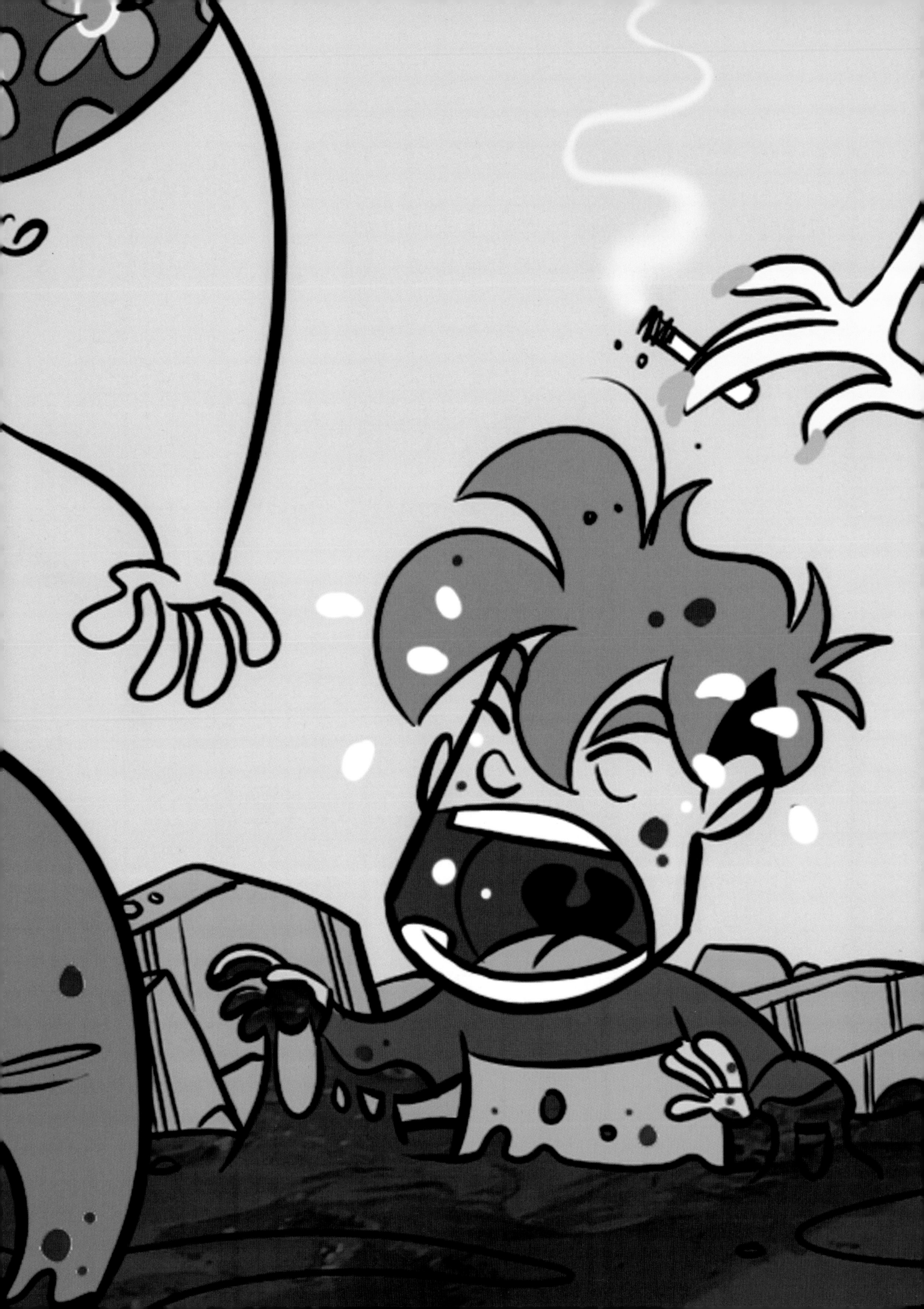

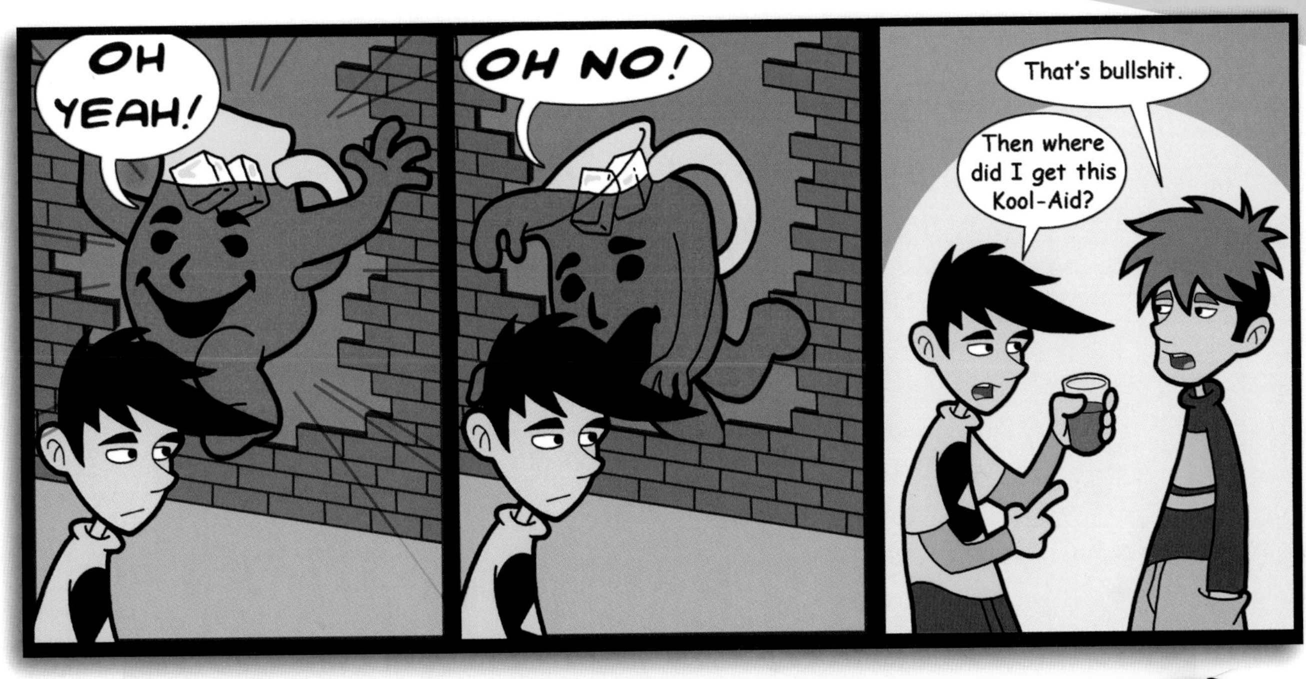
OH YEAH!
OH NO!
That's bullshit.
Then where did I get this Kool-Aid?

Cultural References "R" Us

Wow, what a funny comic!

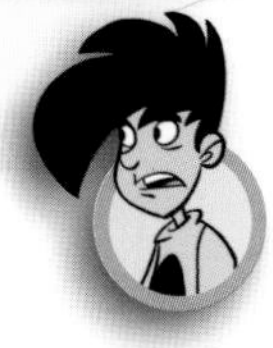

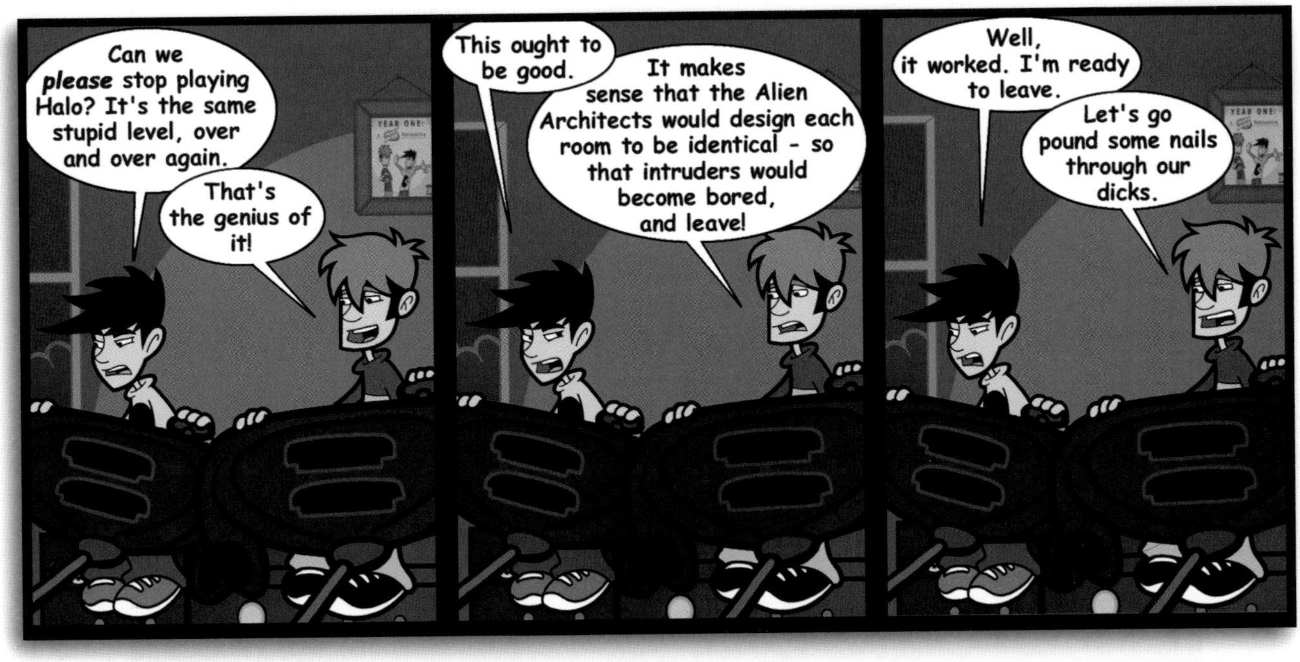
Can we *please* stop playing Halo? It's the same stupid level, over and over again.
That's the genius of it!
This ought to be good.
It makes sense that the Alien Architects would design each room to be identical - so that intruders would become bored, and leave!
Well, it worked. I'm ready to leave.
Let's go pound some nails through our dicks.

The Rest of the Story

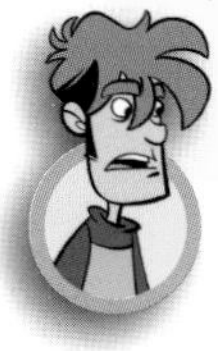

Contrarian opinion is another service we provide, represented notably by this case. For whatever reason, the people we are just end up at odds with prevailing notions. We've gotten used to the sensation of feeling crazy after a while. Occasionally this pressure is released in jpeg form.

We know that many of you are frustrated about Metroid's move into the world of the First Person Shooter. Well, it could have been fucking *worse*.
Zebes
METROID
Retro Studios - a science fiction story
Copyright (c) 2001 by Retro Studios, Inc.
All rights reserved.
You see a metroid (tm).
>shoot metroid
You shoot the Metroid(tm).
You see another Metroid(tm).
LINES-010
TOP
01000
SCORE
00831
NEXT
LEVEL
01
METRIS
Metroid Space Dancer
You know what would be *really* cool? If I was *dead*.

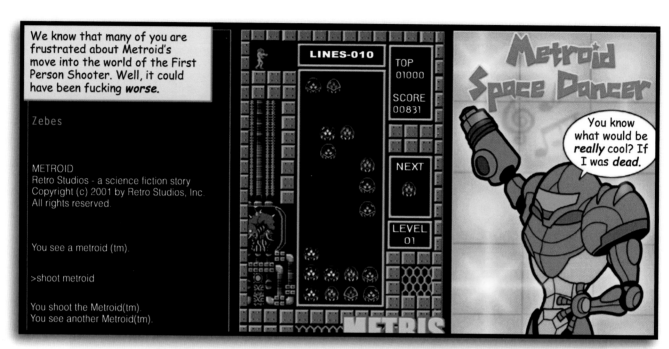

Count Your Lucky Stars

This one's really funny I think.

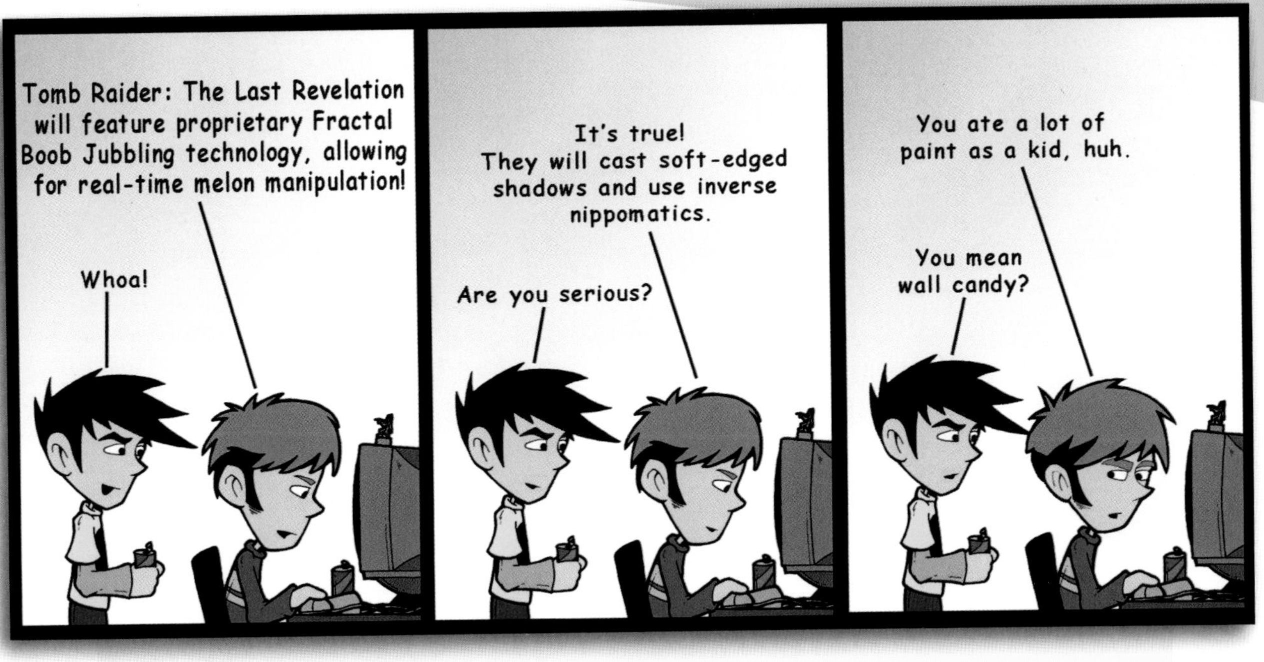
Tomb Raider: The Last Revelation will feature proprietary Fractal Boob Jubbling technology, allowing for real-time melon manipulation!
Whoa!
It's true! They will cast soft-edged shadows and use inverse nippomatics.
Are you serious?
You ate a lot of paint as a kid, huh.
You mean wall candy?

Boob Raider

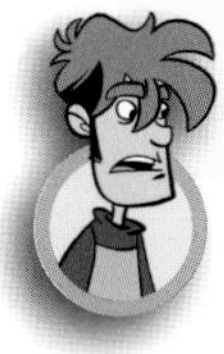

One of my barely hidden fascinations is with the production of new language—wholly new words or phrases that I secretly hope will enter your daily use. There might not *be* that many opportunities to leverage a phrase like *Boob Jubbling,* which is a little sad, but the compulsion to dispense a phrase you might find a use for is irresistible.

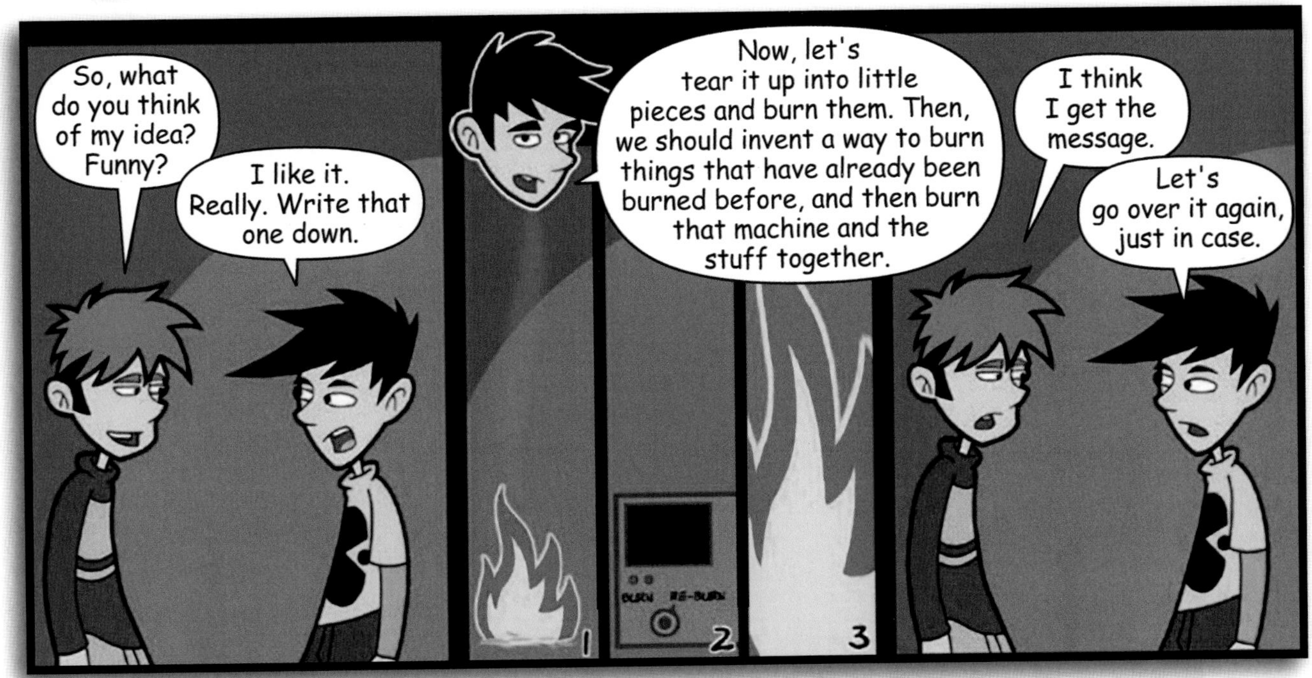
So, what do you think of my idea? Funny?
I like it. Really. Write that one down.
Now, let's tear it up into little pieces and burn them. Then, we should invent a way to burn things that have already been burned before, and then burn that machine and the stuff together.
1
2
3
I think I get the message.
Let's go over it again, just in case.

The Ones You Love

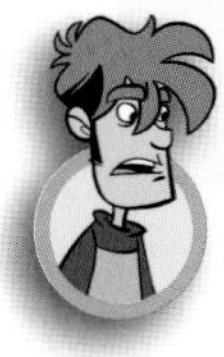

Now that the writing process for some strips is actually cataloged in the occasional podcast, the frequently bizarre, aggressive, and adversarial conversations at the heart of this operation have been laid bare. But then, almost ten years ago, people weren't *casting.* And there were no *pods.* We still wanted to communicate some portion of our working relationship.

TIME LINE **2007 (August) — PAX is forced out of Bellevue due to size limitations and finds its new home in Seattle at the Washington State Convention Center. Thirty-seven thousand people show up.**

What was the worst thing you got this Christmas?
Well, I've got one of those aunts.
You know how everybody has that aunt that thought they were going to turn out gay.
No, I don't have anything like that.
No, I mean like a *weird aunt* that sends you homoerotic stuff all the time, even when it isn't Christmas.
No.

You Know How It Is

Something that happens a lot, though you would never know it because we haven't said, is that the things that *happen* in the strip are real, but they happened to the other person, or someone else we know. We do it either because we think it would be funnier in the context of the strip, or to protect the parties involved, as it is in this case.

WIKIPEDIA
The Free Encyclopedia
article
discussion
edit this page
history
He-Man
From Wikipedia, the free encyclopedia that anyone can ed
He-Man is the most powerful man in the universe. Imbued with incredible magical power by the Sorceress of Castle Graysku he defends Eternia against evildoers with his friends Man-At-Arms, Teela, and the lovable Orko.
Categories: Eternians | Legendary Warri
WIKIPEDIA
The Free Encyclopedia
rticle
discussion
edit this page
history
Editing He-Man
From Wikipedia, the free encyclopedia that anyone can edit.
He-Man is actually a tremendous jackass and no really that powerful. He hangs out with a bunch of jerks like Peela and Dorko, He has a cat who is also dumb and _
Edit Summary:
Save page
Show preview
Show changes

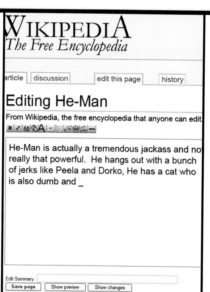

I Have the Power

Taking a somewhat thorny political issue and trying to express the fundamental idea in a way that would be funny to both sides of a conflict is a fun challenge. Jokes of the kind we typically do—that is to say, mean, weird jokes—typically have an obvious "loser." When we're at our best, we can distill the toxic part of the piece out and leave something that is funny, fair to both parties, yet still feels true.

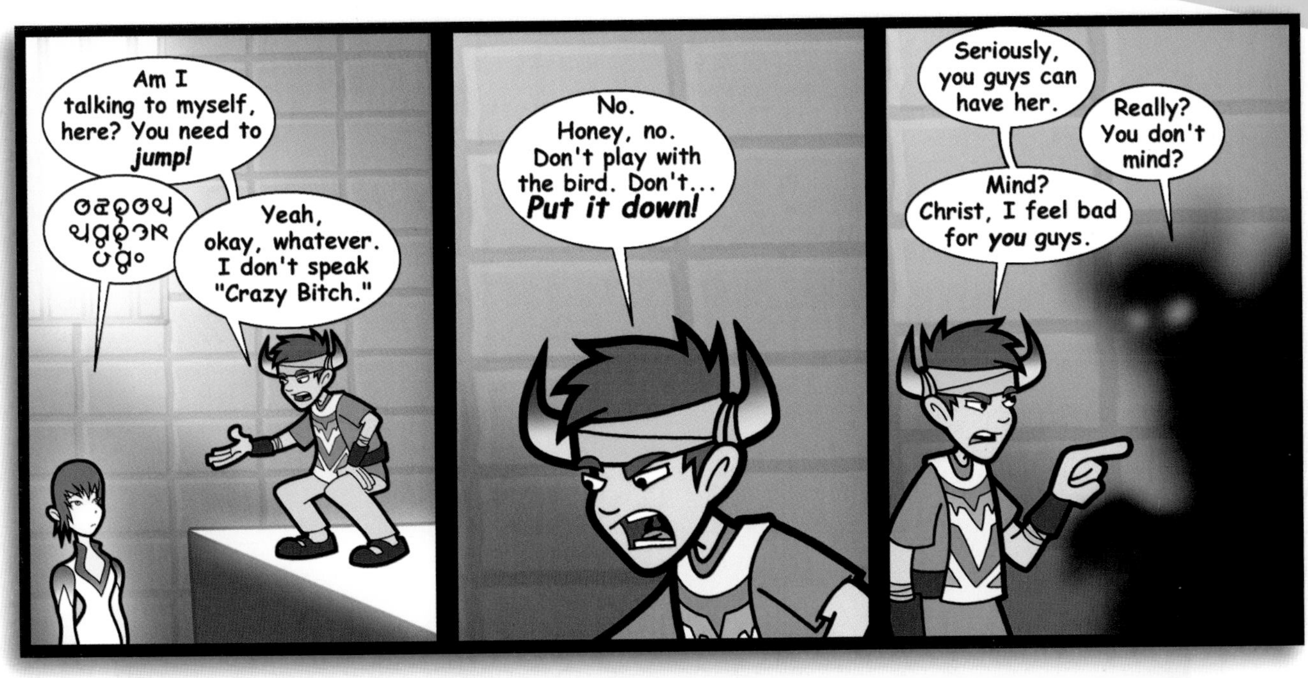
Am I talking to myself, here? You need to *jump!*
Yeah, okay, whatever. I don't speak "Crazy Bitch."
No. Honey, no. Don't play with the bird. Don't... ***Put it down!***
Seriously, you guys can have her.
Really? You don't mind?
Mind? Christ, I feel bad for *you* guys.

The I to the C to the O

HAHAHAHAHAHA!

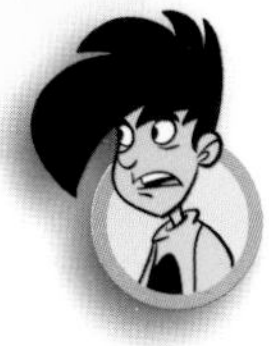

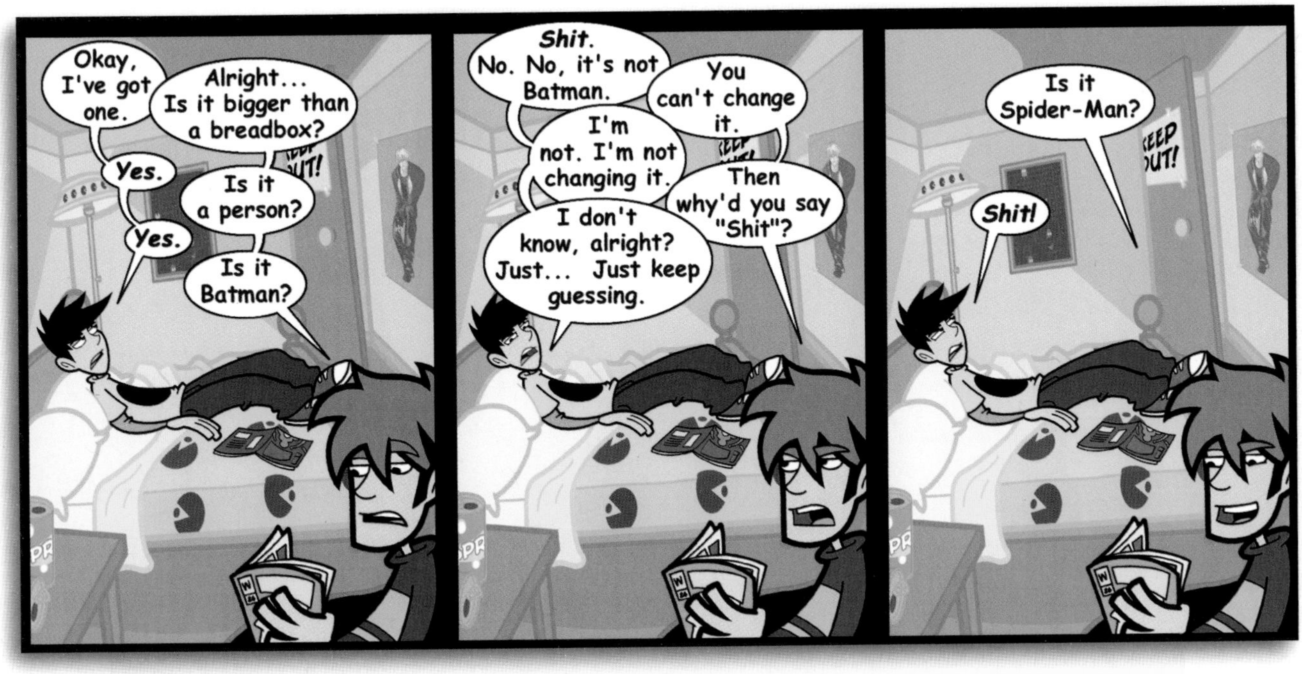
Okay, I've got one.
Alright... Is it bigger than a breadbox?
Yes.
Is it a person?
Yes.
Is it Batman?
KEEP OUT!
Shit. No. No, it's not Batman.
You can't change it.
I'm not. I'm not changing it.
Then why'd you say "Shit"?
I don't know, alright? Just... Just keep guessing.
Is it Spider-Man?
Shit!

NumQuestions = 20

Familiarity is supposed to breed contempt, that's what I've heard, and there may be some measure of that. But familiarity on the level that *we* have developed over more than fifteen years making comics is indistinguishable from *psychic power,* which kind of balances things out.

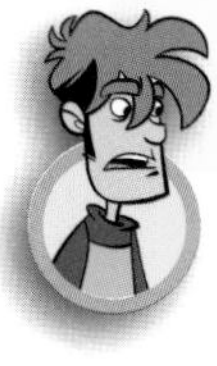

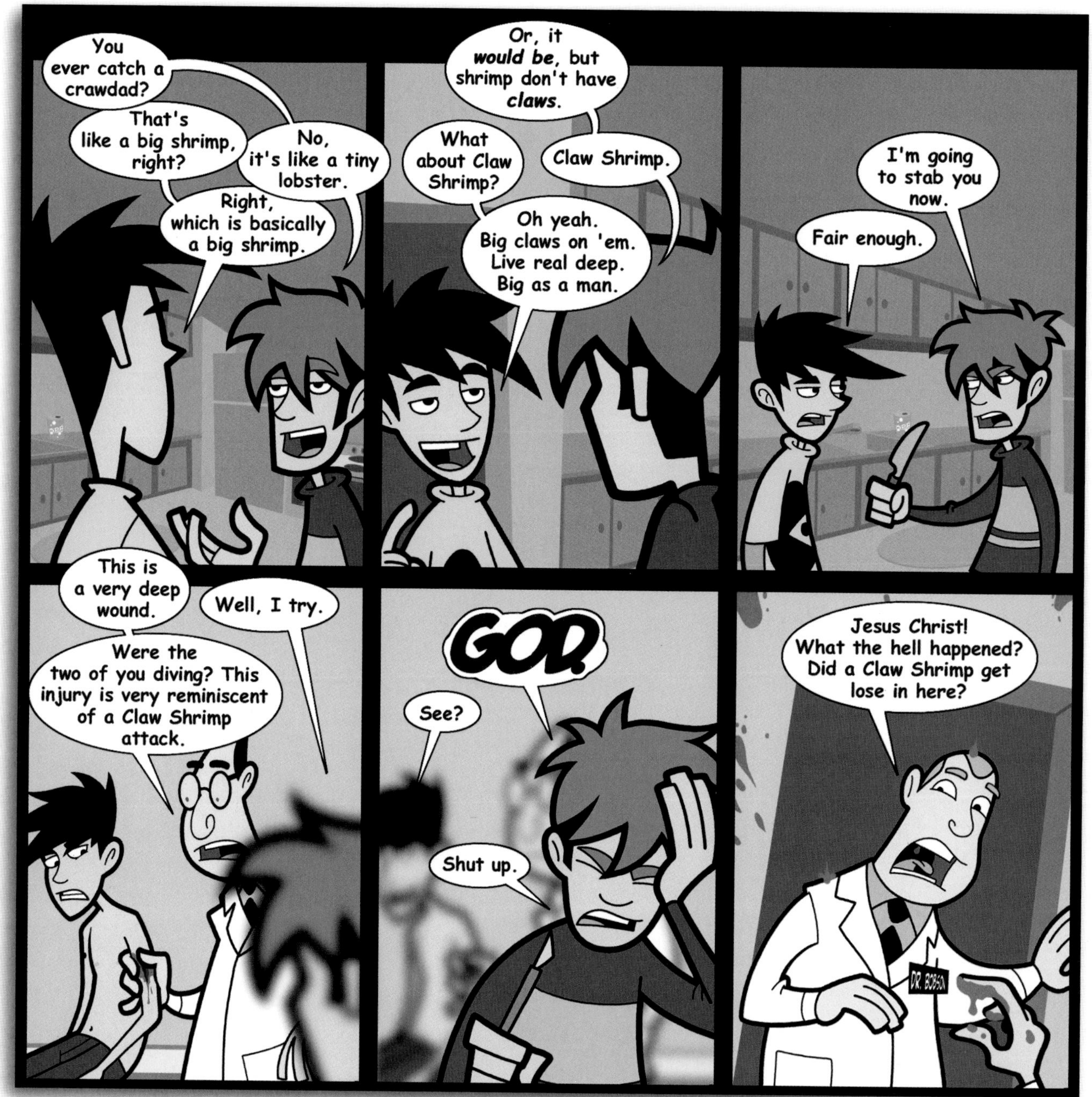

You ever catch a crawdad?
That's like a big shrimp, right?
No, it's like a tiny lobster.
Right, which is basically a big shrimp.
Or, it *would be*, but shrimp don't have *claws*.
What about Claw Shrimp?
Claw Shrimp.
Oh yeah. Big claws on 'em. Live real deep. Big as a man.
I'm going to stab you now.
Fair enough.
This is a very deep wound.
Well, I try.
Were the two of you diving? This injury is very reminiscent of a Claw Shrimp attack.
See?
GOD.
Shut up.
Jesus Christ! What the hell happened? Did a Claw Shrimp get lose in here?

Claw Shrimp!

Claw shrimp! I still laugh at this one.

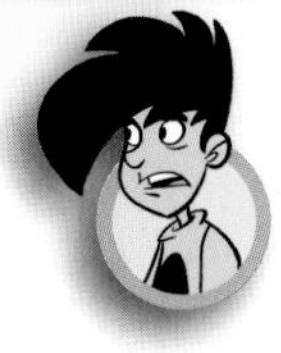

TIME LINE **2008 (January) —** Penny Arcade doubles in size again, with the addition of Paul, Amber, and Jeff.

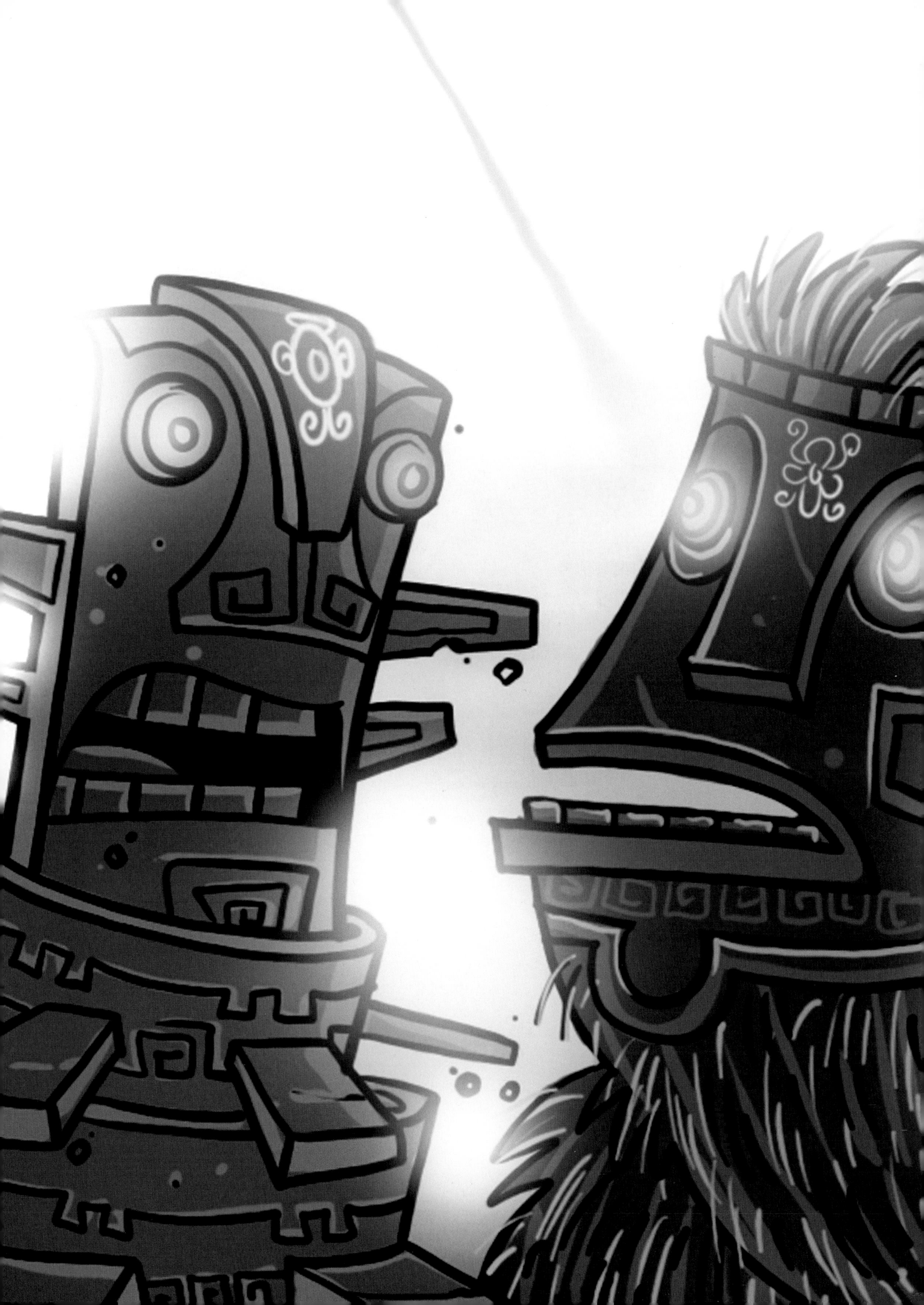

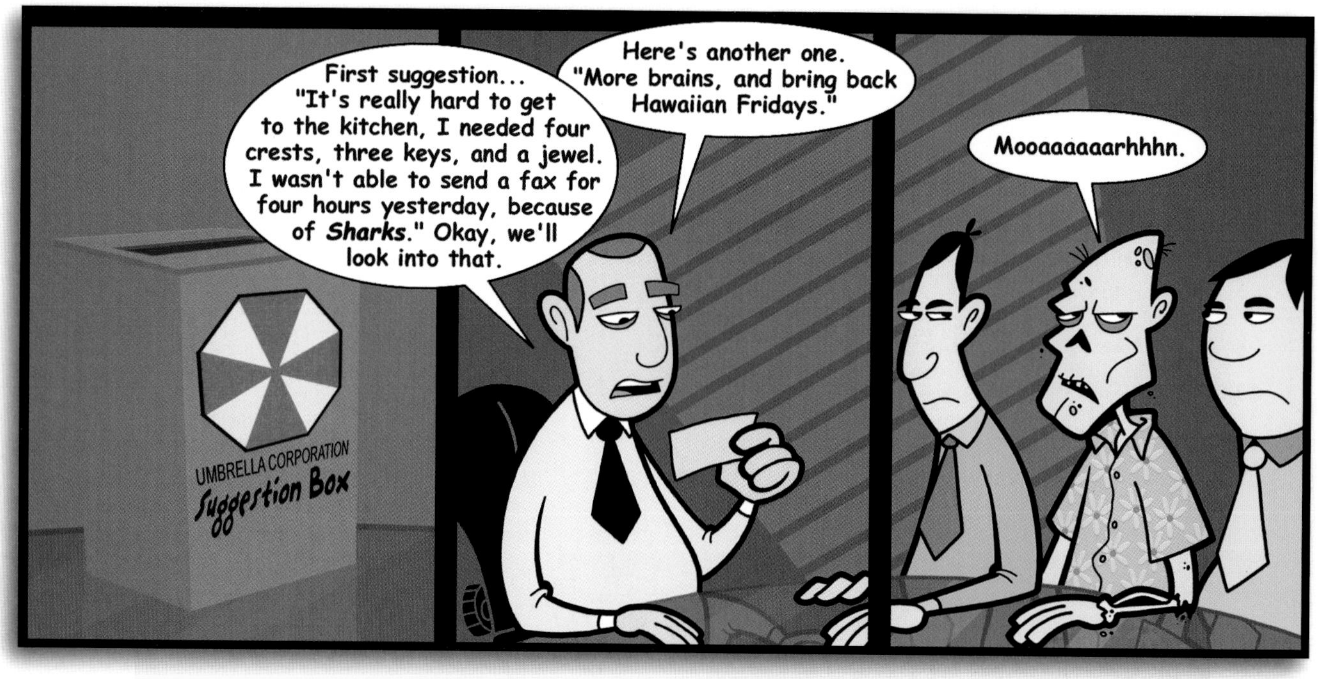
First suggestion... "It's really hard to get to the kitchen, I needed four crests, three keys, and a jewel. I wasn't able to send a fax for four hours yesterday, because of *Sharks*." Okay, we'll look into that.
UMBRELLA CORPORATION
Suggestion Box
Here's another one. "More brains, and bring back Hawaiian Fridays."
Mooaaaaaarhhhn.

Resident Evil Addendum

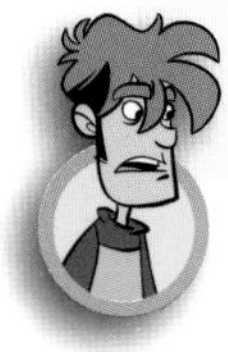

Investigating the lives of the strange creatures who inhabit electronic entertainment is a pillar of the *Penny Arcade* charter, as ratified in 1998. We don't expect our games to resemble real life, indeed, we're often playing a game precisely to have an extraordinary experience. Seriously, though. The Umbrella facilities as presented in Resident Evil bear no resemblance to any place regular people could possibly work, ever.

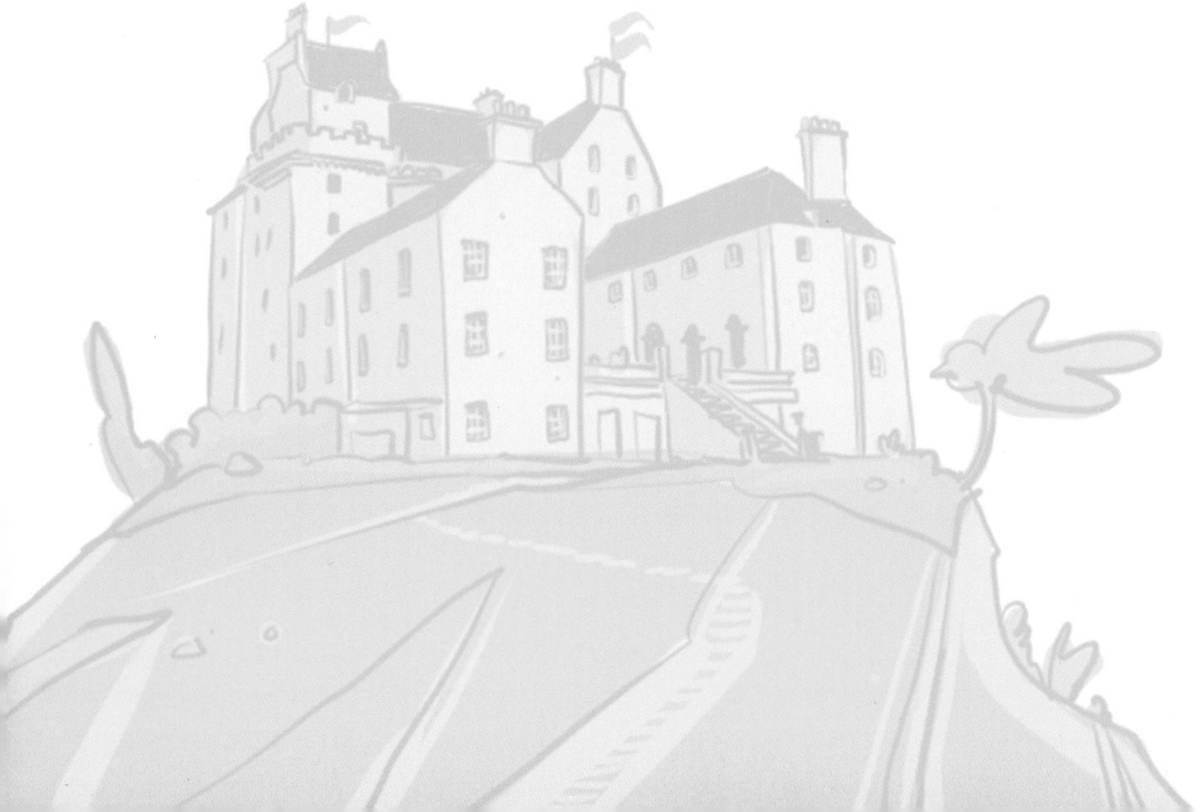

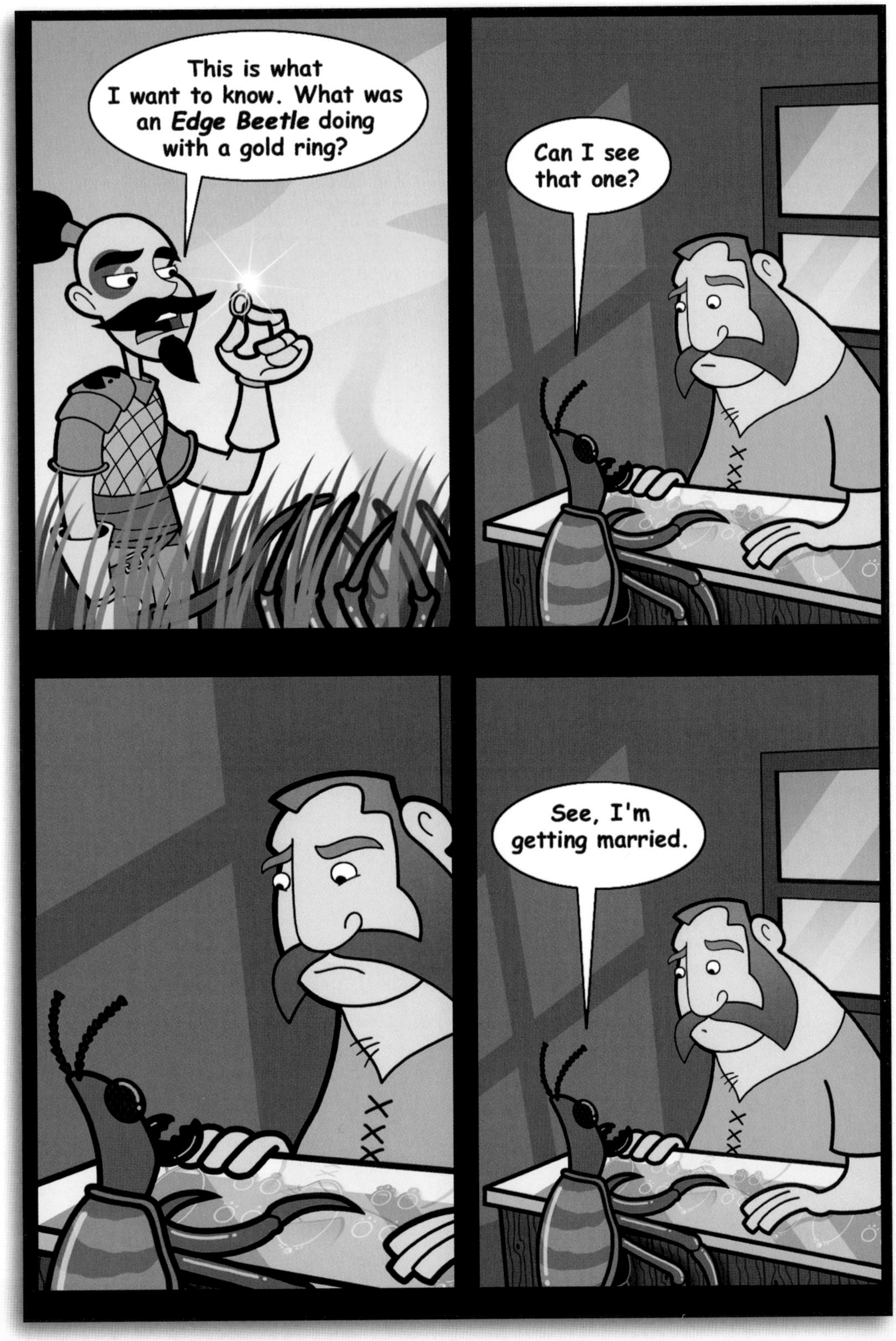
This is what I want to know. What was an *Edge Beetle* doing with a gold ring?
Can I see that one?
See, I'm getting married.

We're Playing Asheron's Call 2

It's funny because, like, why would a bug have a ring!

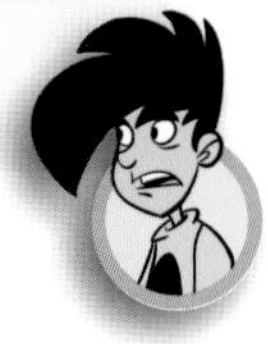

TIME LINE **2008 (March)** — The PAX 10, the annual showcase of independent games, is announced! More than three hundred developers apply.

Did your mom ever tell you that you'd outgrow videogames?
My mom was a drunk. She used to whip me every day with an extension cord.

Sweet and Sour

My mom likes this comic less than I do.

Yeah, I'm one of those "Animal Santas" they have down at the Pet Stop.
You hate animals.
Yes. But I love money.
Kill it!
You've got to kill it!
GRRROWWROR!
So, how was
A dog ate my testicles.

Santa's Little Helpers

Ouch! Right in the balls!

TIME LINE **2008 (April) —** Penny Arcade launches the Greenhouse, a distribution channel for indie game developers.

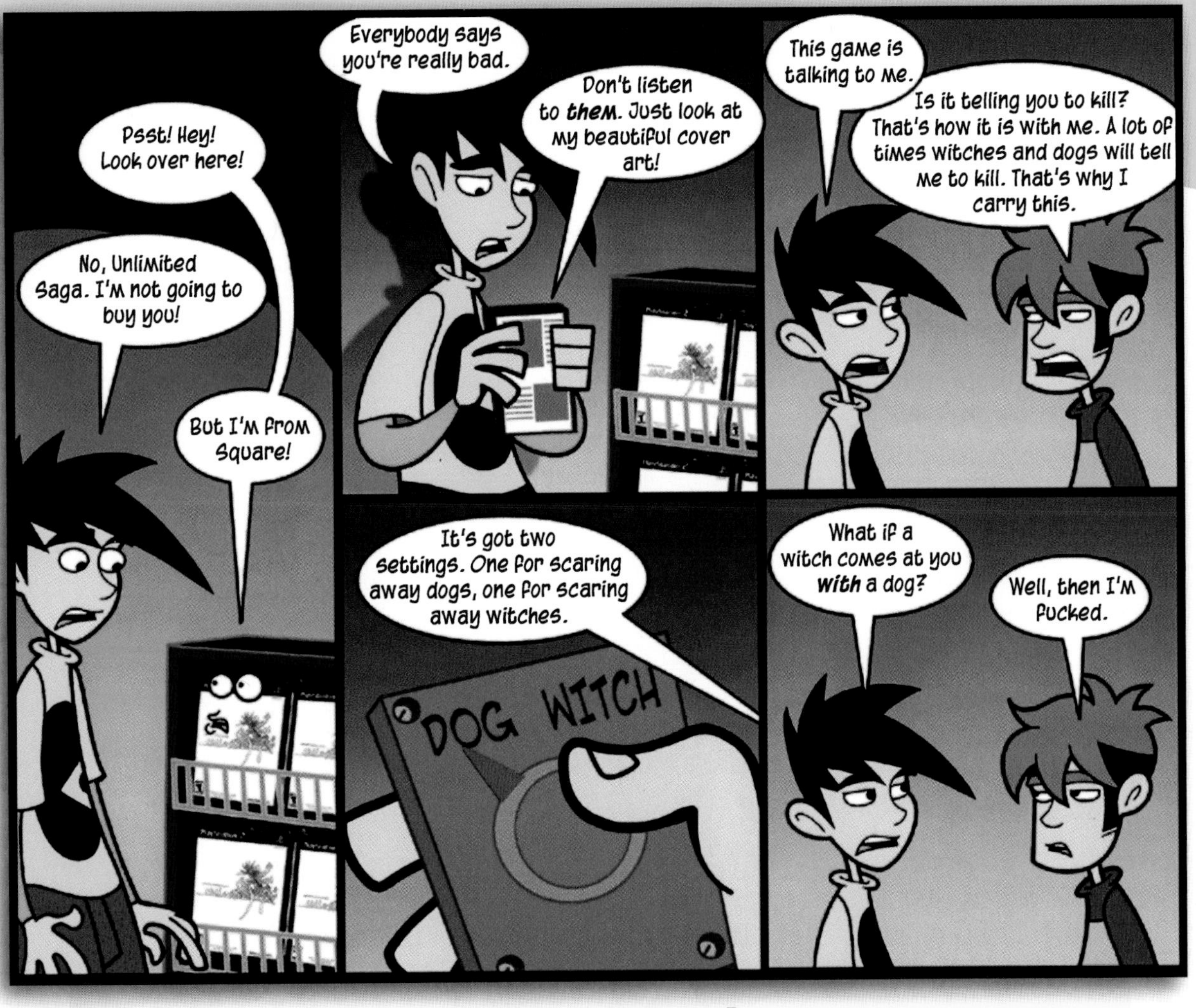
Psst! Hey! Look over here!
No, Unlimited Saga. I'm not going to buy you!
But I'm from Square!
Everybody says you're really bad.
Don't listen to *them*. Just look at my beautiful cover art!
This game is talking to me.
Is it telling you to kill? That's how it is with me. A lot of times witches and dogs will tell me to kill. That's why I carry this.
It's got two settings. One for scaring away dogs, one for scaring away witches.
DOG WITCH
What if a witch comes at you *with* a dog?
Well, then I'm fucked.

A Grave Scenario

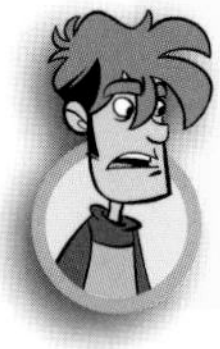

We actually have this Dog/Witch Switch, someone made it for us—it's on the shelf behind me, right by the Neo Geo carts for the arcade cabinet. We've never tried to use it, because we want to believe *it really works,* an illusion that will shatter if the device were ever deployed.

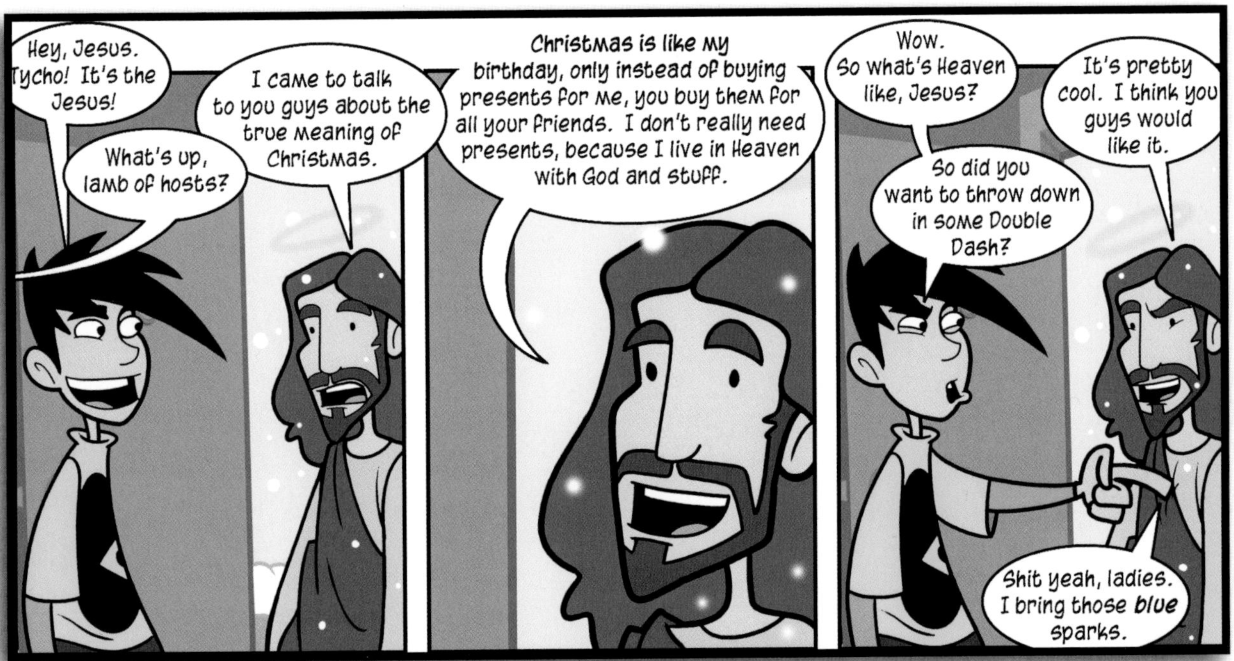
Hey, Jesus. Tycho! It's the Jesus!
What's up, lamb of hosts?
I came to talk to you guys about the true meaning of Christmas.
Christmas is like my birthday, only instead of buying presents for me, you buy them for all your friends. I don't really need presents, because I live in Heaven with God and stuff.
Wow. So what's Heaven like, Jesus?
It's pretty cool. I think you guys would like it.
So did you want to throw down in some Double Dash?
Shit yeah, ladies. I bring those *blue* sparks.

As Foretold In Revelations

Jesus is so awesome.

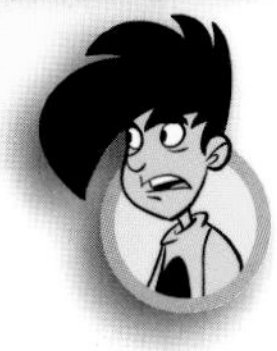

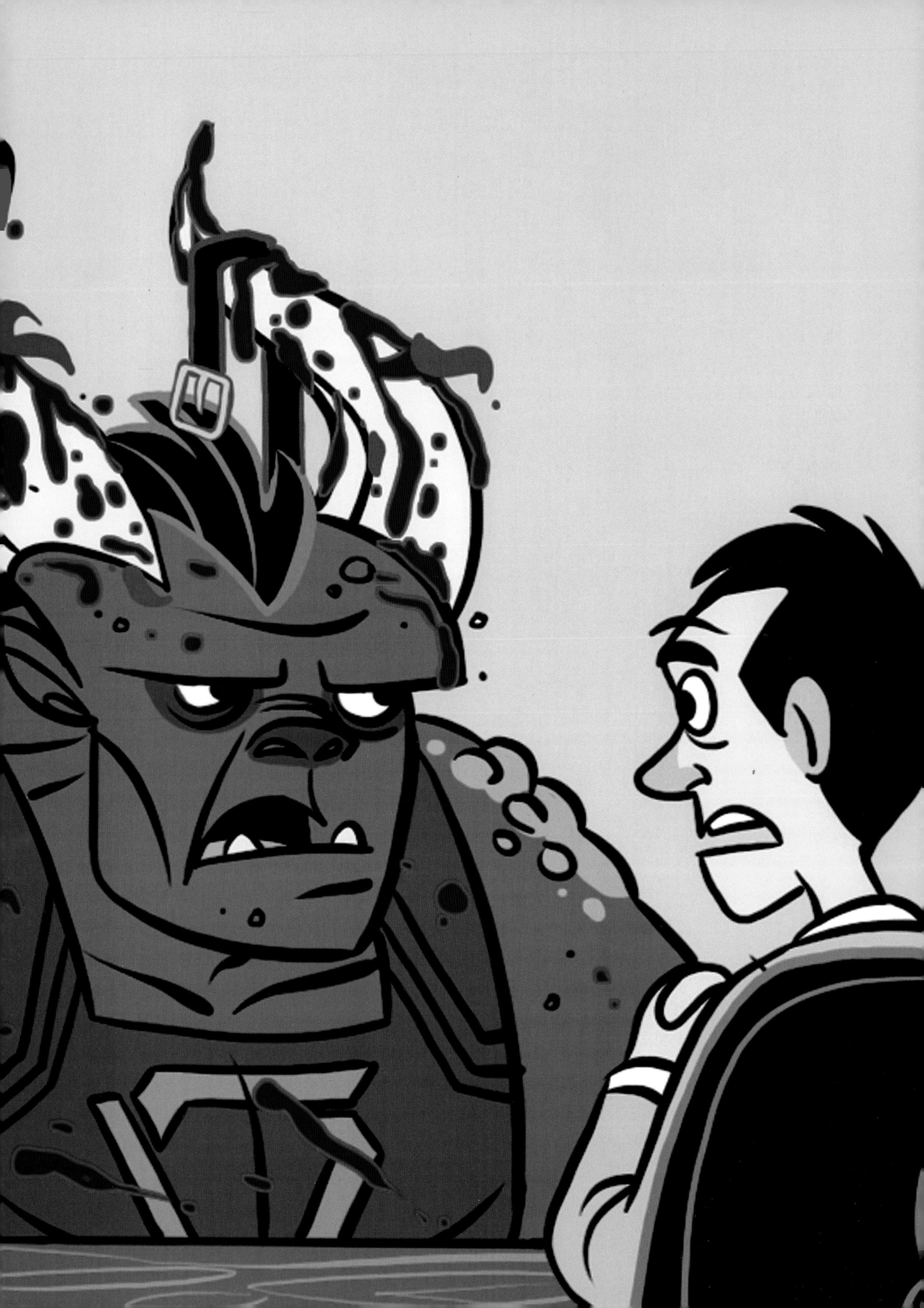

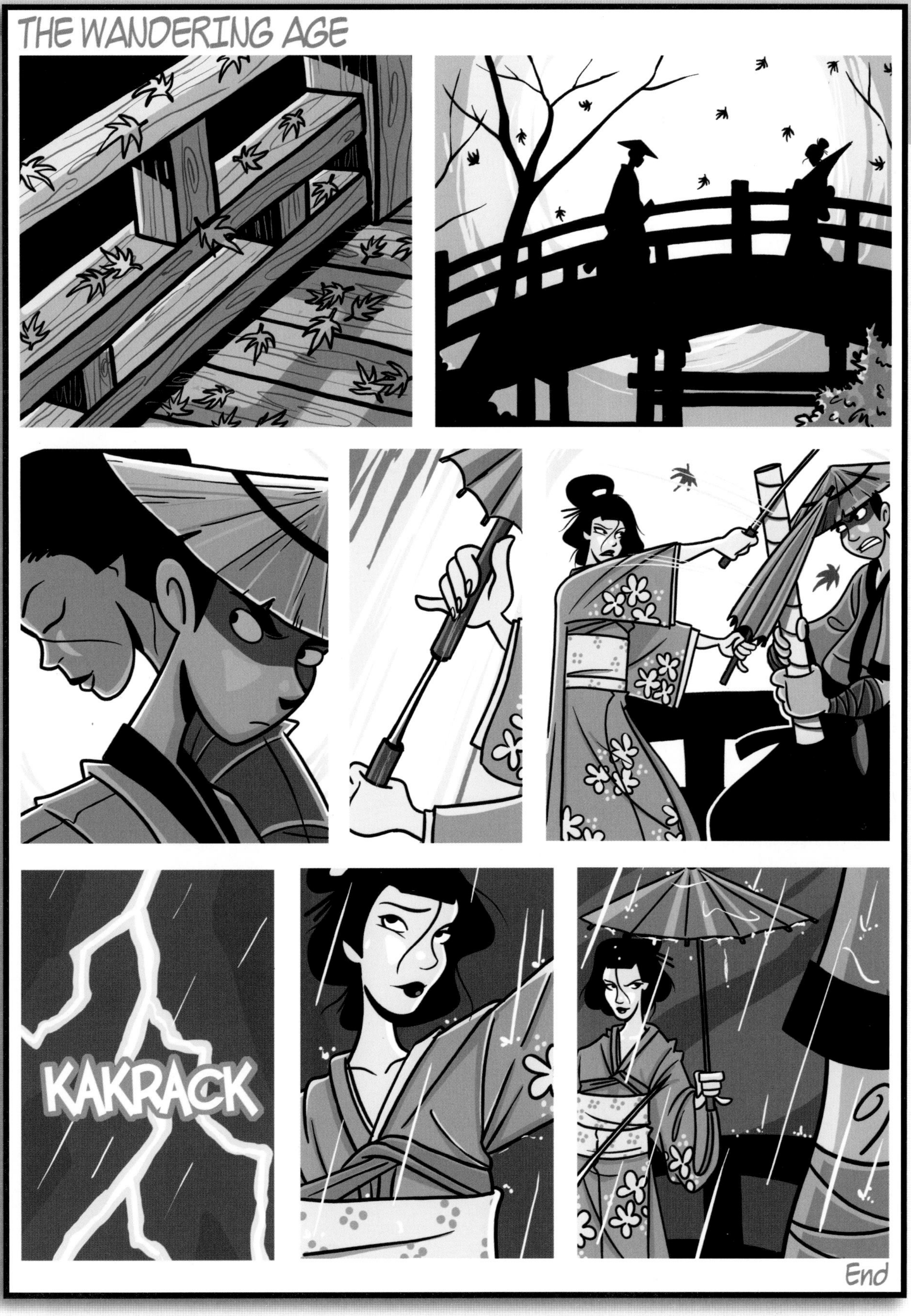
THE WANDERING AGE
KAKRACK
End

The Wandering Age 2

Then again, I also like comics that are entirely self-contained. It's typical of *Cardboard Tube Samurai* strips that they gloss over what would ordinarily be the "most important part," which in this kind of material might be "fighting with swords," and focus instead on something else. Something incidental. I am still learning how to do this, and I suspect that will always be true, but this is the rare case where we were able to do exactly what I wanted to.

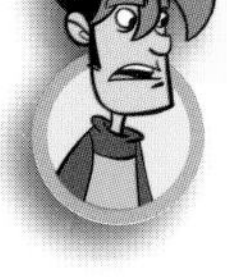

Unreal Tournament 2004 lends incontrovertible proof to John Gabriel's Greater Internet Fuckwad Theory.
Normal Person
Anonymity
Audience
Total Fuckwad
Shitcock
2+3=Cats

Green Blackboards (and Other Anomalies)

It's funny because it's true.

I had the most *wonderful dream*. Nintendo was making a new, *dark* Zelda game!
That's not a dream, actually. They're really doing that.
Wow... Because right after that, I dreamed our world had been conquered by malevolent, spacefaring dog-men, known as the Canid.
Yeah, I was just going to tell you about that. You're pretty much two for two.
Fetch this space frisbee, human. Fetch it, and gaze upon your ruined world!
Man, this fucking sucks.

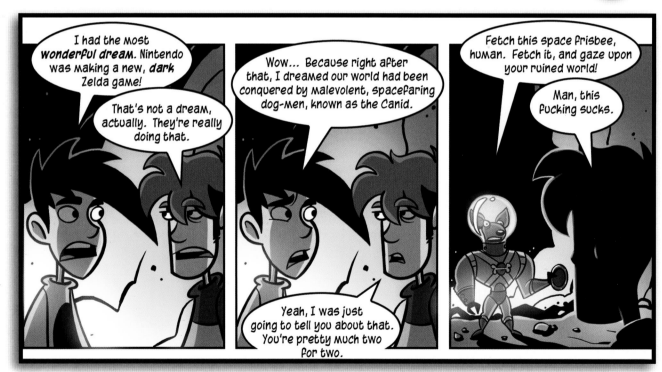

They Hail from Canidon

I like comics that imply some vast secret underlying the universe that for whatever reason never gets explored again—that spacefaring dogs are just doing shit constantly, out in space, and occasionally they raze the earth for our condescension. We play this trick often, and usually they remain non sequiturs, but sometimes these ideas won't sit still. Twisp, Catsby, and the Cardboard Tube Samurai spring readily to mind.

Kevin Smith said his new movie Jersey Girl "wasn't for critics."
Wow! I didn't know you could even do that.
Penny Arcade isn't for critics anymore *either*. Which means we're free to do shit like this!
Good morning! How much does that weigh?
Ham!
I'd bet you'd *love* to criticize that, wouldn't you, you Critics! But you can't.
It's not *for* you.

The Adventures of Twisp And Catsby

Twisp and Catsby, yay!

Hey, man. How did you... No, it's too weird.
I can take it.
I'm nervous about the birth. Do I have any responsibilities, you know... Vis a vis the placenta?
I'll tell you this: the best thing about the placenta is cold placenta sandwiches the next day.

I'm Not Entirely Sure He Knows What That Is

We sometimes have conversations that *are* comics—they're the kind of things that two drawn people would say, peering out from inside their little panels. This was/is one of those times.

TIME LINE **2008 (May) —** Penny Arcade Adventures: On the Rain-Slick Precipice of Darkness, Episode 1, launches.

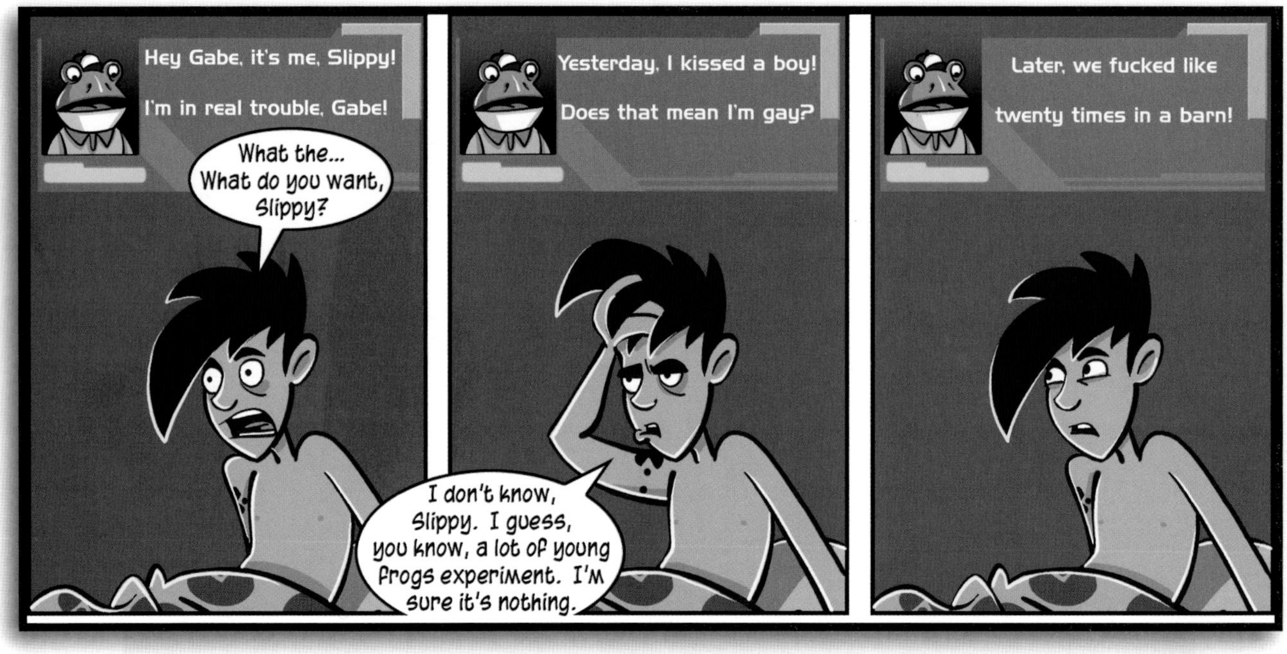
Hey Gabe, it's me, Slippy!
I'm in real trouble, Gabe!
What the... What do you want, Slippy?
Yesterday, I kissed a boy!
Does that mean I'm gay?
I don't know, Slippy. I guess, you know, a lot of young frogs experiment. I'M sure it's nothing.
Later, we fucked like
twenty times in a barn!

On The Matter Of Gay Space Frogs

One of our all-time best I think.

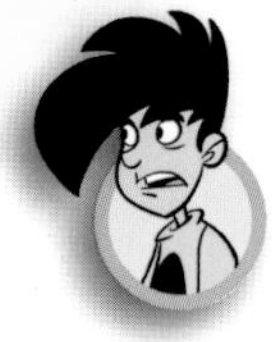

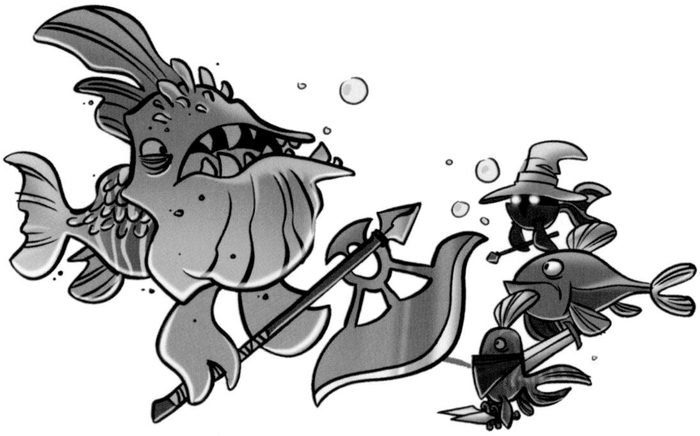

TIME LINE **2008 (May) —** Scott Kurtz from PvPonline joins Mike and Jerry as they promote Dungeons and Dragons, Fourth Edition with podcasts of their play sessions. The series is a massive hit, and the project expands with guest appearances from gaming celebrities from across the industry.

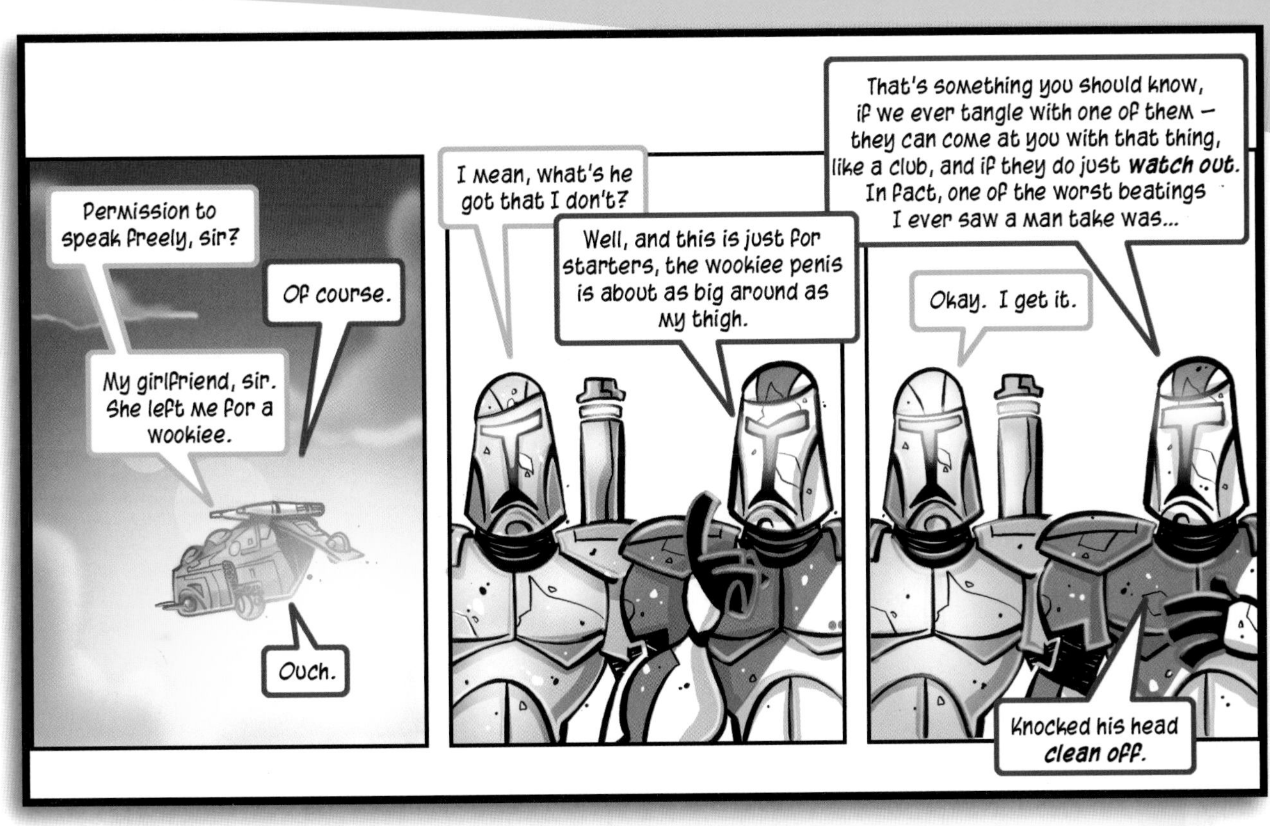
Permission to speak freely, sir?
Of course.
My girlfriend, sir. She left me for a wookiee.
Ouch.
I mean, what's he got that I don't?
Well, and this is just for starters, the wookiee penis is about as big around as my thigh.
That's something you should know, if we ever tangle with one of them – they can come at you with that thing, like a club, and if they do just **watch out.** In fact, one of the worst beatings I ever saw a man take was...
Okay. I get it.
Knocked his head **clean off.**

A Truly Remarkable Circumference

This is a really funny comic.

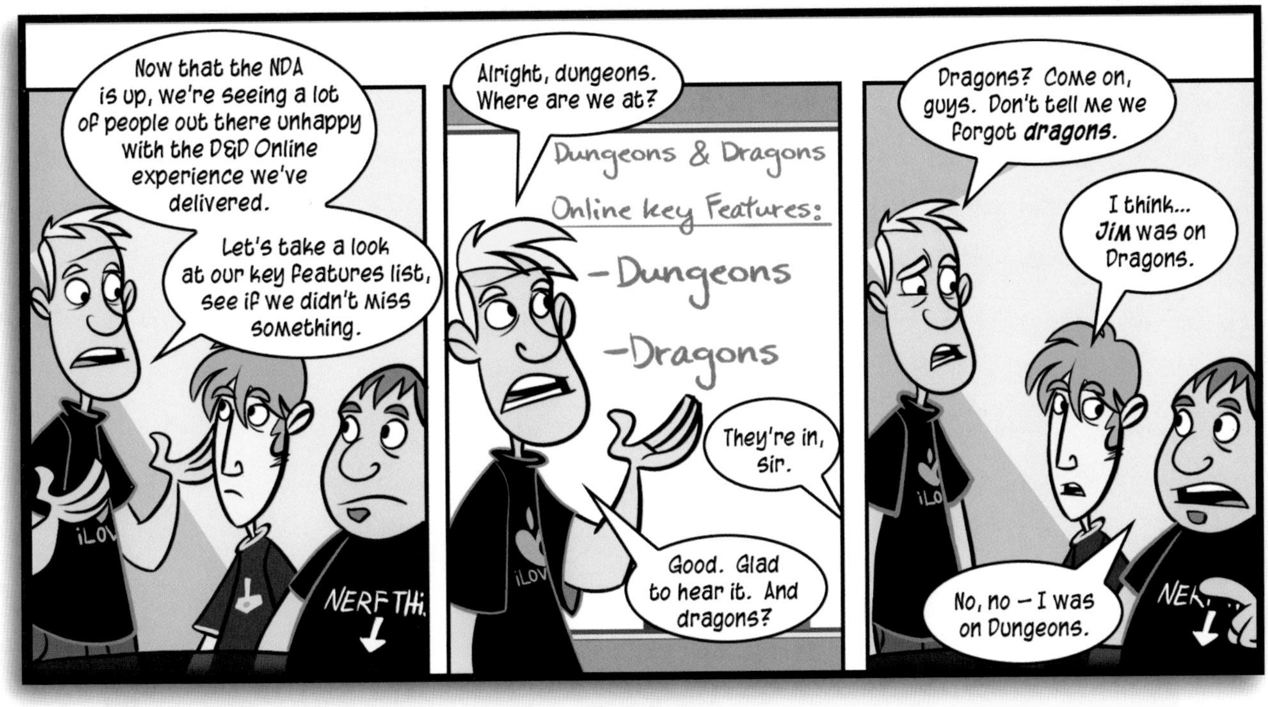
Now that the NDA is up, we're seeing a lot of people out there unhappy with the D&D Online experience we've delivered.
Let's take a look at our key features list, see if we didn't miss something.
NERF THI
Alright, dungeons. Where are we at?
Dungeons & Dragons Online key Features:
-Dungeons
-Dragons
They're in, sir.
Good. Glad to hear it. And dragons?
Dragons? Come on, guys. Don't tell me we forgot **dragons.**
I think... ***Jim*** was on Dragons.
No, no – I was on Dungeons.

DNDA

Another personal weakness, and one I will readily admit to, is an appetite for very simple scripts that feature word repetition or other simple mechanics (like juxtaposition, or reversal). This hews closely to the kinds of conversations we actually have, so when we capture the actual manner of our speech maybe it's just a kind of comfort.

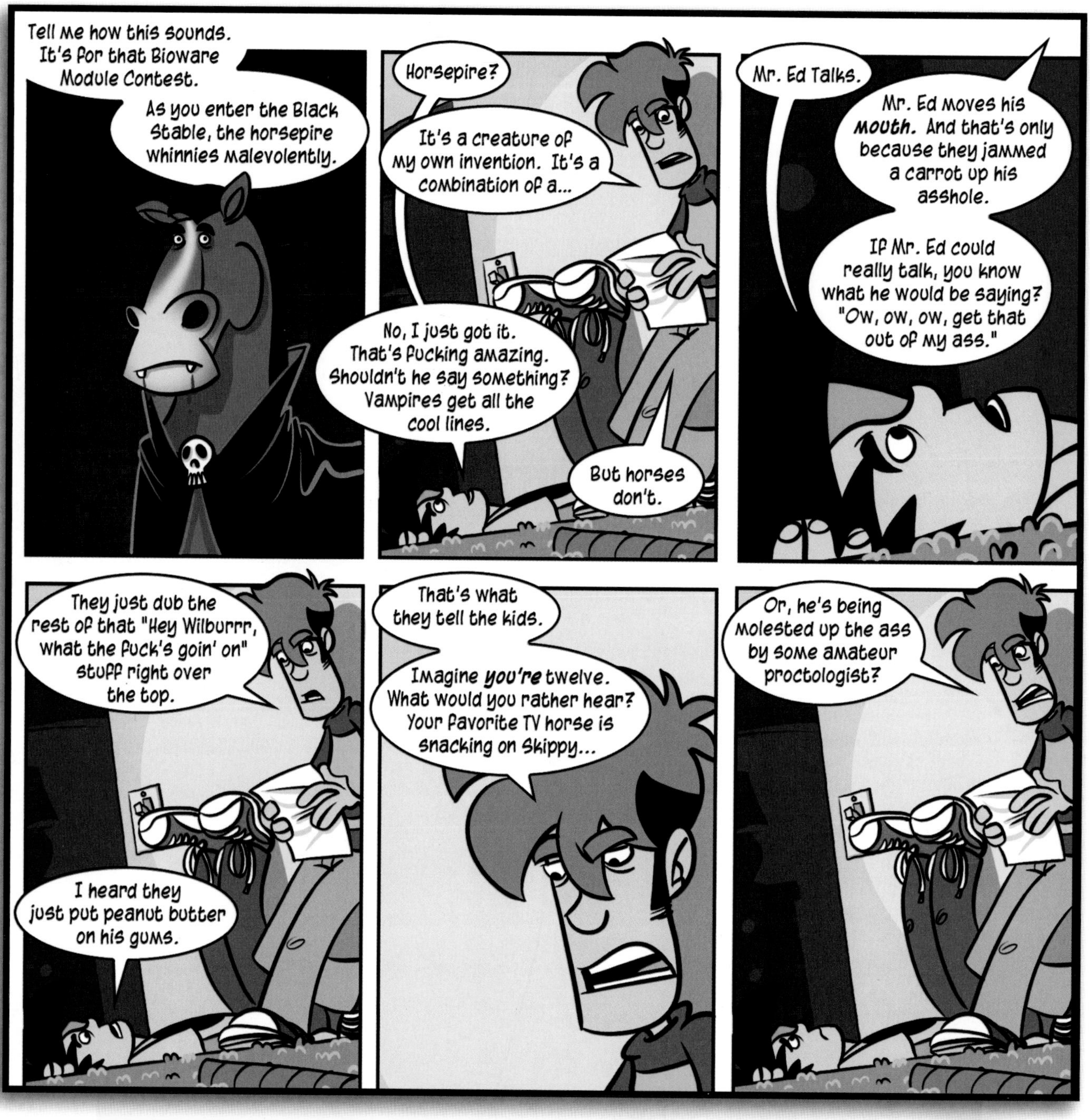
Tell me how this sounds. It's for that Bioware Module Contest.
As you enter the Black Stable, the horsepire whinnies malevolently.
Horsepire?
It's a creature of my own invention. It's a combination of a...
No, I just got it. That's fucking amazing. Shouldn't he say something? Vampires get all the cool lines.
But horses don't.
Mr. Ed Talks.
Mr. Ed moves his **mouth.** And that's only because they jammed a carrot up his asshole.
If Mr. Ed could really talk, you know what he would be saying? "Ow, ow, ow, get that out of my ass."
They just dub the rest of that "Hey Wilburrr, what the fuck's goin' on" stuff right over the top.
I heard they just put peanut butter on his gums.
That's what they tell the kids.
Imagine ***you're*** twelve. What would you rather hear? Your favorite TV horse is snacking on Skippy...
Or, he's being molested up the ass by some amateur proctologist?

Mr. (Penetrat)Ed

I chose this one because it is so funny.

TIME LINE **2008 (October) — Fifteen hundred strips and still going strong.**

Did you see those Warhammer Online shots? More like World of **Warhammer**. Online. Craft.

You never played tabletop games, so I'm going to cut you some slack. Trust me. Just turn around, and walk away.

But they're totally ripping Blizzard off!

Don't say another Goddamn word. Up until now, I've been polite. If you say **anything** else - word **one** - I will kill myself. And when my tainted spirit finds its destination, I will topple the master of that dark place. From my black throne, I will lash together a machine of bone and blood, and fueled by my hatred for you this **fear engine** will bore a hole between this world and that one.

When it begins, you will hear the sound of children screaming - as though from a great distance. A smoking orb of **nothing** will grow above your bed, and from it will emerge a thousand starving crows. As I slip through the widening maw in my new form, you will catch only a glimpse of my radiance before you are incinerated. Then, as tears of bubbling pitch stream down my face, my dark work will begin.

I will open one of my six mouths, and I will sing the song that ends the Earth.

I Hope You Like Text

What's not to like? Words that almost completely obliterate the art!
PROGRESS!

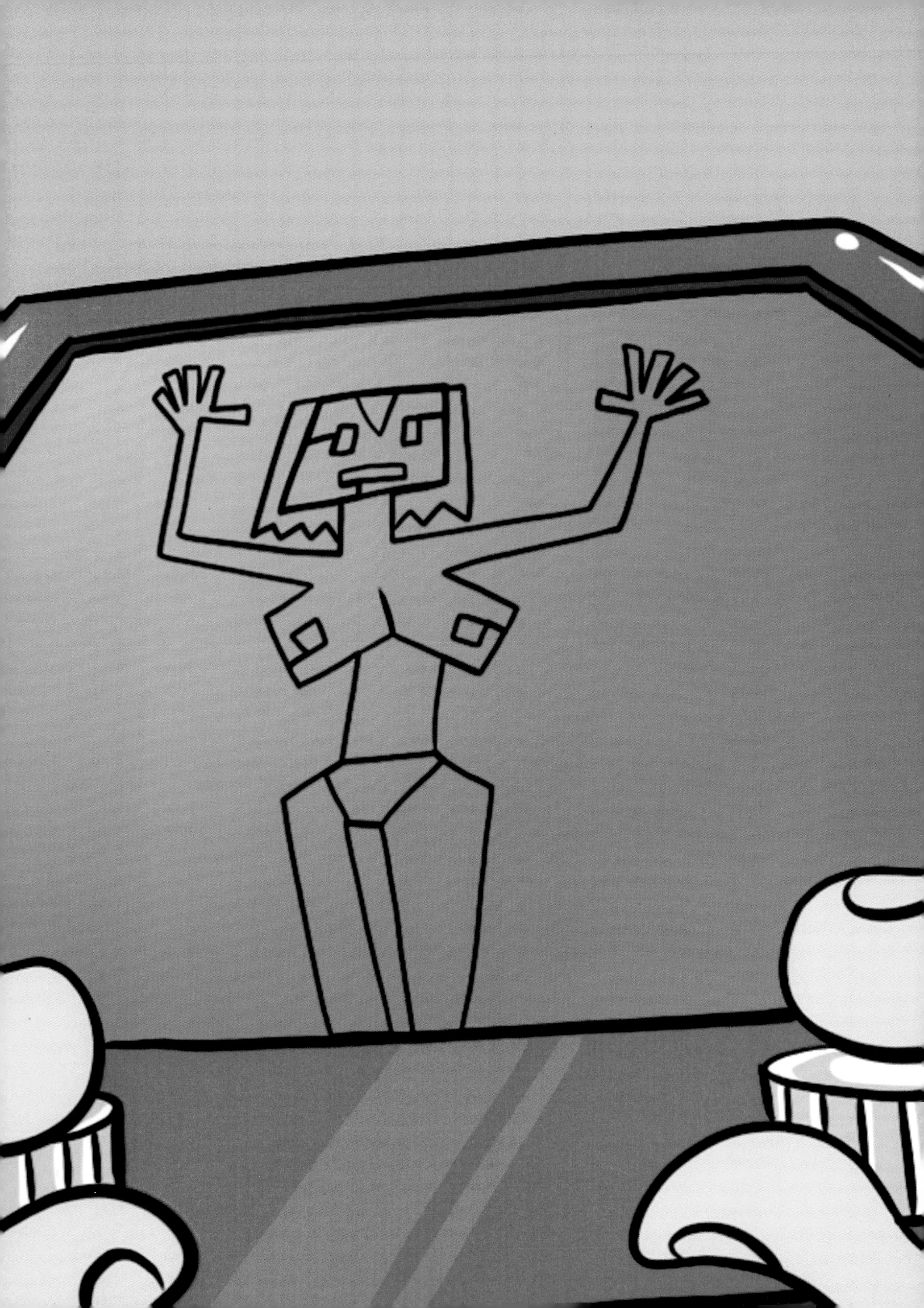

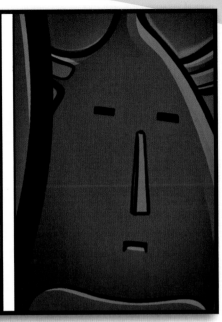

Just for the Elebit

Maybe this is weird behavior for a writer, but wanting the words to obliterate the art isn't actually my goal. I often place pressure on Mike to do comics without writing of any kind, not only because it makes my job *incredibly easy,* but also because I feel communicating without the use of language conforms to some higher ideal. Telepathy, I guess you would say.

Come then, you corrupt things - you creatures of darkness!
For **this** morn, the thirsty blade of Sir Tristram will drink deep!
SKREEEEEEEEEE

An Excerpt from *The Book Of Deeds*

In my opinion this comic is perfect.

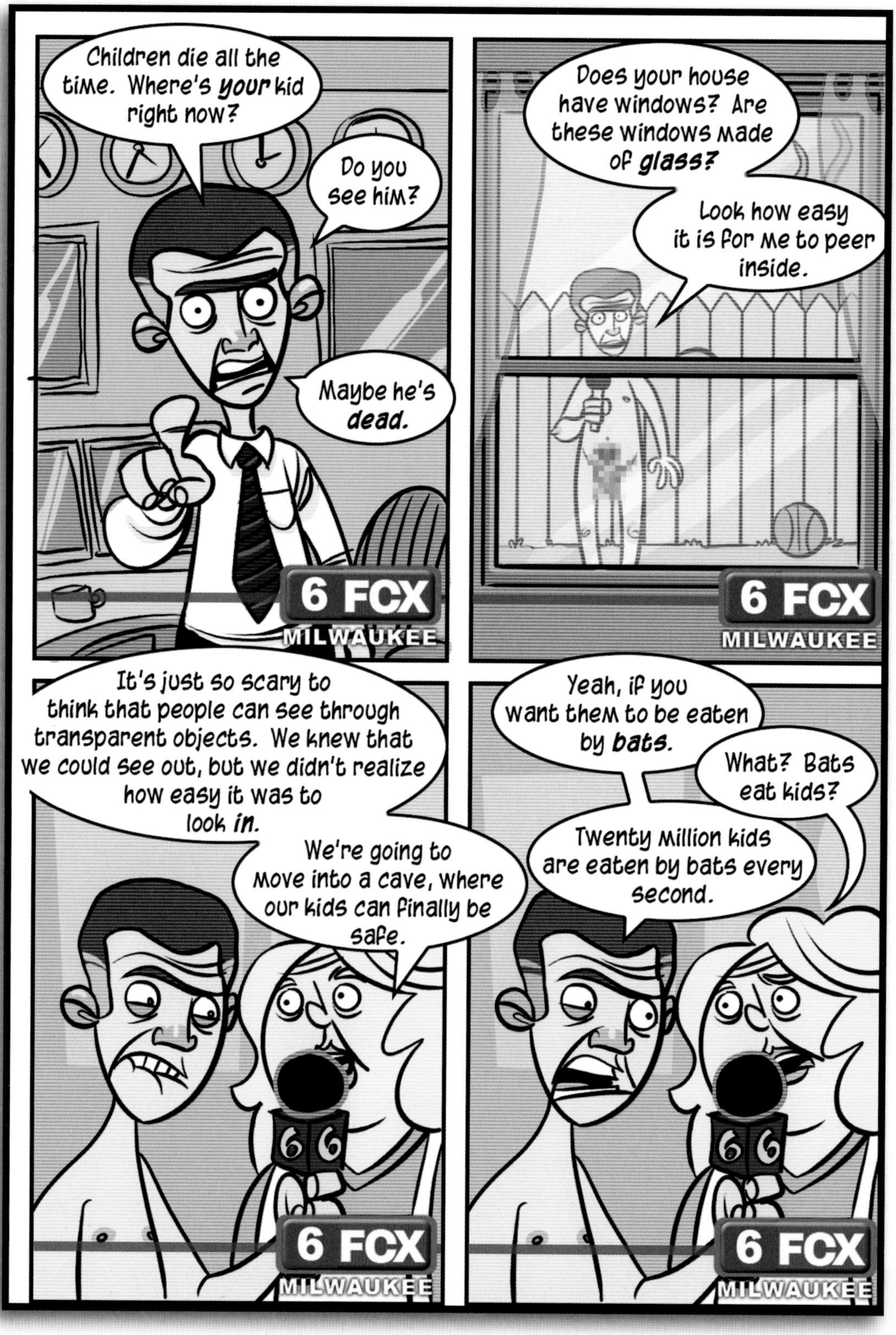
Children die all the time. Where's ***your*** kid right now?
Do you see him?
Maybe he's ***dead.***
6 FCX MILWAUKEE
Does your house have windows? Are these windows made of ***glass?***
Look how easy it is for me to peer inside.
6 FCX MILWAUKEE
It's just so scary to think that people can see through transparent objects. We knew that we could see out, but we didn't realize how easy it was to look ***in.***
We're going to move into a cave, where our kids can finally be safe.
6 FCX MILWAUKEE
Yeah, if you want them to be eaten by ***bats.***
What? Bats eat kids?
Twenty million kids are eaten by bats every second.
6 FCX MILWAUKEE

The Most Recent Catastrophe

"The News" has been lacerated on the site almost since its inception, and we let a number of grisly journalistic acts slide, but once it started to get hilarious again with the portable systems we had to jump back in. The pixilated junk in panel two really works for me, on some level. I don't know why, and I'd rather not dwell on it.

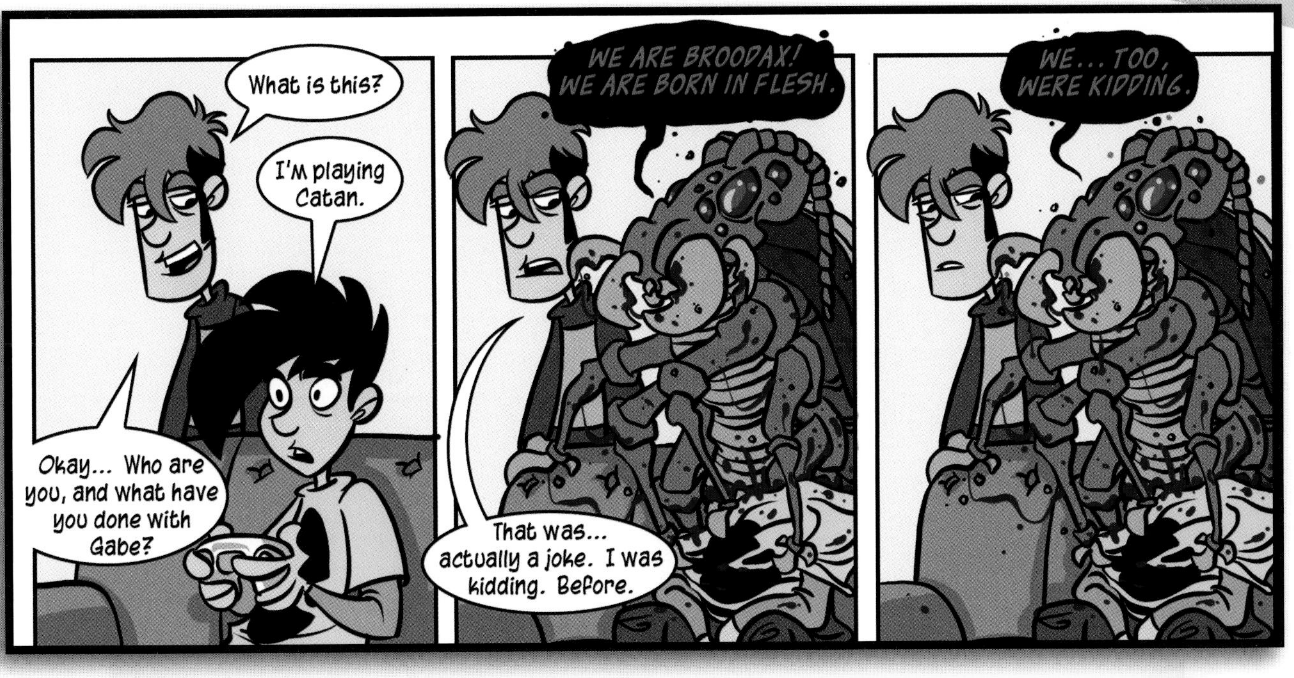
What is this?
I'm playing Catan.
Okay... Who are you, and what have you done with Gabe?
WE ARE BROODAX! WE ARE BORN IN FLESH.
That was... actually a joke. I was kidding. Before.
WE... TOO, WERE KIDDING.

The Broodax Imperiate

LOL

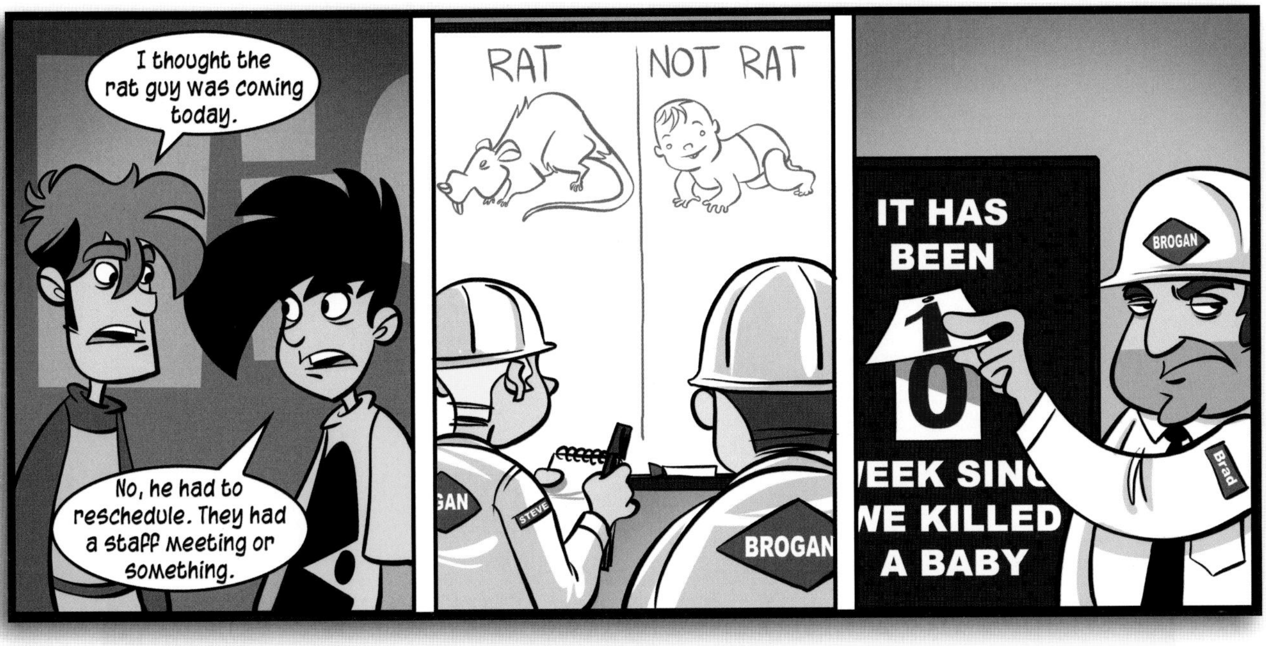
I thought the rat guy was coming today.
No, he had to reschedule. They had a staff meeting or something.
RAT
NOT RAT
STEVE
BROGAN
IT HAS BEEN
10
WEEK SINC
WE KILLED
A BABY
BROGAN
Brad

Bedrock Concepts

This is an example of the strange chains of causality that happen in our "work." Mike had a real rat, at his real house, which led to the creation of this strip, which led immediately into the creation of an exterminator named Carl who knew more than he should about the dark places of the earth. This lead to the return of the Deep Crow, which led to a series of subterranean adventures, which...See what I mean?

TIME LINE

2009 (July) — After eleven years of living rooms, garages, temporary offices, and broken-down walls, Penny Arcade moves into a custom office, thirty times the size of their original digs, Ping-Pong stadium and all.

What do you mean you have "Math Night"?
That's bullshit. Get your deck, and get over here.
Fucking **Math** Night. Fuck you!
Travis is in.
Is he?
Listen, we can do this some other night. This is an old problem. It's hard to get five people together in the real world.
Maybe for pussies like you. I pick up the phone and get **results.**
Kiko. Cards. Here. **Tonight.**
Have the funeral tomorrow! She's not fucking going anywhere.

Cold Calling

Hilarious!

Ahem.
Let us begin.
The stench of **sulfur...**
No. None of that. We're not doing that. We're just playing cards.
You asked me to run this Raid Deck, and I'm running it.
Buckle up.
Descending into the Molten Core, you are assaulted by the heat of a thousand million exploding suns. Lucifron, his hatred forged in this cavern's infinite heat, turns his black gaze upon you.
So, do we take **damage**, or...
YOU ARE SEARED!

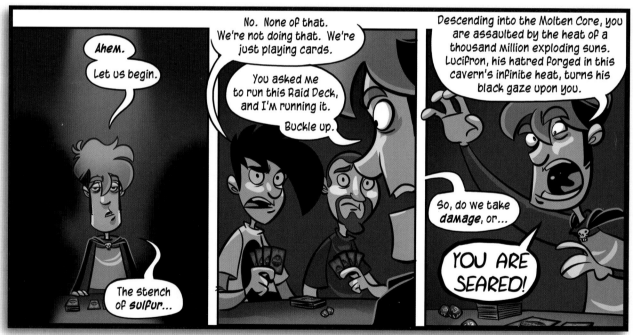

Cloaked in Twilight

Similar to the rest of the archive, this one has meaning for us that is embedded on some secret channel. We got a glimmer of this process at the time, but it's as clear as day now: There's an unbroken line through the Pokémon card game, to the World of Warcraft card game, and on through to Mike's playing (and running) his own Dungeons and Dragons campaign. One of the most rewarding things about writing *Penny Arcade* is that we can record the events of our lives in a way that not only helps us remember, but (hopefully!) entertains as well.

TIME LINE

2009 (November) — Realizing that not everyone can wear a Fruit Fucker shirt to work, Penny Arcade launches their line of gamer apparel, First Party.

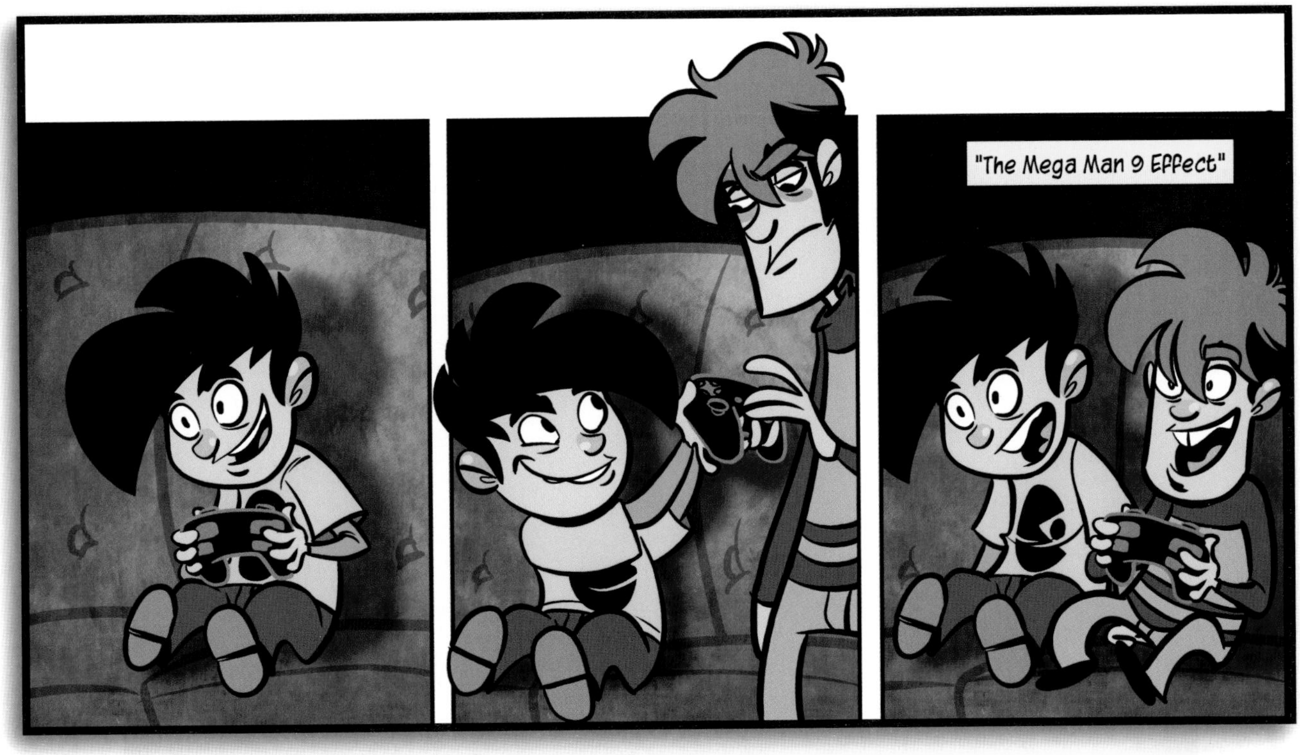
"The Mega Man 9 Effect"

A Trick Of Retrospective

This might be the best comic we've ever done.

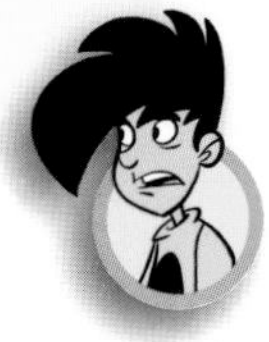

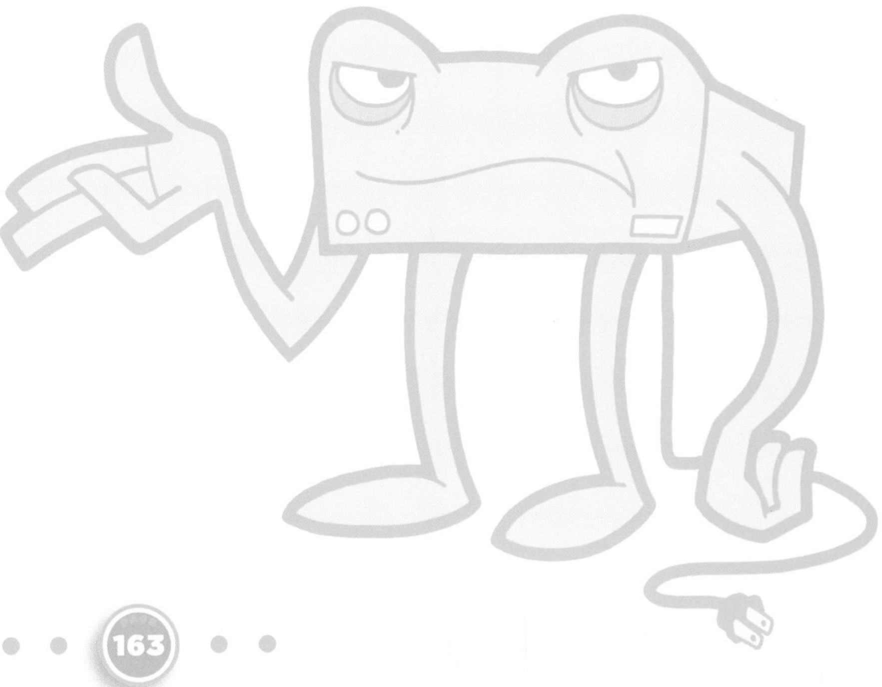

TIME LINE **2010 (March)** — PAX expands their reach with PAX East, a brand-new PAX event held in Boston each spring.

ACKNOWLEDGMENTS

Thanks to everyone who worked on this book!

Writing/Visual Credits

Chris Baker
Jerry Holkins
Kristin Lindsay
Robert Khoo
Mike Krahulik
Kiko Villaseñor

Other *Penny Arcade* Staff

David Coffman
Amber Fechko
Mike Fehlauer
Jeff Kalles
Erik Karulf
Joshua Price
Brian Sunter

Art Contributors

Bill Amend
Sam Didier
Becky Dreistadt
Kazu Kibuishi
Scott Kurtz
Ericka Lugo
Woody Messinger
Stephen Silver
Dirk Erik Schulz

Contest Art Winners

Andrew Hussie
Kevin O'Neill
Joel Timpson

And Thanks to Random House!

April Flores—Publicity
Tricia Narwani—Editor
Ali T. Kokmen—Marketing
Erich Schoeneweiss—Production
Brad Foltz—Design
Scott Shannon—Publisher
Michael Braff—Editorial Assitant
Nancy Delia—Production Editor

Special Thanks

Cary Brisebois
Peta Countryman
Patrick Groome
Kevin Hamilton
Brenna Holkins
Elliott Holkins
Ronia Holkins
Susi Kalles
Paul Kilpatrick
Dawn Krahulik
Don Krahulik
Kara Krahulik
Gabe Krahulik
Don MacAskill
Tom Mathews
Vizelle Villaseñor
All of the Enforcers!

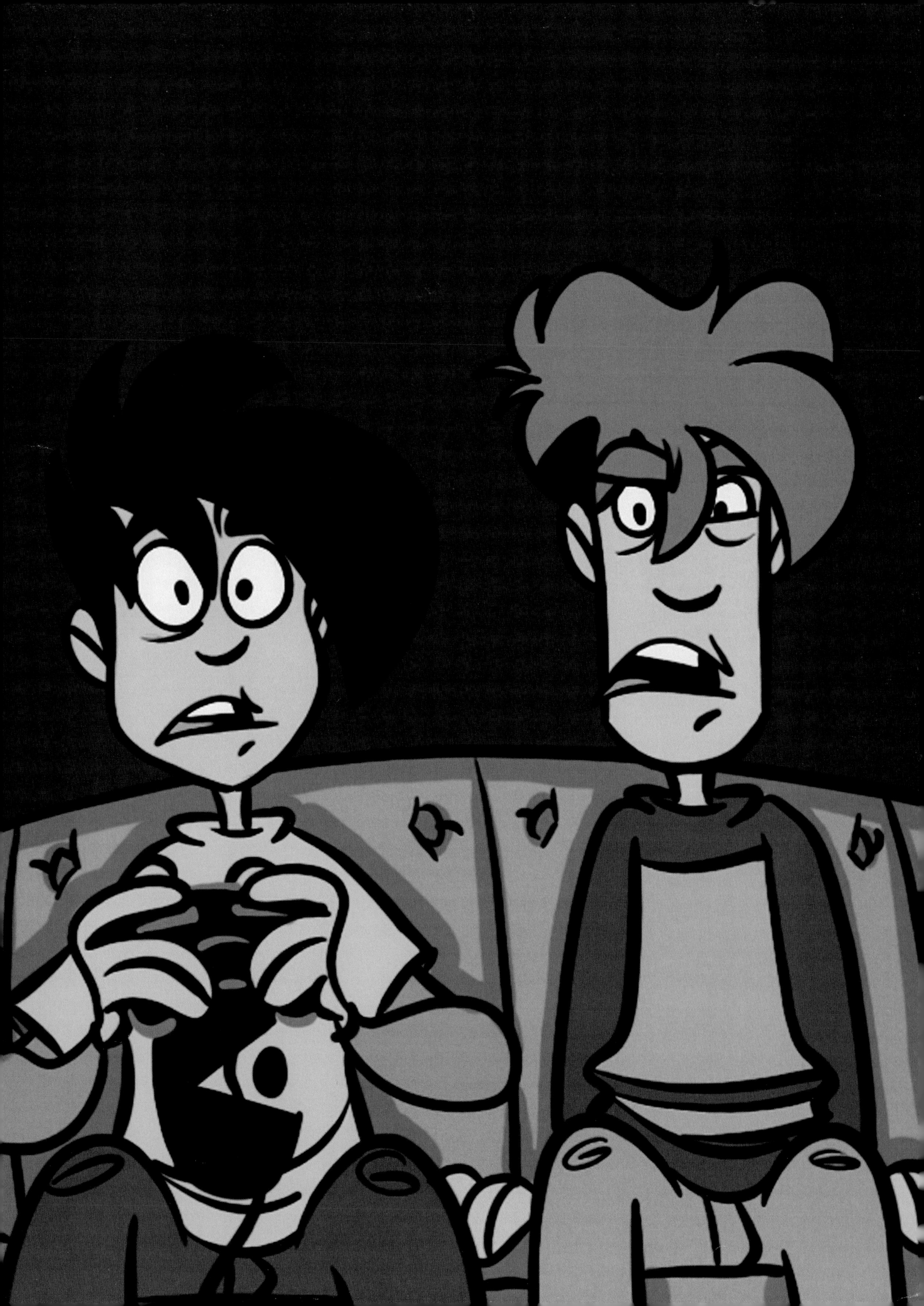

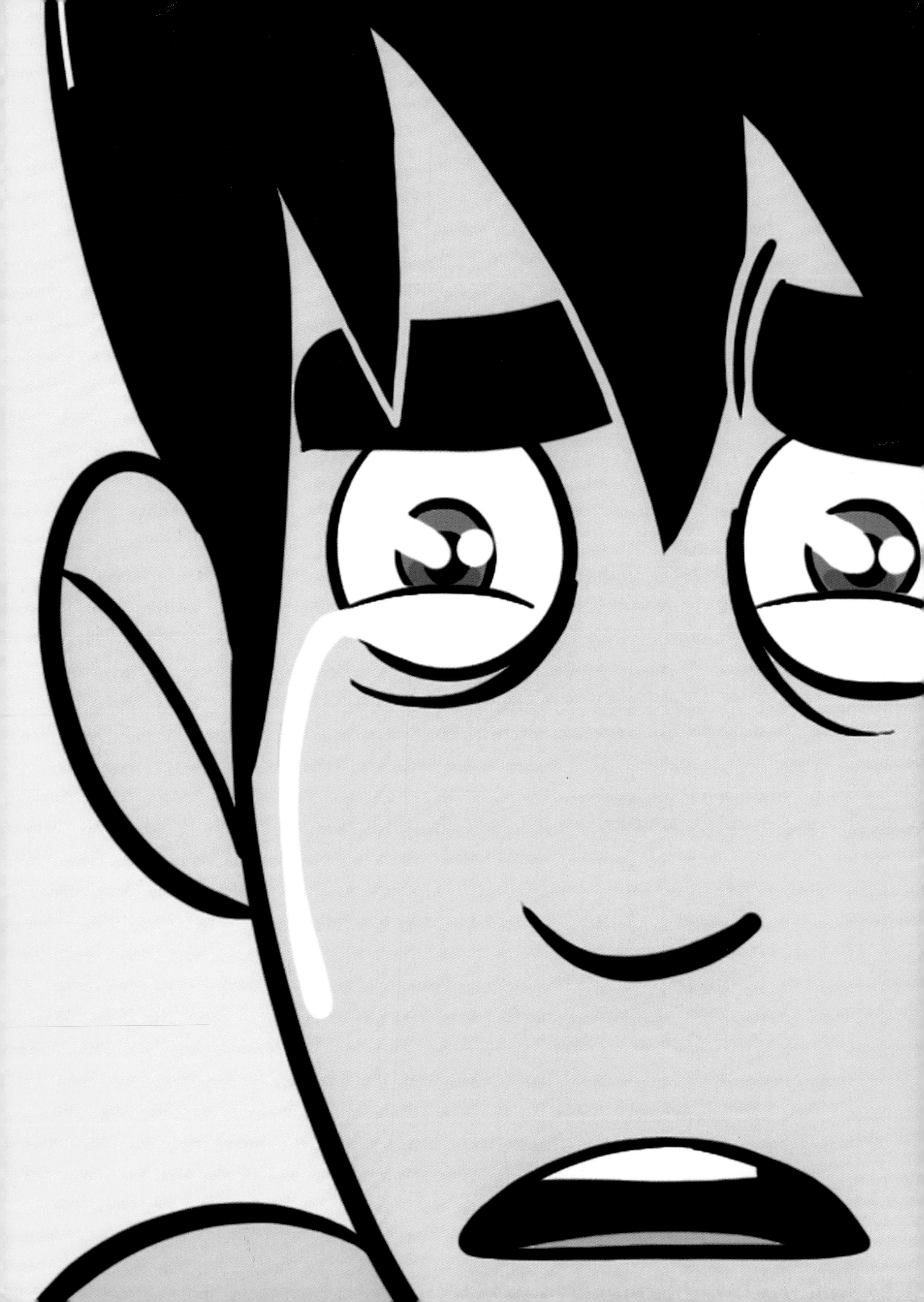

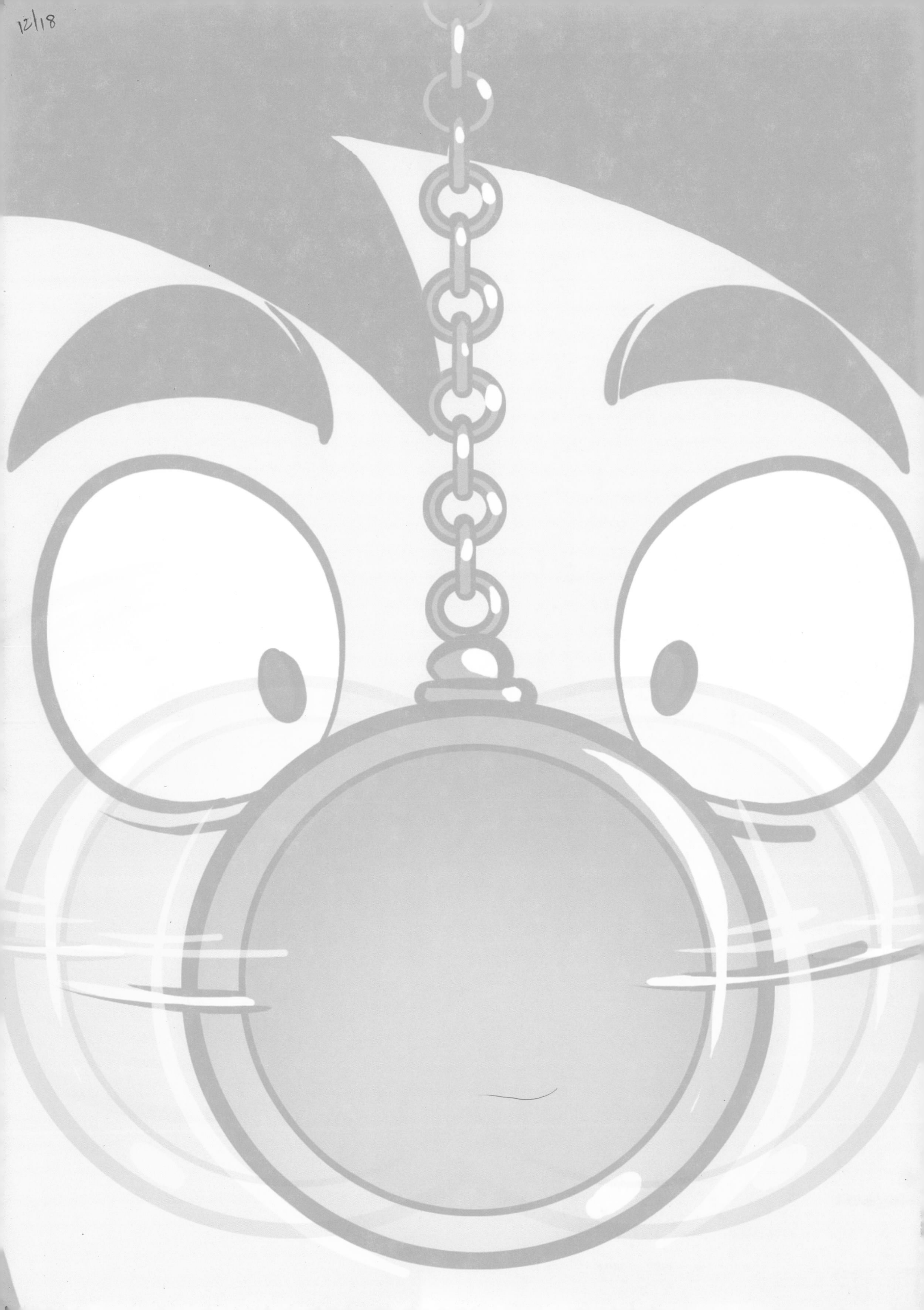